# Ross' Texans & the American Civil War

# Ross' Texans & the American Civil War

Accounts of the Confederate Soldiers
Commanded by General Lawrence Sullivan
Ross

## Ross' Texas Brigade
Victor M. Rose

## The Lone Star Defenders
S. B. Barron

LEONAUR

*Ross' Texans & the American Civil War*
*Accounts of the Confederate Soldiers Commanded by General Lawrence Sullivan Ross*
*Ross' Texas Brigade*
by Victor M. Rose
*The Lone Star Defenders*
by S. B. Barron

FIRST EDITION

First published under the titles
*Ross' Texas Brigade*
and
*The Lone Star Defenders*

Leonaur is an imprint of Oakpast Ltd

ISBN: 978-1-78282-563-0 (hardcover)
ISBN: 978-1-78282-564-7 (softcover)

**http://www.leonaur.com**

Publisher's Notes

The views expressed in this book are not necessarily
those of the publisher.

# Contents

# Ross' Texas Brigade

GENERAL L. S. ROSS

# Contents

TO THE
HERO PATRIOT
GENERAL L. S. ROSS,
THE CHEVALIER BAYARD OF THE WESTERN ARMIES
OF THE CONFEDERATE STATES OF AMERICA, UNDER
WHOSE
ABLE LEADERSHIP THE TEXAS BRIGADE WON
ITS JUSTLY MERITED RENOWN,
THESE PAGES ARE GRATEFULLY
INSCRIBED BY HIS FRIEND
AND COMRADE
THE AUTHOR.

# Salutatory

Victor Hugo says:

Destiny entertains a purpose. It watches mysteriously over the future historian. It allows him to mingle with exterminations and carnages, but it does not allow him to die, because it wishes him to relate them.

Be this as it may, certainly an actor in the scenes he describes should be allowed to possess advantages in the narration of the incidents not possessed by one not so connected.

The author was an actor in most of the events portrayed, and, in addition thereto, he has had the fraternal co-operation of his old comrades—from the commanders down—in the prosecution of this "labour of love."

During the year 1863, Captain Rufus F. Dunn, Company F, Third Regiment Texas Cavalry, was, on account of his feeble health, detailed from operations in the field to write a history of the operations of Ross' Texas Brigade; which design, as the following extract from a letter of General Ross shows, was immediately defeated by the death of Captain Dunn, and permanently impaired by the loss of documentary data, trophies, etc., mentioned. The extract in question reads:

Captain Dunn, whose health had failed, was detailed to write a full and accurate history of the brigade, and I furnished him with all necessary data, orders, papers, etc., to render his duty of easy compliance; but, unfortunately, he died in Alabama, and I received this information simultaneously with the intelligence that my trunk and private papers entrusted to his care had fallen into the hands of the enemy. In my trunk was found twenty stands of colours, and other trophies that we had captured from the Federals.

After many efforts to ascertain the whereabouts of Mrs. Dunn, success was attained in 1878. This estimable lady, Mrs. Parmelia A. Dunn, of Providence, Pickens County, Ala., had, through all these weary years of war and licentious misrule, guarded with fidelity the trust imposed upon her by her dying husband's injunction, and preserved, unscathed, through pillage and sack, the precious manuscript upon which his last care had been expended. To this Cornelia of the South, the surviving comrades of her lamented husband tender their heartfelt thanks.

It is regretted that the orders and other papers alluded to in General Ross' letter were not recovered. Hence, much of the material used has been drawn from other sources; generally, from the memories of surviving members of the command, a necessity that caused delay, and exacted much patience on the part of the author in arranging the many conflicting statements that had grown with time. But it is safe to assert that nothing but absolute truth has been entered on these pages; not the whole truth, for that, alas! may never now be told.

The treatment of a subject should always reflect the object sought to be attained without necessitating any special revelation in regard thereto. In this narrative, called for by the dictates of simple justice to the living and dead, a vindication of their motives is essayed by a brief recapitulation of their services in camp and field. Their courage and chivalry, their heroic fortitude, and manly fidelity to a hopeless cause need no vindication. And, if any were needed, we would turn to the childhood home of the English tongue—the cradle of the Anglo-Norman race—and find such vindications as the eloquent extract which is here reproduced from the columns of the London *Standard*, in the year 1878, when the South was stricken by that pestilential scourge of the tropics—yellow fever:

> The younger among us cannot, perhaps, remember the keen, warm sympathy with which the English of 1861-5 witnessed the heroic struggle maintained by their Southern kinsmen against six-fold odds of numbers, and odds of position, resources, vantage ground, simply incalculable. Even those who, from sympathy with the Northern States were unfavourable to the cause of a great nation revolting against a real tyranny, could not but feel proud of our near kinship with that incomparable soldiery—so designated by their enemies—which, on fifty battlefields, maintained such a contest as no other race has ever, in modern times, maintained; and, at last, when all hope was gone,

held for six months, with 45,000 against 150,000, a slender line of earth-works thirty miles in length; who marched out 28,000 strong, and after six days' retreat in front of a countless cavalry, and overwhelming artillery and infantry pressing them on all sides, surrendered, at last, but 8,000 bayonets and sabres. It is this people, the flower and pride of the great English race, upon whom a more terrible, a more merciless enemy has now fallen. There can be now no division of sympathy, as there is no passion to excite and keep up the courage needed for the occasion. Yet the men and women of the South are true to the old tradition. Her youth volunteer to serve and die in the streets of plague-stricken cities, as readily as they went forth, boys and grey-haired men, to meet the threatened surprise of Petersburg—as they volunteered to charge again and again the cannon-crowned heights of Gettysburg, and to enrich with their blood, and honour with the name of a new victory, every field around Richmond.

Their sisters, wives, mothers, and daughters, are doing and suffering now as they suffered from famine, disease, incessant anxiety, and alarm, throughout the four years of the civil war. There may be among the various nations of the Aryan family one or two who would claim that they could have furnished troops like those which followed Lee and Johnston, Stuart and 'Stonewall' Jackson; but we doubt whether there be one race beside our own that could send forth its children by hundreds to face, in towns desolated by yellow fever, the horror of a nurse's life and the imminent terror of a martyr's death.

And, finally, it is a solemn duty that the survivors owe to their fallen comrades to leave a truthful record of their deeds, upon which shall be predicated the judgment of posterity.

It is to such works as this that the future historian of the American sectional war must have recourse for facts; for the truth of history must rest upon the statements of those who were contemporaneous with the events they detail. Were this, then, the sole object, no further reason would be necessary for the appearance of the work. "*Returning justice lifts aloft her scale,*" and the fame of the Confederate soldier has risen far above the aspersions and calumnies that were sought to be cast upon it; and the descendants of Ross' invincible rangers will piously treasure the record of their services as an invaluable souvenir, and transmit it as an heirloom to their remotest posterity. And to that record the youth of the coming generation will point with pride, and say:

My grandsire fought with Ross at Elk Horn, Iuka, Corinth, Atlanta, and the hundred other fields upon which the 'Old Brigade' signalised itself!

They will rejoice over the recital of our victories, and shed tears over the story of our reverses; and, with the conclusion of the final chapter, over which the sombre legend—"*Conclamatum est*"—hangs like a funeral pall, they will close the volume with Christian resignation, breathing in their hearts the silent prayer: "*Thy will, O God, be done!*"

Indeed, the fame of the Confederate soldier is secure wherever the sway of Southern woman's influence is felt; and if, in succeeding generations, this land gives birth to as noble women as those who sacrificed everything for the cause of Dixie, the treasure of his reputation could be consigned to no safer guardianship. Though out of place, perhaps, we cannot refrain from paying this merited tribute to the matchless women of the South. It was theirs to wish God-speed to father, husband, brother, son, departing for the conflict where the valley was red. And though the yearnings of nature filled their hearts to bursting, while dark forebodings as to the fate of the loved one setting out for the front rose like a nightmare on the mind, yet they *spoke* but words of encouragement and hope. Many a mother bid her only son *adieu* with the sentiment of the Spartan matron holding sway in her heart, though the loving lips refused to utter it:

Take this shield, my son, and bear it back to me thyself, or be borne upon it!

Who rejoiced like they at our ephemeral triumphs? Who shed as bitter tears over our losses and defeats? Their trust in the God of hosts was sublime, and when craven manhood forsook his colours in despair, at the surrender of Vicksburg, and the melting away of Lee's lines before Petersburg, the star of their faith shone still with a constancy akin to its celestial birth, and nothing but the irrefragable evidence itself of the utter subversion of the ill-fated Confederacy, and the surrender of its armies, served to relax their ardour and exertions for the doomed cause. And then, reading upon the lowering clouds of the future the death-knell of all their cherished hopes, they turned to the past, upon angelic missions, among the unlettered graves of their fallen countrymen, and the stranger reads, with a thrill of pleasure, of the ministrations of these angels on earth, as each returning May brings its tributes of flowers for "Decoration Day."

In this, peerless sisterhood, our country recognises its greatest worth; and happy our manhood, our chivalry, to ever kneel as votaries at that pure shrine. A cause that is upheld by such spotless advocates cannot be a bad cause. The doctrines of hell are not propagated by evangels of mercy. But it was the inscrutable will of Providence that their prayers should be of none avail, as this immutable administration had before decreed the elimination of empires from the map of the world.

The genius of Hannibal, the prowess of his legions, and the sacrifices of his devoted countrywomen in defence of right, could not avert the fate of Carthage. The sympathies of the world are now with dismantled Carthagena; and, compared with the dubious ray of starlight that illumines the name of Scipio, Hannibal's is a sunburst of refulgence. And now, when we remember the tragic fate that has overtaken many of those fanatics who preached the doctrine of hate against the South, we recall the story of the Roman victor skulking amid the ruins of his subjugated rival.

The fact is attested by the holy Scriptures that nations are but instrumentalities in the hands of God for the execution of His will upon earth. Thus, commencing with the Babylonian Empire, we descend, by links of nations, down the chain of time, according to interpretation of the writings of the Prophet Daniel, to the Roman and Ottoman Empires. The Chaldean, Assyrian, Medo-Persian, Macedonian, Roman, and Turkish, were each but an instrument in His hands—a medium through which to effect his designs in regard to the advancement of civilization, and the melioration of the condition of mankind. The Roman power was the great disseminator of the truths of Christianity. Being mistress of almost the whole of the known earth when Constantine embraced the true religion, it became but a question of mere time when the gospel should reach, through Roman intercourse, every province and region penetrated for commerce, curiosity, or conquest.

It was for this that the *paladins* of Rome were allowed to subjugate a world. No earthly puissance could stay the onward tramp of the Roman legion in thus executing the will of Him on high. To this the Scipios and Caesars involuntarily contributed until Titus was suffered to raze the walls of Jerusalem to the ground, and, in so doing, he only emphasised the period to the "Old Dispensation." The "New Covenant" was then being taught by the "fishers of Galilee." And so is the United States designed by Omnipotence to serve some great purpose in the administration of His will among the peoples of earth. Of course, all speculation as to that purpose is futile. But with the Government brought back to the pure principles of the Constitution, through that sentiment of the equality of man, under our free institutions, it is thought the zenith of social and political excellence can be attained.

And, in the not very distant future, its effect will be remarked upon the monarchical governments of Europe. Indeed, its effect is felt there now, and has been since their desire to emulate us caused the French to behead their king. Thus, American influence, giving hope to the oppressed of Europe, will go forth as the great evangel of liberty, and subjugate more nations to truth and happiness than were conquered by all the legions of Rome. And, in the fulfilment of this high destiny, the sagacity of Lee and Johnston, Beauregard and Jackson, and the valour and endurance of their men, was futile.

But as the last sigh of the Moor awakes sympathy throughout Christendom for the doomed race whose lofty deeds of daring could not retain for them the rich conquest of Grenada, so, in aftertimes, the "Lost Cause" will gather about its mystic legends a weird tissue of romance and poetry, which, toned and mellowed by age, will eventually develop itself into an epic like the "Cid" or "Henriade." But it is only for the atom of an abstract idea that this apotheosis is invoked by the future Homer. For, barring property, the South lost nothing by the war that is not being regained in the Senate. Her people have adapted themselves to the new order of things, and, hand in hand with the honest Democracy of the West and East, are determined to stand by the rock of the Constitution as vigilant sentinels on the bulwarks of liberty. Of course, in this estimation, our priceless dead are not included. Their loss was incalculable.

And now, but little more remains to be said, in this connection, ere the "narrative" is allowed to speak for itself; whether in a manner commendable to those whose approbation the author is desirous of gaining, or not, the result will demonstrate. He did not regard himself as at all *peculiarly* fitted for the task, and there are, doubtless, many others of his comrades who could have performed the work in a much more satisfactory manner. But one long decade had passed since the colours of the brigade had been forever furled, and another well on its way, and no movement had been set on foot to rescue from oblivion the record of a command as rich in all the material treasured by valour, devotion, and chivalry, as ever graced the pages of history.

Twenty years ago, a friendless wanderer, of eighteen years of age, the writer cast his fortunes with them, and—call them rebels and traitors, revile the cause of the South as much as you will—he is prouder of his course, during those four years, than of any other period of his life. There be some who regard *principle* as of infinitely more value than the catch-words of expediency and policy. There be some who have not *"bowed the pliant hinges of the knee that thrift might follow fawning,"* and to such proud spirits, *"who would break, but never bend,"* the author tenders the result of his labours.

V. M. R.

Victoria, Texas, October, 1880.

*Rebellion! Foul, dishonouring word,*
*Whose wrongful blight so oft' has stained*
*The holiest cause that tongue or sword*
*Of mortal ever lost or gained;*
*How many a spirit born to bless*
*Hath sunk beneath that withering name,*
*Whom but a day's—an hour's—success*
*Had wafted to eternal fame!*

The noblest body of men that ever bared their breasts in defence of a loved land!—General L. S. Ross.

The flower and the pride of the Army of the West!—General Earl Van Dorn.

CHAPTER 1

# Organisation of the Third Regiment Texas Cavalry

The year of grace one thousand eight hundred and sixty-one dawned amidst the most portentous clouds that had ever lowered above the political horizon of America since the stormy period in which the sovereignty of the *States* had their birth, nearly one hundred years before.

Abraham Lincoln had been elected President of the United States by the suffrages of a sectional party whose only vitality and power of cohesion consisted of antagonism against the South and her most cherished principles and institutions; and his induction into the high office was construed by the people of that devoted section as the beginning of the "irrepressible conflict," so long and so often elaborated by Mr. Seward, amid the approving cheers of delighted Northern audiences.

The declaration of Mr. Lincoln himself, that "this country could not remain half slave and half free," had always been regarded south of "Mason and Dixon's line" as a declaration of war; and, now that the aggressive and fanatical Northern Republicans had, by taking advantage of the suicidal folly of the Democratic party, placed themselves in a position to give weight to the declaration, the South recognised the only alternative but submission, left her, and reluctantly accepted the saucy gage of battle thrown, as a forced tender, by her fanatical foe, and proceeded to stake her all upon the brutal arbitrament of arms—a tribunal through whose precedents of unwritten law flow the turbid pollutions of Might and Butchery, and not the limpid stream of Right and Justice relying, with sublime confidence, upon the justice of her cause and the valour of her sons.

21

But it is not our province, here, to recapitulate all those causes that precipitated the tempest of war upon our unhappy country. Suffice it to say, that the sectional administration at Washington gave the South no alternative. Mr. Lincoln and his advisers affected to regard secession, *per se*, as a declaration of war, and the Confederate Government only obeyed the dictates of prudence and reason in anticipating the storm by commencing a vigorous attack upon Fort Sumpter. The first gun on that occasion met an affirmative response from the hearts of nearly all the people of the South, as it also inflamed the rage of those at the North. All hopes of a compromise were now at an end; the line of demarcation was drawn; the work of pacific statesmen had ceased, that of the turbulent soldier was to begin; and, in the South, many original Unionists now accepted the situation of affairs, and cast their lots with their States and people.

It is supposed there are traitors and tories to every cause, and though that of "Dixie" was no exception to the general rule, in the Southern States, properly so styled, there were probably fewer of this nefarious class, *at the beginning*, than ever appeared in any revolution of like proportions and radical character. We say that this was so at the beginning. Degraded human nature never struggles to oppose the flood-tide that promises success. Even venal prosperity never lacks for servile minions to chant its paeans in tones of adulation. And many original secessionists underwent a moderation of their fire-eating proclivities with each Southern reverse, until, with that climax of catastrophes at Appomattox, they had completed the entire circle, and hailed the coming Yankees as original "Houston Union men."

Inquisitive reader, don't ask to glance even at the roll of this Legion of Dishonour. Many now reside in palatial residences, and are families of *influence*—yet they made the poor, bleeding corse of the assassinated Confederacy, the stepping-stone to wealth, position, and power. The tocsin of war met a prompt, affirmative response, and every hamlet, village, and city was soon the scene of warlike preparation. The best elements of society were the first to volunteer. Youth, ever ardent, was conspicuous by its numbers; and schools and colleges dismissed their classes to swell the ranks of the embryo army. And right here, let the fact be recorded, that the best, the bravest, the hardiest, and less complaining soldiers were mere boys from sixteen to twenty years of age.

This period was pre-eminently *the* era of the parlour knight. West Pointers, who had never seen West Point, turned up whenever occasion required it. Scarred veterans from Nicaraugua sprung up as if by magic, and the author, alone, formed the personal acquaintance of at least twelve hundred survivors of the immortal six hundred who charged at Balaklava. Thus, every cross-roads store, where ardent spirits were kept, could boast its own live military man to perfect its "Beauregard Rifles," or "Jeff. Davis Grays," in the manual of arms and evolutions of the line. Whatever became of these "Major Savages," "Colonel Desperades," and "General Seviers"—pronounced "Severe"—is not positively known. It is thought their ardour moderated just before the time for marching, and that they subsequently formed a portion of that delectable fraction of our population who contributed so much to advance the cause through their arduous labours in smuggling cotton to the Yankees. Some ensconced themselves in bomb-proofs about the Quartermaster and the Commissary Departments; while others developed alarming symptoms of disease that found, in the last shots fired, a speedy and radical cure.

At this time, too, the latent fact was revealed that many an old plodding citizen was a real military strategist. Such "natural-born generals" would gather an admiring crowd upon the street corners, and proceed to demonstrate with what ease Washington City could be captured. We never stopped short of the capital in those brave old days; and, perhaps, had the tide been taken just here at the flood, by a dashing leader, the capture of Washington could have been effected. Who knows? The author remembers ascending Red River in the month of May, 1861, fresh from his studies at Centenary College, and anxious to reach his native State and join a company before the war was over; for the eloquent "stump" statesmen did not hesitate to affirm that the end of thirty days would witness the close of the fifth act of the serio-comic drama. On board the same steamboat—the *Texas*—were Colonel Elkanah Greer and Captain Harris, both just from Montgomery, Alabama, the seat of the Provisional Government of the Confederate States, with their commissions.

Colonel Greer, immediately upon his arrival in Texas, issued a call for men, and designated Dallas as the point of rendezvous. The various companies soon arrived, and were mustered into the Confederate service for the period of "one year, unless sooner discharged;" so little did we comprehend the magnitude or duration of the struggle into which we were entering! Those words seemed a bitter sarcasm when twelve months afterward we were sworn in again, without invitation, "for three years, or the war."

The regiment was organised on the 13th of June, 1861, and as two other regiments had been raised in the State (for frontier protection), this was styled the Third Regiment of Texas Cavalry. Walter P. Lane, of Harrison county, was elected Lieutenant-Colonel, and G. W. Chilton, of Smith County, was elected Major. The following companies composed the regiment:

Co. A, Harrison County, T. W. Winston, Captain.
Co. B, Rusk County, R. H. Cumby, Captain.
Co. C, Cherokee County, Frank Taylor, Captain.
Co. D, Hunt County, —— Hale, Captain.
Co. E, Shelby County, D. M. Short, Captain.
Co. F, Kaufman County, Isham Chisholm, Captain.
Co. G, Marion County, H. P. Mabry, Captain.
Co. H, Wood County, Johnson Russell, Captain.
Co. I, Cass County, William Bryan, Captain.
Co. K, Smith County, David Gaines, Captain.

Captain Harris had previously received his commission as Quartermaster; and Captain Armstrong, of Company B, was appointed Commissary of Subsistence. Lieutenant M. D. Ector received the appointment of Adjutant. Dr. Wallace McDougal, of Company C, was appointed Surgeon, and Dr. Daniel Shaw, of Company B, Assistant Surgeon. Abner Rogers, Company G, was named Sergeant-Major. The companies averaged something over one hundred men each, and the regiment thus organised was probably 1,200 strong.

The hospitality of the good citizens of Dallas must not be passed over in silence. Each citizen vied with his neighbour in the warmth of his reception of the various companies and, finally, a mammoth collation was spread, consisting of all the delicacies of the season, by the patriotic and liberal people, around which the soldiers were formed in line and "invited" to charge. The Hon. R. B. Hubbard and Major G. W. Chilton improved this occasion of good cheer by the delivery of eloquent and patriotic speeches to the citizens and soldiers.

Our stay at Dallas was protracted by the non-arrival of the wagon-train, with arms, from San Antonio, until July 6th. Captain John J. Good had organised an artillery company at Dallas, which was attached to the regiment, and, with it, took up the line of march, on July 9, 1861, for the scene of operations in Missouri.

In the MS. of my lamented predecessor in this work, I find that many of the ardent youth of the regiment had become smitten with the charms of the Dallas fair, and tore themselves away from the parting scene with reluctance, hugging the cheering hope of a sacred tryst when the cruel war was over. Alas! how many manly forms came not to the long looked-for reunion! Through tempest and storm, they were true to their troth; and go, maidens, who plighted your vows with the young heroes, to the lines of Corinth, Iuka, Oak Hills, Atlanta, Elk Horn, and where the forlorn hope led the hazardous escalade, you'll find them *"sleeping the sleep that knows no waking"* on *"this side of the river." "No useless coffins enclose their breasts."*

No marble shafts point the pilgrim's steps to the hero-patriots' tombs. Their old, worn blankets were their only shroud; for the weary and struggling Confederacy, stabbed before and behind, was too poor to bury the patriot that she was unable to feed, and fell, herself, a murdered power, as much in the house of her *friends*, as by the hands of her enemies.

The arms received by the regiment were of a very inferior quality—old United States carbines, shot-guns, squirrel rifles, etc. Company A was partially armed with Colt's revolving rifles and six-shooters, while two companies received no arms until within the borders of Arkansas. In arms and ammunition, we certainly were no match for the enemy, who had an abundance of weapons of the latest improvement. Our wagon-train consisted of United States wagons, captured at San Antonio, and the mules bore upon their flesh the plain imprint of Uncle Sam's brand. Even the Mexican teamsters simply continued the service in the Confederate Army which they did not terminate in the United States army.

An idea may be had of the kind of work the average Texas soldier imagined he would be called upon to perform in battle, by the huge knives carried by many. Some of these knives were three feet long, and heavy enough to cleave the skull of a mailed knight through helmet and all. I think they were never used in the butchery of the Yankees, and, ere the close of the first year's service, were discarded altogether. But great was the confidence of the Texas soldier in his own prowess. To whip the Yankees, five to one, was considered the minimum of good fighting, and they seldom encountered on the field a less superiority of numbers; and this was by no means the greatest advantage possessed by the Union forces over their adversaries.

Yet the Southern Cross, time and again, led them to victory, which, alas, was never improved; and their deeds justify the assertion, that, with other counsels at the head of affairs, they would have proven victorious in the end. In fact, they were invincible against any power save that brutal grinding away by attrition, which the enemy was forced to adopt, and decline the combat on the open field, man to man.

Those were brave old days, we have said, and State Sovereignty cropped out on all occasions. To us, Texas was the "nation;" to her alone we owed allegiance. We were *allied* with the other Southern States, not indissolubly *joined*. Each company had a flag, and, in addition to its alphabetical designation, bore some other name suggested by the spirit of the times. Thus, Company A was the "Texas Hunters;" Company G, the "Dead-Shot Rangers," etc.

The regiment proceeded on its march, without incident, until the Red river was reached. We crossed at Colbert's Ferry into the Choctaw Nation, and encamped about a mile beyond. The river was quite low when the men and horses were ferried over. The wagon-train was leisurely crossing, the sky above was without the fleck of a cloud, when suddenly was heard the distant murmur of a coming rise; the murmur deepened into an ominous roar, as the angry waters were precipitated down the mountains, and the flood was upon us. In the brief period of thirty minutes, the swollen torrent reached from bank to bank, and it was with difficulty that the train was saved; indeed, Captain Dunn's MS. records the loss of one or two wagons.

We found our Choctaw allies abreast of the times, and earnestly preparing for war. This people were not behind their Texan compatriots in their hospitality to the men of the regiment, and numbers—men, women, and children—flocked to the camp to see the "warriors." And as the Choctaws were, so were the Creeks, Cherokees, and Chickasaws. Let the record here, once for all, suffice for each and every one of these noble tribes. We brought the conflict upon them, and involved them in the common ruin that overwhelmed us both; but as long as a tattered Confederate flag fluttered in the breeze, these "untutored children of the forest" rallied beneath its folds, with unabated fealty to the cause of the South. But if it be imagined that they are all literally untutored, the fact will not have been attained.

To illustrate: One day, in the Cherokee Nation, a number of men dining at the residence of a prominent citizen, whose daughter, a young and beautiful girl, presided at the head of the table. A gallant young officer was profuse in his compliments to the pretty and intelligent girl. He finally declared that she bore a striking resemblance to the portraits of Anne of Austria, including, even, the world-renowned pouting lips, with their slight vermilion tinge. The young lady, not at all abashed by this comparison with the royal Anne, replied:

26

While I may not boast a regal, or even a patrician descent, I can claim that the blood of three of the most noble nations on earth courses through my veins—the Cherokee, the Creek, and the American.

And this was delivered with a graceful toss of the head that would have done honour to fair Gabrielle d'Estrees, whose siren charms seduced France's greatest king from the path of honour, virtue, and duty.

*En route* for Fort Smith, Arkansas—the country was fertile, well-watered and timbered. Near Big Blue, we passed through a beautiful little Cherokee village, amid the *"vivas"* of the men, and the smiles and waving of handkerchiefs by the ladies—the latter of whom presented the colonel with a regimental flag. From the Big Blue to the Porto, a distance of ten miles, is a hilly, rocky, and broken country.

Here was encamped Colonel Cooper's Indian regiment, and we had the pleasure of witnessing a war-dance one evening. A tree, about six or ten inches in diameter, was denuded of its bark to a height of eight feet, and around this "war-pole" the warriors danced, chanting a deep, guttural, and monotonous drawl the while. The faces of the men were hideously painted, and they were arrayed in habiliments so fantastic that Harlequin himself would have been in the height of fashion. In the dubious moonlight, their weird figures seemed like some phantasm, while the cadence of the low and monotonous chant almost lulled the hearer into a lethargy. When the shrill war-whoop sounds from a single throat, echoed and re-echoed by the rocks and hills, startling the eagle in his eyrie, and the wolf from its covert, immediately upon the dying echoes a thousand braves shriek forth the savage sound, which, reverberating from rock to rock, amid the distant mountains, sounds like the very elements themselves were in discord.

At Fort Smith, we learned that Lyon and Siegel were pressing Price, who was retiring, before their superior numbers, toward the Arkansas line. Here the wagon-train was left, together with the sick men, disabled horses, etc., in command of Lieutenant Milburn, and the regiment, reduced to light marching order, hastened on to report to General Ben. McCulloch, the Confederate commander, whose headquarters were supposed to be somewhere near the Missouri line. Over the Boston mountains the command marched, the picturesque scenery of which extorted exclamations of admiration from all. Arkansas has been styled, with some degree of justness, the Scotland of America, and, perhaps, some future Scott shall spring up in the midst

27

of that romantic landscape and recount, in epic numbers, the deeds enacted there when Titans grappled for the possession of the soil.

Each day, nay, each hour, brought us tidings of the enemy's advance. That grand old Nestor of the Southern cause, Sterling Price, unable to stem the current of dark invasion, was leisurely retiring. As we neared the scene of operations, the demonstrations of welcome, on the part of the inhabitants, became more marked, until the town of Fayetteville was reached, where an enthusiastic ovation awaited us. Men, women, and children were transported with joy, and, amid the booming of "anvil" cannon, deafening cheers, and the waving of kerchiefs, wished us "God-speed."

The next night we encamped near Elk Horn tavern a field destined soon to become famous in the history of the war between the States. The headquarters of General McCulloch were reached about the 1st of August, on Cane Creek. The Missouri State Guard, commanded by General Price, had formed a junction with McCulloch's forces, and the two commanders were awaiting re-enforcements. The Missourians probably numbered 5,000 effective men. McCulloch's immediate command, consisting of the Third Louisiana Infantry and Third Texas Cavalry, did not exceed 2,000 men; and General Carroll, with about 2,000 Arkansas militia, completed the number of effective men under the Southern flag.

All, save the Louisiana regiment, commanded by Colonel Louis Hebert, were poorly armed, the latter, having Mississippi rifles, were a well-uniformed, disciplined, and brave regiment. Thus, we ascertain, that the Confederate forces did not exceed 9,000 men, and they mostly raw recruits, with no drill instruction, and but little discipline. The enemy probably numbered 12,000 men, but this disparity in numbers is of but little moment when the greater disparity of arms, discipline, and munitions of war, generally, are taken into account. The enemy was largely composed of United States regulars, and his volunteer regiments, too, were armed with the latest and most improved weapons. The hostile armies were separated from each other by an interval of about five miles; upon which semi-neutral ground the Missouri cavalry was incessantly engaging that of the Federals in skirmishes and affairs of outposts.

Here were seen, for the first time by our command, evidences of that vandalism which characterized the Federal soldiery throughout the war, and with which we were soon familiarised. A farmhouse, deserted by its inmates at the Yankees' approach—which act proclaimed their Southern sympathies—had been occupied by the soldiers, and the most reckless waste and destruction indulged in, apparently, in a mere spirit of wanton deviltry. Here we filled our haversacks with three days' rations, and drew *ten rounds* of ammunition. When the *eighty* rounds are remembered that we drew daily, and fired away, too, in the Atlanta campaign, this first year's soldiering seems like a "*tempest in a teapot*"—not that we didn't have warm work, for the brave and ill-fated Lyon struggled stubbornly for victory even when all hope had fled his cause.

With the break of day, the advance commenced; the Missouri cavalry in front, the infantry in the centre, and the Texas regiment on the left, or rear. All were in momentary expectation the "ball would open," but the wily Lyon, doubtful as to the numbers of McCulloch's recent re-enforcement, preferred to retire himself, and, by skilful manoeuvring, compel the Confederate generals to discover their real strength. Since crossing the Missouri line, each man had acted as his own purveyor of supplies, and those supplies consisted almost exclusively of green corn, consequently, we were wolfish, and indulged in bright fancies of capturing the Federal army, bag and baggage (that always was the programme in those brave old days), and thereby bettering our commissariat.

Late in the afternoon of August 2, we encamped on the field destined to go down to the latest posterity as the "Battlefield of Oak Hills." Price's army occupied the road leading to Springfield; McCulloch's troops were encamped on, and adjacent to, Wilson Creek, about one and a half miles in the rear of Price. Lyon had retired to Springfield, which town he now occupied. For several days we remained in camp here. Scouting, skirmishing with the enemy's pickets, and procuring forage for man and beast, principally occupied the attention of the men. Captain Frank Taylor, of Company C, made a gallant dash into a detachment guarding a train loaded with supplies for Lyon, routing the detachment, taking a number of prisoners, and capturing the entire train.

On the afternoon of August 9, orders were issued to prepare three days' rations, clean up guns, and be prepared to advance on Springfield, at a moment's notice. The men hailed the order with acclamations of delight, but just about sunsetting, the order to march was countermanded, by reason of the threatening aspect of the heavens, and the men ordered to lie on their arms. This latter order extinguished the fires of enthusiasm, but, as the sequel proved, it was a precaution that saved the army. For, had we been negligently encamped, expecting no advance by the enemy, instead of achieving a victory, we must inevitably have been routed and captured, surrounded and surprised, as we were. And had we advanced upon Springfield, as originally intended, Price's column would have encountered Lyon's main force in the dark of the plutonian night, and been annihilated by it.

The charge has been made, and denied, that the Confederate generals had no pickets stationed that night, in consequence of the expected advance. It does not seem possible that two officers, having the experience and reputation for prudence and caution that both Price and McCulloch enjoyed, would have thus left their commands to surprise. But if pickets were stationed, they were of no service, for the first intimation our regiment had that the enemy was near, was the report of Siegel's cannon and the whistling of shell just overhead.

Lyon and the Confederate commander had conceived the same plan of attack, and resolved to execute the same at about the same time, thus furnishing one of the most singular synchronisms that we ever remember having read of in this or any other war. In pursuance of this plan, Siegel was to turn the entire Confederate position, by taking a circuitous line of march, and open fire at daylight from his position immediately in our rear. Lyon was to advance in command of the main force, leisurely, not discovering his advance to Price until Siegel's signal-gun announced him in position. The entire plan of battle, so far, was carried out to the letter. Siegel formed in our rear, and his cannon boomed our reveille that morning.

On our side, the surprise was complete. Price had intimation that the enemy was upon him a few moments before the artillery opened. Instantly, the command: "To horse!" was given, and the regiment marched out into an open field to await orders from General McCulloch. In passing a rail-fence, the second battalion of the regiment became cut off from the first, and took up position in column of fours near the scene of the late camp. Siegel, however, having changed his position by crossing the creek, now opened upon them a heavy fire of grape and canister. Being without a head, and having no orders to execute, Captain H. P. Mabry, a cool, brave, and determined officer, assumed command, and by a skilful movement, extricated the battalion from its unpleasant position.

By this time, the battle had become general. Lyon had opened upon Price along his entire line, and the Louisiana regiment and Arkansas infantry were engaging Siegel warmly. The rattle of musketry, and the thunder of artillery, were deafening. The hoarse shells groaned their solemn warning high in air, and the whistling minieballs sounded many a poor fellow's requiem; while the shouts of the combatants rose often above the pandemonium of battle. The brave Louisianans would have routed Siegel alone, as they charged his left wing, driving it back in the utmost confusion. Not so the brave, but raw militia. The enemy—United States regulars—were pressing them heavily, and their line was beginning to waver, when General McCulloch rode up to Colonel Greer, and, in a few words, pointed out the state of affairs, and directed him to charge the advancing enemy.

"Boys," shouted Colonel Greer, "remember you are Texans! Forward! trot! gallop! *charge!*"

The enthusiastic shouts that greeted the latter order would have done justice to Cooper's Choctaw warriors. On! irresistibly on! the regiment swept. They were upon the Federals before a bayonet was fixed, and over the routed blue-coats it swept with the impetuosity of an alpine avalanche, as revolver and rifle dashed out many a life.

This sealed the fate of Siegel's command. They were routed and flying before the victorious Confederates, in all directions. Siegel, adopting the cry of the French at Waterloo: "Save himself who can!" succeeded in saving his bacon by the swiftness of his steed, and furnished a literal illustration of the truth of the doggerel:

*He who fights and runs away,*
*Will live to fight another day.*

Siegel disposed of, General McCulloch hastened, with his entire command, to the assistance of General Price, who was hard pressed by his vigorous assailant. Captain H. P. Mabry, in command of a squadron, continued the pursuit of Siegel's broken and demoralized columns. Price and his brave Missourians had sustained the brunt of the battle, unaided, against greatly superior numbers. Charge after charge, the brave and determined Lyon made at the head of his columns, in person. Learning of Siegel's discomfiture, he fought with haste and impetuosity, but kept his men well in hand; and had he not fallen, the issue, possibly, might have been different.

His fall was the signal for the shameful flight of his army, which deserted the dying hero-chieftain to the mercies of his triumphant, but magnanimous, enemy. They were unworthy of their leader; for, however much we may denounce the fanatical views of Lyon, and his intense hatred of everything Southern, there is no question as to his being a strategist of the highest order of genius, and as brave and resolute to execute, as he was cool and sagacious to plan.

He had maneuverer Price out of Missouri, and outgeneraled both Price and McCulloch, at the battle of Oak Hills. Had Siegel maintained his position with any credibility, Lyon could have put into execution other plans, which, doubtless, his fertile resources afforded him. But, as it was, he had no alternative but to strike as hard and rapidly as possible, thus reducing an excellently-planned battle, in which science should have performed a conspicuous part, to a mere brute contest. Though defeated, he displayed remarkable traits of character that stamped him as a master mind; and, had he lived, he certainly would have attained to eminence in the profession of arms. He sealed his convictions with his life's blood—falling within twenty steps of Price's line, where the missiles of death, like the Persian arrows at Thermopylae, were so numerous as to obscure the light of the sun— and his foemen upon that well-contested field, willingly drop this pebble above his tomb.

As tending to further illustrate the subject, and, at the same time, present both sides of the question, as the readiest means of reconciling the discrepant statements of parties attached to different commands, on that memorable occasion, the annexed interview of T. L. Snead, Chief of Staff to General Price, with a correspondent of the Cincinnati *Enquirer*, is reproduced:

Colonel Snead said:

> Lyon was the greatest man I ever knew. That has been my statement everywhere. I always felt it, and always said it. The day we had that memorable interview of six hours with him at the Planter's House, St. Louis, he was Jeff. Davis over again, but not as narrow and prejudiced as Davis. He was Davis, however, in intensity and tenacity, and about the leanness and height of Davis. We were to hold the interview in order to see if war could be prevented. I am the survivor of it. Claib Jackson and Sterling Price were the ablest politicians of Missouri; Price at the head after the death of Colonel Benton. I was the governor's secretary. Lyon came there with Frank Blair, jr., and General Conant. Such was his force, clearness, and real genius, that he met these old politicians at every point, conceding nothing, but never discourteous, his reason and his will equal. The whole party felt him to be the master mind, and the Federal historians do not

err when they put him down as the greatest general they produced—greater than any produced on both sides west of the
Mississippi River. Lyon advanced into that room, a little, red-
bearded, red-haired, precise, positive, plain man. He sat down,
and crossed one leg over the other stiffly, and his face was serious and stern. He spoke each word separate from the other,
pronouncing the little words, like *my* and *to*, with as much em-
phasis as the longer ones. He raised his right arm, automatically,
as the conversation proceeded, and brought it down with a jerk,
the forefinger extended, yet never speaking higher or lower
than at first.

We felt the sense of war and government in all his bearing. 'I
shall take but a small part in this conference,' said Lyon; 'Mr.
Blair is familiar with this question, and knows the views of my
government, and has its full confidence; what he has to say will
have my support.' Yet, in half an hour, he took the case out of
Blair's mouth, and advanced to the front, and Frank Blair was as
dumb as he had been. The United States could never have been
typified by a more invincible mind and presence. It was three
o'clock when the meeting broke up.

The last attempt Jackson made, was to have both sides agree not
to recruit troops in Missouri. Lyon arose: 'Rather than agree
that my government shall concede to your government one
iota of authority as to one man to be recruited, one inch of
ground of this State to be divided in allegiance, or neutralised,
between my government and your government, I will see all of
us under the sod.' Then taking out his watch stiffly, he said: 'You
shall have safe conduct out of my lines for one hour. Meantime,
you can get your dinner.'

It was now three o'clock. We took our dinner in haste, and left
St. Louis by an express-train, and, if we had not burned the
bridges behind us, he would have caught us before we reached
Jefferson City, for he marched at once. Price had soldierly re-
spect for him, and delivered up his body from the field of battle.
It was found deserted a second time in the streets of Springfield.
I then gave it to Mrs. Phelps, wife of the present governor of
Missouri, and sent men to bury it in the grave-yard at Spring-
field. Lyon followed us with a determination unparalleled in
that war, and he went under the sod, in fulfilment of his vow.

(Note: Mr. Snead was Price's adjutant-general at the time of the battle, as McIntosh, of Georgia, was McCulloch's.)

McIntosh was a better soldier than McCulloch, who was indecisive and faint of confidence. Price was a fine old officer, who had never lost a battle, and felt, like all Missourians, that the place to fight Lyon was in Missouri, and not to fall back to Arkansas. McCulloch commanded the Confederate army proper, of 3,000 men. Price commanded the Missouri State Guard of 8,000 men. The Confederate government, including Jeff. Davis, seemed indifferent about Missouri, and did not regard her as having properly seceded. Price was a Major-General—McCulloch only a Brigadier. The latter hesitated about marching upon Springfield, and was inclined to return to Arkansas. One day, Price rode up on his horse. He had a loud voice, and a positive address, and always spoke to McCulloch as if he considered the latter an inferior.

'Do you mean to march into Missouri, and attack General Lyon, General McCulloch?'

'I have not received permission from Mr. Davis to do so, sir,' answered McCulloch; 'my instructions leave me in doubt whether I would be justifiable in doing so.'

'Now, sir,' said Price, still in a loud, imperious tone, 'I have commanded in more battles than you ever saw, General McCulloch; I have three times as many troops as you have; I am of higher rank than you are, and I am twenty years your senior in age. I waive all these things, General McCulloch, and, if you will march into Missouri, I will obey your orders, and give you the whole command, and all the glory to be won there.'

McCulloch said he was then expecting a dispatch from Mr. Davis, and would take Price at his word, if it was favourable. The dispatch came, and the army advanced, with McCulloch in supreme command. After McCulloch had advanced awhile, he again grew irresolute, and, instead of moving on Springfield direct, he halted out at Wilson's Creek, twelve miles or so south of that city. Price rode up to him one day, and found him making diagrams on the ground with a stick. Price bawled out: General McCulloch, are you going to attack Lyon, or not?' McCulloch said that he was undecided. 'Then,' cried Price, 'I want my own Missouri troops, and I will lead them against Lyon, myself, if they are all killed in the action; and you, General McCulloch, may go where in the devil you please.'

McCulloch was thus exasperated into promising an attack. It was arranged to move on the very night that Lyon moved, and by three columns, upon Springfield. In anticipation of this movement, McCulloch drew in his pickets, and, seeing some clouds and threatening weather arising, he ordered the troops to lay on their arms, and did not again advance his pickets. This led to the complete surprise effected by Lyon in the morning. At four o'clock, on the morning of the battle, August 10, 1861, McCulloch rode over to Price's headquarters, which were pitched in a sort of cow-yard, by a little farmhouse down in a hollow.

While Price, McCulloch, Churchill, and Snead were taking breakfast at the earliest dawn, a man came in from the front, where Rains was posted, and said he had an important message. The Yankees were advancing full 30,000 strong, and were on Rains' line already. 'O, pshaw!' exclaimed McCulloch, 'that is only another of Rains' scares.' They then went on eating, until another man came and reported that the enemy was not more than a mile away, and right on Rains' column as they lay on their arms. McCulloch again said it was nonsense; but Price was excited. He thundered out to Snead: 'Order my troops, sir, under arms, and in line of battle at once, and have my horse saddled!'

He had hardly spoken these words, when the little group of men looked up from the cow-yard to where the hills were rising, line on line, above them, and on the clear, morning perspective, they saw Totten's battery unlimbered on the top of a hill, less than three-quarters of a mile distant, and before he had thrown the first shot, Siegel's battery in the rear also pealed out, and the balls from those two cannon crossed each other right over the hollow in which Price's troops were lying. The surprise was perfect. General McCulloch hastened back to his headquarters, and put his troops in motion against Siegel. In a very little time, Siegel was whipped out. Price, in the meantime, had to encounter Lyon. The contest was spirited and deadly, and the weather like fighting in a furnace.

Price's columns were reeling before Lyon's attacks, when he sent Colonel Snead to ask McCulloch if he could spare him a battalion of Missourians that were not properly in McCulloch's command. McCulloch then placed himself at the head of the Missouri column, with certain other troops, and came back over the field to Price's relief. It was this re-enforcement that caused the death of Lyon, as Colonel Snead believes; for, seeing fresh troops advancing on the Southern side, Lyon waved his sword, and led the counter-attack, and was shot dead. It was but a few minutes after Lyon fell before the battle ceased.

The foregoing is reproduced, in justice to the Missourians, for the reader must understand that there was foolish antagonism engendered between the troops of the rival generals, which was fanned into a blaze by a silly controversy conducted through the public journals of the land, by one Mr. Tucker, on the part of General Price, and by John Henry Brown, on the part of General McCulloch, which seriously impaired the efficiency of the army. But, in justice to "Ben McCulloch"—name ever dear to every true Texan—we cannot allow the charge of indecision to rest against the character of him who was decided in all things. His summary disposal of Siegel was the highest evidence of prompt decision.

We would not detract one iota from the well-earned fame of Price and his noble Missourians, but it is but justice to place on record the fact that Ben. McCulloch displayed the high qualities of a command-ing general on that occasion. He comprehended the situation at a glance, and decision came as if by intuition. He shared all the dangers of the field with the meanest of his men. But, as it will be more ap-propriate in a future chapter to dwell at length upon the character of General McCulloch, we will dismiss the subject until that time.

In Company A, Third Texas Calvary, was an unadulterated speci-men from Erin, of the name of B. Thomas. Mr. Thomas rode an in-corrigible horse, who would eat the tether that bound him to a tree, and, being loose, he would devour whatever was eatable in camp. This equine marauder had pursued his evil bent to such an extent, that many of the victims had become exasperated, and declared if Mr. Thomas did not devise means for securing the horse, they would kill him—the horse. As Mr. Thomas would have rather suffered crucifix-ion, head down, than to have been left afoot in Missouri, he procured a chain and padlock, with which he managed to secure the marauder.

When Siegel's battery opened, just before dawn on that memora-ble morning, and the bugle rang out "to horse!" Mr. Thomas discovered that the mechanism of his lock was not perfect, for the "bloody thing wouldn't worruck." Siegel advanced, and the camp-ground became a battlefield. No one thought of Mr. Thomas until the command returned to camp in the evening, when lo! there stood the horse unscathed, and locked securely to a tree that had been literally peeled by the bullets. "Be the vargin!" exclaimed a husky voice from the dense bushes upon the creek; "boys, is the sthorm over till last?" It was Mr. Thomas, who had sought refuge in the bushes from the "inimy;" and, strange indeed, he had been as miraculously preserved as had the horse.

Another member of the same regiment was wounded in the charge upon Siegel's command, and left upon the field for dead. A party of Federal fugitives passing that way, robbed him of hat, boots, money. The ghouls felt his pulse and pronounced him dead, else he believes they would have administered the *coup de grace* with a bayonet. An original character, of the same regiment, was Mr. Brazil, who originally hailed from Buncombe County, Tar River, North Carolina. Mr. Brazil had a dozen ears of green corn on the fire when Siegel opened the matinee, which he swore he wouldn't leave for all the d——d Dutch in hell for, be it known, that Lyon's army was composed so largely of Germans, that they were not called by the Confederates "Yanks," but "Dutch."

When Mr. Brazil was satisfied the corn was cooked thoroughly, he took the dozen ears up in his arm, mounted his "war hoss," and with his old musket, as long as a fence-rail, lying in his lap, went jogging along in the direction he supposed the regiment had taken, while all his faculties were centred on an ear of corn upon which he was munching. "Hello! my man!" exclaimed an officer, as he rode up to one of Siegel' s regiments, "Where are you bound, so early?"

"O, by ——," exclaimed Brazil, with his mouth full of corn, "I'm gwine to ketch me a Dutchman, I am, you bet!"

"Take him in, boys," fell upon the startled ears of the astonished Brazil, like the knell of doom. Mr. Brazil says they did "take him in," and put him through," too, over a hundred miles of rocky road, at double-quick, afoot, to Rollo. The author certifies that Mr. Brazil, on his return to the command, was the worst used up man he ever saw. This episode gave Mr. Brazil a decided distaste to active operations in the field, and he became a teamster, and held the post unto the last. The love of lucre tempted him to substitute for another, after the expiration of his year's service; but he had it expressly stipulated that he was to retain his berth in the wagon-train.

When Siegel's shot began to fly pretty thick, brave, good old Captain Hale, who made no military pretensions, called out to his company: "Git in a straight row, here, boys! This is the war you all have hearn talked about! *Them's* the cannon; *them's* the muskets; that great big screeching thing is a bung-shell; and them little fellows that sing like bumble-bees, are minieballs! Git in a straight row; we're gwine to work, now!" And the brave old man and his gallant "boys" did good work on that memorable day.

The Third Texas Cavalry occupied the town of Springfield the day succeeding the battle, and the regimental flag was hoisted above the court-house, during which ceremony Major Chilton delivered an eloquent address to the assembled citizens and soldiers. Many Southern sympathisers, imprisoned merely for opinion's sake, were released from confinement in the county jail.

The body of the ill-fated Lyon was delivered to Mrs. Phelps, wife of the then member of Congress from the Springfield district, and at the present writing (1878), the Democratic Governor of Missouri, by whom it was interred on the premises of their homestead, two miles north of the town.

The author regrets that he can give no sketch of the life of the gallant, though unfortunate, Lyon.

The Federal loss in the engagement was severe—probably amounting to 1,000 killed, and twice that number prisoners and wounded. The Confederate loss did not exceed 250, all told. General McCulloch, after exchanging for the few Confederates in the hands of the enemy, dismissed the remainder of his prisoners, telling them that he had rather fight, than feed them.

The route of the Federal army was complete, and had the Confederate cavalry pursued, as the Prussians did at Waterloo, not a man would have reached St. Louis, which city— and it was the key to the West—must, undoubtedly, have been occupied by the Southern army. Unfortunately, there is recorded but few instances in which the Confederate soldier improved the advantages of victory. Had the enemy been pressed at Manassas and Oak Hills, Washington and St. Louis would have rewarded the efforts of the Confederates with bright promises of speedy and complete success.

Secession, though it might have been a constitutional remedy, *i. e.*, in conformity to the spirit of the organic law, was a Caesarean remedy, of so radical a nature as to be resorted to only in the extremest case.

By abating no right under the Federal compact, the occupation of Washington would have been the possession of the government.

The true policy, and only hope of the Confederacy, was in a spirited and aggressive warfare. Everything should have been subordinated to efforts calculated to render the army efficient. One year should have ended the war; and it would have done so, could Southern statesmen have foregone the pleasure of splitting theoretical hairs, and came to the aid of the army with a tender of the resources of the whole country. The army performed its duty; the men performed prodigies of valour, and the officers were unsurpassed by any on the planet. But the crisis did not develop a single statesman capable of comprehending the magnitude of the struggle. Happily, now, these issues will arise no more to distract the American people from the high road to prosperity. If this Union is destined ever to be rent asunder, the entering wedge will not be applied by the South. This much is certain.

*BATTLE OF "OAK HILLS."*
*1.*
*At midnight in the drear bivouac,*
*The Southern patriots lay,*
*The storm-cloud with its sombre black,*
*Obscured the dismal way*
*Of the silent sentinel that kept*
*Lonely vigils while his comrades slept.*
*2*
*No camp-fire shed its dubious ray*
*The spectral oaks to define,*
*Or light the stalwart forms that lay*
*With rifles in battle line;*
*For, when the sun o'er the hill should glance,*
*McCulloch'd give the word to advance.*
*3*
*Reposing here, in fitful dream,*
*Of home and loved ones far,*
*By old Wilson's turbid stream,*
*The citizen-knights of war*
*Were eager to meet the foe in fight,*
*Beneath the "Bonnie Blue Flag," for right.*
*4*
*Here waved Missouri's banner'd bear,*

Our lustrous "Lone Star" beside;
The tireless Pelican was there,
Gay Louisiana's pride;
The tocsin Arkansas sounded, too,
And had mustered here her gallants true.
5
Morn at length from the dark night woke—
A streak lit the eastern skies—
When the cannon of Siegel broke
The silence with dire surprise,
Loud then the Federal thunder flew,
And louder the yell of triumph grew
6
To arms, the banded heroes rushed,
And formed their serried front,
With bated breath and lips still hushed,
But eager to meet the brunt
Of battle, rushing with giant strides,
To humble Dixie's patriot pride.
7
As leaps the angry tidal wave
Upon the rock-ribbed shore,
So, when Lyon the order gave,
The Regulars onward pour
Like mad billows from the dark blue sea,
For conquest sweeping the peaceful lea.
8
The shock of battle and the crush
Of ranks, as wild squadrons wheel
And charge, with impetuous rush,
The bright lines of deadly steel;
The cannon's hoarse and murderous roar—
The rifle's deadly rattle, and more—
9
The sabre's flash—the fatal thrust—
The red wound, and ghastly death,
As iron hoofs tramp into dust
The wounded, whose departing breath
Was nursed to give one parting cheer
For the cause the hero deem'd so dear.

*10*

*In vain discipline sought to ride,*
*In haughty victory o'er Patriotism's devoted pride;*
*Vain did the eagle lingering soar,*
*Above this human-created hell,*
*Which Siegel fled, and where Lyon fell.*

*11*

*The pale, cold moon, her timid light,*
*In dubious glances shed,*
*Over the beaten army's flight*
*And over the silent dead*
*Of friend and foe, strewn thick around,*
*WHO WON, AND HELD, IN DEATH, THE GROUND.*

## CHAPTER 2

# Arrival of the Sixth Texas Cavalry

Captain Mabry pursued the routed and flying column of Siegel to a mill, situated on a creek some five miles from the field, capturing 150 prisoners. "And," says the MS. of Captain Dunn, "the road was thickly strewn with dead Federals." Siegel managed to retain possession of one piece of artillery up to this time, but, Mabry pressing him so close, he now consigned the whipped dog of war to the depths of the stream. No official account has been given to the public, so far as we know, of the losses sustained by the enemy in the battle. The fighting was at very close range, and the mortality immense. The dead and wounded literally encumbered the ground. With the exception of Mabry's pursuit, the enemy was allowed to seek safety in flight. An energetic pursuit by 1,000 cavalry would have bagged the whole fugitive mass; for never was defeat more thorough and demoralising. The loss of the Texas regiment did not exceed ten killed and thirty wounded.

After the battle, the sad duty devolved upon the survivors to afford the wounded relief, and give to the dead the poor burial rights that they could. The duty of interring the enemy's killed also devolved upon the Confederate and Missouri soldiers, as the humane Siegel made no proposals to perform that obvious duty himself. Field hospitals were erected for temporary use, at the most convenient points, and the merciless surgical saw and knife commenced their work. The Southern forces occupied Springfield the next day, and to that town the wounded were speedily removed.

The author, being one of the wounded, and in hospital, can certify that the excruciating sufferings of the poor fellows, exceeded the heart-rending scenes of the battlefield itself. Here reclines a poor Arkansian, in a half-sitting position, being supported by rolls of blankets, with a minie-bullet through his bosom. Each laborious respiration produces the fatal death rattle in his throat, and, though science knows the signet of death is fixed upon his clammy brow, the humane surgeons labour to alleviate his pain. Gradually the breathing becomes less frequent, and the horrible gurgling rattle more weird and prolonged. A silence ensues, and then a rustling from his distorted mouth, like the noiseless flapping of angel's wings which we hear, independent of the external sense, and the suffering soldier has passed from earth, with a smile of ineffable sweetness and confidence breaking upon his lips. Did he, in passing the intermediate sphere, with one foot on the shores of Time, catch a glimpse of the cheering promise beyond? None now may know. Many other touching scenes might be added to this; but being in close proximity to the Arkansian, and an eye-witness of his death, the picture has remained stamped upon my mind as vividly as on that August day, in 1861. General McCulloch, with that humanity characteristic of all noble natures, visited the hospitals in person, and had a cheering word for every sufferer.

The Missouri Army commenced an immediate advance, and, to the deep chagrin and mortification of the Confederate army, we were suffered to remain in ignoble quietude, while our brave allies were winning new laurels at Lexington, and on other fields. Whoever in authority was responsible for the fatal course that refused co-operation with General Price, was guilty of the most egregious folly capable of being committed by a man having the least pretension to reason and common sense. Engaged in the same cause, Price's defeat would have been our loss, as his victories were our gain. Yet we remained idle spectators, while the poorly-clad veterans of Missouri's "Old Guard" carried their "Grizzly Bears," from victory to victory, until overwhelming forces checked their splendid career; then, without sustaining a reverse, they sullenly retired, disputing every foot of ground with the giant enemy.

No brighter page will adorn the history of contemporary struggles, than the magnificent campaigns of these bare-footed boys, led by their grand old chieftain. If heroism in the field, and Spartan fortitude in the midst of suffering and privations, had been acceptable sacrifices to the god of war, the rich libation of their blood would have invoked, successfully, the genius of victory to perch upon their banners. But so it was not decreed in the chancery of Heaven.

General McCulloch's forces remained encamped in the southwestern portion of Missouri, doing little else than cooking and eating the wholesome and abundant rations furnished them by the commis-

43

sariat, until Fremont's vain-glorious advance to Springfield, driving Price before him, when the Confederate Army retired to the "Cross Hollows," seemingly a favourite position of General McCulloch. But as the Sixth Texas Cavalry joined us previous to this time, we will now take a brief review of its organisation, regretting that the meagre data available renders it impossible to go into details. For the Sixth deserves the highest eulogium that can be pronounced in its praise. Composed, like the other regiments that early left the State, of the very best young men in the country, it could be relied upon to accomplish any feat of daring within the prowess of human bravery and daring.

In August, 1861, Colonel B. Warren Stone, of Dallas, was commissioned a Colonel, by the President of the Provisional Government, and immediately issued a call, inviting the formation of companies. On the 6th of September following, the subjoined companies were organised as the Sixth Regiment of Texas Cavalry, and were mustered into the service of the Confederate States, at Camp Bartow, in Dallas County, by Colonel Garland:

Co. A, Kaufman County, —— Harden, Captain.
Co. B, Kaufman County, John S. Griffith, Captain.
Co. C, Dallas County, Fayette Smith, Captain.
Co. D, Grayson County, —— Bowen, Captain.
Co. E, Van Zant County, Jack Wharton, Captain.
Co. F, Dallas County, —— Gray, Captain.
Co. G, McLennan County, P. F. Ross, Captain.
Co. H, Bell County, —— White, Captain.
Co. I, Henderson County, H. W. Burgess, Captain.
Co. K, Collin County, J. W. Throckmorton, Captain.

Each company averaged something over 100 men; the regiment aggregating 1,150. An election of field officers was immediately held, the Colonel also submitting his name for the approval of his men. The election resulted as follows:

B. Warren Stone, of Dallas County, Colonel.
John Summerfield Griffith, Lieutenant-Colonel.
Private L. S. Ross, of Company G, was elected Major.
Lieutenant D. R. Gurley, of Company G, was appointed Adjutant.
Captain A. J. White, of Dallas, Quartermaster.
Captain —— ————, of Collin County, Commissary
of Subsistence.

The regiment soon moved up to Collin County, and encamped near McKinney, and while in camp at this place, was reviewed by Colonel Garland. The regiment, being well mounted and well clad, presented a fine appearance, upon which they were handsomely complimented by Colonel Garland. The "sound of resounding arms" had fallen on their ears, and the boys were eager impatience itself to get to the front, and bear a hand in the efforts of Mr. Abraham Lincoln to make history. After a few days' stay at McKinney, the regiment took up the line of march for Missouri, being, for the convenience of obtaining forage, divided into three divisions, of which Major Ross commanded the first, Lieutenant-Colonel Griffith the second, and Colonel Stone the third.

This order of march was continued until Red River was crossed, when the various divisions were consolidated again at Northtown. At this point, information reached Colonel Stone that a large body of hostile Indians were driving the command of Colonel Cooper back. The regiment immediately commenced a forced march in the direction of Fort Gibson. Having reached this place, the news was more definite and confirmatory of the reports before received. Hopotheohola, a veteran chief, who had fought with the hostiles at Talladega and Horse Shoe, had gathered together the disaffected of all the tribes, and, under the designation of "Pin Indians," had taken the field in sufficient numbers as to compel the Confederate Indian Superintendent, Colonel Cooper, to retire before him.

From Fort Gibson, the regiment continued the forced march up the Verdigris. But the wily old chief, hearing of Cooper's anticipated re-enforcement, turned about and retreated in the direction of Kansas, burning and laying waste the country along his route. Hopeless of overtaking the hostiles, as his horses were already much jaded, Colonel Stone countermarched and returned to Fort Gibson. From here the regiment proceeded leisurely to Camp Walker, in Missouri, where were pitched the headquarters of General McCulloch. After reporting to General McCulloch, the regiment then proceeded to Carthage, where General McCulloch was concentrating his cavalry, preparatory to making a raid into Kansas.

On September 28th, the patriot Governor of Missouri, Claiborne F. Jackson, who, like the rejected Son of Man, literally, had not where to lay his head within the broad domain of the Commonwealth over which he was titular Chief Magistrate, with his staff and escort, approached Carthage. Colonel Greer proceeded, at the head of his regiment, to do the honours of the day to the almost fugitive governor, and escort him into town. The governor reviewed the regiment, and took up his quarters in the town. On the night of the 30th, he delivered an eloquent defence of the secession of Missouri, to a large concourse of citizens and soldiers.

Standing upon the steps of the court-house, his silvery hair reflecting the mellow beams of moonlight, he presented a picture of Justice wronged, and the impotency of Virtue, alone, to cope with the minions of Might and Wrong. In this address, Governor Jackson imparted to us the first intimation of the proposed invasion of Kansas. In speaking of the enormities perpetrated by the ruthless Kansas "Jayhawkers," upon the defenceless citizens of the border counties of Missouri, he raised his trembling hand aloft and exclaimed:

> In ten days, we will turn upon them the most ruthless invasion known to man since the razing of Jerusalem to the earth, and burn the accursed land from Dan to Beersheba!

This retaliatory programme, it is supposed, would have been carried out, had not the intelligence reached General McCulloch, at that time, of General Price's retreat from Missouri, closely followed by General Fremont. This general, it is said, assumed the consequence of an eastern satrap, and so encumbered was he with the immense wagon-train necessary to transport the delicacies of his luxurious camp, that he made but a desultory pursuit of General Price, and, like the dog in pursuit of the wolf, was not extremely anxious to overtake him.

The short march, from St. Louis to Springfield, proved enough *active* campaigning for General Fremont, and, in the latter town, he established his court, and remained until the commencement of the winter season in St. Louis, when he removed his court to the gay capital of his satrapy. Hearing of Fremont's departure, General McCulloch hastily placed himself at the head of a cavalry force, of which our Texas regiments and Whitfield's Battalion formed an integral part, and made a rapid march to Springfield, only to find that General Fremont, having rusticated sufficiently, had leisurely returned to St. Louis.

While Fremont was encamped at Springfield, General McCulloch ordered Captain Mabry with his company G, and Captain Cumby with company B, both of the Third Texas, to proceed to Springfield, or as near that town as they could, without risking too much the capture of their commands, and to ascertain approximately the number of the enemy, the number of his guns, and all other information concerning him they could obtain. When within about ten miles of Springfield, these brave officers were met by a regiment of Missouri cavalry that had been skirmishing with the enemy's pickets, the commander of which informed them that Fremont occupied the place with 50,000 men, and that they had better turn back, as their capture would be certain, if they proceeded any further in that direction.

But these brave and conscientious officers did not think they had fulfilled the spirit of their instructions, and resolved to pursue their present course and risk the consequences. They proceeded to within eight miles of the town, and ascertained of a Southern sympathizer, at whose house they had halted to make inquiries, that the enemy was full 35,000 strong, and that his forces were encamped immediately within the limits of the town.

It was judged inadvisable to proceed any further with the men; and, at the suggestion of the dauntless Mabry, Cumby remained in charge of the two companies, and himself, accompanied by Captain Alf. Johnson and a thoroughly reliable guide, set out, determined to obtain the information desired by General McCulloch. They proceeded without incident to within one mile of Springfield, and here fastening their horses, entered the town afoot, and made for the house of a well-known Southern lady. From her they learned that the enemy was reported to be 30,000 strong. Dispatching the guide for a Southern gentleman, from whom the desired information could be obtained, Mabry and Johnson proceeded to regale themselves with a warm supper that had been prepared for them.

After supper, Mabry went out into the front yard to ascertain if all was right, and his quick eye immediately discovered the fact that the house was surrounded by Yankees. Turning to re-enter the house, he was accosted by a party of five or six, who demanded his surrender and the yielding up of his arms. Pretending to comply, the dauntless man drew his bowie knife and plunged it into the heart of the spokesman, who dropped dead at his feet. This was the signal for a terrific onslaught. The infuriated Yankees closed in on him, while revolver after revolver rung out its murderous report.

Mabry slashed right and left in the darkness with his trusty knife, and other foemen, undoubtedly, felt the keenness of its edge. But he is now shot through the right hand and the friendly knife drops from his nerveless grasp at his feet. Drawing his revolver with his left hand, he retreats around the house to where Johnson is engaged with a number of the enemy; for, upon the first report of fire-arms, Johnson jumped out of the window, and was met by a number of men, who demanded his surrender. His only reply was from the muzzle of his shot-gun. Emptying both barrels of which, he, too, drew his six-shooter and continued the bloody fray. Mabry having rejoined him, the two kept the enemy at bay as they retired from the scene, Johnson supporting himself upon the shoulder of Mabry, as he was severely wounded in the hip.

The indomitable men proceeded thus until they reached their horses, when they made for Captain Cumby and the two companies. The faithful guide, hearing the uproar, immediately retraced his steps, and procuring their overcoats, letters, etc., rejoined them at camp. Take this episode in all its bearing, and, I suppose, it stands unparalleled in all the hairbreadth escapes of the war for cool courage and indomitable will. Julius Caesar was no braver than H. P. Mabry, and the writer has often thought that, if Mabry had commanded at Vicksburg, there would have been no surrender of that place, and, *ergo*, no necessity for the sad finale at Appomattox Court-house.

After reaching the command, the two wounded heroes had time and leisure to realise how hazardous had been their mission, and how narrow their escape. Their clothing was literally perforated by the enemy's balls, and it seemed that the hand of death had been averted only by a miracle. Of Captain Mabry's subsequent career, our narrative will deal. Captain Johnson was afterwards appointed to a Colonelcy, for his gallantry on this occasion, and was the commandant of Arkansas Post, when that place fell into the hands of the enemy. He was taken prisoner and died in St. Louis. After the reconnaissance, at Springfield, General McCulloch retired toward the Arkansas line, and, about December 6, 1861, the various regiments went into winter-quarters.

The winter encampment of the Third was selected at the mouth of Frog Bayou, on the Arkansas River, and that of the Sixth a few miles below. Captain Harris, the energetic Quartermaster of the Third, procured a saw-mill, and soon material for the erection of comfortable shanties, was in abundance. As there were no rumours of war here, the boys commenced a life of pleasure and social dissipation in the fashionable circles of Frog Bayou. Dances—regular old-fashioned "brandances"—were the order of the night; and animated jig and reel followed the lively twanging of many an Arkansaw Ole Bull's fiddle.

Many of the boys here obtained furloughs for the purpose of visiting their homes. General McCulloch went to Richmond, Virginia, the permanent capital of the Confederacy, and Colonel Greer obtained leave of absence to visit his home, which left the army in command of General McIntosh, and the regiment in command of Lieutenant-Colonel Lane.

# CHAPTER 3

# Death of Captain Harris

Early in December, the Third Regiment was called upon to mourn the loss of their good old quartermaster. In superintending the sawing of timber, Captain Harris carelessly allowed his clothing to be caught by the teeth of the circular saw, and, ere the team could be stopped, his body was fearfully mangled. He survived a day or two, and died. No regiment in the service had the good fortune to possess a better quartermaster than he, and his loss was long and seriously felt by the men.

The festivities alluded to in the preceding chapter were at their height—like the celebrated ball at Brussels, immortalised by Byron—when the rude blast of war broke upon the diverting scene, and summoned the gay Adonis from blushing sweetheart and nimble-toed jig, to ruder scenes in the march, the bivouac, and the deadly charge. The irrepressible Hopotheohola, daring the rigors of winter as he had braved the frosts of time, had again flung his seditious standard to the breeze, and defiantly thrown down the gage of battle to General Cooper, who immediately commenced a periodical retreat. Simultaneously with the reception of the intelligence, Colonel McIntosh ordered out the cavalry, consisting of the Third, Sixth, and Eleventh (Young's) Texas Regiment, and Whitfield's Battalion (Texas), the latter two of whom had but recently joined us.

Placing himself at the head of the column, McIntosh gave the signal for the march to commence. At Van Buren, where the command crossed the Arkansas River, McIntosh's regiment of mounted infantry fell into line. A forced march was here begun, which terminated only when Fort Gibson was reached. The weather, previously very pleasant, now became extremely cold. The ground was frozen, and the men suffered much from the bitter cold. Passing through Fort Gibson, the command crossed a large prairie, and entered the woods beyond, through which flowed the Chustenahlah Creek, a beautiful and wild mountain brook. From this point, the smoke from the enemy's camp-fires was plainly visible, rising from the summits of the mountains in the distant perspective.

The command halted on Chustenahlah Creek until midnight, when Colonel Lane, throwing forward Company E (Third Regiment), Captain D. M. Short commanding, as an advance-guard, the command resumed the line of march. The march was continued all night without an incident to vary the dull monotony. About 9 p.m., Captain Short came upon the enemy's pickets, and drove them rapidly in upon the main body. The command soon arrived upon the scene, when it was discovered that the enemy was posted upon the summit of an almost inaccessible mountain.

The sagacious and experienced Hopotheohola had selected a position impregnable by nature, and the veteran chieftain, with his more youthful lieutenant—Halleck Tschustenuga—were riding up and down the lines, speaking words of confidence, and imparting hopes of promise, in an effort to rouse their warriors to as sublime a devotion to the cause, and reckless disregard of consequences, as filled their own stoical bosoms. The warriors, painted in the most hideous manner, and clad in the most outlandish garbs, were perpetrating fantastic antics before high heaven, and the cat-like enemy ready for the fatal spring below. Some gobbled, in imitation of the turkey-gobbler; others, fired by a spirit of emulation, apparently, rivalled the coyote in howling; the game Viking of the barnyard would have recognised his "cock-a-doodle-doo," in the wild pandemonium of sounds, as would the panther, the catamount, and even the domestic dog.

Colonel McIntosh determined to charge the almost perpendicular mountain, on horseback. Upon the side next us there was but little timber to afford us shelter from the unerring marksmen covered by their works, but there were large, craggy rocks to be scaled, and bottomless gulches to be passed. The command was immediately deployed into line. The Sixth, commanded by Lieutenant-Colonel John S. Griffith, on the right; the Third, commanded by Lieutenant-Colonel Lane, in the centre; the Eleventh, commanded by Colonel Wm. C. Young, on the left; Macintosh's battalion of infantry supporting the line. Slowly the command marches to the very base of the last elevation, and the enemy's sharpshooters are commencing to fire. But the impetuous McIntosh, who cannot brook a tardy skirmish salutation, orders the charge, and the intrepid Lane and Griffith, responding, call on their men, and a thousand frenzied yells reply, as a thousand excited horses plunge madly up the steep ascent, and a thousand rifles pour such a leaden hail into the ranks of the astounded and terrified Indians, that no effort is made to hold the works, and the victory is won ere the battle had fairly begun.

A vigorous pursuit was immediately commenced, and many hand-to-hand fights to the death occurred; for, however impotent the Indian may be *fettered* by disciplined organisation, individually, he knows no personal danger, and, taking his life in his hand, will accept the challenge to mortal combat with the odds against him of ten to one. The Indians scattered in all directions—having Kansas, however, for the objective point—and built fires, or rather made "smokes," in order to divert the pursuers, and cause them to relax the pursuit. One instance of their stoical indifference to death will suffice: An old warrior fired upon a party of eight or ten from behind a tree.

The men did not wish to kill him, and used even entreaties to induce him to surrender; but, with death imminent, he continued to load his old rifle with a sublime indifference never attained by the Cynic philosophers of Greece, and, having loaded, he coolly proceeded with the priming, when his admiring foes were compelled to dash out his brave old life. "Only an Indian killed!" but who knows what the hopes were that this old man had founded upon his cause? Go, votaries of the "Lost Cause," to the crumbling stones of your dismantled altars, and invoke, if ye can, the spirit of 1861. It is dead! dead in soul and body, and no wraith even represents it in the phantom processions of the shadowy land of Weir!

The victors at Atlanta and Appomattox hold it even lighter than you regard the cause of the poor old warrior, lying there in the silent wilderness before you, with his crimson life-tide ebbing and splashing away! Unhappy man, in the brief span of life, is but a puppet! The Roman emperor weighs not more in the balances of Divine justice than does the savage Indian; each leaves the impress of his foot upon the sands of time, and the first returning wave obliterates all trace of empire and tribe alike.

An inventory of the captured prisoners and property showed: Two hundred and fifty women and children; forty or fifty negroes; five hundred head of ponies; seventy or eighty wagons; one hundred head of beef cattle; five hundred head of sheep; ten thousand (more or less) dogs; besides buffalo-robes, beads, belts, and other trinkets too numerous and infinitesimal to name. One article found among the trinkets, invaluable by reason of its age and antecedents, was a silver medal, struck in commemoration of a treaty of peace concluded between the Creeks and the British Government, in the year 1694. What became of this souvenir, the author knows not; but hopes it has been returned, ere this, to its original owners.

The loss of the command was slight, but no correct list, it is thought, of the casualties, is now extant. Lieutenant Durham, a young and promising officer of Company B, Third Regiment, was mortally wounded, and died soon after. Company A, of the Third Regiment, was ably commanded by Orderly-Sergeant R. B. Gause, whose many noble qualities deserve that he should be mentioned; but the author knows no eulogium that he could pronounce in his praise more appropriate than that pronounced by the great Napoleon on Baron Larry: *"He was,"* said the emperor, *"the most virtuous man I ever knew."*

That the United States had stirred up this revolt among the Indians, the United States rifles with which they were largely armed, amply demonstrated. But the emissaries of the Federal Government were powerless again to cause the Indian to offer himself as food for powder and lead. The crushing defeat of Chustenahlah put a period to all hopes of creating a diversion in that direction. Poor old Hopotheohola, who had done all that individual sagacity and intrepidity could, with the limited means at his command, fell a victim to his discomfited warriors' desire for revenge and blood. He was assassinated by unknown parties soon after the battle. The campaign proper terminated with the Battle of Chustenahlah, and the command of Colonel McIntosh returned to their respective quarters.

In the case of the Third Regiment, the boys were glad enough to return to their comfortable quarters, and resume the social duties and pleasures that had been so unceremoniously broken up by the late call to arms. Colonel Greer, soon after this, returned, being accompanied by his charming and good lady. We have spoken elsewhere of the angelic ministrations of Mrs. Greer, at the bedside of the sick soldiers, and would again repeat all that we there wrote; and did the language admit of more positive expressions, they should be employed in commendation of her Christian deeds.

About the latter portion of February, the men who had been home on furlough reported for duty, and many fresh volunteers came, also, to swell the ranks of the regiment. Of course, these neophytes in the art of war looked upon their veteran friends of twelve months' service as perambulating military encyclopaedias of useful knowledge. The veteran felt his importance, and, oracle-like, delivered his replies to the many questions by metaphorical allusions, and with an air of freezing indifference. A new recruit, upon one occasion, desired to be informed, by a veteran friend, how many Yankees he had killed. The impossibility of ascertaining this fact, in a general engagement, was shown by the veteran. "Did you ever kill *one?*" persisted the recruit. "Did you ever shoot one, and see the blood spout out—see it, yourself?"

"It is better," replied the veteran, "to be in doubt whether we ever killed *one*, than to have the conscience tormented with the belief that we killed them all." This was satisfactory.

While in winter-quarters, as Adjutant M. D. Ector was attempting to suppress some boisterous noise in the camp of one of the companies, he was assaulted by two of the men, who were subsequently court-martialled, and sentenced to be dishonourably discharged and drummed out of the regiment. The sentence was severe, and the unfortunate men, who had proved themselves good and brave soldiers, felt the disgrace deeply.

The negroes, and a portion of the women and children captured at Chustenahlah, were kept under guard at this post for several weeks. What ultimately was the fate of the poor unfortunates, we know not. They presented a forlorn and pitiful picture—bereft of all they held dear and the author's heart, on more than one occasion, went out in sympathy to them.

## INCIDENTS, ETC.

On the evening of the 25th, as the Third Texas was busy in the work of pitching camp, two hundred warriors, as if they had emerged from the bosom of the earth, were discovered in line of battle, not exceeding one-half mile, in the immediate front of the regiment, calmly contemplating the actions of the busy and unconscious men before them. Major Chilton rode out about halfway toward them, and signified, by signs, for one to approach him, which request was immediately complied with. The Indians refused to speak the American language, by which token Major Chilton was soon convinced that they were hostiles, and abandoned the conference; whereupon, the silent cavalcade as mysteriously disappeared in the mountains as it had appeared.

Just before night, on this evening, Sam. Martin, an old Indian fighter, discerned the smoke of the hostile encampment rising above the summits of the mountains, in the dim distance, and forthwith reported the fact to Colonel Lane, and from this moment, all fears of the enemy's retreat were dispelled.

Hopotheohola had, at one time, exercised the functions of Chief of the Creek Nation, and was displaced by the able and favourite "White King," McIntosh, who was succeeded by his son, Chili, who, as chief, concluded a treaty with General Pike, on the part of the Confederate States, in 1861. A bitter feud existed between Hopotheohola and the McIntosh family, and for Chili McIntosh to espouse the cause of the South, was sufficient reason why his hereditary enemy should cast his fortunes on the opposite side. The full-bloods generally sided with Hopotheohola, while the wealth and intelligence of the tribe arrayed themselves under the banner of the legitimate chief, McIntosh, who proved himself an able leader, a sagacious ruler, and a man of unswerving fidelity to the cause he had espoused. Indeed, there were instances in which the civilized Indians signalised themselves for high courage, fortitude, and chivalry, that would have reflected credit on knights of the "Round-Table;" conspicuous among whom must always stand the names of Chili McIntosh and Colonel Stan Waitie.

Colonel McIntosh's plan of campaign comprised the capture of the enemy as well as his defeat; and, to this end, Colonel D. H. Cooper, commanding an Indian brigade, to which was temporarily attached to the Ninth Regiment of Texas Cavalry, and Whitfield's Texas Battalion—both of which organisations, subsequently, were integral parts of "Ross' Brigade"—marched up the Arkansas River with the object of cutting off the retreat of the enemy, while the command of Colonel McIntosh, as before stated, marched up the Verdigris, and attacked Hopotheohola on the heights of Chustenahlah. The immediate object of the movement was defeated by the precipitancy of the attack, and the immediate giving way of the Indian line.

But the indefatigable Whitfield, the gallant Colonel Sims of the Ninth, and Colonel Cooper, with his brigade of friendly Indians, pursued them far into the inhospitable plains. The pursuers were forced to turn back, as their rations were consumed, and they had already tested the quality of broiled horse-flesh. The plains were utterly destitute of game. The weather was intensely cold, and, in addition to the pangs of hunger, the men suffered no little from this cause.

Major G. W. Chilton, of the Third Texas Cavalry, while acting with conspicuous gallantry, was wounded by a rifle-ball, slightly, in the head; but, disregarding which, he remained at his post until the last gun was fired. Major M. J. Brinson, of the Ninth Texas Cavalry, bore himself, throughout the engagement, with marked gallantry; and, by his fearless demeanour, contributed no little to the final result. The author's friend, Harry Bell, of Company A, Third Texas Cavalry, was severely, though not mortally, wounded by a frightful bullet-hole in the right breast.

At Fort Gibson, Lieutenant-Colonel Lane obtained leave of absence, and returned home, leaving Major G. W. Chilton in command of the Third Texas Cavalry, which leisurely continued the march to winter-quarters. At Van Buren, Major Chilton munificently "stood treat," and purchased a barrel of choice whisky, which the boys of the regiment disposed of by drinking frequent "potations pottle deep," and all got as merry as merry could be, and many didn't get home till morning, and some, only after the lapse of two or three days; but, in the case of these latter, whether their absence was attributable to the effects of Arkansaw corn-juice, or to Arkansaw belles, deponent sayeth not.

One of the unostentatious heroes of Chustenahlah, was B. S. Triplett, the author's friend, and to whom he was indebted for many an act of kindness. Brave and loyal "old Tripp," after passing through the hundreds of battles and skirmishes of the four years of war, fell just at its close by the hands of an assassin. Perhaps it was better so! He never lived to look upon the "conquered banner," and to feel that experience of death in life that he had outlived his usefulness. Death is generally accounted the ultimate loss; but death often relieves life of many burdens too grievous to be borne; and, it is doubtful, if we should not look upon the white horse and his spectre rider as friends of humanity, instead of remorseless foes.

Organisation, and First Year's Service of the Ninth Texas Cavalry.

To its gallant and noble Colonel, W. B. Sims, now a leading merchant of Jefferson, Texas, the author is indebted for the data from which is evolved the subjoined brief reference to the organisation of the Ninth Texas Cavalry, and its services up to the first day's fight at Elk Horn, on March 6, 1862. The regiment was originally organised for State service, at Brogden's Springs, about twelve miles north of Sherman, Grayson County, October 2, 1861, with the following officers:

Colonel—W. B. Sims, Red River County.
Lieutenant-Colonel— —— Quail, Tarrant County.
Major—N. C. Towns, Red River County.
Surgeon— —— Robinson, Titus County.

Assistant Surgeon— —— Prewitt, Titus County.

Adjutant—Dudley Jones, Titus County.

(D. W. Jones was elected Colonel at the re-organisation of the regiment at Corinth, Mississippi, in May, 1862.)

Quartermaster—W. B. Sims, Red River County.

Commissary—J. D. Wright, Lamar County.

Co. A, Tarrant County, Thos. G. Berry, Captain.

Co. B, Fannin County, Sid. Smith, Captain.

Co. C, Grayson County, J. E. McCoole, Captain.

Co. D, Tarrant County, M. J. Brinson, Captain.

Co. E, Red River County, J. C. Hart, Captain.

Co. F, Titus County, W. E. Duncan, Captain.

Co. G, Hopkins County, L. D. King, Captain.

Co. H, J. D. Wright, Captain, who was appointed Commissary of Subsistence at Horsehead, and E. L. Dohoney was elected Captain.

Co. I, Titus County, Chas. S. Stewart. Captain.

Co. K, Hopkins County, J. P. Williams, Captain.

The regiment was mustered into the Confederate States' service October 14, 1861, by Colonel W. C. Young; and, in a very short while, Colonel Sims received orders to report, with his command, to General Ben. McCulloch, whose headquarters were located in Southwest Missouri. *En route*, in conformity to these instructions, Colonel Sims received, at North Forktown, in the Indian Territory, orders from General McCulloch directing him to proceed to the assistance of General D. H. Cooper, who was being pressed by a superior force of hostile Indians. In compliance with this order, the command was turned, and soon Colonel Sims received an urgent appeal from General Cooper to the effect that he should forward five hundred men, in charge of Lieutenant-Colonel Quail and Major Towns, by forced marches, to his assistance.

Volunteers were called for, and, the whole regiment responding, Colonel Sims caused the requisite number to be detailed, when the march was immediately commenced. Arriving at General Cooper's quarters, Lieutenant-Colonel Quail was directed to have his men cook seven days' rations, and otherwise prepare for assuming the offensive. The night was spent in making the necessary preparations, and, with the early dawn, the march was resumed. Hopotheohola, a veteran ex-chief of the Creeks, was in command of the hostiles. These burned the grass, and destroyed everything eatable, in the line of the Confederate advance; and, as the boys were novices in campaigning, and knew not the necessity of economising their rations, the consequence was that the supply was soon exhausted.

On the fourth day out, the village of Hopotheohola was sighted, and Lieutenant-Colonel Quail immediately made dispositions for battle. This was on November 19. The regiment was divided; a portion in charge of Lieutenant-Colonel Quail, deflecting to the right, in the edge of the timber, and the remainder, under Major Towns, obliqueing to the left through the prairie. In a short time, Lieutenant-Colonel Quail came upon the enemy, and attacked him vigorously. This battle was quite stubbornly contested by Hopotheohola, but Colonel Quail finally drove them from the field, and won the victory of Round Mountain. Captain Stewart, of Titus County, was killed while gallantly leading his men, and several of the men were killed and wounded.

The Indians fired the grass in such a manner as to throw the glare upon the whites, while the shadow of the dense smoke afforded them a friendly cover. The command camped upon the field with horses saddled and arms in hand, and, in the early dawn, set out upon the trail of the retreating foe. Several of the Texans had been taken prisoners at Round Mountain, and were tortured and killed by the savages on their retreat. Their mutilated bodies—always scalped—were properly interred by their comrades.

On December 9, another engagement was had with Hopotheohola, on Bird's Creek, in which Colonel Sims again defeated him, with but slight loss on the part of the whites. The battle was spirited, and continued for the space of three hours. The next day, Colonel Sims received orders to report at Fort Gibson, and to assume command of that post until further orders. The Ninth remained at this place until the arrival of Colonel McIntosh, when the Chustenahlah campaign was inaugurated, as elsewhere recounted in these pages. The fugitives from that fatal field were pursued by the regiment of Colonel Sims, the battalion of Major Whitfield, and the Indians of General Cooper's immediate command, far into the bleak and inhospitable plains of Kansas, whose death-brooding alkali soil nourished nothing for the subsistence of man or horse. The men, in consequence, suffered no little from the pangs of hunger and cold, and were forced, finally, to the alternative of starving outright, or eating "mule-beef."

On returning to Fort Gibson, Colonel Sims was ordered to proceed to Van Buren, Arkansas, and from there the regiment marched to Horsehead bayou and went into winter-quarters. The men had, however, scarcely completed their cabins, and were beginning to feel comfortable, when the regiment was ordered to report to General McCulloch, at Fayetteville. This was the opening of the campaign that terminated in the drawn Battle of Elk Horn, or Pea Ridge, as the Union historians have named it. Colonel Sims opened the fight, on the part of McCulloch's corps, by a splendid charge upon a Federal battery, which he captured, with the loss of about twenty men and twice that number of horses.

The gallant Sims, while intrepidly leading his men in the charge, had his right arm broken by a grape-shot, and was forced, reluctantly, to quit the field. In about the space of one hour from this time, Colonel Sims received the intelligence of General McCulloch's fall, and immediately dispatched his ambulance for the body of the general. This he conveyed to Bentonville, Arkansas, and delivered it into the charge of Major Brown, of McCulloch's staff.

After the battle, the regiment leisurely fell back to Van Buren, at which place it remained several days, and until orders were received for dismounting of the men, and their transfer to the Cis-Mississippi department. The regiment embarked for Memphis, Tennessee, at Des Arc, April 16, 1862, and were soon transported by rail to Corinth, where they were brigaded with the Sixth Texas, and other regiments which constituted Phifer's Brigade, of Maury's Division. Of their subsequent services, the narrative speaks in connection with those of the other regiments which constituted the "Texas Brigade," which was first commanded by Brigadier-General J. W. Whitfield, and, subsequently, by General L. S. Ross.

The Ninth was a splendid body of young men, who signalized their valour and devotion to the cause of their section on many of the bloodiest fields of the war.

## CHAPTER 4

# Van Dorn Arrives and Assumes Command

The peaceful, semi-domestic scenes that characterised the sojourn in winter-quarters, were of short duration, for soon the summons came for us to mount and go forth, to meet a more powerful foe than the one so recently vanquished on the heights of Chustenahlah. The heroic Price had made a winter campaign into Missouri, and the "Old Guard" had added fresh laurels to their fame by the victory of Drywood, and on other fields. About the middle of February. General Curtis took the field, at the head of about 40,000 men, magnificently equipped, and abundantly provided with all the murderous machinery of war. Price had halted at Springfield, purposing to spend the remainder of the winter there, in the re-organisation of his army. In an address to the people of Missouri, he eloquently exclaimed: "Give me 50,000 men, and Missouri shall march to victory with the tread of a giant!"

At Carthage, in the autumn past, a quorum of the Missouri Legislature had convened, and formally severed her connection with the United States, and, in conformity to this "Act," General Price was mustering the State Guard into the Confederate service; and, in the midst of his labours, he was apprised of the enemy's advance. The brave old man did not move until the enemy was upon him. Then, placing his raw recruits in front, with the immense wagon-train, that he had filled with supplies from the fertile fields of Missouri, he commenced his slow and stubborn retreat. And woe to the enemy's column that had the temerity to beard the old lion in his den when he defiantly stood at bay, as he often did, to give his train time, for they were invariably driven from the field by the dauntless veterans of Lexington and Drywood. Dispatches announcing the warlike situation of affairs beyond the line, were sent General McCulloch, and soon his forces were *en route* for the theatre of action.

Intelligence reached us that the enemy had driven General Price beyond "Cross Hollows," and that he was making demonstrations on the town of Fayetteville. In passing the Boston mountains, the weather was intensely cold, and the men, though warmly clothed, suffered no little. On either side of the road, the precipitous mountains rose hundreds of feet overhead, while gigantic icicles hung pendant from the overhanging rocks, like huge stalactites, and, glittering in the brilliant rays of the cold winter sun, looked like the suspended spears of giants. On entering Fayetteville, the Third Regiment passed the bivouac of the Third Louisiana, our old comrades on the field of Oak Hills, who now welcomed us with extravagant demonstrations of joy. Between these two regiments there was an affectionate spirit of *comraderie*, from the battle of Oak Hills unto the last. Brigaded together during the Iuka and Corinth campaigns, the bonds of friendship became more earnest and binding with daily association.

The intrepid regiment, in the veins of many of whose members the best blood of Louisiana coursed, constituted a portion of the ill-fated garrison of Vicksburg, and occupying a bastion during the siege that was blown up, its ranks were literally decimated, and but few of the intrepid and generous Frenchmen lived to return home and recount the proud story of their heroic career. The author is grateful that he has been allowed to offer even this inadequate tribute to their worth. Great was the contrast between our entry into Fayetteville, now, and eight months before. Then, the people had faith in the puissance of the Confederate soldier, and they hailed the flag of Dixie as the harbinger of protection. Now, since defeats had destroyed the prestige of Southern arms, they looked upon our advent with apathy, seeming to think that the hand of fate was upon them, and that no earthly prowess could avert the blow.

Like the French, our people grew despondent with reverses. They did not remember the high old Roman way: While the legions of Hannibal were encamped before the city, the very ground occupied by them was put up for sale to the highest bidder, as a means of obtaining funds for the prosecution of the war, and brought fabulous prices. But the despondency of the good people of Fayetteville, in the present instance, was not without foundation, for the Missouri Army was in retreat, and McCulloch's infantry yet remained in position on the Van Buren road, in the Boston mountains. Halting in the town, we had the opportunity of "reviewing" the Missouri Army as it denied past us *en route,* for the new position in the mountains. General Price, assuredly, had the most *multitudinous* and *variegated* wagon-train ever concentrated on the continent. Every species of wheel vehicle, from the jolting old ox-cart to the most fantastically-painted stage-coach, rolled along the road.

The men were well clad, and presented a fine, soldierly appearance. Starting out, originally, as militia, the Missouri army had an entirely disproportionate number of brigadier-generals, and the facetious boys cried out, "Here's your army of brigadier-generals and stagecoaches!" The cavalry were assigned to the duty of picketing in front of the enemy, and various skirmishes, of but little interest, took place. Finally, the cavalry was withdrawn, and the enemy's cavalry occupied the town of Fayetteville for a week or two, and then fell back on Bentonville, at which place, also, was the division of Siegel. General Curtis, with the main portion of the army, occupied a very strong position, near Elk Horn tavern.

The Confederate forces, in the Boston mountains, occupied the main road leading from Van Buren to Fayetteville. The Missouri Army took up position on the "Cane Hill" road. The two armies remained substantially in this position until Major-General Earl Van Dorn assumed command of both Price's and McCulloch's divisions, about March 1st, 1862. And thus a period was put to the unseemly wrangling as to precedence, that had formerly characterized the intercourse of Price and McCulloch with each other, and which, at times, very seriously impaired the efficiency of both armies. About this time, two expeditions were started to the enemy's rear, with the object of destroying whatever material of war access could be had to. Companies G and I, of the Third Regiment, commanded by Major L. S. Ross, of the Sixth Regiment, composed one of the detachments, and Company F, of the Third, was ordered to report to Major Whitfield, which, with his battalion, constituted the other.

Major Ross was ordered to ride around the enemy's left wing, and Major Whitfield around the right. Ross succeeded in reaching the rear of the main force, and, at Keitsville, captured a number of prisoners, horses, and mules, and burned an immense train, containing a vast amount of military stores, and brought off his men in safety, with no loss. Major Ross won the highest compliments from the commanding General, for his dashing gallantry and skilful conduct throughout the affair. The skill and sagacity displayed in this raid, by Major Ross, gave token of that splendid career which the near future had in store for him.

Major Whitfield was not so successful, as his horses were too jaded to perform the long and rapid march necessary in affairs of this nature. On the 28th of February, General Van Dorn arrived, and assumed command of the combined Missouri and Confederate forces, and immediately preparations for an advance was then made. The army, took up the line of march on the 2nd of March. The weather was bitter cold, but such spirit had the new commander infused into the hearts of the men, by his energetic actions, that the signal to advance was hailed with enthusiastic shouts, and other demonstrations of joy. General Van Dorn accompanied Price's column, while General McCulloch had command of the infantry portion of his late army. General McIntosh, who had recently received his commission of Brigadier-General, commanded the cavalry.

During the advance, the Sixth Regiment captured a commissary train and fifty prisoners. The march proceeded without incident, until the morning of the 5th. The weather continued cold, and snow had been falling for a day or two, and the earth was covered by the cold, white carpet, to the depth of three or four inches. Price's division had made a detour to the right, for the purpose of turning the enemy's left flank, and gaining his rear—a move that was crowned with success. McCulloch advanced upon the main road to Elk Horn tavern. McIntosh, on the left, headed for Bentonville. From the highlands, two miles south of the town, we could see Siegel's infantry retreating.

Quick as thought, we obliqued to the left, and passed around the town, having for an object the cutting off of Siegel's division. But the cunning old fox, calculating exactly where we would enter the road again, placed his division, 10,000 strong, in ambush, and the first intimation we had of the position of affairs, was the firing upon our advance-guard, Company B, Third Regiment, Captain Cumby commanding. The Third Regiment was in the advance, and the men apprehensive of no danger. Many were walking, leading their horses, to get warm by the exercise. *Bang! bang!* went the guns, fired at Cumby's company, and, quick as thought, McIntosh drew his saber and ordered the bugle to sound the charge. It may be imagined that the regiment was thrown into great disorder.

Yet, the impetuous young general led the assault, sword in hand, up to the very muzzles of Siegel's guns. A deafening roar of artillery, and rattling of musketry, greeted the charging column, and minie-balls, grape and canister chorused through the air. *The regiment was repulsed!* Had such a thing been whispered before as possible, every man in the regiment would have denounced him as a calumniator, who mouthed the suspicion. The intrepid McIntosh, amid a shower of balls, grasped the flag, and, waving it above his head, implored the men to rally for another charge.

But brave, simple-hearted old Captain Hale stood up in his stirrups, the tears trickling down his snow-white beard, and exclaimed: "*This here rigiment are disgraced forever! I'd a ruther died right thar than to a give arry a inch!*" Brave old Captain Hale! He was a diamond in the rough, and his men regarded him more in the light of a kind father than that of an officer, and when the time came for the election of officers, after the first year's service had expired, his "boys" begged him to remain with them as their captain. We were serving, then, as infantry, and the feeble old hero informed them that he could not make one day's march afoot. Whereupon, the "boys" held a consultation, and it was determined upon that they would purchase their beloved old captain a horse and buggy! Did ever man govern before with such unanimous and full consent of the governed? The loss of the regiment in this affair was ten men killed and twenty wounded.

The command camped at "Camp Stephens" the night of the 5th. The snow fell all night. The command was in motion two hours before day, and all felt assured that a few hours would usher in the first act of the drama. *En route* to the field of battle, we passed the Indian Brigade of General Pike, all of whom were painted, in conformity to the horrid custom of their people. Soon the thunders of Price's guns announced that the "Old Guard" were in position, in the enemy's rear, and General McCulloch at once advanced a brigade of infantry, composed of the Third Louisiana and several regiments of Arkansas troops, against the Federal left. As McIntosh, at the head of several cavalry regiments, came on the field, marching by fours, in the following order: Third Texas on the right; Sixth Texas on the right centre; Ninth Texas on the left centre; and Brooks' battalion on the left, through an open field, in parallel lines, by fours, a Federal battery, supported by a brigade of infantry, opened upon us at a distance of about 500 yards.

General Ben. McCulloch was just passing the Third Regiment, with a Confederate battery, and, as the first Yankee shell went crashing through our ranks, commanded, "Wheel that battery into line!"— probably the last order ever uttered by this true and staunch son of

Texas. The gallant McIntosh ordered the bugle to sound the charge, and, waving his sabre overhead, led the furious and irresistible charge. Like the impetuous rush of an avalanche, the mad columns swept over the field, in the midst of a tempest of iron hail, the thunders of artillery, the yells of the combatants, and the groans of the dying and wounded. They are upon the enemy! and the iron dogs of war are hushed.

The combatants become intermixed, and the gunners are cut down at their posts. The Stars and Stripes go down, and the Red Cross of the South waves in triumph above the scene of destruction. But the work of slaughter does not stop here. The infuriated cavaliers charge the supporting infantry, in the teeth of a most destructive storm of musketry, and, routed, they fly from the field! The Third Regiment did not engage in the brilliant affair, as it remained to support the Confederate battery before alluded to. By this time, McCulloch's infantry were warmly engaged with the enemy, about eight hundred yards in front of Pea Ridge, and the interminable volleys of musketry told how hotly contested was the fight. The Third Regiment was dismounted, and placed in line of battle just behind the crest of Pea Ridge, as a support to the infantry, and with orders not to abandon the Ridge under any circumstances.

General McCulloch, very early in the action, imprudently ventured too far in front of his own lines, to reconnoitre the enemy's position, and this was the last ever seen of the brave and conscientious old Texas chief in life. The impetuous McIntosh, who was at home only amidst the raging of wild elements, and who courted the missions of danger with a fondness not surpassed by the affection of a lover for his mistress, led an Arkansas regiment of infantry against the enemy, soon after his dashing cavalry charge, and fell at the very muzzles of their guns, sword in hand.

The author regrets exceedingly that he has no *data* upon which to predicate any sketch of the life of this daring young Georgian. He was the soul of honour and chivalry; the *beau sabreur* of the Western Army; and, had he lived, would have written his name high upon the memorial roll of Fame. With McIntosh, there was no intermediate rest between death and glory. To add to the misfortunes of the Confederate forces, on this ill-starred field, Colonel Hebert, of the Third Louisiana, who, after McIntosh, was the next ranking officer in McCulloch's division, was taken prisoner. It was evident, from the firing, that the brave old Missourian was slowly driving the main force of the enemy before his indomitable "Grizzly Bears," and the unbroken succession of the volleys from cannon and rifles, which sounded like one continuous roll of thunder, proclaimed the deadly nature of the conflict.

And had McCulloch and McIntosh lived; had Hebert been spared us; or had Colonel Greer known that the carnival of death and misfortune had devolved the command upon himself; the enemy before us, too, would have been driven back upon a common centre, where but the alternative of surrender or destruction awaited the Federal army. As it was, these brave Louisianans and Arkansians, without a head, manfully breasted the terrific storm of shot and canister poured into their ranks by an enemy who outnumbered them in the ratio of five to one, throughout the entire day, and yielded never one foot of ground. The continued absence of Generals McCulloch and McIntosh excited the suspicions of Colonel Greer that all was not right, and he dispatched private John N. Coleman, of Company A, Third Regiment, to go in quest of the generals, and ascertain if no further disposition of the reserve was to be made, for that experienced officer well knew that the brave and weary Louisianans and Arkansians in our front should be re-enforced, or relieved by a fresh division entirely.

Mr. Coleman soon returned, saying that he could ascertain nothing in regard to the whereabouts of either Generals McCulloch or McIntosh, but that he had seen the adjutant-general of each, neither of whom could give any account of their chieftains. Mr. Coleman, however, stated that he had met Lieutenant-Colonel Lane, who had been detached from his regiment, and placed in command of another cavalry corps; that Lane wished Greer to meet him at a log-house, immediately in rear of his brigade, where they could hold a consultation, and arrive at some determination as to what course should be pursued in the strange and anomalous state of affairs. Thither Colonel Greer repaired, without the loss of any precious time. It was decided by these officers, to withdraw the troops to the main road, about one-half mile in rear of our present position, and dispatch a courier to General Van Dorn, announcing the critical condition in which this wing of the army was placed.

At 11 p.m., with no guard but the friendly darkness, Mr. John N. Coleman set out on his hazardous mission, in the prosecution of which it was necessary to describe the semi-circumference of the circle of which the enemy's centre was the pivot, and pass his flank, all the while exposed to imminent danger of being captured by the cavalry covering that wing of the army. Coleman arrived at General Van Dorn's head-quarters at one o'clock, with the dispatches, which imparted the first intelligence to the general that all was not right with McCulloch's division. General Van Dorn instructed his assistant adjutant-general, Major Dabney H. Maury, to write Colonel Greer an order, directing him to withdraw the entire division, and lead it around the enemy's right flank, to the position occupied by the Missouri division. Coleman, with a sagacity superior to that of his chief, refused to bear the order in writing, for, if he was captured, and unable to destroy the paper, the enemy would come into possession of the fact that some calamity had occurred to that division, and at once inaugurate measures to prevent the desired concentration, when General Van Dorn consented that it should be transmitted verbally.

Coleman returned about 2 a.m., and Colonel Greer at once undertook the hazardous task of complying with the directions of General Van Dorn. Mr. Coleman, for the eminent services rendered on this occasion, was recommended by Colonel Greer for promotion, and was, accordingly, commissioned Regimental Commissary of Subsistence, with the rank of Captain. Subsequently, on the formation of the Texas Brigade, he was named Commissary for the Brigade, with the rank of Major. He deserved the highest meed of praise for the cool courage, devotion to the cause, and penetrating sagacity manifested on this occasion.

Major Coleman had the misfortune to lose both his feet, a few years ago, by a railway accident. He resides in the city of Marshall, Harrison County, Texas, respected by all his neighbours, and beloved by his comrades of the old brigade. The division reached the headquarters of General Van Dorn about daylight, and, after a few sporadic charges on the enemy, and some desultory firing, apparently without spirit or object, the "Army of the West," which had never before turned its back to the foe, sullenly retired from the scene, leaving the defeated enemy in possession of the field.

Van Dorn was urgently pressed by General Beauregard, the Department Commander, to re-enforce him at Corinth, Mississippi, with all his available force, for almost simultaneously with the Battle of Elk Horn, the terrible tragedy of Shiloh had been enacted, and General Beauregard was now confronted by an overwhelming force, commanded by Major-General Halleck. Van Dorn acted with haste, but so consummate had been all his preparations, that, had it not been for the death of McCulloch and McIntosh, the Battle of Elk Horn would have been one of the most crushing defeats to the enemy known in modern times; for, surrounded as he was, defeat meant capitulation or destruction. Even had he organised a continued and vigorous attack by the combined divisions, the evening of March 8th, 1862, would have ushered into history a splendid Confederate victory.

The soldiers, every one of whom felt that the beaten enemy was not entitled to the possession of the field of battle, and its necessary sequence—the meed of victory—quitted the contest with reluctance, feeling that they had been defrauded of their well-earned dues, and many were the anxious glances turned to the rear by the retreating army, in the vain hope that the enemy would attempt a pursuit. But nothing was more distant from the intentions of General Curtis and his lieutenants. They had had sufficient work, and were content to let "good enough alone."

"By the gods!" exclaimed "Colonel" H. McBride Pridgen, a private of Whitfield's battalion, in describing the battle to friends at home, "we whipped them! we butchered them! we exterminated them! and I don't believe there was but one man that escaped to tell the tale, and *he* stole my blankets!" Upon this statement of the gallant "Colonel" Pridgen, "hangs a tale."

Whitfield's battalion had been dismounted, in order that it could participate in the battle as infantry, which it did, and, as the Third Regiment was marching to the battlefield, on the morning of the 6th, "Colonel" Pridgen, who, foot-sore and weary, had sat down by the roadside, enveloped in a huge, grey, double blanket, in one corner of which was worked, in scarlet worsted, "H. McBride Pridgen." Being acquainted with nearly every man in Company A, he desired someone to allow him to ride behind him to the battlefield. Robert R. Wright invited the fatigued man to mount behind him, which he did, and rejoined his command on the battlefield. In the heat of the action, his huge blankets became too cumbersome, and he laid them on the ground, but the line being forced back by the enemy, the "Colonel's" blankets were not recovered. He gave them up for lost, and, at the dreary bivouac fire, often afterwards spoke in touching terms of his friendly blankets.

Time wore on, and Van Dorn's command was transferred to Mississippi, and had the honour of whipping the *corps d'armée* of "Headquarters-in-the-Saddle" Pope, at the Battle of Farmington, capturing his camp and all its contents. After the battle, the boys engaged, to a moderate extent, in pillaging his deserted stores. Imagine my surprise, when the redoubtable "Colonel" Pridgen rushed up, holding a large, double, grey blanket in his hands, in the corner of which still shone the legend in crimson letters: "H. McBride Pridgen!" "By the gods!" he exclaimed, "I have found the blankets I lost at Elk Horn, Arkansas." This was a strange coincidence, but the circumstance is true.

The bodies of the slain generals were recovered from the field by members of their respective staffs. It is believed that the body of the lamented young Georgian was buried in Van Buren, Arkansas, and that of General McCulloch, conveyed to Texas, by Colonel Brown, his old friend, and a member of his staff. General Ben. McCulloch came to Texas, at a very early day, and fought at the Battle of San Jacinto. He was a celebrated Indian fighter, and, among other creditable affairs with the savage foe, defeated the daring band of Comanches that burned Linnville, in the Battle of Plum Creek, in the year 1840. Subsequently, he engaged in the Mexican war, as commandant of a guerrilla battalion, that performed many eminent services during the war.

As a citizen, Ben. McCulloch had the respect and confidence of all who knew him. He filled several public positions of trust, and acquitted himself, in the discharge of his duties, with as much credit to the probity of his character as to his business capacity. He was among the first appointments of Mr. Davis, receiving the commission of Brigadier-General, and was assigned to the command of the Arkansas District—a command involving, probably, more vexatious questions for solution than any other in the Confederate States.

To say that General McCulloch acquitted himself with credit in his administration of the affairs of his district, and that he retained the confidence of his government to the last, is eulogium sufficient to satisfy his most exacting friend. General McCulloch was very abstemious in his appetites, and indulged in none of the small vices. The character of none of the sons of Texas could more properly be chosen as an exemplar for the youth of the land. Ben. McCulloch was dear to all true Texans. May the grass grow green above his soldier-mound!

# CHAPTER 5

# Retreat from Elk Horn

The soldierly conduct of Private Polk Dye, of Company F, Third Texas Cavalry, in the battle of Elk Horn, deserves mention. Having lost his horse, he joined temporarily a company of the Third Louisiana Infantry, and stood the brunt of battle with that noble regiment all day. In the last of many charges made by the regiment, his arm was broken by a minie-bullet. He was assisted to his own regiment by his comrades of the day, who paid him high compliments for his coolness and courage.

As our wagon-train had been ordered back to the Arkansas River, when Colonel Greer made the move to rejoin General Van Dorn, the command was without rations, and the men presented the most gloomy and dejected appearance possible to conceive. By some unaccountable oversight, the entire park of artillery belonging to McCulloch's late division, in withdrawing from the field, were suffered to take a road leading to the north. Just as we had bivouacked, after the third day's march, hungry, gloomy, and dispirited, orders came for the Third Regiment to saddle up and return in quest of the artillery, which had been heard from, and to escort it to the army. Mechanically the men obeyed, and were soon retracing their march in gloomy silence.

In the morning we met Captain Good, having in charge his own and other batteries. Instead of losing our own artillery, as many feared was the case, we ascertained that we had brought off one more piece than we had carried on the field.

Finally, after many days' wrestling with the "grim and unrelenting enemy," hunger, we reached our winter-quarters, where the wagon-train awaited us, with an abundance of rations. Replenishing the inner man, we hurriedly resumed the march for Little Rock, and from thence to Duvall's Bluff, at which place, to our utter astonishment, we were ordered to be dismounted, our horses sent to Texas, and the men embarked on a steamboat and transported to Memphis, Tenn., *en route* to Corinth, Miss. Notwithstanding the fact that we regarded this order as a breach of faith, totally at variance with our contract, yet the men being impressed with a correct idea of the critical condition in which recent reverses had placed the Confederacy, yielded their own inclinations, with patriotic zeal and devotion to the cause, and complied.

The Third Regiment embarked on board the steamboat *Scotland*, and soon were steaming down White River. The stream was flooded to overflowing, as was the "old father of waters." After a trip without incident, the regiment arrived at Memphis, and encamped in the suburbs of the city for several days. Finally, we departed by train for Corinth, and soon reached that disease-infected point. Here General Beauregard was in command of an army variously estimated at from 35,000 to 75,000 men. We opine the former figures came nearest the truth.

Without memoranda or *data* of any nature of the other regiments that subsequently composed the brigade, a narrative of whose services we are purposing now to commit to paper, cannot be followed through all their individual movements, as can that one of which the author was a member; and if, seemingly, more prominence is given the Third than to the others, the author would beg his comrades to assign the effect to the cause just stated. He would not detract one iota from the well-earned fame of any. To him the Legion—Ninth, Sixth, and Third—are one, and he only wishes he could be invested with the means of according even-handed justice to all, as assuredly he has the will to do so. At Corinth, the Third Regiment was placed in a newly-organised brigade, over which was placed Brigadier-General Hogg. General Hogg was a Texas gentleman of many commendable social and domestic qualities, and was a veteran of the Mexican war, having served as a private in Wood's regiment. General Hogg soon fell a victim to the brooding malaria of that plague-infected place.

Colonel Louis Hebert, of the Third Louisiana, though a prisoner in the hands of the enemy, was promoted Brigadier-General, and to this brigade the Third Texas Regiment was transferred. The brigade, in the absence of General Hebert, was commanded by Colonel J. W. Whitfield, of the First Texas Legion. This brigade did not participate in any of the actual fighting at the battle of Farmington, in which the vain-glorious Pope was driven back, in disgrace, by one division of Van Dorn's *corps d'armée*, and his camp captured, though it did an unpleasant amount of marching, with the object of cutting Pope off from the ford of Hatchie creek. But that doughty warrior was too fast for us, as we arrived just in time to witness the crossing of his rear-guard.

Thus, time passed in drilling, skirmishing, and *physicing,*—for fully one-half of the men were prostrated by camp dysentery—until May 8, 1862, which day had been designated as the time for the re-organisation of the regiment, by the election of field and company officers: Captain Robert H. Cumby, of Company B, was elected Colonel; Captain H. P. Mabry, of Company G, Lieutenant-Colonel; and Captain Barker, Major. Dr. Zeb. Shaw was appointed Surgeon; J. N. Coleman, Captain and Commissary; E. P. Hill, Quartermaster; O. N. Hollingsworth, Adjutant, and Wm. H. Gee, Sergeant-Major.

A. B. Stone, Captain Co. A; Giles S. Boggess, Captain Co. B; James Jones, Captain Co. C; R. S. Dabney, Captain Co. D; Preston B. Ward, Captain Co. E; R. F. Dunn, Captain Co. F; S. C. Noble, Captain Co. G; J. W. Lee, Captain Co. H; —— Green, Captain Co. I; Sid. S. Johnston, Captain Co. K.

As both Colonel Cumby and Lieutenant-Colonel Mabry were in bad health, and unable to assume the command, Major Barker requested Colonel Lane to retain command of the regiment awhile longer, to which request Colonel Lane consented.

During this campaign, the enemy advanced his lines slowly and with the greatest caution; for he had been made to feel the steel of his less numerous opponent on the sanguinary field of Shiloh, and to respect his prowess. Disease was the insidious and fatal enemy that the Southern army had to yield to, finally. Day by day, the ranks of the men on duty grew thinner and thinner. The hospitals were crowded, and thousands were sent to asylums far in the rear. The evacuation was voluntary, on the part of General Beauregard, and dictated by the soundest policy. The movement was affected in the face of the enemy, without confusion or the loss of a cartridge.

Preparatory to this retrograde move, the trains were so taxed, in the removal of supplies and munitions of war, that many of the sick could not obtain transportation, and these poor unfortunates were the 10,000 prisoners alleged to have been captured by Major-General "Headquarters-in-the-Saddle" Pope, over which he crowed so lustily in the papers of the North, and for which he was considered the hero to instruct the Army of the Potomac in the ways to victory—with what success, the reader knows who has perused an account of his passage at arms with brave old "Stonewall" Jackson, at second Manassas.

Previous to the retreat, there transpired many acts of daring and intrepidity on the part of Southern commands in the innumerable skirmishes, and affairs of outposts, that daily occurred. In one of several, the cool courage and soldierly bearing of the Third was so marked as to call from the commanding general a complimentary notice that was read on parade to the entire army. On June 29th, heavy skirmishing was going on in our immediate front, and the regiment was ordered out to support the skirmishers. On the advanced skirmish line the command was drawn up in line of battle, and an advance ordered by Lieutenant-Colonel Lane, who, on the right, led the men in person, while the brave and young Major Barker, performed a similar duty on the left.

The firing increased in volume as the regiment advanced, until Colonel Lane ordered the charge, which was responded to by deafening yells on the part of the men. A deadly volley of musketry was poured into the line of yelling, charging Texans, who, with bayonets fixed, rushed, with the impetuosity of a tornado, over all obstructions, and, though numbering but 256 rifles, drove the Eleventh Ohio and Eighteenth Missouri infantry regiments, numbering full 1,000 men, in confusion and dismay, from the field. The regiment sustained a loss of thirty killed and fifty-five wounded. Among the former was the brave young Major Barker, whose high soldierly bearing on this and former occasions, won the admiration of all. The contest was warm, short, and decisive, as thirty minutes would have covered the whole time of the entire action.

The author cannot refrain from reproducing, in this connection, a vivid description of this gallant action, from the pen of Judge Hogg, who was a member of the Third Texas Regiment:

On the morning preceding the evacuation of Corinth by the Confederates under Beauregard, in May, 1862, we made a considerable demonstration on the front of our lines, in order to hoodwink the enemy, while the *matériel* and main bulk of the troops were withdrawn. Among the forces ordered out was the Third Texas Cavalry, dismounted, under command of Colonel W. P. Lane. About sunrise on the 28th of May, the regiment was ordered to "double-quick" to re-enforce the skirmishers, who were being heavily pressed by a force of the enemy of vast numerical superiority.

After passing through an immense abatis and over a formidable *chevaux de frise,* we came up with our advanced skirmishers, and in full view of the enemy's position, which was in a valley about three hundred yards distant, covered by a jungle of black-jack underbrush that completely veiled them from our view, while our position afforded no cover except large oaks, and we were denied their protection when it interfered with our alignment. As soon as we were discovered by the enemy, a galling fire was opened upon our line, and from the volumes of smoke that boiled up from the copse, and the deafening roar of the musketry, we were apprised of the fact that the encounter would be stubborn and deadly. The battle opened in earnest, now, and the firing became terrific. There were only 246 of our regiment well enough to participate in the engagement, and, owing to the enemy's heavy overbalance of numbers, and their more advantageous position, it behoved every man to avail himself of whatever protection the timber afforded.

Each man took his tree, and, after discharging his fire-lock and re-loading in that position, would advance to the next cover and repeat the performance. Colonel W. P. Lane, Major James A. J. Barker, and Adjutant Orlando Hollingsworth were the only mounted officers on the field, and, thus exposed, were excellent targets for the enemy's sharpshooters.

We advanced but a short distance in the aforesaid manner, when Lane's favourite command, "Charge!" was given, to dislodge the enemy from his stronghold. At the spell-word, "charge," each Texan quit his cover, and dashed with wonted impetuosity upon the opposing ranks. The forest resounded with their dreadful shout, which sent a chill of terror to the hearts of the invaders. In full run, the Texans, with the fury of madmen, close on the lurking enemy, whose skill and power are spent in vain to check them.

Over three thousand rifles are belching forth their death-fraught charges into the slim line of the brave 246—still they come! Their wake is covered with the best blood of the nation—yet on they rush! They reach the fire-breathing thicket, and, without a halt, they plunge into its thorny bosom, when, in one chaotic stampede, the gallant brigade of Indianans, that Uncle Sam had entrusted with honour's post, made their shameful exeunt, leaving about forty of their dead and a like number of their wounded on the field. The flying enemy was pursued until the sound of the "long roll" in the main camp, warned the impetuous Lane that prudence counselled a halt. Of the boys from Cherokee, we found the brave young Abner Harris dead; Wallace Caldwell—the beloved, the noble Wallace—languishing under a mortal wound, and John Lambert severely wounded.

Many were lamented on that day, but none more than that prince of nature's nobleman, the talented and chivalric Major James A. J. Barker, the pride of his regiment. He fell while gallantly cheering his men on to victory, as he had done on many a well-fought field. His gallantry and general superiority was the theme of every tongue that knew him. His name was inseparably connected with our ideas of valour, magnanimity, truth, candour, and fidelity.

The major had a presentiment of evil, and so informed his intimate friends on the morning of the battle. The dying hero fell into the arms of John Myres and Lem. Reed, who bore his inanimate form from the field of his death and his glory."

The author made many attempts to obtain a copy of the complimentary address issued to the army, by General Beauregard, on this occasion, but regrets that all his efforts were unavailing. If such a copy is extant, he hopes to be able to procure it, should a second edition of this work be demanded.

# CHAPTER 6

# Retirement

General Beauregard executed the movement of retiring from Corinth in a masterly manner. Captain S. S. Johnston, Company K, of the Third, was on picket duty at the time of withdrawal, and, in the hurry of the moment, Colonel Lane neglected to relieve them. The army had proceeded some miles when the absence of gallant old Company K was remarked. The courier who bore Captain Johnston the order to "fall back," found him, with his twenty-five Texans, boldly confronting Halleck's 100,000. Texas had many brave and daring sons to be proud of, but not one more deservedly so than Captain Sid. S. Johnston—now the modest, unassuming citizen of Tyler, Texas.

General Halleck seemed satisfied with the occupation of Corinth, and halted his victorious legions at that point.

The Confederate Army retired to Tupelo, on the Mobile and Ohio railroad. The greater portion was soon transferred, under General Bragg, to Tennessee. One *corps de armée* remained at Tupelo, composed of the divisions of Generals Maury and Little, the whole commanded by Major-General Sterling Price. For several months, the corps remained here, with no incident to break the dull monotony save the daily "guard mounting" and drill. About the time General Bragg commenced his advance into Kentucky, the camp was removed up the railroad to Saltillo, about fifteen miles north of Tupelo. From this point General Price made a rapid march on Iuka, where General Rosecranz was posted with about 10,000 men General Grant being at Corinth, fifteen miles above, with as many more.

So complete was the surprise, that General Rosecranz evacuated the town without removing or destroying any of his immense stores collected there. Consequently, the Confederates revelled on "Yankee" rations during their short-lived possession of the place. Price's position was an extremely hazardous one here, and not a night passed but an alarm was sounded. Our cavalry was extremely inefficient, and the enemy was expected on either of three fronts. When the crisis came, after a week of anxious watch, the army was drawn up in line of battle on the Corinth road, about three miles from Iuka, awaiting the enemy, who, it was reported, was advancing on that road. When, suddenly, a breathless courier dashed up to General Price with the astounding information that the enemy was advancing on Iuka from the south side, and that nothing interposed between him and the town save a company of cavalry, who could offer him no opposition.

Hebert's Brigade, composed of the First Texas Legion, Third Texas Cavalry (dismounted), Third Louisiana Infantry, and Fortieth Mississippi Infantry—the whole commanded by General Louis Hebert—was ordered to "double-quick" to the threatened point. Arriving, the Third Texas was deployed as skirmishers, and drove the Federal sharpshooters back on the reserve. The brigade was now formed in line of battle, and King's (Confederate) battery opened fire. This was immediately responded to by the enemy's artillery; at the same time, the firing of small arms became general, and, as the opposing lines were not exceeding three hundred yards apart, considerable execution was done.

As Generals Price and Little were conferring, just in the rear of the Third Texas, the latter received a rifle-ball in the forehead and fell from his horse into the arms of Sergeant T. J. Cellum, of Company A, Third Texas, dead. General Price dismounted and hastened to the side of the fallen general, whose spirit, alas, had already flown. To Cellum, the old hero said, with moistened eyes and husky voice: "Bear his body from the field, my son; and remain with it, yourself, until I can join you." That night, when the storm of battle had lulled, the form of General Little was consigned to a hastily-dug grave, "by the light of the lanterns dimly burning."

A forward movement was now ordered, and as the brigade marched with slow and solemn tread down a slight declivity in the direction of the enemy, a little dog was observed trotting along in advance of the line, apparently oblivious to the thunders of artillery, the rattle of rifles, and the *whizzing* of missiles that literally filled the air. The fate of the brave little rebel dog was never known. Arriving at the base of the declivity, the command "double-quick," was given. The enemy now redoubled his exertions. Nine pieces of artillery were brought to bear, and the threatened point re-enforced. "Charge!" was the next command uttered by brave little creole Hebert, and the Confederates, yelling like demons revelling in a saturnalia of death, pushed forward at the top of their speed. They are met, full in the face, by the iron contents of the nine cannon, and, like a tree torn by the hurricane, waver for a moment.

"On, men, on!" shouts the impetuous Frenchman, and the Confederates distinctly hear the command of the enemy: "Double charge of grape and canister!" They know what the result will be if the cannon are not taken before they can be again fired. Their comrades lie around them dead and dying. Of five colonels, not one remains. Death is abroad in his fury; *but to retreat is more dangerous than to advance!* The men hesitate but a moment, and raising again the demoniac yell, dash madly forward and reach the guns just as the double load is being driven home. In vain did the infantry support attempt to come to the rescue of the guns—their charges on the Confederate line were as impotent as the beating of the waves on the sides of Gibraltar. The Confederate loss was simply terrible. In the Legion and Third Texas, one-third of the men were killed or wounded. Their loss was greater from the fact that their position was immediately in front of the death-dealing artillery.

Where all displayed such heroism, it would seem invidious to make distinctions; but the author cannot refrain from mentioning the name of brave young Lieutenant Dan. H. Alley, of Company G, Third Texas, who he witnessed, in the hottest period of the charge, sword in hand, calling to his men; "Come on, boys!"

Colonel H. P. Mabry, commanding Third Texas, received a severe wound that fractured an ankle; Colonel J. W. Whitfield was wounded severely in the shoulder; Colonel Gillam, of the Third Louisiana, received a half-dozen wounds, that incapacitated him for active service. Captain Odell, Brigade Commissary, was killed.

The author feels excusable in mentioning the death of his friend, John Sherrod, who was killed at his side—a grape-shot passing entirely through the body.

Night put an end to the carnage. General Price became convinced that General Grant had re-enforced General Rosecranz, and that his retreat would be cut off, resolved to anticipate events, and about 9 p.m., commenced a retrograde movement in the direction of Baldwin, Mississippi. The enemy did not attempt a pursuit, as he was satisfied with the test of metal at Iuka. All the wounded, unable to march, fell into the hands of the enemy. But, at this period, the humane system of paroling prisoners was in operation, and it was not until some months later that both sides disgraced the American name, and libelled humanity, in their inhuman treatment of prisoners.

A characteristic anecdote is told of Colonel Mabry, who fell into the enemy's hands. The printed parole offered him to sign, read "the so-called Confederate States," etc. The punctilious officer refused to attach his name to the instrument, alleging that the Confederacy was an established fact; and as Colonel Mabry was about as firm in his convictions as old Cato of Rome, he was given a parole in which the obnoxious words did not occur. And all Confederate soldiers will remember that their paroles, at the general surrender, read "Confederate States," etc.—a phraseology of respect accorded to the punctilious honour and manly firmness of Colonel H. P. Mabry, of Texas.

An incident in regard to General Hebert: As the Third Texas was being thrown forward as skirmishers—the enemy still advancing and firing—an officer of the regiment asked of the general, who was superintending the movement, "General, must we fix bayonets?"

"Yes, sir!" shouted the impatient officer; "What for you have ze bayonet, if you no fix him? Yes, by gar; fix him! fix him!"

At Baldwin, General Price was met by General Earl Van Dorn, who had advanced from Vicksburg with about 5,000 men—General Price's force was about twice as many. With this force, General Van Dorn, who now assumed the command, commenced a rapid advance on Corinth—probably the strongest fortified place in the South—occupied by General Rosecranz and 30,000 men. The fatiguing march was attended by no incident until the morning of the first day's fight, when, just at daybreak, three distinct shocks of an earthquake were felt, and construed by many as of ominous import.

It is not the province of the author, in this connection, to give the details of operation unconnected with the immediate operations of the four regiments that composed Ross' Brigade; and as that brigade had not yet been organised, difficulty is experienced in correctly drawing the line. Suffice it to say, the four regiments participated in this fatal battle, and bore themselves, as they always did, with soldierly daring and bravery. They charged the outer line of breastworks, over *abatis* of fallen timber; they scaled the works through bristling rows of *chevaux de frise*, and silenced the siege guns on the ramparts by capture. During the night of the first day's fight, the Confederate army was drawn up in line of battle, Price occupying the centre, and bivouacked on their arms. The signal for attack the next morning was a discharge of ten pieces of artillery by Price.

As agreed upon, the ten cannon were discharged simultaneously, just at daybreak, and the army rose to its feet as one man. A desperate charge was immediately made upon the inner lines, which were also taken in many places, though at a fearful cost of life. All know how short-lived was this ephemeral success. It is enough to recount the catastrophe, without attempting to designate the cause. The charging columns were not supported as they should have been, and were, consequently, driven from the town, to which they had penetrated in the frenzy of the charge, and back across the breastworks, which they had purchased at such a fearful cost, only to lose again. That someone was culpable, is not to be disputed; but to designate the individual is the province of the general historian, and not the author of this circumscribed narrative.

A disorderly retreat was now commenced, with the enemy in close pursuit. Villepigue's Brigade, only, of the whole army, preserved sufficient discipline to interpose any impediment in the way of the triumphant enemy.

In advancing on Corinth, General Van Dorn had left the wagon-trains at the bridge on the Hatchie River; and the Texas Legion, consisting of about 500 efficient men, together with other detachments, numbering possibly 500 more, constituted the guard left to preserve the sole means of retreat, and secure the train from capture. And now, to add to the gravity of the situation, Generals Hulburt and Ord came down from Grand Junction with a corps about 10,000 fresh men, rendered enthusiastic by the news of the victory, and gained possession of the bridge, after an obstinate contest with the guard; in which action the "Old Legion" bore itself with conspicuous gallantry, and suffered heavily in killed, wounded, and prisoners.

Previous to the capture of the bridge, however, Colonel L. S. Ross, in command of a brigade numbering not more than 700 rifles for duty, were thrown across the stream to support the Confederate guard, commanded by Brigadier-General Moore, who was overwhelmed by numbers, and his heterogeneous force almost disorganised, ere the arrival of Ross. Moore urged Ross to retire behind the stream, and pointed out the futility of his sustaining an attack from the advancing enemy, who numbered near 10,000 fresh men. Colonel Ross maintained his position, however, until his superior in rank, General Maury, ordered a retreat. To extricate his brigade from the hazardous position it now occupied, demanded prudence, skill, and courage, and that Colonel Ross effected this delicate manoeuvre, in the face of overwhelming numbers of troops flushed with victory, speaks volumes in his praise.

The triumphant enemy now held the bridge, and nothing intervened between him and the Confederate wagon-train but Ross and his little brigade, who maintained their position with a heroism not excelled by either side during the whole course of the war. Finally, General Maury brought up the brigades of Generals Phifer and Cabell, and this force kept the enemy at bay, during a brief crisis in the history of the Army of the West, that momentarily threatened a disastrous catastrophe. The routed and disorganised columns of Van Dorn and Price, closely pursued by Rosecranz, were now arriving upon the scene in a state of demoralization that made "confusion worse confounded." In the rear of this straggling mass, the gallant Villepigue, at the head of his brigade, was offering such opposition to Rosecranz as his paucity of numbers would justify. But neither Villepigue nor Maury could hope to maintain their positions, against such fearful odds, long.

It appeared that the "Army of the West" was confronting its fate at last on the banks of this turbid and impassable stream. Events had reached a crisis, and disaster seemed imminent. Generals Van Dorn and Price hold a hurried interview. The head of the column is turned to the left of the road, and the forlorn retreat is resumed down the river. A mounted detachment is hastened down the stream to a point some ten miles distant, where the remains of an ancient mill-dam are said to exist. Upon this foundation, the "pioneers" hastily improvise a bridge ere the head of the column appears. Over this providential bridge the army passes, and frees itself from the enveloping folds of the enemy.

A sigh of relief escapes ten thousand hearts when they realise their escape from the very jaws of destruction. Strange to relate, not a wagon was lost, not a gun—though so demoralized was the army that, had the enemy maintained a vigorous pursuit, the consequences must have proved fatal to the Confederates. General Rosecranz, with the humanity characteristic of the brave, caused the Confederate dead, upon the fields of Corinth and Hatchie, to be properly interred. The brave Colonel Rodgers, of the Second Texas Infantry, who fell, sword in hand, upon the death-swept ramparts, the foremost man in one of the deadliest assaults of modern times, was accorded a soldier's burial, with all the honours of war, by his admiring enemies.

Such acts as this, half redeems the depravity of man, and partially beguiles the horrors of war. The beaten army retired to Holly Springs; where, however, it was not suffered long to remain, as General Grant, who has been rather appropriately styled the "Modern Sphynx," placed his legions in motion, with the city of Vicksburg as the objective point.

It was evident to the most obtuse, that the fortunes of the Confederacy in that quarter were desperate, and that, unless something extraordinary was attempted, Vicksburg must become the prey of the Federals. The defeated army contained, in its own ranks, the medium through which its deliverance was to be obtained. Three thousand five hundred cavalrymen were destined to achieve this result an exploit unsurpassed in the annals of war, and which revolutionized the art of war in America, at least, by assigning the cavalry-arm to a position of importance it had never before occupied.

For his defeat at Corinth, Major-General Earl Van Dorn was superseded in the command of the "Army of the West" by Lieutenant-General J. C. Pemberton.

*ROSS' BRIGADE.*
*1*
*No more the bugle's ringing blast,*
*Now sounds "to horse!" throughout the camp;*
*No more the charger, dashing fast,*
*In gore his quiv'ring fetlocks tramp;*
*No more the "Red Cross" proudly waves*
*Defiance to the haughty foe;*
*No more the crimson battle waves*
*Of human blood, now ebb and flow.*
*2*
*No more as when the "cool Old Chief,"* (General Ben. McCulloch)
*His life gave up in sacrifice,*
*Does glory lead the path to grief,*
*Where tears and sobs may not suffice;*
*No more as when the "dashing boy,"* (General McIntosh, killed at Elk Horn)
*A stranger, came to do and dare,*
*Is life exchanged for fame's alloy,*
*Like empty bubbles, light as air.*
*3*
*Still we recall those scenes with pride,*
*And mark each incident, though light;*

*The bivouac, the cheerless ride,*
*The skirmish, and the deadly fight.*
*First in the front of each advance,*
*Last in the rear of each retreat;*
*The Cossack Ranger's ready lance,*
*Was ever poised the foe to meet.*
4
*And when the "modern Sphynx" arrayed—*
*With will to match against the fates—*
*His legions which had ne'er essayed*
*In vain the storm of city gates,*
*Delay'd, proud Vicksburg, was thy doom,*
*By spectral men on noiseless wings,*
*Who lit, with lurid glare, the gloom,*
*That hung a pall o'er Holly Springs.*
5
*A pandemonium, Spring Hill heard,*
*When Whitfield led, through shot and shell,*
*The "Legion," "Sixth," the "Ninth," and "Third,"*
*And triumphed o'er a mimic hell.*
*With Yazoo glories, bursts enlarge,*
*As recompense for all our loss,*
*Where fortune, in the dashing charge,*
*Conferr'd the "wreath and stars" on Ross.* (insignia of a general officer)
6
*Around the lines of Corinth, where*
*Disease, an ally of the foe,*
*Rode on the pestilential air,*
*And claimed its dues of death and woe;*
*And 'round Atlanta's ditches red,*
*Where Valour failed to cope with Might,*
*We left at rest our priceless dead,*
*Athwart the field from left to right.*
7
*No marble shaft may point the way,*
*No epitaph the tombs disclose,*
*Where death's still line, in grim array,*
*Unheeded find their last repose.*
*But far beyond, the phantom line*
*In silence holds the dim parade,*

*Where radiant suns forever shine,*
*"Across the river in the shade."*

★★★★★★

Note:—Among the bravest and best that ever shouldered a musket for the cause of Dixie, was the author's friend, comrade, and confident, Alonzo P. Hope, of Company A, Third Regiment, who, although wounded in the hip at Corinth, continued at his post, rejecting all tenders of a discharge from the service until the end. Mr. Hope now resides near Marshall, Texas, upon his farm, respected by all who know him.

## Chapter 7

# Tupelo

While encamped at Tupelo, the following orders were issued, relative to the remounting of the Texas Brigade:

> Headquarters, District of the Tennessee,
> Tupelo, Mississippi, August 23d, 1862.

Special Orders, No. 19—Extract.

Brigadier-General Little will detail two commissioned officers and three men of the Third Texas Cavalry (dismounted), Colonel Mabry commanding, to bring from beyond the Mississippi river, the horses belonging to that regiment.

By Order of Major-General Price.

> James M. Loughborough, A. A. G.

> First Division, District of the Tennessee,
> Headquarters, Post at Saltillo, Mississippi, August, 1862.

Special Order, No. 16.

Captain J. N. Goleman, A. C. S.; First Lieutenant Logan, Company K; Sergeant-Major W. H. Gee, private Robert I. Haywood, Company G; and private J. D. Davis, Company E, are hereby detailed to bring from beyond the Mississippi River the horses and men belonging to the Third Texas Cavalry.

By Order of Brigadier-General Little.

> W. C. Shamburg, A. A. G.

> Headquarters, Third Texas Cavalry,
> Camp Near Saltillo, Mississippi, August 23d, 1862.

Special Order, No. 1.

The men belonging to this command, who were detailed under order No. —, issued by Major-General Van Dorn, Des Arc,

Arkansas, April, 1862, to carry the horses belonging to this command to Texas, are required to report to Captain John N. Coleman, at Marshall, Texas, for duty.

H. P. Mabry, Colonel, Commanding Third Texas.

Captain Coleman will receive recruits for the various companies as follows:

Company A, Captain A. B. Stone, five men.
Company B, Captain J. W. Wynne, five men.
Company C, Captain J. A. Jones, twenty men.
Company D, Captain R. S. Dabney, twenty-two men.
Company E, Captain P. B. Ward, fourteen men.
Company F, Captain R. F. Dunn, nine men.
Company G, Captain E. S. Noble, ten men."

At Lumpkin's Mills, another brief halt was obtained, and while here the Texans, who were brigaded together at Holly Springs, learned of the arrival of the anxiously-expected horses. Alexander Selkirk hailed not with greater joy the first glimpse of the white sails that were to bear him from solitude, than did these men hail the arrival of their horses. It was announced that the horses were but a few miles distant. Orders arrived to prepare for another retreat; retreat had become a word nauseous, and the men were actually ashamed to retreat further. Brigades, divisions, *corps* passed the Texan camp. They had concluded, after consultation, not to march without their horses. When the drums beat to "fall in," the sound was absolutely drowned by the deafening cries, "*Horses!*" "*Horses!*" General Whitfield, the brigade commander, made them an appeal to duty, but the boys knew that "Old Whit" wished them mounted, and, at all events, that he "was with them" in anything short of desertion. General Maury now appeared, and appealed to the men to proceed. Their sole reply was "*Horses!*" "*Horses!*" In despair the general turned away, and rode to overtake his retreating division.

Colonel Griffith, who was, at the time, in command of the Sixth Texas Regiment, had his regiment called into line, and, after a calm review of the military situation, he showed how necessary it was for the maintenance of discipline; how infectious and fatal insubordination would prove, and appealed to the men not to tarnish their own honour, and place a bar sinister upon the escutcheon of Texas. He promised them that they should be mounted soon, and without the loss of honour, and concluded by inviting all who were disposed to

GENERAL JOHN S. GRIFFITH.

remain at the post of duty, to return to their camp and prepare for the march. All responded but one solitary individual. To him, Griffith said: "Go, sir, and obey orders, or I will run you through with my sabre!"

The effect of Griffith's appeal had the influence necessary to lead all the other regiments into the performance of duty, and saved them the lasting disgrace that such mutinous conduct, if persisted in, was sure to attach to their names. Heretofore, he had led them to victory over their enemies; he had, in this instance, led them to triumph over their baser passions; and the moralist would not hesitate to say that the latter was the most splendid victory of the two. Happily, the old brigade was never afterwards pervaded by so mean a spirit.

Similar orders to the foregoing were issued in regard to the other regiments of the Texas Brigade; but, like much other data referring to this work, was inaccessible to the author. This is regretted, and was sought to be obviated, by every effort that promised the slightest success, but only to be met with defeat.

Footworn and weary, the defeated army took up the line of retreat from Holly Springs, for what point they knew not, for it was but too apparent that General Grant could drive the Army of West Tennessee into the Gulf, if he so wished. Never did the Confederate Cross trail in the dust as. at this time. The army was demoralized by the crushing defeat at Corinth; a defeat that burst upon them like a cyclone from a cloudless sky, in the very moment of victory. General Price took up the line of march from Abbeville to Grenada, as soon as it was evident that General Grant intended another advance. General Van Dorn had already made Oxford his head-quarters. Just before Price evacuated Abbeville, Colonel Griffith, in command of the Texas brigade, occupied the left wing, which rested on the Tallahatchie, near Toby Tuby ferry.

This energetic and restless officer kept a vigilant watch on the enemy's movements, and, discovering a detached column of some five hundred cavalry, on the extreme right of the Federal position, asked and obtained permission of General Van Dorn to attack them. Returning to his command, Griffith caused forty rounds of ammunition to be issued to each man, and, after completing other necessary arrangements, was in the act of crossing the river, when orders arrived from General Van Dorn, countermanding the previous one, and directing Colonel Griffith to proceed down the Tallahatchie, *via* Panola, cross the Tokona, and thus place himself in the rear of General Washburne, who, at the head of an unknown force, was threatening

Grenada, with a view of intercepting General Price's retreat. General Van Dorn's directions were for Griffith to harass Washburne, by unexpected attacks upon his rear, and thus retard his movements, until General Price could bring off his large wagon-train, wounded, artillery, etc.

With his usual energy, Griffith made the necessary dispositions for the care of his wagon-train, and, within an hour, was ready to set out upon this unexpected expedition. The Brigade consisted of the Legion, Third and Sixth Texas Cavalry, and Captain McNally's battery of four guns. After a forced march to the Tokona, it was discovered that all the fords were strongly guarded, and that it would be impossible to penetrate the enemy's rear. In this dilemma, Griffith boldly determined to throw his little brigade in Washburne's immediate front, and risk the safety of Price's retreat upon the issue. The odds were terrible, but he argued that if his brigade was cut to pieces, that the salvation of the army would have been purchased cheaply enough—a disinterested decision, worthy a hero. In pursuance of this resolution, he proceeded up the Tokona, and hastily communicated this decision to General Van Dorn, who immediately replied, in the following brief dispatch, which, however, gave Colonel Griffith full authority to act as he should elect:

Headquarters,
Department of Mississippi and East Louisiana,
Oxford, Mississippi, December 1st, 1862.
Colonel Griffith: I am directed by the general commanding, to say, that if you carry out what you propose, it will be what he desires. He has no instructions to give. The army has now fallen back, and will be tonight on the Tokona.
I am, respectfully,
R. W. Memminger, A. A. G.

But the readiness of Griffith to assume grave responsibilities, when he deemed that the interest of the cause was to be subserved thereby, as exemplified in his charge, contrary to orders, at Chustenahlah, now asserted itself, and he was deep into the practical execution already of his project to strike Washburne in front, when the above dispatch reached him. The Tokona was passed, and the head of the column was nearing the enemy, in the neighbourhood of Oakland. From a few stragglers from the enemy's ranks, it was learned that General Washburne was in command of eight or ten thousand infantry, and about two thousand cavalry. Griffith's brigade numbered not more than twelve hundred effective men. It was a bold stroke, conceived by the daring Texan, but demanded by the exigencies of the occasion.

In consequence of the rapidity of the march, the battery was left in the care of a number of the men whose horses were too jaded to proceed. On the night of the second, learning that the enemy's cavalry were occupying Preston, the irrepressible ranger dashed into that place, but only to discover that the "blue-coats" had retired to Mitchell's Cross Roads, on hearing of the arrival of the Confederate cavalry at Grenada.

On the morning of the third, learning that Washburne, at the head of his whole force, was moving on the town of Oakland, Griffith immediately determined to meet him at the junction of the road he was marching upon with the Charleston road, and a half mile beyond town. Colonel Boggess, of the Third, was directed to make a demonstration on his left and rear; Captain Jack Wharton, commanding the Sixth, took position on the Charleston road; Colonel Hawkins, commanding the Legion, together with Major J. H. Broocks, temporarily commanding three detached companies, constituted the centre. Major Broocks, being in the advance, speedily opened the engagement by a vigorous attack, which was met by the enemy with a spirited return. Colonel E. R. Hawkins dismounted his men under the cover of a slight natural elevation, and moved up in excellent order on the right of Broocks.

\*\*\*\*\*\*

At the Battle of Oakland, Sergeant Cellum, of the Third Texas, at the head of thirty men, penetrated the enemy's rear, and captured several wagons loaded with commissary supplies, killing several of the guard, and making some twenty prisoners.

\*\*\*\*\*\*

The battle was now general, and the gallant Hawkins, and the veteran Legion, maintained their position against a force outnumbering them in the ratio of ten to one. The artillery of the enemy literally poured into their devoted ranks grape and canister with a rapidity and precision of aim rarely exceeded. Griffith, true to the boldness of his original conception, ordered a charge upon the battery, and the brave fellows, responding with a yell of triumph, irresistibly charged in the wake of their gallant leaders, and took the murder-dealing guns; and, without a moment to re-form their disordered line, attacked, and drove from the field, the infantry that was supporting the battery.

The enemy now planted another battery on their right, and opened a crossfire upon the Legion. Colonel Griffith ordered Captain Wharton to dismount his men, and take the battery. The brave Wharton was eagerly complying with this order, when intelligence reached Colonel Griffith that the enemy was outflanking his left.

The Texans were immediately summoned to horse, as the safety of the command demanded a speedy withdrawal from the enfolding lines of the enemy's superior numbers. This delicate manoeuvre was performed, under fire, in perfect order, and line of battle re-formed in the suburbs of Oakland. The spirited engagement had continued fifty minutes, and the loss on the side of the enemy was considerable. The Texans lost ten men. General Washburne did not wish another repetition of the dose, and, with the friendly cover of the night, retired to the crossroads.

This engagement, small in itself, was of vital consequence to the army of Price, in that it drove from its rear an army of 12,000 Federals. General Washburne evidently imagined that he was confronted by a division of Van Dorn's army, for had he known the inconsiderable number of his assailants, it is not probable that he would have turned his back to them. The boldness and spirit of Griffith's attack was sufficient data upon which to predicate such a hypothesis. Of course, during the presence of Washburne's force in the rear of General Price, the trains on the railroad had ceased to run. Colonel Griffith immediately forwarded to General Price some fifteen trains, with which to facilitate his retreat. Thanks to the boldness of the victors at Oakland, the brave old Missourian was enabled to save all his stores, and reached Grenada, on the south of the Yallabusha River, in due course.

The distracted and suffering army of West Tennessee was now allowed a respite from the alarums of battle; but how long it would continue, no one presumed to know; all feared that the victorious Grant would soon push onward. General Van Dorn was, at this time, superseded in the command of the army by Lieutenant-General J. C. Pemberton. Of the organisation of a cavalry corps, to be commanded by General Van Dorn, and the conception of the Holly Springs expedition, *vide* "Biography of General Griffith," in this book.

The army of General Pemberton, numbering about 25,000 illy-disciplined, poorly-clothed and fed men, occupied the town and vicinity of Grenada. General U. S. Grant was in command of 75,000 disciplined, and thoroughly-supplied and equipped men, accustomed to victory, and occupied the town of Coffeeville. Memphis was General

Grant's base of operations, and Holly Springs an intermediate depot, where had been accumulated immense stores of supplies and munitions of war. This latter place was garrisoned by about 2,500 men. In compliance with orders from General Pemberton, Colonel Griffith reported to General Van Dorn for duty, with his brigade, on December 12, 1862, composed and officered as follows:

Ninth Texas Cavalry Colonel D. W. Jones, commanding.
Third Texas Cavalry Lieutenant-Colonel J. S. Boggess, commanding.
Sixth Texas Cavalry Captain Jack Wharton, commanding.
First Texas Legion Calvary Major J. H. Broocks, commanding.

In addition to the Texas Brigade, General Van Dorn's command comprised the brigade of General W. H. Jackson, composed of Tennessee and Mississippi cavalry, and the Missouri Brigade of Colonel McCulloch, the whole aggregating about 3,500 men. The object and purposes of the expedition were enveloped in absolute secrecy, and Van Dorn set out from Grenada, it is believed, on the night of December 19, and pursued the hasty march all night and the next day.

Passing through the beautiful town of Pontotoc, the hungry troopers were enthusiastically welcomed by the noble and patriotic citizens of the place; and trays, dishes, and baskets of the choicest edibles were offered on all sides, and pitchers of wine and milk as well. No halt was allowed, and the men pursued their mysterious way munching the welcomed "grub" dispensed by the fair hands of Pontotoc's good, and beautiful, and noble heroines.

Oh peerless ladies of Pontotoc, though the mists of twenty years becloud the mind's eye, and interminable leagues intervene between us, the courtly Griffith, and his. surviving "rebels," salute you! You who were radiant maidens, then, and had, perchance, plighted your vows with those of a soldier lover, are matrons now. Time despoils the cheek of its damask, but the heart, like old wine, grows the better from the effects of age. May your clime continue to produce a type of womanhood as noble and exalted as your own; for emulation will find, at the standard of your excellence, an *ultima thule* beyond which there can be no progression!

General Van Dorn had dispatched a trusty spy, well acquainted with the place, to Holly Springs, to ascertain the number and position of the enemy, and to accurately locate the picket on the Ripley road. The command proceeded at a brisk pace, in a northerly direction, and crossed the Holly Springs road three miles north of the Ripley road. Here the Federal scouts, hitherto hanging on the Confederate rear, returned to their camp, satisfied that having passed Holly Springs so far to the left, that the object of the rebel raid was to be found in Tennessee. The command halted at 3 p.m., on the 21st, and the men regaled themselves on broiled pork and luscious sweet potatoes.

General Van Dorn summoned Colonel Griffith to his presence, and imparted to him the plan of the purposed attack. The spy returned with accurate data as to all necessary information, and further stated that the Yankees, apprehending no danger, were preparing for a grand ball. The command was disposed of as follows: Jackson's Brigade on the right, Griffith's the centre, and McCulloch's the left. At nightfall, Van Dorn counter-marched, and proceeded back to the Ripley and Holly Springs road, and thence to Holly Springs, moving by columns of fours, and guns uncapped. Silently, Jackson leads his brigade to the right, and McCulloch his to the left, and the meshes of fate are encircling the unconscious Federals.

Guards had been left at all the houses in the immediate vicinity of the line of march, and other precautions taken to prevent the possibility of the intelligence of Van Dorn's return passing into the city. Slowly and cautiously, the command moves along through the darkness, like some monster serpent, conscious of its ability to seize and crush its prey. Lieutenant Hyams, of General Van Dorn's staff, was dispatched on the delicate mission to capture the picket, without the discharge of a gun, for one pistol-shot would apprise the slumbering Federals of the presence of their enemy. That the mission of this young officer was an entire success, speaks volumes in praise of his bravery, coolness, and sagacity. The enterprise contained the elements of ninety-nine failures to one of success.

General Van Dorn directed Colonel Griffith to charge at the head of the Sixth and Ninth into the town.

"And take care," added the general, "that you do not find a hornet's-nest at the square!"

With drawn sabre, Griffith places himself at the head of the charging column. "Forward, at a gallop!" he commands, and the squadrons move down the road; and, as the suburbs are reached, the bugle's shrill, harsh blast sounds the charge upon the crisp morning air, and shouting, yelling rebels disturb the slumbers of Federal soldiers and citizens, alike. The former emerge from their tents to be informed that they are prisoners of war; and the latter—mostly women and children—to shout: "Hurrah for Van Dorn! Hurrah for the Confederacy!! Hurrah for Jeff. Davis!!!" Little children bring forth miniature Confederate flags that they have been forced to conceal since the "Yankees" came; beautiful young ladies wave their handkerchiefs, and matrons implore the protection of God for the charging soldiers. Tears of joy gush forth from many an eye, and manly voices grow husky from emotion. O, that entry into Holly Springs was the incident of a lifetime!

Colonel Griffith posted the Third, under Colonel Boggess, in the square, and detailed the Legion, at the instance of General Van Dorn, to guard the prisoners. Colonel Broocks faithfully performed this duty, as indeed he always did, and kept his men well in hand, and none of the Legion engaged in the subsequent plundering of the stores that ensued. Colonel Broocks had four men detailed from each company at a time, and, in a decent manner, these procured whatever they wished of the captured property. This conscientious officer allowed no prisoner to be robbed of his individual property, and, while he thus honoured himself and his State, kept the bright escutcheon of the Confederacy untarnished.

A regiment of Iowa troops were seen forming line just out of town, and Colonel Griffith ordered Colonel Jones to form his regiment—the Ninth—so as to charge them down the street. A flag of truce was now raised in a camp to the left, and Griffith dispatched an aid to receive the surrender; in the meantime, placing himself by the side of the gallant "boy colonel," Jones, they lead the Ninth in a headlong charge against the Iowa warriors; disperse them, take their colours, and many prisoners.

Colonel Griffith now dispatched to General Van Dorn: "The 'hornet's-nest' is ours!" and joined Colonel Boggess in the square.

Many ladies—some still in *dishabille*—throng the square; all rejoicing, all excited, and none looking to future consequences. They point out to Griffith the house occupied by Mrs. Grant, the paymaster, and the chief quartermaster. Colonel Griffith sent guards to arrest all the officers domiciled in houses, and to the house occupied by Mrs. Grant, at which were several of the general's staff. Griffith detailed ten men, in the special charge of Colonel Boggess, as a guarantee that the ladies should be treated with deference and respect. But a few minutes elapsed when a messenger from Boggess announced to Colonel Griffith that three ladies denied him entrance to the house. Griffith, fearing some rudeness might be committed, repaired to the scene immediately, when Colonel Boggess exclaimed: "I cannot execute your orders without the exercise of violence to these ladies!"

Mrs. Grant, stepping forward, said: "And you, sir, make war upon women, do you?"

"On the contrary, madam," replied the knightly Griffith, doffing his plumed *chapeau*, and bowing profoundly to the lady; "we leave that to our enemies!"

But the ladies continued to "hold the fort," and Griffith, addressing the soldiers, said: "Men, offer no rudeness to the ladies; if they will not allow you to pass through the gate, tear off a picket from the fence, and flank them; if you are denied admittance at the door, go around them, and find ingress through a window. You must search the house for concealed prisoners, but do not touch the hem of the garment of one of these ladies."

The men commenced tearing off the pickets to the right and left of the gate, when Mrs. Grant relented, and politely invited them to enter through the gate, at the same time protesting that there were no men in the house. One officer was found in the house. Colonel Griffith placed a guard over the house, for the protection of the ladies, while the command remained in town.

McCulloch's Brigade now arrived at the square, and some of the men broke into a sutler's store, and commenced an indiscriminate pillage. Colonel Griffith, knowing that the infection would become contagious, appealed to the men, in the absence of their officers, to desist. His appeals to the Missourians were, however, futile; and soon Tennesseans, Mississippians, and Texans, vied in the work of pillage; the latter *nationality*, however, always keeping a sharp look out for their commander. Of course, all this was wrong, was destructive of discipline, and would have proved fatal in its consequences had a few hundred Federal troopers dashed into town; but the poor, ragged, half-starved fellows, deserved all they got, and more.

Never did an army undergo as complete a transformation, in external appearances, in so short a time. The grimy, ragged rebel of a moment ago, now appears" with the uniform-coat of a Federal colonel on his back, a plumed hat on his head, and his feet and legs are encased in patent-leather cavalry-boots. *In vino veritas!* at least one would have imagined as much to judge from the frequent and liberal potations indulged in by, alas! too many. Cigars were plentiful, and about three thousand of them were kept puffing at a time. The property captured and destroyed was estimated at over $5,000,000 worth.

Besides the stores that were filled with the goods of the sutlers and the government, immense quantities of bacon, pork, flour in sacks, hard bread, coffee, etc., etc., were stacked in piles as high as a man's head, and in rows a quarter of a mile long, at the depot. Great quantities of arms and ammunition were found. The court-house was the magazine, and contained an immense quantity of ordnance stores, bomb-shells, powder, etc. This was fired as the command left the city, and the exploding pieces sounded, at a distance, as if a battle was in progress.

The dream of John S. Griffith was realised the blow had been struck, and it only remained to be seen what effect it would have in causing the great Federal captain to change his plans for the reduction of Vicksburg.

As the fifth act of the drama, in this connection, does not properly pertain to our narrative, it will only be remarked, *en passant*, that the result was all that had been hoped for. General Grant withdrew his forces from that front, to Memphis, and inaugurated his celebrated movement down the Mississippi river, directly against Vicksburg, and the Texas Brigade was summoned, from the mountains of distant Tennessee, to attend the obsequies of the Army of West Tennessee, on July 4, 1863.

The following incidents attracted the attention of the author during the brief sojourn of the distinguished Southern party at the headquarters of General Grant. Our fortunes had undergone such remarkable changes in the last few hours, that nothing now could possibly surprise us. We had stepped from privation to plenty, and many were disposed to inaugurate a jubilee, inspired by the spirit of John Barleycorn, Esq.

Here comes Pennington, of the Third, with $20,000 in crisp, new greenbacks that he has discovered. He'd dispose of the batch for five dollars in silver. Despairing of drinking all the whisky, and having engagements elsewhere, the rebels knock the heads of the whisky-barrels in, and the streets of Holly Springs, literally, are flooded with whisky. A big, red-headed Irishman, in his shirtsleeves, but wearing a Federal officer's trowsers, called Colonel Mulligan whether derisively or not, *quien sabe?*—takes advantage of the sudden decline in liquors, and drinks confusion to his enemies with the pillaged whisky of his friends.

"Ye coom like thaves in the dark!" cries the melodramatic Colonel Mulligan. "Is this the way to make warr on a civilized people? But ye'll nivir, no nivir, escape!"

"Release the prisoners in the jail," is the next order. We find many

Federal soldiers incarcerated, some of whom join the ranks of their liberators. Many citizens imprisoned without a charge being preferred against them. But, shade of Brian Boru! who have we here else than Mr. B. Thomas! O, inimitable son of the Emerald Isle! My old comrade, whose loyal friendship was as true as steel, and whose aversion for guard duty was stronger than his hatred of the devil, what fate hath befallen thee since we parted so long ago under the "Stars and Bars?"

Mr. Thomas informs us that he is under sentence of death as a spy. "And if ye hadn't a come, it was shooting me they would the day afther the morrow. I'm glad to see yez, boys, and glad yez canteens are full."

*"O, I am not fond of wurruck,*
*It was nivir the gift of the Bradies,*
*But sure I 'd make a most illegant Turruck,*
*For I'm fond of tobaccy and ladies!"*

Mr. Thomas did not exaggerate his case a particle. He was discharged from the Third Texas after the conclusion of the first year's service, as being over the age of re-enlistment; whereupon, he engaged in the business of a sutler to the regiment. In quest of necessaries for his shop, Mr. Thomas ventured into the enemy's lines as affording a more varied market from which to select his purchases, with the result already remarked.

Colonel Griffith, as elsewhere stated, commanded the "Texas Brigade" in this, perhaps, most remarkable campaign of the war, and was second to no officer, in the corps, in contributing to its unparalleled success. He charged at the head of the Texans into the city, and his black plume waved in the thickest of the fight at Middleburg and Davis' Mill. Cool in the hottest fever of battle, he was brave even unto rashness. But happily, his temerity and impetuosity were held in subjection by a sagacious intelligence, and prudence characterised all his actions.

General Griffith is no less a gentleman of letters and culture, than of action on the field, and he would grace any civil position in the State—that he would consent to occupy—with profit to the people and honour to the office. His friend, the author, looks forward to his civil preferment with happy anticipations; knowing, full well, that Texas has no truer son upon whom she could confer her honours in part compensation for the arduous services that he has rendered her, on distant fields, which made the Texan name glorious.

Upon the immediate capture of Holly Springs, an indescribable scene of pillage ensued. In some commands, soldiers no longer recognised their officers, and, apparently, all subordination and discipline were lost sight of. It was, doubtless, a diverting scene to the prisoners, who longed in their hearts to see a few hundred of their blue-coated comrades come charging into town, and route the greedy rebels who were sacking it. And, in truth, this would not have been impossible, had the evil continued unchecked. But seeing some of his own brigade catching the disgraceful infection, Colonel Griffith appealed to them to remain at their posts of duty, and not disgrace the fair fame of the Confederacy by such riotous conduct. But some of the men not heeding the soldierly appeal to their noble natures, the determined chieftain drew his sword, and, in language more forcible than polite, vowed that he would constitute himself the custodian of Confederate honour, and drove the delinquents, at its point, back into the ranks.

The Texans bore the brunt of each engagement on this expedition. Wherever opposition was encountered, the gallant Griffith led his Texans through the revel of death, and wherever the conflict deepened most, his sable plume, like the *oriflamme* of Henry of Navarre, was seen. To the sterling soldierly qualities of Colonel John S. Griffith, was the Confederate cause indebted, in no small degree, for this success, which, in its results, exceeded those of many of the most stubbornly-contested battles of the war.

The prisoners captured in Holly Springs numbered between 2,800 and 3,000. But of infinitely more value than the paroling of these, or the destruction of the vast accumulation of supplies, was the rendering of Holly Springs a strategic point of no further importance in the "Great Captain's" campaign against Vicksburg.

About four o'clock in the afternoon, and as soon as the work of paroling the prisoners was accomplished, the command resumed the march northward. Nothing occurred, worthy of mention, until the fortified position of "Davis' Mill" was reached, just beyond the Tennessee line. Here a force of some three or four hundred Federals were ensconced in a palisade fort, having an impassable stream in its front, across which the assailants must move over a foot-bridge, exposed to the fire from the fort.

A curious contrivance, employed here, was a cannon mounted on a hand-car, which, from the facility with which it could be shifted from position to position, caused the Confederates considerable injury and annoyance. The Texas Brigade was dismounted, and marched to the attack in fine spirits, led by the intrepid Griffith. Colonel Griffith ordered Colonel Broocks, with the Legion, to cross the stream above the bridge on some logs, and assail the position in flank.

This movement the gallant Broocks executed in excellent order, and had General Van Dorn not called Griffith from the attack in front, to resume the march into Tennessee, the place must inevitably have been taken by the Confederates. The engagement was warm, and the Texans left about twenty dead upon the field, and twice that number wounded. At the bridge, in going to the attack, and in retreating from the field, volley after volley was poured into their ranks, wholly exposed to the enemy's aim, as they defiled across the narrow causeway, and deployed into line on the other side of the stream. The engagement continued, without intermission, for about three hours, when General Van Dorn, seeing the futility of his attacks on the fortified position without guns, called off the men. Again must the gauntlet be run at the fatal bridge, and again did the vigilant enemy improve the occasion by a free use of their rifles. A Confederate hospital was erected on the field, and left in charge of Assistant-Surgeon Eugene Blocker, of the Third Texas.

Northward, again, the indefatigable Van Dorn led the march, and, in the afternoon of the next day, came in the neighbourhood of Bolivar, Tennessee, at which place was a considerable force of the enemy. General Van Dorn amused them by a skirmish with the Tennesseans and Mississippians, while the Texans attacked a strongly-fortified position at Middleburg, a few miles distant. One prominent feature of this position was a block-house, absolutely impregnable to attacks by small arms. The position was stormed again and again, but no foothold could be gained, and General Van Dorn, despairing of success, abandoned the undertaking late in the afternoon.

The author omitted to state, in its proper connection, that the railroad track was torn up at various points between Holly Springs and Bolivar, and the telegraph wires cut. The object of the expedition was now attained, and the column turned to retrace its way by a circuitous route. The Federal cavalry were making superhuman efforts to capture Van Dorn, and endeavouring to intercept the column—a force of cavalry and mounted infantry, not far short of 10,000 men, were employed. Frequent skirmishes were had with this force on the return, the last of which occurred at Ripley, Mississippi.

The month of January was passed by the Texas Brigade in doing picket duty, and in scouting expeditions in and about Water Valley.

There being no longer any immediate need of cavalry in Mississippi, the command of General Van Dorn was ordered to Tennessee. Before commencing the long and fatiguing march, Van Dorn issued his celebrated "Order No. 5," in which he prescribed the minutest rules for the government of his corps, whether in camp or on the march. Proper distances were prescribed to be observed on the march between companies, regiments, brigades, and divisions; a regular system of bugle calls was formulated; challenges and replies of videttes, etc., etc.—the whole concluding with the impetuous declaration:

"Cavalry knows no danger—knows no failure; *what it is ordered to do, it must do!*"

The seemingly interminable march to Tennessee was wearisome in the extreme, and utterly devoid of interesting incident. The army of General Bragg was encamped at Tullahoma and Shelbyville. His left flank was threatened by a force of about 10,000 men, under General Granger, at Franklin. The object of Van Dorn was to confront this force, and prevent, if possible, its further advance in the direction of Duck river. This stream was crossed over a pontoon-bridge at Columbia, and the column proceeded to Spring Hill, on the pike connecting Columbia and Franklin. Several skirmishes were had with the enemy in the neighbourhood of Franklin; when, finally, about March 5, 1863, General Granger determined to put a period to Van Dorn's annoyances, and, affecting to despise the prowess of his adversary, dispatched Colonel Coburn, with 3,000 infantry, a battery of artillery, and about 500 cavalry, to drive the audacious rebel across Duck River.

Van Dorn met the expeditionary column at Thompson's Station, near Spring Hill; and, while engaging him in front with the Texas Brigade, dispatched General Forrest—who had reported to him for duty—to gain the enemy's rear. The Texans made charge after charge, upon the line of the enemy, and the author would bear witness to the bravery and soldierly bearing of Colonel Coburn, who fought with a velour worthy of a better issue. Outnumbered, surrounded, and being attacked by the impetuous charges of the Texans every moment, he finally raised the white flag, and surrendered to General Van Dorn in front of the Texas Brigade. The prisoners surrendered were about 3,000, as the cavalry and artillery escaped. Again, the author regrets that he is unable to present anything like an accurate estimate of the Confederate loss. A comrade of the author, in a late letter, says:

I think all the estimates place the loss of the Texas Brigade too

COLONEL JACK WHARTON.

low. The Legion carried into the battle 225 men, after leaving one-fourth of the whole to hold the horses; and, my recollection is, that the killed and wounded of the Legion numbered seventy-five. Company E came out of the fight with only half its number (twenty-eight), unhurt. Those true gentlemen and splendid officers, Captain B. H. Norsworthy (afterward promoted Major), and Lieutenant Lipscomb Norvell, being of the severely wounded.

That victory was indeed dearly bought by our brigade, no matter from what other quarter attempts have been made to appropriate the honours of it. With feelings of mingled pride and sadness, I continually, in my mind, look back upon the scenes of that day, and hear voices that are no longer of this world. Captain J. W. Bazer, commanding Company H of the Legion, with kindness of heart, intelligence, and iron nerve stamped on his countenance, severely wounded, but continuing duty on the field until shot dead.

Lieutenant Alley, of Company G of the Legion, always the gentleman and soldier, in fact and bearing, his black plume waving in the thickest of the fight until mortally wounded. Captain James A. Broocks, commanding Company C of the Legion, with his clear, ringing voice: "Come on, Company C!" The author would bear testimony to the daring and chivalry of Captain Broocks, who, upon that occasion, seemed to court the missions of danger like a Saladin bearing a charmed life. But he was struck down in his ripe manhood. To Colonel John H. Broocks, his brother, the dying patriot said:

John, take this sword (their venerable father had given it to him), and tell father that I died in the performance of my duty.

Noble words—example worthy the emulation of Southern youth for all time! Lieutenant C. H. Roberts, Company C of the Legion, true and brave, was killed at the head of his company. Privates Spoon, Elezer Davis, and John Bryant, of the Legion, and Drew Polk, and David B. Nicholson, of Company E, Third Texas Regiment, always distinguished for soldierly qualities, were all slain in close propinquity. The engagement continued, without intermission, about five hours; and, so deadly and stubborn was the nature of the contest, that at times bayonets actually clashed, and hand to hand fights to the death were not uncommon. Here fell one of nature's noblemen—Wyndham, First Sergeant of Company A, Third Texas. In the morning of manhood, he left his Louisiana home, and came to tender his services, and his life, to the cause of the South. Pure in his character, of a high and lofty nature, and talents far above mediocrity, Wyndham was justly regarded by his friends as a young man of great promise. Alas, what fond, proud hopes went down with him! He sleeps all alone, far from the home and friends of his youth, without a slab of marble to mark the spot; but he lives in the hearts of all who knew him,

*For none knew him but to love,*
*None named him but to praise!*

If the capture of Holly Springs was the most important cavalry exploit of the war, the Battle of Thompson's Station was not by any means the least. As an effort has been made to detract from the hard-earned fame of the Texas Brigade on this occasion, the author refers to a "defence" published in the Waco *Examiner and Patron*, and which has been endorsed by a number of officers of the Texas Brigade as being correct and just in all particulars, save that the loss in killed and wounded is underestimated.

Though not exactly in its proper connection, the original organisation of Whitfield's Legion will be given here, together with a statement of its participation in the Battle of Iuka. As this data came anonymously by mail, the author does not know to whom his thanks are due for the same:

Whitfield's Legion was organised April 2, 1862, by the addition of nine new companies to Whitfield's Battalion, the companies of the old battalion, to-wit: A, Captain E. R. Hawkins; B, Captain Murphy; C, Captain John H. Broocks; and D, Captain John T. Whitfield, carrying with them into the Legion the same letter designations respectively, that they had in the battalion. Major J. W. Whitfield was elected Colonel without opposition. The organisation was not completed until April 19, when Captain E. R. Hawkins was elected Lieutenant-Colonel, and Private S. Holman, Major. The command was composed of eleven companies from Texas and two from Arkansas, up to, and a short time after, the reorganisation, when the Arkansas Company B—Captain W. Catterson—was transferred to an Arkansas command.

At the 're-organisation' (May 8, 1862), all the field-officers were re-elected, and the companies were commanded by the following officers: A, Captain J. N. Zackry; B, Captain W. Catterson (*vice* Captain Murphy); C, Captain John H. Broocks; D, Captain John T. Whitfield; E, Captain B. H. Norsworthy; F, Captain Ben. Griffin; G, Captain Ed. O. Williams; H, Captain ———; I, Captain Jesse M. Cook; K, Captain ———: L, Captain ——————; M, Captain O. P. Preston; N, Captain———. Major Holman resigned, and Captain John H. Broocks was promoted in his stead. On May 9, 1863, Colonel Whitfield was appointed Brigadier-General, after which, Lieutenant-Colonel Hawkins was promoted Colonel, Major Brooks, Lieutenant-Colonel, and Captain John T. Whitfield, Major.

On September 19, 1862, the Legion participated in the Battle of Iuka. It occupied the position on the right of the brigade. When the skirmishers were driven back, Colonel Whitfield ordered a charge. The Third Texas, which had been thrown forward as skirmishers, seeing us advance, fell into ranks with us, and thus formed—as one regiment—we captured the Ninth Ohio Battery, driving the enemy before us. The Forty-Second Iowa attempted to make a right-wheel, so as to enfilade the line, but three companies, and about seventy men of the Third Texas, charged, and drove it in confusion from the field.

In this engagement, the three Cook brothers, of the Legion, greatly distinguished themselves for cool intrepidity and loyal devotion to the flag of the Confederacy. Ensign Ivey Cook was shot down, severely wounded, when his brother, Samuel, seized the regimental colours, and waved them with a cheer of triumph. But he advanced but a few steps, when he, too, was shot down; when a third brother, young Andrew Cook, grasped the staff from his relaxing hold, exclaiming: 'The flag shall wave, though the entire Cook family is exterminated in the attempt!' Colonel Whitfield was severely wounded. The loss of the regiment was 107 killed and wounded. On October 5, 1862, the Legion participated in the engagement at Hatchie Bridge, while the Battle of Corinth was in progress. We were first formed on the north bank of the river; were then moved to the south bank, and formed in line, with the river in our rear. We were attacked by an overwhelming force and driven back. Our loss was very great in prisoners, as the bridge was torn in pieces by the enemy's shell, and the means of passing the stream was difficult and dangerous. Our loss, during the engagement, was ninety-seven in killed, wounded, and prisoners.

The author regrets that he does not know to whom he is indebted for the above extract; but, knowing the general correctness of the statements given, he has no hesitation whatever in embodying it in the narrative of the services of the Texas Brigade.

*A Texan's Estimate of General W. S. Hancock, U. S. A.*

1

*Hancock, the smiling Muse lights on thy name,*
*With stylus ready to record thy fame;*
*The legend reads upon the tablet traced—*
*In letters that may never be effaced.*

2

*In war the superb soldier's matchless blade,*
*Gleamed first and last along the lines array'd;*
*When Peace arose with crown of olive wreath,*
*His tempered steel was first to seek its sheath.*

3

*Though others in the drama bore conspicuous part,*
*He won the fortress of his foeman's heart;*
*The civic chief, by all the sections blest,*
*Who knew no North, no South, no East, no West!*

★★★★★★

NOTES:—

During the march of the 20th, Colonel Griffith galloped to the head of the column, and rode with General Van Dorn an hour or more. Griffith represented to the general that, inasmuch as he was the originator of the expedition, he should be granted the post of honour; or, in other words, bear the brunt of the fighting; that his regiments, having served as infantry, would be more efficient than those drilled purely as cavalry. General Van Dorn readily acquiesced, and took occasion to thank the colonel for having, in such complimentary terms, suggested himself as the commander. He also complimented Colonel Griffith on the conception of such a bold *ruse de guerre*, which promised such sterling results to the cause.

Upon the entry of the Confederates into Holly Springs, Colonel Griffith was informed that General U. S. Grant had just departed, on a special train, for Memphis; and the locomotive that bore the modern Caesar and his fortunes, could even then be located by the smoke escaping from its chimney. A delay of five minutes, on his part, would have materially cheeked that tide in his affairs, that was bearing him on to fortune and to fame.

At the instance of Colonel Broocks, their regimental commander, honourable mention is made of the following officers and men of the "Legion," as their due for soldierly qualities exhibited on all occasions:

Lieutenant Thompson Morris, Company I, First Texas Legion.

Captain J. M. Cook, Company I, First Texas Legion.

T. M. Bagby, Company F, First Texas Legion.

Lieutenant Snell, Company F, First Texas Legion.

Sergeant M. McQuistain, Company G, First Texas Legion.

Captain Dave Snodgrass, illegally promoted from a lieutenancy in his own company, to the captaincy of another, by virtue of General Bragg's autocratic ukase of 1862.

John F. Pleasants, Company C, First Texas Legion.

Captain Adam Adams, Company E, First Texas Legion.

Captain Ed. O. Williams, Company G, First Texas Legion.

Lieutenant W. B. Walker, Company D, who lost an arm in the battles around Atlanta, while at the post of duty.

Rev. R. W. Thompson, the able and efficient chaplain of the Legion.

The author cheerfully adds to these the names of Ulysses Hairgrove, Company K, Third Texas Cavalry, who was as brave as he was always willing and ready for battle. First Sergeant Thomas J. Cellum, Company A, Third Texas Cavalry, who was always at his post, and ready to take a hand in anything that might turn up. Hays Alston, R. A. Godbold, Fannin Montgomery, and Jack Phillips, of the same company and regiment, recur to the mind; but, where all were actuated by motives the most disinterested and patriotic, it would seem invidious to make distinctions by the special mention of any.

## CHAPTER 8

# Chapter Title

After the Battle of Thompson's Station, the brigade encamped near the village of Spring Hill, on the Columbia and Franklin pike, for a week or ten days—a respite from service of which both horses and men stood much in need. But General Granger finally moved down the pike with an overwhelming force. Van Dorn retired in the direction of Columbia, sullenly disputing every inch of ground. As the recent heavy rains had caused the streams to rise, and more rain threatened, General Van Dorn very sagaciously crossed the wagon-train and battery of artillery over the river. General Granger's force now occupied the position of a horseshoe, extending from the river on the right of Van Dorn, to the river on his left. The Confederates were enveloped in the folds of the anaconda-like enemy; and, to complete the picture of their seemingly wretched condition, the pontoon-bridge was swept away, leaving a swollen, roaring torrent in their rear.

General Van Dorn recognised the desperation of the situation, and addressed himself at once to redeem it; and, on this occasion, he unquestionably showed those qualities of quick perception, rapid decision, and indomitable pluck, that characterizes the captain of genius. An attack, in force, was made on the enemy's extreme right, which forced him to draw re-enforcements from the left to come to the rescue of the threatened wing, thus leaving an outlet which the sagacious Van Dorn was not slow to improve. Placing himself at the head of the Third Texas Cavalry, the general led the way, followed by the remainder of the corps. Granger was surprised and chagrined to see his wily adversary elude his grasp, in what he, doubtless, deemed the moment of victory.

Van Dorn took up the line of march for Shelbyville, and, crossing the river at that point, returned to Columbia. The pontoon was soon repaired, and the corps was, ere many days, in front of Franklin, to which post the discomforted Granger had retraced his steps. The brigade, while here, was engaged in doing very arduous picket duty, and in foraging almost under the guns of the enemy. Frequent skirmishes, and partial engagements, took place; though the redoubtable Granger did not again venture out of his stronghold. The Legion, while doing picket duty in an advanced and very exposed position, was surprised one night by the enemy, and suffered some loss.

While encamped here, the assassination of General Van Dorn occurred. This was one of the severest blows to the Confederacy. Cavalry, pre-eminently, was the arm upon which the South should have relied, as by rapidity of movement, the deficiency in numbers could, in a measure, have been obviated. Van Dorn, Stuart, and Forrest, with 10,000 well-mounted and well-armed men, would, undoubtedly, have accomplished great results. As we have seen, Van Dorn frustrated Grant's army of 75,000 men with barely 3,000 troopers, and the results of the capture of Holly Springs was just the same as if Pemberton had driven Grant to Memphis; and, in a humanitarian sense, much greater, since the butchery was avoided. Forrest, with 5,000 men, fell upon Smith and Grierson, and crushed them, though they had full 15,000. men. Had this column joined Sherman at Meridian, as doubtless was the intention, the Georgia campaign had never been, for Sherman would have marched to Mobile, and the end would have been.

The circumstances attending the killing of General Van Dorn belong to history, and the public have a right to demand the whole truth, and, whatever delicacy of feeling we may have in regard to invading the sacred precincts of the domestic circle, vanish, when circumstances have invited the inexorable stylus of history to secure a record in the case; yet the author has no relish for such episodes, and is glad that another has kindly performed most of the unpleasant duty of reciting the causes of the homicide, and so relieved him of a very uncongenial task. There were no witnesses to the unfortunate act. The writer was encamped within three hundred yards of the house at the time, and can but give the report as current then. The headquarters of General Van Dorn were at the residence of Major Chairs, a few rods from the house of Dr. Peters.

On the morning of the homicide, the general rose from the breakfast-table in advance of his staff, and proceeded, alone, to his office, where he found Dr. Peters waiting. The latter presented a pass to Franklin, to the general, for his signature. Van Dorn took the paper, sat down to the desk to sign it. Peters, standing behind him, awaited the final stroke of the pen, when he drew a Smith & Wesson revolver and fired, the ball entering the back of the head, and lodging just under the surface above the right eye. The assassin, licensed by the pass, mounted his horse, and a few minutes' gallop passed him through the enemy's lines. Peters was subsequently apprehended, and tried in Mississippi before a Confederate court, and acquitted. The following account of his arrest, as given by Lieutenant Dan. H. Alley, Company G, Third Texas Cavalry, will prove of interest:

I was in command of General W. H. Jackson's scouts, and, in 1864, with five men, was on a reconnoitring expedition in Bolivar county, Mississippi. One evening we had struck camp— that is to say, we had scattered out among the houses of the immediate neighbourhood, two or three in a place, so as not to crowd or impose upon the citizens. Walter Boster and another man, whom I do not now recall, but think he was John Nelson, went to a house about a mile distant, and, in a very short time, Boster came back to me, and reported that he thought Dr. Peters was at the house where he was stopping, but was not sure. I instructed him to return, and keep out a strict watch during the night, and ascertain, if possible, if the suspected person was Peters; and that if he ascertained, beyond doubt, that it was Peters, to arrest and hold him. After supper, the ladies of the family and Dr. Peters were engaged in a game of cards.

The lady of the house was a niece of Peters. Accidentally, one of them called his name, so as to leave no doubt, on the mind of Boster, as to his identity. Shortly after this he laid off his pistols, a pair of Smith & Wesson, with one of which he killed the General. Boster now arrested him. He made no resistance— probably because they 'had the drop on him.' He appeared very much incensed at such a procedure, and forthwith dispatched a negro messenger for me, desiring that I 'come over' and explain. I sent Boster instructions to guard him until morning, when I would come over 'and explain.'

I went over early the next morning. He demanded my authority for causing his arrest, etc. I informed him that I was a Confederate officer, and that I arrested him for the killing of Major-General Earl Van Dorn, and that there was a standing order for his arrest. He desired to know what disposition I would make of him. I informed him that I reported to Brigadier-General W. H. Jackson, and that he was destined to that officer's headquarters.

He stated that he knew I was a Texan, and that I intended to kill him, as he had learned that the Texas Brigade had vowed vengeance against him. I assured him that he should be protected so long as he conducted himself docilely. He slept none, but was engaged in writing the greater part of the night. I presumed he was writing his will, as he evidently believed we would kill him. On our way to headquarters, he talked freely about the affair; abused his wife, and General Van Dorn, but was more bitter against Mrs. Peters than the general. He said that he had parted with her once before for a similar offense, committed in connection with a man other than General Van Dorn. He stated that he only condoned her fall from virtue on account of his children. He told me that he had caught Van Dorn at his house two nights before the killing; that Van Dorn ran out of, and under the house; that he pursued, and dragged him forth by the hair of the head.

Van Dorn was intoxicated at the time, and begged for his life, which he spared on condition that he would visit his house no more, and that he would sign writings to that effect; and also admit, in writing, that he (Van Dorn) had been too intimate with his wife. On the morning of the murder, he stated that he visited the office of Van Dorn to have him comply with these promises, and that Van Dorn exclaimed: 'Take the door, you ——— Puppy!' whereupon, he drew his pistol and fired.

I took him to General Jackson's headquarters, which were situated about fifteen miles from Canton, Mississippi. Efforts were made to take him from me by writ of *habeas corpus*, but I informed them that I would oppose any such attempt with force, and that, if they forced me to extremities, I would kill him myself, in preference to surrendering him. General Jackson had him conveyed to Meridian, where the court was in session for the trial of all military causes. I learned, subsequently, that he was tried and acquitted, and that he returned home, and took to his bosom the twice-discarded wife. Of this latter statement, however, I cannot vouch, as it is merely hearsay.

As well as I can remember, the scouts with me at the time were: Walter Boster—killed near Atlanta, Georgia, in a personal difficulty, (he was as brave a man as ever lived) Edgar Dade, J. W. Grimes, and John Nelson; the former were Texans, the latter, a Mississippian. Very much of his conversation in regard to Mrs. Peters and Van Dorn was unsuitable for print, and I have, consequently, omitted the greater portion of it.

The funeral of the dead general was very impressive and solemn. The command was mounted, and drawn up on either side of the street. The body, in a metallic casket, was laid in the hearse; on the head of the coffin reposed his Mexican *sombrero*, bearing a gold Texas star; along the breast reposed his gold-hilted sword, a present from the State of Mississippi; at the foot of the coffin, stood his military boots. Following the hearse was his horse, bridled and saddled. As the hearse passed down the lines, the officers and men saluted their dead chieftain with the sabre; and, though extremest silence reigned, many an eye was moist. Especially did his escort seem to realise their loss. They were men of the old army, who had followed the fortunes of the dashing "Major" into the Confederate Army, and had come to look upon the general as little children do a father.

We repeat, that the death of General Van Dorn was a great calamity to the Confederacy. Upon the death of the general, the cavalry corps was broken up; General Forrest, with his division, remaining in Tennessee, and the brigades of Whitfield (Texas), Cosby, and Ferguson, were organised into a division, over which was placed Brigadier-General W. H. Jackson, a cultured gentleman, and a brave, efficient officer, and a native of the State of Tennessee.

Grant had now inaugurated his titanic operations against the heroic city of Vicksburg, and Jackson's Division was ordered to the scene of operations. Probably a month was consumed in the arduous march, which afforded no incident worthy of note. Several days before we arrived in the vicinity of the doomed city, the terrible artillery duel, that was progressing day and night, could be distinctly heard. The city being closely invested, there remained but little for the cavalry to do but cover the front of the relieving army being organised by General Joseph E. Johnston. Preparations were finally made for crossing the Big Black River—and Breckinridge's Division, with the pontoon-train, were actually on the bank of the river—when intelligence came of the surrender. Immediately, the Confederate infantry fell back to Jackson, and the cavalry was left to dispute the advance of General Sherman, who marched on Jackson at the head of near 30,000 men.

During these operations, the Texas Brigade was commanded by General J. W. Whitfield Colonel Ross being in temporary command of another brigade, and operating in the Tennessee valley.

During the three days of Sherman's march from Vicksburg to Jackson, the command was under fire incessantly, and often and again did the impetuosity of their attacks force Sherman to deploy a division to clear the audacious troopers from his front. The "siege of Jackson," so-called, the retiring of Johnston to Brandon, and, eventually, the departure of Sherman for Vicksburg, are all too well-known to require repetition here. *Vide* conclusion of this chapter for additional details.

During the remainder of the summer and autumn, the Texas Brigade remained in front of Vicksburg, having an occasional skirmish to break the dull monotony of camp-life.

About this time—in the fall of 1863—General Whitfield, whose health was feeble, sought service in the Trans-Mississippi Department, and Colonel L. S. Ross, of the Sixth Texas Cavalry, was named Brigadier-General, and assigned to the command of the Texas Brigade. So identified did the general become with his brigade, that ever afterward it was known as Ross' Brigade. General Ross was quite young when the "wreath and stars" were conferred upon him, but he had been inured to war from his youth up. His father, Captain S. P. Ross, was, in the early days of Texas, a compatriot of Ben McCulloch, Hayes, Chevallie, and did good service on the exposed frontier against savage Indian and marauding Mexican.

Under the brave father's lead, the no less gallant son took his first lessons in war, and the truthful incidents connected with the youth of General Ross, if presented in print, would appear as a romance. The strong individuality of General Ross marked him from the commencement of the civil war, while his magnetic nature, and noble qualities of head and heart, made him almost the idol of the whole brigade. The boys were proud of their dashing young general, and I doubt if he would have accepted a Major-General's commission, unless conditioned that the old brigade should remain with him. As one instance, among hundreds that could be given, I copy from a recent letter from B. P. Simmons, who was a gallant soldier of the Sixth Texas Regiment of Cavalry, showing the affection that existed between the general and the men:

> I was with the command at the Battle of Corinth, where I was wounded; and, right here, I wish to make mention of General

Ross (God bless him!), who assisted me in getting off the field of battle. I had the calf of my leg shot away in a charge we made on Friday evening, when I was conveyed back to the hospital— I suppose some three miles to the rear—and was placed on a blanket between Goodson King and Spearman, both belonging to Company D, Sixth Texas. Both of them had their legs shattered by grape-shot. King died that night, and Spearman the next morning, about eight o'clock. As the army retreated on Saturday morning, General Ross placed me on his own horse, and carried me safely out of danger.

This is an incident that we read of in the exploits of ideal heroes in romances; but how seldom do we ever come upon the incident verified, as in this instance?

General Ross was fortunate in the selection of his staff officers. Captain D. R. Gurley, than whom a more perfect and accomplished gentleman does not exist, was the Assistant Adjutant-General, and served his chief, throughout the war, with intelligence, fidelity, and signal courage. Next to the general, I doubt if Captain Gurley was not the most popular man in the brigade.

In January, 1863, the brigade wag sent to guard a train, loaded with arms for the army, in the Trans-Mississippi Department. The weather was bitter cold, the smaller streams being frozen over. The men were thinly clad, and suffered terribly. The roads in the swamp being found impassable by wagons, the rifles were taken from the boxes, and each man, from the general down, took two guns and carried them to the river, where, with much difficulty, they were crossed over—an artillery duel, between a gun-boat and the Confederate battery, being in progress all the while. Sherman was now preparing for his celebrated raid through Mississippi, and General Ross hastened to the theatre of operations.

An expedition of gun-boats and transports, started up the Yazoo River about the same time that Sherman set out. To this latter expedition, General Ross paid his attention. The enemy landed at Satartia, and attacked Ross' Brigade, which was drawn up in line of battle just out the village. The Texans repulsed the enemy, who were mostly negroes, with white officers, and closely pursued them to the water's edge, when Ross retired from the guns of the boats. The action was sharp, hot, and decisive. General Ross was at the head of his column, encouraging his men by word and example. The repulsed enemy steamed up the river. At Liverpool, General Ross attacked the enemy in his floating fort.

The Texan sharpshooters soon caused the port-holes to be closed, and the enemy turned, and retreated down the river. Had not General Ross been called to the assistance of General Polk, who commanded the Confederate Army in front of Sherman, it is not at all problematical that he would have driven the enemy down the Yazoo, and forced him to seek refuge behind the walls of Vicksburg. A double-quick march now commenced for General Polk. General Ross fell in Sherman's rear, and, by many annoying and persistent attacks, materially retarded that general's march.

At Marion, Ross engaged the greater portion of the Union army all day in skirmishes, as if intending to attack in force. Here Sherman, doubtless, intended awaiting the arrival of General Smith, who, with 15,000 men, was *en route* from Memphis join him, intending, perhaps, when thus re-enforced, to march against and capture Mobile. Smith was advancing down the Mobile & Ohio Railroad, confronted by the indomitable Forrest. Ross was ordered to proceed, with the utmost dispatch, to General Forrest's assistance. Off the Texans started; but, on the second day, intelligence reached Ross that Forrest had routed his enemy, and that the demoralised army of Smith was flying in confusion toward Memphis. This startling intelligence was sufficient to cause General Sherman to retrace his steps, also. General Ross was now ordered to the Yazoo, to complete the job he had just commenced when, ordered away—*i. e.,* clear the river and valley of the enemy.

The column took up the line of march for Bentonville—distant from Yazoo city about ten miles, and being connected with it by a plank-road. The brigade passed through the village, and were encamping—two regiments, in fact, had gone into camp, and the battery was planted facing down the Yazoo road—when, like a clattering apparition, two of the Texan scouts dashed into camp hotly pursued by about two hundred negro cavalry. The battery gave them a startling salute that emptied several saddles, when General Ross mounted his horse, and shouting: "Charge them!" went clattering down the road, followed by his men, in enthusiastic confusion. The "black apes," as the boys called the negro soldiers, were pursued into the lines of Yazoo city, and the weary and victorious Texans camped about a mile in front of their lines.

★★★★★★

Note.—During the operations on the Yazoo, two young men of the Sixth Texas were brutally murdered by the enemy, after surrender; and thus was inaugurated an informal "war to the knife," which claimed many victims who otherwise would only have experienced the rigors of captivity.

******

Finally, after one or two days spent in skirmishing, General Ross determined to attack them. A detachment of ten men from Company A, Third Texas, drove in the pickets, which movement was followed up by the advance of the whole brigade. The enemy was driven into their bomb proofs, which were so effectually sealed by the Texan sharpshooters, that not a Federal gun could be heard. The Texans charged into the city, and drove the enemy aboard of the gunboats, and these iron monsters found it convenient to ride at anchor in the middle of the river. The guns of the boats were practically useless at such short range, as the river being higher than the country immediately around, the shells passed harmlessly over the heads of the Texans into the hills.

Night closed the scene, and General Ross drew off his men to the camp of the previous evening, intending to pay his respects to the enemy again in the morning. But the commander of the "black apes" did not wish another repetition of the "sealing-up process," consequently, he discreetly slipped aboard his boats, weighed anchor, and steamed for Vicksburg, to compare notes of failure and disappointment with General Sherman. The remainder of the campaign was confined to repelling raids from Vicksburg until about the last of April, when General Ross was ordered to re-enforce the army of General Johnston in North Georgia. This long march was prosecuted in a somewhat leisurely manner, the command often halting, for several days, to recuperate. One of these halting-places was Tuscaloosa, Alabama, at which point two members of Company A, Third Texas—Harvey Gregg and —— Gray were drowned in the Black Warrior River.

Ross' Brigade reached the army of General Johnston as it was crossing the Etowah River, and was immediately assigned to duty at the front. From this time on, to the fall of Atlanta, the brigade was daily under fire. For two months the men did not change their apparel, partook of only cold rations, and, during most of the time, were exposed to heavy rains—both from the clouds, and from the throats of the enemy's guns. The engagement at New Hope Church was a brilliant action, and reflected lustre on Texan arms. General Ross brought on the engagement, and the brigade, with those of Granberry and

115

Ector, repulsed, with heavy loss, a greatly superior corps of the enemy. General Johnston warmly congratulated the troops engaged, upon the immediate field of battle.

The lines of Sherman were now fast closing around Atlanta, yet the wily old chief of the Confederates disputed, stubbornly, each inch of ground, and every advance of the Northern army was dearly paid for. Sherman became impatient, or doubted the eventual success of his movements in front, and had recourse to cavalry raids in the rear of the Confederate position, with a view to cutting their lines of communication. General McCook, with an expeditionary force of cavalry numbering about 5,000, passed the left flank of the Confederate position, and gained the rear; but so closely was he pursued by the Texas Brigade and the Eighth Texas Cavalry (the Terry Rangers), that but little opportunity was allowed him to destroy the railroad.

Finally, he was brought to bay near Jonesboro, and attacked so vigorously, that his forces were demoralised, many were captured, and the remainder put to flight. Not being fully satisfied with the result of McCook's failure, General Sherman dispatched General Kilpatrick on a similar mission. (In this engagement fell William L. Thornton, the pride of his regiment and friends. Texas never possessed a son who gave greater promise than he. Daring and brave to a fault, he was sensitive, and refused promotion frequently rendered).

The Legion was on picket. This brave old regiment, handled by its gallant Colonel, John H. Broocks, contested the ground to the last, but was compelled to yield to overwhelming numbers, and Kilpatrick turned the flank of the Confederate position, and proceeded to the rear; but the vigilant Ross soon had his men in the saddle and in pursuit. A little after daylight, Ross struck the enemy in the flank, and inflicted considerable loss on him. But the innumerable attacks made on this raiding column by Ross' Brigade, are now impossible of description. Suffice it to say, that no opportunity for attack was allowed to go unimproved. Finally, Kilpatrick attempted to enter Lovejoy Station, and finding a division of infantry there, retired. General Ross had formed his brigade in the enemy's rear, expecting to be supported by the brigades of Cosby and Ferguson—neither of which put in an appearance.

Finding the infantry too strong for him, and meeting with an unexpected attack from Ross in the rear, Kilpatrick attempted to intimidate the Texans by a furious shelling, and then charged through the line—a feat by no means remarkable, when we consider that Ross did not have exceeding five hundred men, and Kilpatrick as many thousands. Add to this the fact that the Texans were dismounted, and armed with short guns—not having a bayonet in the brigade—and it will not be wondered at that they did not repulse a cavalry charge of ten times their number. Ross lost two or three men killed and wounded, and about thirty prisoners, many of whom escaped the first night.

Scarcely had the charging column passed the line, when the indomitable Ross had his bugler to sound the rally, and, in an incredibly short space, renewed his unceasing attacks upon the enemy's rear. From this time on, Kilpatrick found no rest, and, evidently, was bent upon the sole plan of making the best of his way out of a bad scrape. He was somewhat more fortunate than his predecessor, McCook, and made Sherman's lines in pretty good order. As the author was captured in the charge at Lovejoy Station, the remainder of the narrative is told as it was told to him. Nothing like a minute description has been attempted in the hasty tracing of the Georgia campaign. Each day was a battle, without characteristics to distinguish it from the battle of the day before, or that of the next day; and that campaign, being, as it was, one series of contests, will always defy the efforts of the conscientious historian. He may deal with it in the concrete—in the abstract, never.

### Addenda in Regard to the Siege of Vicksburg, and Other Operations of the Year 1863.

The Texas Brigade, in command of General J. W. Whitfield, took up the line of march from Maury county, Tennessee, for the purpose of re-enforcing the army of General Johnston, who was attempting the deliverance of Pemberton's beleaguered legions in Vicksburg, on May 19, 1863. On arriving in Mississippi, Colonel L. S. Ross was placed in command of a brigade composed of his own regiment, the Sixth Texas Cavalry, and Colonel Pinson's regiment—the First Mississippi Cavalry—and dispatched on an expedition in the Tennessee valley. The remainder of the Texas Brigade commenced duty on the line of the Big Black, which service consisted of frequent skirmishes with the enemy on the other bank, picket duty, scouting expeditions, etc. The headquarters of General Whitfield were established at Bolton's Depot.

The vigilant and courageous Colonel Broocks, and his veteran Legion, signalised themselves upon this field by valuable and conspicuous services rendered on more than one occasion; among which, we are enabled to record the following: One day the Federals were grazing some one hundred and fifty beeves in threatening proximity to

LIEUTENANT-COLONEL JOHN H. BROOCKS.

the line of demarcation—the river. Colonel Broocks, upon his own motion, silently crossed the river, and, by a rapid movement, dispersed the guard and captured the cattle; all of which he delivered to the Commissary of the brigade, much to the gratification of his not over-fed comrades of the other regiments.

On July 5, the Legion went on picket duty in its turn. On the 6th, General Sherman commenced advancing eastward, and 16,000 of his men crossed at Messenger's Ferry. The Legion was posted, in a slightly-elevated wood, on the east side of the river, and commanded an open field through which the enemy must pass. The position was one eminently adapted to a stubborn defence, and the gallant Broocks improved its natural advantages by a determination truly heroic, to hold his ground until re-enforcements should come to his aid, or he be driven from the field by the mere momentum of overwhelming odds. For four hours did the Legion hold the position against all efforts of the enemy to dislodge them; and it was only after the Federals had gained a foothold on the eminence, and, despairing of assistance, that the iron-willed officer consented to lead his men from the field rendered glorious by their valour; a movement which the brave Texans executed with perfect order.

The report of prisoners taken on the field, represented the Federal loss as very heavy, and rumour stated that General Osterhaus was wounded, or killed. The primary cause of the stubborn resistance of the Legion, was the appearance of an impostor, who represented himself to Colonel Broocks as a Confederate officer, and showed a dispatch purporting to come from General Johnston, in which the commander doubted the fall of Vicksburg, and urged Colonel Broocks to dispute the advance of the enemy until he could ascertain the strength of the force in his front. The Legion leisurely fell back to the line of the Ninth Texas Cavalry, about two miles distant, which regiment had come forward to relieve the Legion. Although his men and horses sadly needed rest, food, and sleep, Colonel Broocks complied with the urgent request of Colonel Jones, of the Ninth, to form the Legion in supporting distance of his regiment.

The enemy soon began the advance, and opened upon the Ninth with artillery and deafening volleys of small arms. Colonel Broocks hastened to the assistance of his brave young comrade, Colonel Jones, and continued to dispute the ground with the enemy, foot by foot, from position to position, until ten o'clock at night, when the storm of battle lulled. The contestants slept upon the field, in the midst of their respective killed and wounded, separated by but a few hundred yards. General Whitfield, with the Third Regiment, came up in the night, and, with the early dawn of the morning, the contest was renewed with redoubled exertions on either side. On every foot of ground, from Bolton's Depot to Clinton, a distance of eight miles, did the brave old Whitfield, and his indomitable veterans, struggle with the overwhelming numbers of Sherman, and force them to pay dearly for every advantage gained.

At Clinton, the brigade remained two or three days, as the enemy did not advance. At the end of this time, and when one-half of the brigade was absent from camp in quest of forage for the horses, excepting the Legion, the Federals resumed the offensive. General Whitfield dispatched Colonel Broocks immediately to the support of the skirmishers, and soon the Legion, formed in an open field upon a slight elevation, the cynosure of hundreds of admiring eyes, was engaged with the enemy. With such coolness, tact, and decision, did the gallant Broocks handle his men on this occasion, that he elicited the thanks of his superiors in command, and won for himself, and his incomparable Legion, the admiration of all. A young Mississippian, who was in the lines of the enemy, and present in the field-hospitals the night of the engagement, subsequently reported the killed and wounded of the enemy as approximating near one hundred. The loss of the Legion was slight.

Late in October, 1863, the Legion, commanded by its brave and efficient Colonel, E. R. Hawkins, together with Company E, of the Third (Lieutenants Soap and B. T. Roberts), were ordered to report to Colonel L. S. Ross, commanding the temporary brigade before mentioned, to which had been added Willis' Battalion of Texas Cavalry. It had been the original purpose of the expedition for Ross to re-enforce General Forrest, and, together, attempt the capture of Memphis. But, at Grenada, Ross learned that General Forrest was otherwise engaged, and had, consequently, abandoned his purpose in regard to the original conception. Colonel Ross was summoned, with his command, to Pontotoc, Mississippi, by General S. D. Lee; and his brigade, together with that of General Ferguson, and some companies of artillery, were organised into a division. The command was reviewed at Pontotoc by General Joseph E. Johnston, and there witnessed the hanging of a Federal spy, who was dressed in Confederate uniform, and who, probably, was a member of the Fourth Illinois Infantry.

From Pontotoc, the division moved into North Alabama, where

General W. T. Sherman, at the head of some 30,000 men, was marching along the railroad, up the Tennessee river, *en route* to re-enforce the beaten army of Rosecranz, at Chattanooga. General Lee proceeded to dispute the passage of the valley with the enemy, and so skilfully did he employ the limited means at his disposal, that General Sherman found it impossible to make the celerity of movement necessary to arrive at Chattanooga in time to succour his comrades there. The fighting was incessant, and the weather bitter cold, which called upon the thinly-clad men for the exercise of all the fortitude and endurance that they could summon.

Colonel John H. Broocks, with nine companies detailed from the Sixth Texas, Legion, and First Mississippi, was dispatched to destroy the railroad from Bear Creek, eastward. This was an arduous and fatiguing task, but the men performed it faithfully—burning the ties, heating the rails, and bending them double. While in the performance of this duty, Colonel Broocks was apprised of the fact that General Lee had fallen back on Bear creek, and was preparing to give battle. Broocks promptly repaired to the scene at the head of his nine companies, and participated in the spirited engagement which ensued. But it was in vain that General Lee attempted, with his small force, to check the progress of Sherman's legions. He was driven from the field by the mere weight of numerical superiority. General Sherman crossed the Tennessee thirty-five miles below Tuscumbia, and thus avoiding the lion in his way, proceeded to his destination.

Colonel Ross now set out for Mississippi with his command, and, at Okolona, the Legion left for the brigade proper, which was now commanded by Colonel H. P. Mabry, of the Third General Whitfield having, in consequence of continued ill-health, gone home. The Legion reported to Colonel Mabry at a point about twenty miles west of the town of Canton. General Ross, with the remainder of the brigade—Sixth Texas, First Mississippi, and Willis' Battalion—moved northward from Okolona to intercept a body of Federal cavalry who were raiding in that section. Ross met the body in battle, defeated it, and drove it into Memphis, when he returned to Canton, and assumed command of the Texas Brigade; Colonel H. P. Mabry, at the same time, being assigned to the command of a brigade in the cavalry corps of Lieutenant-General N. B. Forrest. From this period, until the termination of the war, it is believed Colonel Mabry remained with the cavalry corps of General Forrest; commanding, at first, a brigade, and, subsequently, a division.

The author regrets, exceedingly, that he has no data upon which to predicate a narrative of the sterling services of the gallant Mabry while attached to this command. But to have won the confidence and esteem of the incomparable Forrest to such a degree that he would not consent to part with his Texan Lieutenant, should have sufficed for the ambition of any man. Of Colonel H. P. Mabry, it can be truthfully said that he possessed all the higher qualities that enter into the heroic composition; and, through his accomplishments as a ripe scholar and profound jurist, he is no less conspicuous in the walks of civil life than he was on the field. Colonel Mabry has a future that will yet shed a lustre on the annals of Texas.

In the progress of the fight with McCook, Lieutenant T. J. Towles, of Company G, Third Texas Cavalry, was dangerously wounded, and remained, for some time, within the lines of the enemy. Says Lieutenant Towles:

> As I was sitting, with my back to a tree for support, my clothing saturated with blood, from the loss of which I was very faint and weak, General McCook, accompanied by some members of his staff, halted in front of me, and the general remarked: 'Major, you appear to be suffering.' I replied that I thought I was mortally wounded, and requested surgical aid. The general replied that he could not even give his own wounded the necessary attention, and said, apologetically: 'You have been a soldier long enough to know how these things are, and you must not think hard of me.' He wished to know what forces were opposing him on the immediate field. I replied that he could form as correct an estimate of their numerical strength as I could, as the divisions of Jackson, Wheeler, and Roddy were present; whereupon, he remarked to his staff: '*We must get out of this!*' and immediately rode away."

This revelation of Lieutenant Towles explains the panic with which McCook's men were seized, when General Ross, soon after, bore down upon them in the headlong charge which routed and dispersed them. Too much praise cannot be accorded this brave officer for his fortitude and loyal devotion to his country's cause, though suffering from excruciating pains that amounted to agony. Captain Towles is now a prosperous merchant of Camden, Van Zandt County, Texas, and is worthy the homage of all who love the true, the noble, and the brave. Long may his voyage of life be fanned by the breezes of prosperity, is the wish of his friend, the author.

Lieutenant T. J. Towles was long the brave, vigilant, and efficient commander of the brigade scouts, and as such, was the eyes and ears of the command. In the discharge of this hazardous service, he won the confidence of his commanding general, and we always slept with a sense of security when the faithful Towles was on duty. Lieutenant Dan. H. Alley performed a similar duty for the division commander, General W. H. Jackson, and was always equal to any emergency that might arise. Of him we have spoken elsewhere.

During the Mississippi campaign, the chivalrous Lieutenant Hill Taylor commanded the brigade scouts, and during the intervals between his engagements with the enemy, found time to cement one upon the basis of love with a *faire ladie* of Silver Creek, whom he led to the hymeneal altar when the "cruel war was over."

Distinguished as solitary scouts, or spies, the names of B. S. Triplett, and J. W. Montgomery—the present efficient Sheriff of Rains County—were pre-eminent. Triplett fell at the hands of an assassin, as elsewhere stated, but Wiley Montgomery is winning as many encomiums in the civic walks of life, as he did in the more hazardous paths of war. He is worthy of all the honours his fellow-citizens may confer upon him.

# CHAPTER 9

# The Beginning of the End

During these latter days, when the fate of the Confederacy was trembling in the balance, and Titans grappled for the possession of the "Gate City," the scene shifts so frequently that the *camera* fails to retain an impression. The visit of President Davis; the removal of General Johnston; the placing of General Hood in command of the army, are events yet remembered. Then came Sherman's erratic move to the rear, which sealed the fate of Atlanta. In all these rapid movements Ross' Brigade bore its banner with honour, and signalised its prowess on twenty of the bloodiest fields of the tragic drama.

It was theirs to lead the Confederate advance; theirs to participate, as infantry, in the stubborn fight, and theirs, finally, to cover the gloomy retreat. While the infantry were enjoying short respites of repose in camp, from their arduous duties in the field, Ross' men formed a cordon of safety between them and the enemy—where sleepless vigilance was the price of security. No historian will ever recount the many acts of individual heroism performed in the wild mountain passes of North Georgia by the Texas scout; no record will ever keep for admiring posterity the midnight attack and repulse.

The future will but know the general legend, that Ross and his braves were tried by ordeals that taxed to their utmost the highest qualities of our nature, and that they came forth from the fiery saturnalia of demoniac war as gold purified from the crucible. True to every trust, their sublime devotion wavered not, nor did their heroic exertions relax even when the hand of Fate had written the Confederacy's epitaph above the hopes of its people, and craven manhood deserted the colours of their allegiance, and sought ignoble security behind the devastating lines of the enemy. The last rally of the bugle found them as ready to mount as did the first, when cheered by the smiles of wives and sweethearts in far distant Texas.

It is not our province to follow the rapid moves of the columns on this gigantic field of war. Sherman commenced his "march to the sea," and Hood set out for Nashville. General Ross was ordered with his brigade to take the advance, and to proceed to the vicinity of Decatur and Tuscumbia, Ala. This march was performed quietly enough, as no enemy at all was encountered. At Decatur, General Ross awaited the arrival of General Hood, who, with the main army, arrived in a few days, and went into camp, remaining there nearly a week, to allow rest and refreshment to the tired men. During the halt, however, activity reigned in the commissary and ordnance departments; and the necessary ammunition and provisions were gotten ready for the purposed campaign.

Again, Ross was ordered to take the advance. The Tennessee river was crossed, and the column headed for Nashville. At the Tennessee River the enemy's cavalry was encountered; but, after several spirited engagements, General Ross drove them from his front. The march was necessarily slow and tedious. The cavalry of the enemy was re-enforced by overwhelming numbers, and, no sooner had Ross driven a body from his front, than he was attacked by a fresh contingent, which arduous service told heavily on men and horses. Even the night brought but little relief, for both general and men were in arms during the entire night. Thus Ross led the advance into Tennessee, literally cutting a pathway through the multitudinous enemy for the march of Hood's army.

A few miles south of Pulaski, Tenn., a large force was descried drawn up in line of battle, and occupying a very advantageous position. Ross did not hesitate a moment, but commenced preparations to attack, though it was evident that they out-numbered the Texans in the ratio of ten to one. The Legion was deployed to the left; the Ninth to the right, and the Third and Sixth advanced as the centre. All thought a hotly-contested engagement was imminent. But, after some heavy skirmishing, the enemy, evidently thinking discretion the better part of valor, left the field precipitately, and fell back on Pulaski. At this place, General Ross discovered the enemy posted in force, and so dispatched General Hood, in the meantime, however, annoying the Federals with his skirmishers and sharpshooters. Hood came up with the army, and directed Ross to turn the left flank of the enemy, and gain his rear.

Seeing Ross in the execution of this movement, the enemy abandoned his position, and once more retired in the direction of Nashville, to which point all the clouds of war seemed now converging for the coming storm. Ross pursued the retreating Federals; and, from Pulaski to Columbia, scarce a moment passed that the eager Texans were not on their heels. In this pursuit many prisoners were taken, and some wagons. At Columbia it was understood that the enemy would give battle. Cheatham's Division had been sent lower down the river to cross, so as to gain the enemy's rear.

Arriving in front of Columbia, General Hood directed General Ross to cross Duck River some miles above the city, and gain the enemy's rear—a move he executed with neatness and dispatch, taking position on the pike between Spring Hill and Franklin. General Ross at once dismounted his men, and attacked the enemy in his front (Federal rear) with vigour. Simultaneously with the report of Ross' guns, General S. D. Lee attacked the enemy in Columbia. It evidently was Hood's design that Cheatham should have re-enforced Ross' Brigade with his division of infantry, and capture the army of Schofield at Columbia. Lee drove the enemy into town; and Schofield bent his energies now to drive Ross from his rear—now become his front—that he could retire. All that day the unequal contest raged. The brave young hero was dismounted and at the head of his columns; and his clear, ringing voice was often heard above the din of conflict, encouraging his men to maintain the unequal grapple.

Anxiously, but in vain, did Ross look for Cheatham. He felt that his skeleton brigade could not much longer stand up before the terrible odds pitted against it. The long hours seemed interminable in their weary course; and the guns of the enemy thundered their vomitings of iron hail into the decimated ranks of the Texans. The field of battle was the narrow turnpike, and the vast numbers of the enemy did not avail as they would on the open field. To the deafening volleys of the enemy's fifty guns, the unerring rifles of the Texans defiantly replied. In vain did the Federal infantry charge the position time after time, as if to sweep, by mere weight of numbers and momentum, the audacious Texans from their path. But Ross, sword in hand, his face blackened with the smoke of battle, met them each time with a counter-charge, to retire, when the spasmodic death grapple was over, sullenly to his old position.

Ross appeared as personating the character of Leonidas in the pass of a western Thermopylae. Finally, the sun set as if ashamed to witness the scene of slaughter. As the thunders of battle lulled temporarily, the groans of the wounded piled—on the narrow pike indiscriminately with the dead—were heard, often begging in piteous accents for water. Ross learned from a citizen that General Cheatham was not more than a mile distant. Assuredly, then, the long and anxiously-expected re-enforcement will soon arrive. This hope imparts to the indomitable young chieftain new resolution, and nerves his heart with determination to hold the pass at all hazards. He communicates the high and unselfish resolve to his men, and is answered by cheers of enthusiasm. They feel that they hold in their hands the key of the position; and that the muse of history is contemplating their acts. They appreciate the magnitude of the trust reposed in them, and swear to be faithful at the price of life itself.

Doubtless, General Hood imagined that it was the legions of Cheatham that were staying the progress of Schofield's divisions, and felt that victory was in his grasp. And, if Cheatham had come, how different would have been the result. Hood did all that it was in the power of mortal man to do. His orders were disobeyed, and Napoleon himself would have failed, under similar circumstances. But the lull in the storm of battle was only temporary. Again the enemy, with re-enforcements drawn from the front of Lee, where the combatants had ceased for the night, renewed the contest with redoubled efforts. He was struggling for existence, and desperation characterized his attempts to extricate himself from the enveloping lines of the determined Confederates.

The darkness of the night was lit up by the lurid glare of a hundred cannon, and their thunders reverberating among the rocks and hills, sounded as if pandemonium had settled upon the earth. Volley after volley of musketry rattled along the lines; the groans of the wounded; the piles of the dead; the shrieks of the combatants, formed a picture in the stygian darkness terrible and sublime! Charge after charge the enemy made on the Texan position; but the indomitable Ross never failed to accept the gage, and always met them on halfway ground. Often the combatants were mixed in inextricable confusion, and friend could not be distinguished from foe.

Thus, throughout the entire night did the demoniacal conflict rage; but *Ross held the pike!* With the morning's dawn the enemy ceased firing in front, and concentrated all his available force of infantry, cavalry, and artillery upon the position held by Ross, who, by the mere force of numbers and the utter exhaustion of his men, retired sorrowfully from the pike that had witnessed his unparalleled defence. The Texans retired but a short distance from the field, and sought that repose so much needed, while the army of Schofield was pouring through the gap thus formed, and leading Hood on to the fatal field of Nashville. Had Cheatham re-enforced Ross on the pike, the campaign would have closed at Columbia in a glorious Confederate victory.

Having rested the greater portion of the day, the shades of evening found Ross and his men in the saddle. The enemy was retreating on Franklin; and being stretched along the single pike presented a tempting opportunity to a daring leader to make reprisals an opportunity that Ross did not neglect. The night was spent by the Texas Brigade in making sudden attacks upon this line; and many prisoners, and wagons containing commissary and quartermaster stores, were captured. The town of Franklin was well fortified, and, doubtless, General Schofield imagined he would be allowed to remain here unmolested—a supposition not justified by the result, for General Hood, immediately upon his arrival, made preparation for an assault. General Ross was dispatched to the right, and up Big Harpeth River, which he crossed.

The Texans were here encountered by Brownlow's celebrated "Gray Horse," an excellent body of cavalry. The Ninth Texas was thrown forward as skirmishers; the General holding well in hand the Third, Sixth, and one battalion of the Legion, the remainder of that regiment having been left across the creek as a support. The enemy attacked the Ninth furiously; and, by force of numbers, drove them back. Ross, seeing the condition of affairs, placed himself at the head of his men and charged. The "Gray Horse" met the onset gallantly by a counter-charge, and the two opposing lines absolutely passed through each other; probably an incident without parallel in the whole course of the war.

★★★★★★

In his desperate encounter with the "White Horse," Colonel Jones, of the Ninth, ran his sword through a Union trooper, and broke it off at the hilt, the blade remaining in the body of his adversary. No one was more conspicuous for daring bravery, in this engagement, than Lieutenant W. J. Cavin, of Company A, Third Texas Cavalry. Sergeant T. J. Cellum, in this engagement, slew in single combat a Union officer, who refused to surrender; himself receiving three pistol-shot wounds in the deadly duel.

★★★★★★

Many hand-to-hand fights ensued; and several of Ross' men were afterward mounted on grey horses captured in the fight. Especially worthy of mention was a personal combat between a Federal non-commissioned officer and J. C. Pritchett, of Company E, Third Texas. Mr. Pritchett killed his man and captured his steed. Again, the "Gray Horse" prepared for another charge. The liberty is taken to quote the language of Lieutenant B. T. Roberts, Company E, Third Texas, to whom the author is indebted for the incidents of the Tennessee campaign:

General Ross told his men to stand firm; that he was there to lead them. He called on the Ninth to rally on him, which was readily done. The enemy, in the meantime, were bearing down on our line furiously; when General Ross, standing straight in his stirrups, shouted 'Forward!' and with drawn saber led the charge in person. At once the opposing lines clashed, and for some time it seemed doubtful which would yield. Ross was ubiquitous, and seemed to bear a charmed life; and was heard to exclaim at the crisis of the engagement, 'Boys, if you don't run, they will!' And they did. The Texans pursued Brownlow until the fugitives found refuge in night.

While Ross was engaging the "Gray Horse," Hood was storming the ramparts of Franklin. Upon the retreat of the enemy from Franklin, Ross was still kept to the right, and in advance, following the enemy to the very suburbs of Nashville. While General Hood was investing Nashville, General Ross was ordered to cut off re-enforcements to Thomas, expected from Murfreesboro. This he did effectually, capturing stockades and stations between Nashville and Murfreesboro. The result of this brief campaign was three hundred and fifty prisoners, and an immense train loaded with commissary supplies—an invaluable acquisition to General Hood at the time. But General Hood's successes—dearly bought—were at an end. The disastrous Battle of Nashville dissipated the hopes of an advance. Indeed, the issue now was the existence of his routed columns.

Ross covered the retreat, and hung on the rear of Hood's demoralised army, a barrier to the eagerly-pursuing Federals. This, says Lieutenant Roberts, was the severest service experienced during the war. It being late in December, the weather was intensely cold freezing all the time the men were thinly clad, poorly fed, and dejected and disheartened. The Texans were called upon to repulse twenty charges of the enemy's cavalry a day. Nor did night relieve them of their arduous duties; for often they were compelled to stand in line of battle throughout the cold night. But Ross and his men were true to the trust reposed in them, and interposed, as a barrier between the beaten army and its victorious enemy, until the Tennessee River was crossed, which ended the campaign, and virtually, the services of Ross' Texas Brigade. The author would say no more; but point to the record contained in this imperfect narrative of their services.

## ADDENDA

Through the kindness of Rev. John Hudson, of Hutto, Williamson county, Texas, the author was given access to the diary of his brother, Rev. Edward Hudson, who had been appointed by Colonel Griffith, Chaplain of the Sixth Regiment, Texas Cavalry. Mr. Hudson served some time as a private in Captain "Pete" Ross' company, and bore all the dangers, privations, and hardships, incidental to that position, until promoted Chaplain. In an engagement between Ross' Brigade and the command of General McCook, in July, 1864, near Noonan, Ga., Chaplain Hudson, who accompanied his regiment into the engagement, discovered one of his acquaintances dangerously wounded. He called to a comrade to assist him in removing the wounded man to a place of safety.

The two men dismounted, leaving their horses in the care of a third, and immediately proceeded to succour their wounded friend. Having accomplished this humane act, they returned for their horses, but discovered that the enemy had advanced considerably, and that their horses were gone. Chaplain Hudson caught, upon the field, the horse of a Union trooper, mounted him, and proceed in a line diagonally across the field in quest of the missing horses. He was fired upon by a body of the enemy, his horse killed, and himself dangerously wounded. In a recent letter to the author, Rev. John Hudson writes:

At his own request, General Ross had him carried to a private house, and there he remained until the close of the war. Levi Fowler remained with him, and finally brought him home. General Ross (although I never met him) and Levi Fowler occupy a very warm, sacred place in my heart, because of their kind, humane, brotherly treatment of my dear brother. He remained but a short time near Waco; received a suit of clothes and some money from the boys of his old regiment, as a token of their esteem, and went from there to Kemp, Kaufman county, and taught school four years.

He resumed preaching soon after settling in Kaufman; but was compelled, in consequence of the result of his wounds, to occupy a sitting posture whenever doing so; and he so continued to preach until his death, which occurred August 17, 1877. He preached a great deal; rode two years as a missionary in the bounds of the "Bacon Presbytery." But he was a great sufferer all the time. His health finally failing, I brought him to my home in Williamson county. He bore his affliction with great fortitude and resignation. His death was one of great peace and triumph; not a dimming veil or cloud obscured his mental horizon.

From Mr. Hudson's diary the following facts in regard to General Ross' campaign in the Tennessee valley, in 1863, are gained; and for which the author is specially thankful, inasmuch as all his efforts to obtain data, upon which to predicate a narrative of this brilliant campaign, have been unavailing. As little else than the dates, and briefest mention of movements, in a general way, are given, the brief story of one of the most successful cavalry expeditions of the war must remain, for the present, at least, but partially told. But to the diary:

On September 26, 1863, the Sixth Texas Cavalry, and the First Mississippi Cavalry, left Richland, Mississippi, under the command of Colonel L. S. Ross. At Pontotoc, the command was reviewed by General Joseph E. Johnston. Taking up the line of march again, the brigade passed Tupelo, the scene of our infantry encampment the previous summer. From this town, on the Mobile & Ohio Railroad, the brigade proceeded to Tuscumbia, Alabama, on the Tennessee River, where the Fifteenth (Union) Army Corps was stationed. General Ross immediately inaugurated a system of surprises, attacks, etc., that annoyed the enemy intolerably for the space of six days, during which period, night and day, the confused enemy knew not at what moment we would attack him, nor from what point of the compass the attacking party would come.

Finally, the Union corps, though numbering nearly ten thousand men, were forced to retire from the Memphis & Charleston Railroad, which it was their duty to hold, and leave it in the possession of their adversary, who could not count over twelve hundred rifles. The enemy was forced to cross the Tennessee River at Eastport, and fall back upon Corinth; thus retarding their purposed re-enforcement of General Rosecranz's army, which was operating against the army of General Bragg in East Tennessee. After considerable manoeuvring, the brigade made a rapid dash on Moscow, where we had a very spirited fight with the enemy there posted; thence, back, via Holly Springs and Grenada, to Canton, where the remainder of the old brigade were encamped. We here parted with our comrades of the First Mississippi than which no regiment was composed of more perfect gentlemen or braver soldiers.

After this expedition, a feeling of *comraderie* always existed between the Sixth Texas and the First Mississippi. Soon after the arrival of the Sixth Regiment, the brigade moved, in charge of a train of wagons loaded with arms and ammunition for the trans-Mississippi Department. Mention of which is made in its proper place in the narrative.

While the brigade was encamped at Canton, many horses were afflicted with a malady somewhat resembling "blind-staggers," which, in most instances, proved fatal. The general cause assigned, was grazing on a vegetable called "sneeze-weed," of all which the author is ignorant, save only the effects.

Mr. J. Wylie Montgomery, of Company A, Third Texas Cavalry, and at present the efficient sheriff of Rains county, Texas, deserves special mention for his daring bravery in battle, and for his sagacity as a scout, in which peculiarly dangerous service he was long employed, and rendered services of incalculable value to the brigade and division commanders. He is deserving, in all respects, the confidence of his fellow-citizens.

# Biographical Sketches

GENERAL JOHN S. GRIFFITH.

In that galaxy of glorious stars, whose effulgence yet lights the memory of the "Lost Cause," though its sun has forever set, none shines with a steadier glow than that consecrated to the name and fame of John S. Griffith. Where paladins seemed to contend in generous emulation for the plaudits of fame, and individual heroism was the daily rule, it would seem invidious to make distinctions. But we can accord all the honours, that are so eminently his due, to this gifted son of Texas, without the disparagement of anyone.

Unselfish in his characteristics; brave, though sagacious, as becomes a commander; patriotic in all his impulses; had health been vouchsafed to him, a career of glory and usefulness would have crowned his efforts with success. As it was, by his consummate address on the hardly-contested field of Oakland, and as the central figure of the Holly Springs campaign, he gave ample evidence that he possessed, in a pre-eminent degree, those lofty, necessary qualities that can only fit a man for command in battle. General Griffith was more than a dashing cavalryman, for his analytical mind penetrated far beyond the immediate shock of battle, and took in the salient features of the campaign as a whole.

It was he who conceived that master stroke of policy, and was the most efficient agent of its execution "the Holly Springs Raid." He saved the army of Pemberton, indubitably, by the movement; and, consequently, delayed the fall of Vicksburg many months. On the field of Oakland, he performed for the same army duties, of scarce less vital moment. But we anticipate. John S. Griffith was born in Montgomery County, Maryland, on the 17th day of June, A. D. 1829. His father, Michael B. Griffith, was the son of Captain Henry Griffith, of the Revolutionary army, and a lineal descendant of the historical Llewellen ap

Griffith, of Wales. To the influence of his pious mother, who was a daughter of General Jeremiah, and Elizabeth Crabb, a beautiful, cultured, and accomplished lady, whose energy, will, and fortitude were sufficient to surmount the many obstacles and misfortunes that beset her path amid the vicissitudes of life, the subject of this sketch has ever attributed whatever success, under Providence, he has achieved.

His parents started in life in affluent circumstances. But forced by some losses in his business (mercantile) Mr. Griffith removed to Jefferson City, Missouri, in the year 1835; and from the latter place to Portland, Missouri, in 1837. Misfortune attended all his efforts to improve the long series of losses, until, when reduced to the paltry capital of one thousand dollars, he removed, April 15th, 1839, to San Augustine county, Texas, with a family of six children, three of whom were girls.

In common with the pioneers of early Texas colonization, theirs was a lot of hardship and privation. Flour cost twenty-five dollars per barrel, and bacon fifty cents per pound. In this situation of affairs, which would have impaired the energies of a man more accustomed to the smiles of success, the father seemed for a space to despond; but the heroine wife and mother rose superior to the occasion, and her high qualities of energy and endurance and above all, hope eternal, though its realization had been so often deferred, shone with a noontide glow that promised to dispel the lowering clouds of adversity that hovered above the devoted heads of her little ones.

Such a mother! Is it wonderful that her heroic son should now recall, with moistened eye, her unequal struggle in that frontier home? Her example, though subserving its immediate objects, had a result far more distant and lasting, for it moulded in the nature of the boy the admirable qualities that made John S. Griffith a leader of men. How true is the saying of the great Napoleon, that the mother's qualities, good or bad, are always imparted to the son!

This struggle with adversity was accepted without a murmur by young John S., the second son, and, doubtless, he there learned many practical lessons, which had much to do in forming the character of the man. He received, chiefly at home, the rudiments of an English education; and, in 1850, commenced business as a clerk in a mercantile establishment. In the following year, he set up on his own account as a merchant, operating wholly on borrowed capital. Thanks to his industry and economy, the business prospered remarkably; and our young merchant, in December, 1857, was united in marriage to Miss Emily, daughter of John J. and Mrs. Jane Simpson, of Nacogdoches county, Texas. His business affairs continuing to prosper, he removed, in the year 1859, to Kaufman county, where he engaged in the raising of live stock in connection with his mercantile pursuits.

At the sound of the first tocsin of war, in 1861, Captain John S. Griffith was called to the command of a volunteer company of cavalry raised at Rockwall, Texas. Captain Griffith tendered the services of his company to Colonel E. Greer, whose regiment, the Third Texas Cavalry, however, was already full. So ardent were the Rockwall boys, that their liberal captain offered Colonel Greer to defray their expenses for three months out of his own purse, if allowed to become attached to the regiment for that space.

Why they were not allowed to do so, and as many other companies as desired, must always remain a mystery—seeing that General Price was being driven out of Missouri by an overwhelming Federal force, and that General McCulloch, with a few Arkansas militia, was awaiting the arrival of the only two regiments coming to his assistance, the Third Texas Cavalry and Third Louisiana Infantry. Of course, Colonel Greer had no option in the premises, as his authority extended no further than the organisation and command of his own regiment. But it is of interest to discover right here, at the inception of the contest, the commencement of that fatal series of maladministration which contributed more to the wreck of the Confederate cause than the armies of the invader.

The Battle of Oak Hills was won through a combination of fortuitous circumstances; and the South relapsed into fancied security. Had we been beaten there, the result may have aroused the Southern administrations to a sense of the magnitude of the struggle in which they were actors, or hastened the final catastrophe; either of which conclusions was preferable to the protracted, often desultory, and seemingly hopeless manner in which the war was waged on the part of the South.

But Captain Griffith had not long to wait; as soon as Colonel B. Warren Stone commenced the organisation of the gallant old Sixth Texas Cavalry, the Rockwall boys were incorporated in this regiment as Company B, and was officered as follows:

John S. Griffith, Captain.
Amos Dye, First Lieutenant.
E. P. Chisholm, Second Lieutenant.
James Truett, Third Lieutenant.

F. M. Nixon, Orderly-Sergeant.

M. B. Cannon, Second Sergeant.

A. C. Richardson, Third Sergeant.

F. Chisum, Fourth Sergeant.

A. W. Hedges, First Corporal.

A. Cummins, Second Corporal.

B. L. Williams, Third Corporal.

John R. Briscoe, Fourth Corporal.

John O. Heath, Ensign.

Allen Anrick, Bugler.

Upon the organisation of the regiment, Captain Griffith, who was already a popular favourite with his comrades, was elected Lieutenant-Colonel. The regiment proceeded, as elsewhere stated in these pages, to Arkansas, and reported for duty to General Ben McCulloch. The service here consisted of foraging, scouting expeditions, picket duty, etc.; though the gallant Price and his immortal "Old Guard" were struggling under the "Grizzly Bears" against overwhelming odds. Had the Texans been consulted, they would have sped to the assistance of their struggling Missouri allies. In December, 1861, Colonel McIntosh, in command of a battalion, each from the Third and Sixth Texas Cavalry, the former commanded by Lieutenant-Colonel W. P. Lane, and the latter by Lieutenant-Colonel J. S. Griffith, Whitfield's (Texas) Battalion, and Young's Regiment, Eleventh Texas Cavalry, and a battalion of First Arkansas Cavalry, marched to the relief of General Cooper, who was being driven back by superior forces of hostile Indians. The enemy was encountered on the heights of Chustenahlah, and routed (as elsewhere detailed). The following letter from the gallant and heroic General W. P. Lane will be of interest:

Marshall, Texas, February 4, 1881.

Victor M. Rose, Esq.:

My Dear Sir—I delayed answering your letter, hoping to find some one more conversant with the incidents of our fight at Chustenahlah than myself; but failing to find anyone who would volunteer to do so, I will endeavour to present my recollections of the campaign. On Christmas day, 1861, we moved from camp to attack the Indians, who, we learned, were some ten miles distant. Our force consisted of battalions of Third. Sixth, and Eleventh Texas Cavalry, and Captain Bennett's company, all under command of McIntosh.

My battalion being in advance. I detached Captain D. M. Short, with thirty men, to reconnoitre, and to drive back a small party that the enemy had sent out to review us. Finally, Captain Short sent me word that the Indians were posted on the hills in force, and were complacently awaiting our attack. Colonel McIntosh then placed his force in the following order: Sixth Texas, Lieutenant-Colonel Griffith commanding, on the right; Third Texas, Lieutenant-Colonel W. P. Lane commanding, in the centre; the Eleventh Texas Cavalry, Colonel Young commanding, together with Bennett's company, on the left. He then ordered me, with the Third, to charge the hill on horseback.

The hill was very steep, and just possible for a horse to ascend. I replied, that I would do so with pleasure; and added, 'but if I do not carry the position?' He replied, that, in that event, he would dispatch the Sixth and Eleventh to my aid. I replied, 'All right, but if I do not carry the position I will be at the bottom before the re-enforcements can arrive.' I gave the order for the men to dismount and tighten girths. I then informed the boys that when the command to charge was given, the quicker we got among the Indians the fewer empty saddles we would have. We charged in good style, carrying the hill, and throwing the Indians into confusion. At the same time, Colonel Griffith, on my right, and without orders, led his battalion in a gallant charge, and the Eleventh, and Captain Bennett's company, simultaneously swept around the hill on the left, thus completing the discomfiture of the enemy. Our loss was small; some eight or ten killed, and eighteen or twenty wounded. In my battalion, Lieutenant Durham was mortally wounded, and Major G. W. Chilton slightly. The battle effectually broke up the Indians. We took several hundred prisoners, horses, cattle, sheep, and other property, too numerous to mention.

Yours, truly,

Walter P. Lane.

When Colonel McIntosh placed the Sixth in position on the right of the line, his instructions to Colonel Griffith were to *await further orders*. But Colonel Griffith, seeing the intrepid charge of Lane had dislodged the Indians, who were retiring across a deep gulch to the right, very correctly decided that the opportune moment had arrived for striking a decisive blow. Not a moment was to be lost; and, with sabre in the left and revolver in the right hand, he led his command in a dashing charge over a seemingly impassable ravine, and spurred his horse up its almost precipitous banks, and was the first of the command to engage in the desperate hand-to-hand encounter that ensued. Emptying his revolver, he borrowed another of one of his captains, and continued the running fight until it was also emptied, when he had recourse to his sabre.

During the *melee*, Colonel Griffith became separated from his men, and encountered an Indian who was loading his rifle. The colonel charged upon him, and the Indian recognising the absence of fear in his opponent, seized his gun as a club. It had been the intention of Griffith to run him through with his sabre as he passed him; but now decided to ride him down; and with that purpose reined his horse full upon him, but the Indian agilely stepped aside, and aimed a tremendous blow at his opponent, which knocked the plumed hat of the colonel to the ground. But simultaneously with the Indian's blow Griffith dealt him a terrible stroke with his sabre on the side of the head. Lieutenant Vance opportunely came up and dispatched the Indian.

Griffith now, after a hasty survey of the field, discovered that the enemy were re-forming their lines upon an eminence in front; and that his own men were scattered, everyone acting on his own hook. The rally was sounded, and line of battle being formed, when Captain J. W. Throckmorton (since Governor of Texas) rode up to the colonel and informed him that Lieutenant Gabe Fitzhugh had fallen. Colonel Griffith loved his brave young subaltern, and the announcement of his untimely death brought a tear to his eye. "Comrades!" he exclaimed to the eager men, "Fitzhugh has been killed, and there are his slayers!"

About three hundred of the Indians now occupied the rocky eminence in front, and were fully prepared for the threatened attack. "Forward, my brave men!" exclaimed the colonel, as at their head he dashed up the steep, and among the painted, howling savages, as trusty rifles and repeating pistols were dashing out lives on every side. The men, animated by the ardour of their commander, and by the recklessness of his bearing, fought as if the issue depended upon each individual's exertion. Driven from this position, it was only to retire a short distance and take up another position; and thus four separate charges brought Griffith and his gallant rangers into a hand-to-hand contest with the enemy.

At four o'clock in the afternoon Griffith called in his weary men.

They had been engaged incessantly since morning, and were now six miles from the heights of Chustenahlah, where Colonel Lane had so gallantly opened the ball. The enemy had had enough, and were in full retreat. In returning, Colonel Griffith gathered up many wagons, teams, ponies, and other livestock, together with many negroes, women and children, and arrived at camp about night-fall.

Colonel Griffith soon reported to Colonel McIntosh to apologise for his disobedience of orders. Said Griffith: 'Colonel McIntosh, I felt so well assured that you would have ordered me to do just what I did, had you been present, that I unhesitatingly assumed the responsibility; and since the merit of the move has been tested by its success. I shall in my official report of the engagement state that I moved in conformity to your direction.' McIntosh replied that success was vindication; and he further took occasion to compliment the gallantry of Griffith throughout the series of actions. This compliment coming from a man absolutely a stranger to fear, was no idle frame-work of unmeaning words.

In the battle or battles, for it was a series of separate encounters, of Chustenahlah, Colonel Griffith had his horse shot under him, his clothing was perforated by rifle-balls, and a tuft of his whiskers shot away; yet, Saladin-like, as if bearing a talismanic charm, he escaped unhurt, save the blow received with the clubbed rifle, at the hands of the Indian.

At the reorganisation of the regiment, near Corinth, in May 1862, Colonel Griffith, against the solicitations of many friends, and, possibly, in violence to the promptings of a commendable ambition, declined to become a candidate for the colonelcy, and was re-elected to his former position of Lieutenant-Colonel. Colonel Griffith took this decision in consequence of failing health, and the necessity of his visiting home for a brief space; it being understood, at the time, that the lieutenant-colonel, or major, would be detailed to return to Texas on recruiting service.

During General Price's retreat from Abbyville, the Federal General, Washburn, at the head of a considerable force, undertook to intercept the retreat, by marching upon the. rear of the Confederate position, and threatened the trains and wounded of Price's corps. Colonel Griffith commanded the Texas Brigade at the time, and attacked Washburn on the field at Oakland, inflicting a heavy loss on him, and driving him from the field—(*vide Battle of Oakland*). For the daring gallantry displayed on this occasion, he was the recipient of complimentary letters from Generals Maury, Price, Jackson, and others. The result of the battle at Oakland gave General Price an open road to Grenada, which town he reached in safety, and his weary men were soon seeking the respite from toil, vigilance, and privation, which they so much needed. The campaign was now virtually concluded for the winter; and Colonels Broocks and Griffith often conversed upon the most profitable employment that the cavalry could be assigned to.

It was self-evident, that, as matters now stood, they were only consuming the supplies that should be economized for the infantry, which was less able to forage independently. They agreed that the Confederate cavalry, of the Army of the West, should be "massed," and moved into the enemy's lines, where they could repel all smaller bodies, and escape any force too strong to encounter in battle. Thus was the system of heavy cavalry-raiding first advocated. Colonel Griffith adopted this conclusion, and sought to apply it practically to the existing situation of affairs. The Confederate Army, beaten in battle, outnumbered by the enemy in the ratio of five to one, poorly clad, poorly fed, pay in arrear, was discontented, not to say demoralised. General U. S. Grant confronted them at the head of a force that was puissant; and the coming spring must inevitably witness another contest against fearful odds, and the army of West Tennessee again defeated, driven into Vicksburg, where its doom would be but a question of time.

Colonel Griffith became convinced that of Grant's long line of communication, with his base of supplies at Memphis, the most vulnerable point was Holly Springs, at which place immense quantities of army stores had been collected, and a garrison of about 2,500 men left to guard it. Griffith brooded over this subject, and reviewed it in every conceivable light. A cavalry corps should be organised; the enemy's rear entered, and Holly Springs taken, and all the supplies destroyed; then the railroad should be destroyed as far in the direction of Memphis as possible.

Surely this would draw Grant out of Mississippi, and give the Confederate authorities ample time to devise some plan for the defence of the country, and to concentrate sufficient forces with which to execute it. Becoming assured of the feasibility of his project, Colonel Griffith determined to broach the subject to the Commanding General, Lieutenant-General J. C. Pemberton, although he had no acquaintance with him. To this end, he drew up the following letter, which many of the field officers of the brigade also signed at his invitation:

Headquarters Texas Brigade,
Camp Wharton, Miss., December 5, 1862.

Lieutenant-General J. C. Pemberton:

The undersigned, officers of the First Texas Brigade of Cavalry, disclaiming any desire to dictate to the Commanding General my plan, or line of operations he should pursue, would yet beg leave modestly to suggest the propriety of a cavalry expedition into the enemy's rear. We are the more bold to do so, and have less fear of the misconstruction of our motives, when we remember that you have been so recently placed in command over us; and that the multitudinous cares incidental to your responsible position have necessarily, thus far, precluded an examination of the position of the enemy, and as to what is the best employment in which the cavalry, under your command, can be engaged.

We, therefore, respectfully submit, if you will fit up a cavalry expedition, comprising three or four thousand men, and give us Major-General Earl Van Dorn, than whom no braver man lives, to command us, we will penetrate the rear of the enemy, capture Holly Springs, Memphis, and other points, and, perhaps, force him to retreat from Coffeeville; if not, we can certainly force more of the enemy to remain in their rear, to protect their supplies, than the cavalry could whip if we remained at the front.

Very respectfully,

John S. Griffith,
Commanding Texas Cavalry Brigade.
E. R. Hawkins,
Commanding First Texas Legion.
J. H. Broocks,
Major First Texas Legion.
Jiles S. Boggess,
Lieut-Colonel Third Texas Cavalry.
D. W. Jones,
Lieut-Colonel Commd'g Ninth Texas Cavalry.
Jack Wharton,
Captain Commanding Sixth Texas Cavalry.

Colonel Griffith forwarded this letter immediately to General Pemberton, and, no one not acquainted with the restless energy of the man, can imagine the night of consuming anxiety and suspense that he passed in awaiting a reply. To his sagacious mind, the memorial suggested the last card left the Confederacy to play with any chance of winning on this board. The Army of West Tennessee must be inevitably crushed whenever Grant should place his legions in motion to execute the fiat of his will. General Pemberton promptly replied the next day, in the following letter:

Headquarters Department Mississippi,
Grenada, December 6, 1862.

Colonel:

You will furnish me with a report of the events subsequent to the engagement of Oakland. I wish to see you personally, if circumstances will possibly admit of it.

Very respectfully,

J. C. Pemberton,
Lieutenant-General.

The commanding general desired a personal interview with the bold ranger who dared to chalk out a campaign to his chief. In the interview which followed, General Pemberton informed Colonel Griffith, that the proposition commended itself to his consideration with much force, and that he would give it careful consideration, etc.

About the 12th, or six days after the interview with General Pemberton, Colonel Griffith received orders to report to General Van Dorn, who was now actively engaged in preparing for the long-desired expedition in rear of the enemy.

General Van Dorn's command consisted of the Texas Brigade, Colonel Griffith commanding, 1,500 men; Jackson's Tennessee Brigade, 1,200 men; McCulloch's Missouri Brigade, 800 men. The whole amounting to about 3,500 men. For an account of this famous expedition, the reader is referred to the proper chapter in the body of the narrative.

The services exacted of him, on this expedition, proved so great a demand upon his vital forces that the health of Colonel Griffith, never robust, was seriously impaired; and, in the summer of 1863, he tendered his resignation, and returned to Texas.

The following testimonial from the officers of the "Whitfield Legion," will serve to show, in some degree, the esteem in which Colonel Griffith was held by his comrades:

Camp First Texas Legion,
Near Spring Hill, Tennessee, May 10, 1863.
Lieutenant-Colonel John S. Griffith:

Dear Sir—We, the undersigned, officers of the First Texas Legion, having learned that, in consequence of continued ill-health, you have tendered your resignation, we cannot, in justice to our feelings, permit you to quit the service without this testimonial of our appreciation of your services while commanding the brigade, of which our regiment is a part. You were ever the faithful and efficient officer, and, at the same time, the kind and courteous gentleman. Rest assured, sir, that whether you go to some other branch of our country's service, or to your home in the State that we all love so well, you will carry with you the confidence and esteem of the officers and men of the First Texas Legion. With heart-felt wishes for your future welfare, we remain respectfully,

J. H. Broocks,
Lieut.-Colonel Commanding Legion.
John T. Whitfield,
Major Texas Legion.
B. H. Norsworthy,
Captain Company E, First Texas Legion.
C. D. Preston,
Company M, First Texas Legion.
J. N. Zachry,
Captain Co. A, First Texas Legion.
J. M. Ingram,
Captain Co. C, First Texas Legion.
B. M. Irwin,
First Lieutenant Co. A, Texas Legion.
W. T. Rogers,
Second Lieutenant Co. A, Texas Legion.

Upon his return to Texas, Colonel Griffith was elected a member of the Tenth Legislature; in which body he occupied the responsible position of Chairman of the Committee on Military Affairs. On March 1st, 1864, he was appointed Brigadier-General of State troops, by Governor P. Murrah, and placed in command of District No. 2, which was composed of the counties of Kaufman, Ellis, Navarro, Hill, McLennan, Limestone, Freestone, Leon, Robertson, Falls, Bell, Williamson, Milam, Burleson, Brazos, Madison, Coryell, Bosque; Erath, Hamilton, Comanche, Lampasas, San Saba, Brown, Eastlant, Callahan, Coleman, McCulloch, Mason, Kimble, Menard, Concho, Runnels, Taylor, and Johnston.

The duties of the brigadier-generals of the State were, "to encourage and form volunteer companies and organisations, of such persons as are not subject to militia or other duty, for local defence, and all necessary police regulations in the counties where such companies may be raised." In his efficient and faithful discharge of the onerous duties incumbent on him in this position, Colonel Griffith elicited the complimentary mention of Governor Murrah, in his message to the Eleventh Legislature. General Griffith continued in command of the "Second District" until the termination of hostilities.

The result of the war left him comparatively poor, he having some twenty-five or thirty slaves; but, with indomitable will, energy, and pluck, upon which his vital forces expend themselves, General Griffith entered the race of life again, and, by dint of industry and good sense, he has accumulated a handsome fortune, and resides in Terrell, Kaufman county, Texas, once more in affluent circumstances.

In 1876, he was elected a member of the Fifteenth Legislature, upon which body devolved the duty of placing in operation the "new constitution." He was appointed Chairman of the Committee on Public Printing, and was successful in defeating the printer in an effort to obtain illegitimate gains at the expense of the State. So assiduous were his labours in this body, that he earned the reputation of being an industrious and untiring legislator. He was, indeed, a "watch-dog" over the public treasury; and lobbyists, shysters, and *chevaliers d'industrie*, shunned him as if his presence was a fatal upas. He was attacked in the newspapers by the printer, who became exasperated at being foiled in his "little game."

Griffith responded, and demonstrated the proposed fraud; and, backed by the opinion of the attorney-general, he had the satisfaction of seeing the "printer" leave the ring demolished in reputation, and all his calculations "pied." Several statutes bear the impress of his statesmanship—especially that one making drunkenness in civil officers a misdemeanour. This statute alone is a living monument to his probity of character, and is a work of which he may justly feel proud.

In conclusion, but little remains to be said. General Griffith is yet, comparatively, a young man; and the author, his friend, hopes that he may be spared, by the grim spectre of the glass and scythe, yet many years, in which event, he will make much more biography for the second sitting. General Griffith is a gentleman of pleasing address, and his heart is as big as Texas, and as open as his sleeve; of an ardent temperament, he is often impulsive, but never rash nor unjust; his mind is acute, penetrating, and sagacious, and thoroughly analytical in the examination of practical details, while his judgment is clear and perspicuous.

In short, General Griffith is a Napoleonic embodiment of restless energy and indomitable will, guided by an equally balanced mind, who would not have occupied a subordinate position in whatever sphere of life his lot had been cast. In the management of his private estate, he has proved himself to be a consummate business manager— commencing with nothing, and having accumulated two fortunes.

In his conduct of the operations of the command at Oakland, Chustenahlah, and Holly Springs, he appeared to the world as a natural-born general, and overlapped West Point in its own peculiar province. As a legislator, he stood *primus inter pares*, and left the lobby-lined chambers with hands unsmirched and reputation clean. Though unsolicitous for office, and retiring in his disposition, General Griffith would shed honour on the chief magistracy of the State, and his administration of the people's affairs would certainly be in the interest of the people. The following anecdote is illustrative of the general's impetuosity: Upon one occasion he was detailing the exciting scenes attendant upon the Confederate entry into Holly Springs, and especially the earnest welcome extended the rebels by the ladies, when his auditor asked: "And how did you feel, General?"

"Feel!" exclaimed the excited veteran; "I felt as if I could have charged hell, and captured the devil, if the Almighty had commanded me to do so!"

Of one thing certain, if the general ever does enlist under the banner of the Lord, he will be one of the last to think of giving up the fort, for he goes into everything with his whole soul—he is never a half-measure man. As a further testimonial of the regard in which General Griffith was held by his brother-officers, the following letter, from the gallant Jackson, will speak for itself:

Headquarters First Cavalry Corps,
Spring Hill, Tenn., May 8, 1863.

Lieut.-Colonel J. S. Griffith:

Colonel—Permit me to offer the testimonial of my high appreciation of you as a gallant, competent, and meritorious officer of unexceptional moral character. It affords me great pleasure to refer to the valuable services rendered by your command at Oakland, Mississippi, in repulsing, and routing, a superior force of the enemy, advancing upon Grenada, *and thereby saving our* retreating army; also the gallant and signal service of yourself, while we were together, and commanding separate brigades, on the raid to Holly Springs and West Tennessee. Please accept the assurances of my highest consideration, and with many regrets that your continued ill-health compels you to leave this corps, and a wish that you may soon regain your health sufficiently to enter the service again.

I remain, very respectfully,

W. H. Jackson,
Brigadier-General Commanding Cavalry Corps.

## Hon. O. N. Hollingsworth

Orlando N. Hollingsworth was born in Calhoun county, Alabama, April 5, 1836, and removed, with his mother, to Rusk county, Texas, in December, 1845, his father having died the earlier part of the last-mentioned year. He laid the foundation of his education in the common schools of the country, and graduated from the University of Virginia, in 1859. He responded, among the earliest, to the call of the South, in 1861, for volunteers, and enlisted as a private soldier in the company of Captain R. H. Cumby, which comprised many of the best young men of Rusk county.

His soldierly qualities, and executive capacity, soon secured him promotion to the responsible station of adjutant of his regiment, the Third Texas Cavalry, in which position he served with credit to himself and profit to the service, until he was seriously wounded in the assault on Corinth, in 1862, and permanently unfitted for service in the field. He returned to Texas, and became interested in the cause of education—a cause in whose behalf he has expended much pecuniary means and the best years of his life. Coronal Institute, located at San Marcos, Texas, was founded by Captain Hollingsworth, in 1864-6, and was long presided over by himself.

Subsequently, he was elected Superintendent of Public Instruction, and, on the abolition of that office by constitutional amendment, he was appointed Secretary to the State Board of Education, a position which he now most efficiently fills. In addition to his clerical labours in connection with office, Captain Hollingsworth founded, and conducts, the *Educational Journal*, a timely and invaluable adjunct to the cause that he has espoused. Mr. Hollingsworth is comparatively a young man; has had some experience in practice at the bar, and served one term in the State legislature.

Of a benevolent disposition, kind in all his impulses, and highly intellectual, he has always exercised a wholesome, moral influence wherever his services have been required. If merit meets with a just reward, Mr. Hollingsworth may be regarded as a man with a future, and to whatever position he may be called in the service of the State, the people may rest assured of having at least one pure, and honest, and industrious public servant.

## Colonel Elkanah Greer.

Colonel Greer was born in Marshall County, Mississippi, in the year 1825; received a liberal education, which was just completed at the breaking out of the Mexican War. Though but twenty years of age, he was among the first to volunteer as a private in the First Mississippi Rifles, the colonel of which regiment was Jefferson Davis. Upon the organisation of the command, it reported for duty to General Taylor, beyond the Rio Grande.

At the Battles of Monterey and Buena Vista, in both of which it participated, so signal were its services, that a grateful country expressed admiration for the conduct of both officers and men. Colonel Greer returned home with the regiment on the expiration of their term of service; and, though but twenty-one years of age, was prevailed upon, by his admiring fellow-citizens, to become a candidate for Major-General of militia, defeating General James D. Alcorn, a very popular man, for the position. Under General Greer's control, the militia was organised, drilled, and properly disciplined.

In 1848, he removed to Texas, and soon after, was united in marriage to Miss Anna Holcombe, of Marshall, Texas, eldest daughter of Colonel B. L. and Mrs. Anna Holcombe, a beautiful young lady, possessed of rare charms of both mind and heart. General Greer located at Marshall, and devoted his attention to the civil pursuits of planting and merchandizing. Being an ardent State's rights Democrat, he was deeply interested in the weighty events of 1859 and 1860, which seemed to be culminating into war. General Greer, at this time, probably enjoyed a political influence not surpassed by that of any man in Texas. He was appointed, in 1859, "Grand Commander" of the secret organisation known as the "K. G. C's.," for the State of Texas, and employed himself in the organisation of subordinate *commanderies* throughout the State. He manfully opposed the conservative policy of Governor Sam Houston, in 1860, and was urgent in his advocacy of a call for a sovereign convention.

Upon the formation of the provisional government, at Montgomery, Alabama, Colonel Greer received the first colonel's commission issued to a Texan, and proceeded immediately to organise the Third Regiment of Texas Cavalry. Of his services in connection with that regiment, the foregoing narrative speaks. At the expiration of the first year's service, Colonel Greer declined re-election to the colonelcy of the regiment, though he would have had no opposition (so high was he held in the esteem of the men), and returned to Texas.

Of his services in the Trans-Mississippi Department, the author cannot speak. Colonel Greer was brave, cool in danger, quick to grasp the situation of affairs in the most critical juncture, and as prompt to act. To these high qualities as an officer, he combined those of the gentleman kindness and conscientiousness. Since the conclusion of the war, Colonel Greer has lived quietly, and somewhat retired, upon his estate near Marshall, Texas, respected and loved by his neighbours.

## COLONEL H. P. MABRY.

Colonel H. P. Mabry was born in the village of Laurel Hill, Carroll county, Georgia, October 27, 1829. His father, whose Christian name he bears, originally came from North Carolina, settling in Georgia in 1805. He was a soldier in the war of 1812, and in the campaigns against the Creek Indians. The father died while yet the son was but a youth. Young Mabry was deeply impressed with the necessity for an education; and as his patrimony was inconsiderable, he encountered many privations and hardships in the prosecution of his cherished object. After attending this "country-school" for a few months, young Mabry was prepared to enter college—prepared intellectually, but by no means financially. To obviate this difficulty, he entered a store as salesman at a salary of five dollars per month, and in addition to this, he soon found night employment in the post-office.

By the most rigid economy, he was enabled, after two years' incessant labour, to enter the University of Tennessee, located at Knoxville. Here, by his studious habits and gentlemanly deportment, he won the confidence of the college faculty, and the respect of his fellow-students. But his means were not sufficient to bear him through the entire course, and he was compelled to lay aside his cherished books, and go forth into the world to earn, sufficient means to defray his collegiate expenses. Thus did the indomitable boy earn an education by his own industry and perseverance. This indomitable will, and fixedness of purpose, thus early displayed, continued, in after years, to be the most marked characteristics of the man. Not many years after the completion of his education, he removed to Jefferson, Texas, and engaged in mercantile pursuits. In 1854, he was united in marriage to Miss Abbie Haywood—a most estimable lady, worthy to be the wife of a hero— the daughter of W. H. Hay wood, Esq., a planter living near Jefferson.

Soon after his marriage, Colonel Mabry commenced the study of law. was admitted to the bar, and at once entered upon a lucrative practice. He was elected to a seat in the Legislature, in 1856, and again in 1859, and was re-elected to the same position, and held a seat in the House of Representatives, in 1861. Upon the secession of Texas, Colonel Mabry returned home, and organised a military company, at the head of which he marched against Fort Wichita. The Federal forces abandoned the fort at his approach, and retired. Captain Mabry occupied the place until May 28, when he was relieved, and, with his company, reported to Colonel Greer for duty, and his company was assigned the position of Company G, in the Third Texas Cavalry, the first regiment that left the State of Texas.

As captain of Company G, and as colonel of the regiment, the foregoing narrative deals. He was absolutely fearless, and cool to indifference in the midst of danger, and his indomitable will seemed able to grapple with fate itself in the formulation of destiny. He ought to have been a lieutenant-general, and placed in command of Vicksburg. The "Modern Sphynx" would have found in H. P. Mabry a foeman worthy of his steel. General Robert Toombs, of Georgia, has been credited with the saying, that West Point defeated the Confederacy. Certainly, proven merit did not receive reward by promotion at the hands of Mr. Davis, as justice and the efficiency of the service required. As better illustrating the respect and esteem in which Colonel Mabry was held by those best qualified to judge his merits, the following communications to the Secretary of War are introduced:

Headquarters, Snyder's Mills,
Yazoo River, March 30, 1864.

Hon. James A. Seddon:

Sir—I have the honour to recommend for promotion to the

rank of Brigadier-General, P. A. C. S., Colonel H. P. Mabry, Third Regiment, Texas Cavalry; having been near him in the field since July, 1861; having had him under my command, in my brigade, for many months; having seen him tested in camp, on the inarch, and on various hard-fought fields, I can, unhesitatingly, and do, cheerfully, recommend him for a higher rank, as a meed to merit and distinguished service.

He was severely wounded in Missouri, in 1861, and still more severely at the battle of Iuka, on the 19th of September last, when he and his gallant regiment most heroically bore what I considered the brunt of the fight. As a man of correct principles, of soldierlike deportment, of good finished education, of unquestioned coolness, bravery, and sagacity, of systematic and determined character, and as a disciplinarian, I can fully recommend him as highly fitted to take command of a brigade, and I feel sure that his success would be satisfactory to the War Department, the President, and the country.

I remain, sir, very respectfully your obedient servant,

Louis Hebert,
Brigadier-General, P. A. C. S.

Headquarters Texas Cavalry Brigade,
March 27, 1864.

Hon. James A. Seddon:

Sir—Having learned that the interest of the service demands the appointment of another Brigadier-General in Major-General Lee's Cavalry corps, the undersigned officers of the Texas Brigade cheerfully recommend to your favourable consideration, the peculiar claims of Colonel Mabry, Third Texas Cavalry. He has been faithfully engaged, in the service of his country, since July, 1861; twice severely wounded, and by gallantry and rigid discipline, has won the universal approbation of his superior officers. For force of character, resolution, prudence, indomitable courage, energy, and ability, he has no superior in the cavalry of the Department.

L. S. Ross, Brigadier-General.
E. R. Hawkins,
Colonel First Texas Legion.
D. W. Jones,
Colonel Ninth Texas Cavalry.

P. F. Ross,
Lieut.-Colonel Sixth Texas Cavalry.
Jiles S. Boggess,
Lieut.-Colonel Third Texas Cavalry.

Headquarters Armstrong's Division,
Near Canton, Miss., March 29, 1864.

General S. Cooper,
Adjutant and Inspector-General, Richmond, Va.:

General—I have the honour to recommend Colonel H. P. Mabry, Third Texas Cavalry, for promotion, to be placed in command of a brigade now in my division. Although Colonel Mabry has never served under my immediate command, I can recommend him, as he commanded a regiment (Third Texas Cavalry, dismounted), in General Hebert's Infantry Brigade, in which I commanded the Third Louisiana Regiment. I consider him an excellent disciplinarian (especially needed in the cavalry), and one of the most competent, in every respect, that can be selected. His regiment, which is the best qualification, is one of the best disciplined, and most efficient, in the service.

I have the honour to be, with respect,
your obedient servant,

Frank C. Armstrong,
Brigadier-General.

Headquarters Lee's Cavalry Department,
Canton, Miss., March 29, 1864.

General S. Cooper,
Adjutant and Inspector-General, Richmond, Va.:

General—I have the honour to recommend that Colonel H. P. Mabry, Third Texas Cavalry, be appointed Brigadier-General, and assigned to the command of the brigade recently commanded by Brigadier-General Adams. Colonel Mabry entered the service when the war first broke out, and has continued therein ever since, except when temporarily absent on account of two wounds received in battle. I consider him the best disciplinarian in my command.

He has distinguished himself in most of the engagements of the West, and has often been complimented for his gallantry and good conduct. I desire Colonel Mabry as a permanent commander of the brigade to which he is now temporarily assigned.

I am, General, yours respectfully,

S. D. Lee, Major-General.

Meridian, Miss., June 23, 1864.

General S. Cooper,

Adjutant and Inspector-General, Richmond, Va.:

General—I have the honour to enclose a return of the brigade commanded by Colonel H. P. Mabry. It is the brigade recently commanded by Brigadier-General Wirt Adams, who now commands a division consisting of the brigades of Generals Gholson and John Scott, in East Louisiana. Mabry's Brigade was in his command, but is now in North Mississippi. General Adams has immediate charge of the country from Grenada to New Orleans. I consider Colonel Mabry one of the best officers I have met in the army, and much, desire his promotion. Should it not be deemed proper to appoint him in this Department, and to his present brigade, I trust he may be promoted and assigned elsewhere.

Yours, respectfully,

S. D. Lee, Major-General.

### GENERAL J. W. WHITFIELD.

General J. W. Whitfield was born in Williamson County, Tennessee, in the year 1818, and received such limited education as the "log school-houses" of the time afforded. Early in life he pursued the calling of a farmer, but his strong individuality, and marked character, soon called him to public station; and, for eighteen years, with scarce an intermission, he represented his district in both branches of the State Legislature. He served, with marked gallantry, through the Mexican war, and upon its cessation, was appointed Indian Agent to the wild tribes in Kansas. General Whitfield was a resident of Kansas at the inception of the slavery troubles attendant upon the application of that State for admission into the Union, espousing the proslavery side of the controversy.

Whitfield was the first delegate sent from Kansas to the Federal Congress, defeating the anti-slavery candidate, Reeder, by a handsome majority. In the turbulent era of murder and pillage that ensued, the greater portion of his property was swept away; and when, finally, Kansas was given over to abolitionism, Whitfield, impoverished, removed to Lavaca county, Texas, and resumed the avocation of a farmer. The rude blast of internecine war, however, soon broke upon the quiet scenes of his pastoral life, and the brave old veteran responded by buckling on his sword, and summoning his neighbours to follow him. Starting out as a captain of a company, his command was augmented to a battalion of four companies by the time he reached General McCulloch's quarters. During, and after the campaign that culminated in the Battle of Elk Horn, his battalion was increased to a legion of twelve companies, than which, there was not a braver, or more efficient, organisation in the Confederate Army. General Whitfield relinquished the command of the brigade in 1863, and retired to the Trans-Mississippi Department. In personal appearance, General Whitfield was marked, being over six feet in height, and straight as an arrow—he looked every inch the soldier. Of his services in the Trans-Mississippi Department, the author has no data upon which to predicate a narrative.

After the termination of the war, General Whitfield continued to reside on his farm, near the village of Vienna, in Lavaca County, Texas, engaged in peaceful pursuits through the evening of life, until the autumn of 1879, when he responded to the summons of the spectre with the hour-glass and scythe, and took up his solitary march across the river into that undiscovered country in which his departed comrades had pitched their silent camp. There, with Van Dorn, McCulloch, McIntosh, Jones, and others, he awaits the arrival of the rearguard upon the scene to complete the grand reunion of the Texas Brigade, in the shade of the lotus-trees of the Summerland.

## COLONEL D. W. JONES.

Colonel D. W. Jones was, it is thought, a native Texan, and was born about the year 1842, as he was but eighteen years of age at the commencement of the war.

At the first notes of the approaching storm, he quitted his studies at Maury Institute, Columbia, Tennessee, and proceeded to his home at Mt. Pleasant, Titus County, Texas. He entered the Ninth Texas Cavalry, Colonel W. B. Sims, commanding, it is thought, as a private soldier, and served as such during the first year of the war, through the campaigns in the Indian Territory and in Missouri.

Upon the reorganisation of the Ninth Texas regiment, near Corinth, Mississippi, in 1862, though a beardless boy of scarce twenty years of age, D. W. Jones was triumphantly elected colonel of the regiment; and that he was worthy to be the recipient of this very high honour, the author can bear positive testimony, based upon personal observation.

It was a familiar sight, in the "Army of the West," to see the bronzed and bearded faces of the veterans of the gallant old Ninth following the lead of their handsome and chivalrous boy colonel. The losses of this regiment were unusually severe, and, at the close of the struggle, nine out of every ten men, who had started, failed to respond at roll-call.

The author again expresses deep regret that he was unable, after the most assiduous efforts, to obtain data upon which to recount the immediate services of the regiment.

Colonel Jones' served in the first Constitutional Convention of Texas after the war, and died soon afterward in the city of Houston, where he lies buried in a neglected grave.

Peace to his ashes!

### Colonel Jack Wharton

Colonel Jack Wharton was born December 1, 1832, in Washington county, Maryland, and, at an early age, studied law under the celebrated Otho Scott, practicing his profession until 1857, with considerable success in the courts of his native State. At this period, he located in Kansas, where the political feeling was of such a nature, that no Southern man, with any degree of pride for the land of his nativity, could rise in his profession. With all the vim and vitality of a man determined not to be subdued by the passions and prejudices of this eventful period, he started for Salt Lake City, in 1858, with General Harney, who, being ordered back, he left for California under Captain W. S. Hancock—now Major-General—acting as Quartermaster of the Sixth Regiment of Infantry.

After remaining some time in California, he returned to Baltimore, where he remained several months, visiting old friends. It was at this period he established, in Texas, an extensive horse ranch, on the line of Kaufman and Van Zandt counties, about two hundred miles west of Shreveport. Here he remained until the war commenced, when he enlisted, as a private soldier, in a company organised in his neighbourhood, and which, subsequently, became attached to the Sixth Texas Cavalry. Upon the definite organisation of the company, Wharton was elected captain. Henceforth, the history of the man, and of the regiment, are indissoluble. He served through all the campaigns, battles, advances, and retreats in which the regiment and brigade were engaged, until the final catastrophe.

Upon the appointment of General L. S. Ross to the rank of Brigadier-General, Wharton, who had been elected Lieutenant-Colonel of the regiment, was promoted to the Colonelcy. After the conclusion of the war, he returned to his stock ranch in Texas, where he remained until 1867, when he was invited by the Southern Pacific Railroad Company, to take charge of their works from Shreveport, Louisiana, to Marshall, Texas, with headquarters at the former place. After the completion of the railroad, he came to New Orleans, where he has resided since 1868.

Colonel Wharton has held many important offices of honour and trust in the State—such as Assessor of Taxes, Secretary of State under Governor Warmouth, Adjutant-General under Governor Kellogg, which place he held until the meeting of the Packard Legislature, when he resigned the office of Adjutant-General, and accepted the position of Clerk of the Superior Civil Court, an office just created, and which was the most lucrative in the gift of the governor. After the downfall of the Packard Government, he was appointed, by President Hayes, Marshal for the State of Louisiana, from June 15, 1878, which office he holds at the present time, and for four years from the date of commission. Colonel Wharton has an agreeable personal appearance, is a fluent conversationalist, and always a boon companion, and welcomed by *bon vivants*. As an officer in the field, he was surpassed by none in personal courage, sagacity, and devotion. We believe the colonel never married.

## Colonel John H. Broocks

The subject of this sketch was born in the town of Jackson, County of Madison, State of Tennessee, October 12, A.D., 1829; was the son of the late General Travis G. Broocks—a native of Virginia—and of Mrs. Elizabeth A. Broocks, a native of Alabama. General Broocks removed, with his family, to San Augustine, Texas, in the year 1837. John H. was educated at the Wesleyan College, at San Augustine, and at the San Augustine University. His acquaintance, however, with the practical relations of life, was formed in the counting-room of his father, who did an extensive mercantile business in San Augustine. At the commencement of the Mexican war, young Broocks joined, as a private soldier, the company of Captain O. M. Wheeler, of Colonel Woods' regiment of Texas Cavalry, and rendered efficient services in this new and stirring field of operations until the cessation of hostilities. Returning home, Mr. Broocks entered into the mercantile business at San Augustine, at which place he continued to reside until about the year 1852, when the spirit of adventure and enterprise led him to migrate to California in company of his brother, the late Captain James A. Broocks, and Captain A. D. Edwards, now of Terrell, Texas. In this virgin field, the young Texans first essayed mining, and then worked as hired hands on a hay and small grain farm; and, finally, as merchants, operating under the firm name of J. H. Broocks & Co., at "Shaw's Flat," in Ptoulumne county. While in this business, they did their own freighting with ox-teams, over execrable roads, a distance of sixty-five miles.

Having been quite successful in his business pursuits, Mr. Broocks returned to San Augustine, Texas, in 1854, and was united in marriage to Miss Elizabeth J. Polk. In 1855, he retired from mercantile pursuits to his farm near San Augustine, where he has continued to reside ever since. When Texas called upon her sons to march to battle in defence of constitutional government, in 1861, she found not one more ready to respond to the summons than John H. Broocks. A company was formed in San Augustine, and adjoining counties, of which he was elected captain. Captain Broocks at once set out at the head of his company to join the army of General Ben McCulloch, in Missouri.

Before, or at the time of reaching the army, a battalion was formed of the four detached companies, commanded by Captain J. H. Broocks, Captain J. W. Whitfield, of Lavaca county, Texas, Captain Murphy, of Arkansas, and Captain Brooks, of Arkansas. Captain Whitfield was elected Major of the battalion. Subsequently, Captain Brooks' company was transferred to Colonel McIntosh's Arkansas regiment, and Captain E. R. Hawkins' Texas company joined the battalion. Under this organisation, the battalion served in the campaigns against the hostile Indians in the winter of 1861, and at the Battle of Elk Horn, in March, 1862.

After the campaign in March, an accession of eight more companies was had, and the First Texas Legion was organised with J. W. Whitfield, Colonel; E. R. Hawkins, Lieutenant-Colonel; and ——— Holman, Major. Major Holman resigned soon after his election, and Captain John H. Broocks was promoted Major. Subsequently, in 1863, Colonel Whitfield was promoted Brigadier-General, Lieutenant-Colonel E. R. Hawkins, Colonel, and Major Broocks, Lieutenant-Colonel. Captain J. T. Whitfield was promoted Major. We reproduce, in this connection, Colonel Broocks' statement in regard to the action at Oakland, Mississippi, as tending to elucidate, in some measure, the account of the same in the body of the narrative. General Price was retreating from Abbeville, followed by a large supply-train. A considerable force of the enemy was disembarked from transports on the Mississippi River, and by rapid marches, sought to strike the train in flank.

Generals Hovey and Washburne, we believe, commanded this expedition, which amounted to about 4,000 infantry, 500 cavalry, and 12 guns. Nothing interposed between the unprotected train and this daring Federal column, but the Texas Brigade of about 1,500 men. Lieutenant-Colonel John S. Griffith, of the Sixth Texas Cavalry, was in temporary command of the brigade. Colonel Griffith realised the gravity of the situation, and appreciated the value of prompt action. Says Colonel Broocks:

> The Legion, Colonel Hawkins commanding, and three companies as an advance-guard, under my immediate command, fought Washburne's advance fifty-six minutes, near Oakland, Mississippi. We charged, and captured two guns, one of which, only, we brought off the field, as the team attached to the other were killed. Lieutenant-Colonel Griffith, commanding the brigade, was present, and in the charge, bearing himself most gallantly, and but for an accident, we perhaps would have captured Washburne. The Legion was driving the enemy in some confusion. The Sixth Texas had arrived, dismounted, and were ready to join in the fight. The Third Texas, Lieutenant-Colonel J. S. Boggess commanding, had been dispatched to the enemy's rear, and directed to dismount and attack. At this interesting stage, Colonel Griffith received a report (false) that we were being outflanked.
>
> Placing credence in the report, he retired his men, and firing ceased. Colonel Boggess, who was just ready to attack in the rear at this time, hearing the firing no more in front, did not attack. Thus an excellently-planned engagement was suffered to pass by default. But the Legions' spirited attack had discomfited the enemy, and, undoubtedly, saved from capture the wagon-train of General Price. Had Colonel Griffith's original plan been carried out, it is probable we would have captured the greater portion of the Federals present. Some idea may be had of the spirited nature of the engagement, from the fact that sixty-four cannon-shots were fired during the fifty-six minutes of action. After we were called off from the charge, the en-

emy recovered from the confusion caused by our unexpected charge, and their long lines of infantry, "double-quicking" into position, revealed too much force for Colonel Griffith to again venture an attack.

The enemy accorded the Texans equal respect, and immediately retired from the field, and returned to the protection of their ironclads on the Mississippi River.

Owing to the ill-health of the gallant Hawkins, Colonel Broocks was very often left in command of the Legion, in which responsible station he acquitted himself always with credit, and won the love of his men and the confidence and respect of his superiors in rank. The Confederacy bore upon its rosters the name of no braver, or truer man to its cause, than that of Colonel John H. Broocks. Colonel Broocks has, since the termination of the war, lived a somewhat retired life on his farm, in the midst of his many friends, and surrounded by his interesting family.

His name has been repeatedly mentioned in connection with a seat in the State Senate; and, though eminently fitted to grace the councils of State, he has persistently declined the honours which his fellow-citizens would gladly confer, contenting himself with the laborious and unremunerating position of Chairman of the Democratic Congressional District Committee. Colonel Broocks is an educated gentleman—a man of firm will, fixed opinions, and the courage to advocate the same at all proper times. Though it seemed that the moral obliquity of "our army in Flanders" had seized the Confederate Army, yet the author can testify to the Roman simplicity and stern exercise of morality by Colonel Broocks, at all times; and never did he hear a profane expression escape his lips. These pages, though in an inadequate manner, testify to the heroism of Colonel Broocks; but of the many high qualities, both of head and heart, of which he is possessed, none may know except those who are drawn into personal contact with him.

If heroic services on the battlefield, augmented by capacity, probity, and patriotism, entitle a man to civic preferment, then is Colonel John H. Broocks entitled to the highest office in the gift of the people of Texas. His friend, the author, cheerfully pays this simple tribute to his sterling worth, with the confident hope that he will yet respond to the solicitations of his fellow-citizens, and give to the councils of the State the benefit of his ripe experience, and practical knowledge of men, and political and economical questions.

Texas, though her annals be brief, counts upon her "roll of honour" the names of many heroes, living and dead. Their splendid services are the inestimable legacies of the past and present, to the future. Of the latter, it is the high prerogative of the State to embalm their names and memories as perpetual examplars to excite the generous emulation of the Texan youth to the latest posterity. Of the former, it is our pleasant province to accord them those honours which their services, in so eminent a degree, entitle them to receive.

Few lands, since the days of the "Scottish Chiefs," have furnished material upon which to predicate a Douglas, a Wallace, or a Ravens wood; and the adventure of chivalric enterprise, errant quest of danger, and the personal combat, were relegated, together with the knight's armorial trappings, to the musty archives of "Tower" and "Pantheon," until the Comanche Bedouins of the Texan plains tendered, in bold defiance, the savage gauntlet to the pioneer knights of progress and civilization. And, though her heraldic roll glows with the names of a Houston, a Rusk, Lamar, McCulloch, Hayes, Chevallie, which illumine the pages of her history with an effulgence of glory, Texas never nurtured on her maternal bosom a son of more filial devotion, of more loyal patriotism, or indomitable will to do and dare, than the subject of this brief sketch.

Laurence Sullivan Ross was born in the town of Bentonsport, Iowa, in the year of our Lord, one thousand eight hundred and thirty-eight. His father, Captain S. P. Ross, removed to Texas in 1839, and cast his fortunes with the pioneers who were blazing the pathway of civilization into the wilds of a *terra incognita,* as Texas then was. Captain S. P. Ross was, for many years, pre-eminent as a leader against the implacable savages, who made frequent incursions into the settlements. The duty of repelling these forays usually devolved upon Captain Ross and his neighbours, and, for many years, his company constituted the only bulwark of safety between the feeble colonists and the scalping-knife.

The rapacity and treachery of his Comanche and Kiowa foes demanded of Captain Ross sleepless vigilance, acute sagacity, and a will that brooked no obstacle or danger. It was in the performance of this arduous duty that he slew, in single combat, "Big Foot," a Comanche chief of great prowess, and who was for many years the scourge of the early Texas frontier. The services of Captain S. P. Ross are still held in grateful remembrance by the descendants of his compatriots, and his memory will never be suffered to pass away while Texans feel a pride in the sterling worth of the pioneers who laid the foundation of Texas' greatness and glory.

The following incident, as illustrative of the character and spirit of the man and times, is given:

> Captain Ross, who had been visiting a neighbour, was return-ing home, afoot, accompanied by his little son 'Sul,' as the gen-eral was familiarly called. When within a half mile of his house, he was surrounded by fifteen or twenty mounted Comanche warriors, who commenced an immediate attack. The captain, athletic and swift of foot, threw his son on his back, and out-ran their ponies to the house, escaping unhurt amid a perfect shower of arrows.

Such were among the daily experiences of the child, and with such impressions stamped upon the infantile mind, it was but natural that the enthusiastic spirit of the ardent youth should lead him to seek adventures upon the "war-path," similar to those that had signalised his honoured father's prowess upon so many occasions. Hence, we find "Sul" Ross, during vacation from his studies at Florence Wesleyan University, Alabama, though scarcely twenty years of age, in command of 135 friendly Indians, co-operating with the United States cavalry against the hostile Comanches. During this campaign the dashing Major Earl Van Dorn led an expedition against the hostiles in the Wichita mountains, which culminated in the hotly-contested battle of the Wichita, in October, 1858.

In this engagement, the red warriors of Captain "Sul" Ross, led by their intrepid young white chief, performed prodigies of valour, and to the sagacity, skill, and bravery of Ross was the complete annihila-tion of the hostiles, in a great measure, attributable. In the moment of victory, Ross was felled to the earth by receiving two dangerous wounds, by a rifle-shot which pierced his arm and side, and was borne from the field on the shields of his faithful and brave Indian retainers. In the heat of the engagement, and before being shot down, Ross dis-covered a little white girl, a captive, among the Indians. Immediately upon her discovery was her rescue determined upon, and, after a mur-derous *melee*, was effected. For the particulars of which, as well as of the fortune of "Lizzie Ross," *vide* the concluding pages of this memoir.

For conspicuous gallantry on this occasion, Major Van Dorn, upon the field of battle, drew up a recommendation, which was signed by all the officers of the gallant old Second United States Cavalry, addressed to the Secretary of War, asking the promotion of Captain Ross, and his assignment to duty in the regular army. The venerable General Winfield Scott, Commander of the United States Army, wrote an autograph letter to the wounded young leader, complimenting, in the highest terms, the noble qualities displayed on that trying occasion, and tendered him his friendship and assistance. Captain Ross made no attempt to use the recommendation of the United States officers, whatever, but, as soon as his wounds admitted of travel, he returned to college, and graduated in 1859.

Immediately upon his return home, Captain Ross was placed in command of the rangers on the frontier, by appointment of Governor Sam Houston, and repaired forthwith to his post of duty. In December, 1860, at the head of sixty rangers, Captain Ross followed the trail of a large body of Comanches, who had raided through Parker County, to their village on the headwaters of Pease River. Though proverbial for vigilance and cunning, Captain Ross succeeded in effecting a complete surprise, and in the desperate encounter of "war to the knife" that ensued, *nearly all the warriors bit the dust.* So signal a victory had never before been gained over the fierce and warlike Comanches, and ever since that fatal December day, in 1860, the dispirited Comanche "brave" dates the dissipation of that wand of invincibility which it seemed the "Great Spirit" had thrown around them. The blow was as sudden, and as irresistible, as a thunder-bolt from a cloudless sky, and as crushing and remorseless as the hand of fate itself.

Ross, sword in hand, led the furious charge of the rangers, and Peta Nocona, chief of the tribe, arose from his last sleep on earth, aroused by the demoniacal saturnalia, in the midst of which his warriors were melting away like snow-flakes on the river's brink, to strike, at least, an avenging blow ere the night of death had drawn its sable curtains around and above his devoted tribe. Singling out Ross, as the most conspicuous of his assailants, with eyes flashing and nerves steeled by the crisis of fate, Peta Nocona rushed on the wings of the wind to this revel of death. The eagle eyes of the young ranger took in the situation at a glance, and he welcomed the redoubtable chief to the contest with a smile. Desperate was this hand-to-hand grapple, for there was no alternative but victory or death.

Peta Nocona fell covered with wounds at the feet of his conqueror, and his last sigh was taken up in mournful wailings by the fugitives fleeing from this village of blood and death. Many of these latter perished on the inhospitable plains, in a fruitless endeavour to reach their friends and allies on the headwaters of the Arkansas River. The immediate fruits of this victory were 450 horses and all their accumulated winter supplies. But the subsequent results are not to be computed on the basis of dollars and cents. The spirit of the Comanche was here broken, and to this crushing defeat is to be attributed the pacific conduct of these hitherto implacable foes of the white race during the civil war a boon to Texas of incalculable value.

It was in this engagement that Captain Ross rescued "Cynthia Ann Parker," after a captivity of twenty-five years, or since the capture of "Parker's Fort," in 1830, near the site of the town of Groesbeck, Limestone county. General Ross corrects the statement of Mr. Thrall, to the effect that Cynthia Ann Parker was dressed in male attire, nor was there much doubt as to her identity, as in conversing with her, through the medium of his Mexican servant, who had also been a captive to the Comanches and perfectly conversant with their language, there was but little doubt on the part of Ross as to who his captive really was; and he dispatched a special messenger for her uncle, Colonel Parker. In the meantime, sending Cynthia Ann to Camp Cooper, so that Mrs. Evans, the wife of Captain (afterward Lieutenant-General) N. G. Evans could properly attend to her necessities.

After the carnage had ceased, Captain Ross discovered a little Indian boy lying concealed in the tall grass, expecting, in conformity to the savage customs of his own race, to be killed immediately upon discovery. Ross, with kind words, placed the little fellow upon his horse behind himself, and took him to camp. The little captive was named "Pease," in honour of Governor E. M. Pease. Captain Ross took "Pease" home, and properly cared for him, and he is now with his benefactor, a full-blooded Comanche Indian, though a civilised and educated gentleman.

Captain Ross sent the shield, bow, and lance of Peta Nocona to Governor Houston, who placed them in the archives at Austin, where they now remain, encrusted and stained with his blood. In a letter, recognising the great service rendered the State by Captain Ross in dealing the Indians this crushing blow, Governor Houston says:

> Your success in protecting the frontier gives me great satisfaction.
> I am satisfied that, with the same opportunities, you would rival, if not excel, the greatest exploits of McCulloch or Jack Hays. Continue to repel, pursue, and punish every body of Indians coming into the State, and the people will not withhold their praise.

But the tempest of sectional hate, that had so long been distracting the country, was now culminating into a seething, whirling cyclone of war, and such a spirit as Ross could not remain confined to the mere border foray, when armed legions were mustering for the titanic strife; he, therefore, tendered his resignation to Governor Houston, who, in recognition of the services rendered by Ross, had appointed him his *aide-de-camp*, with the rank of colonel. Ross' resignation drew from Governor Houston the following letter, than which a more gratifying testimonial of his worth and services could not be tendered a young man of scarce twenty-three years of age:

Executive Department, Austin, Texas,
February 23, 1861.

Captain L. S. Ross,
Commanding Texas Rangers:
Sir—Your letter of the 13th, tendering your resignation as captain in the ranging service of Texas, has been received. The Executive regrets that you should think of resigning your position, as the state of the frontier requires good and efficient officers. He is, therefore, unwilling to accept your resignation. . . . . The Executive has always had confidence in your capacity as an officer; and your deportment, as a soldier and gentleman, has met with his entire approval. It is his desire that you at once increase your command to eighty-three, rank and file, and take the field again.

Very respectfully,
(Signed)                                    Sam Houston.

Captain Ross called Governor Clarke's attention to the necessity of entering into treaty stipulations with the Indians on our frontier; and Major Van Dorn also urged the same measure upon the Governor, and suggested Captain Ross as the most proper person to conduct the negotiation on the part of the State, as it was well known he had the full confidence of the "Texas Indians," whom he commanded in the Wichita campaign. In response to these suggestions, Governor Clarke wrote Captain Ross as follows:

Austin, July 13, 1861.

Captain L. S. Ross:
Dear Sir—When you were here, a few days ago, you spoke to me of the disposition of the Indians to treat with the people of

Texas. At the time you did so, I was so crowded with business that I was unable to give to the subject the consideration its importance demanded. I, nevertheless, concluded and determined to adopt and carry out your suggestions. I would be pleased for you to inform me whether it may now be in time to accomplish the objects you spoke of, and, if so, whether you would be willing to undertake its execution. You mentioned, I believe, that a day was fixed by the Indians for the interview, but that you informed them that by that time Texas could not be ready.

Very respectfully,

(Signed)                                        Edward Clarke.

In pursuance of this programme, Captain Ross received his credentials from the governor, and, taking with him Mr. Downs, of the Waco *Examiner*, and two or three more young friends, set out for the plains. Arriving at Gainsville, Ross met an Indian trader, whom he knew, named Shirley, whose brother was an interpreter, and both of whom lived in the Indian country. He was about to engage the assistance and co-operation of these men, when he learned that General Pike had been commissioned, and was then *en route* to Fort Sill to enter into treaty stipulations with the Indians, on the part of the Confederate Government.

Captain Ross, deeming that the interests of Texas could be best subserved by non-action, as certainly all expense and responsibility was obviated, did not attend the interview; nor, indeed, did he allow to transpire the nature of his business in that section, at all, though, through the medium of Shirley, Jones, Bickle, and one or two other white men living with the Indians, all of whom were well known to Ross, the Indians were fully prepared and anxious to enter into friendly relations with the South; so, that when General Pike arrived, the ground lay fair before him, and he found no difficulty in arranging the terms.

Captain Ross, who had been in correspondence with the above-named white residents of the Indian section, realised the importance of prompt action on the part of the South, before commissioners of the United States could have opportunities for seducing the Indians from their natural friends. Finding that the Confederacy was moving to the accomplishment of the same object, Ross possessed too much sagacity to invite a conflict of authority between Texas and the Confederacy, as was the case in some other States by a too liberal

LIEUTENANT-COLONEL P. F. ROSS.

interpretation of the sovereign prerogative of the States; and, while saving Texas the expense of the negotiation, and all responsibility in the matter, silently contributed to the accomplishment of General Pike's mission.

The value of this treaty to the South cannot well be overestimated. It not only obviated the necessity for the presence of a considerable force on the frontier which was required elsewhere, but it actually contributed to the augmentation of the Confederate ranks. This great service rendered Texas, and particularly to the immediate frontier, was wholly unselfish and gratuitous, and it is believed the true statement of the case, now, for the first time, finds itself in print.

Seeing the consummation of this important affair well under way, Ross returned to Waco and joined, as a private, the company of Captain P. F. Ross, his elder brother. This company was, with others, consolidated into the Sixth Regiment of Texas Cavalry, at the city of Dallas, Texas, and L. S. Ross was elected Major, and commissioned as such September 12th, 1861. In this same regiment, ex-Governor J. W. Throckmorton was Captain of Company "K," and John S. Griffith Lieutenant-Colonel, Colonel B. Warren Stone being the Colonel. The regiment immediately took up the line of march for General Ben McCulloch's army in Missouri. The regiment participated in the Battle of Chustenahlah (Creek Nation) with distinguished gallantry, December, 1861, and in the three days' battle at Elk Horn, or Pea Ridge, Arkansas. Just previous to this latter engagement, Major Ross was dispatched upon a raid, at the head of a detachment of about 300 men, composed of companies of the Third and Sixth Texas Cavalry, in the enemy's rear. This delicate expedition, demanding the consummate address of a prompt and decisive commander, was attended with eminent success, General Ross capturing numbers of prisoners and destroying immense quantities of quartermaster and commissary stores.

The "Army of the West," composed of the divisions of the lamented McCulloch and General Price, were transferred to the Cis-Mississippi Department to re-enforce General Beauregard at Corinth, Mississippi, where he was confronted by an overwhelming force of the enemy. The Sixth Texas, as were the other cavalry regiments, was dismounted, and their horses sent to Texas. At Corinth, the command was engaged in a number of outpost affairs until in May, when the first year's service having expired, the regiment was reorganised, and Major L. S. Ross was elected Colonel. Immediately upon his election he was assigned to the command of the brigade in which his regiment was incorporated, in the following order from division headquarters:

Headquarters Jones' Division,
May 26, 1862.

Special Orders No. 11—Extract.

1. Colonel Laurence S. Ross will immediately assume command of Roane's Brigade, Jones' Division, Army of the West.

By command of

L. Jones, Major-General,
Charles S. Stringfellow, A. A. G.

Colonel Ross, with his characteristic modesty, declined the honour, and prevailed with General Jones to allow him to remain in command of his own regiment, and General Phifer was subsequently placed in command of the brigade. The summer of 1862 was spent in the camp at Tupelo, Mississippi; the time being principally employed in drilling the regiments, in the case of the dismounted Texans in transforming natural troopers into unwilling infantrymen. The next engagement of importance was the storming of Corinth, and the struggle at Hatchie bridge for the temporary salvation of the "Army of the West." And, as an authorative elucidation of the part borne by Ross and his men, on those two trying occasions, the following letters from General Dabney H. Maury and General Pryor are adduced:

Headquarters Department of the Gulf,
Mobile, Alabama, October 6, 1863.

My Dear Colonel:

General Jackson asked me to have some colours made for his division. Please send me, at once, the names of the battles in which my old Texas regiments were engaged prior to coming under my command, as I wish to have them placed on their colours. I always think of the behaviour of the Texans at Corinth, and at the Hatchie, next day, as entitled to rank with the very "gamest" conduct displayed by any troops in this war. It does not seem to be generally known, but it is a fact, that the fragment of my shattered division withstood the attack of Ord's corps , and successfully checked it until the whole train of the army had changed its line of march.

For about an hour the remnant of Phifer's Brigade, commanded by Colonel L. S. Ross, held the Hatchie bridge, and with the light batteries, kept the enemy back. Then Cabell's Brigade came up, and the fight was maintained exclusively by my divi-

sion until we were ordered to retire, which was done in a delib-
erate and soldierly manner. I often reflect, with satisfaction, on
that fight as one of the most creditable to the troops engaged
of which I have any knowledge, and I do not believe anything
is known of it outside of the division. No regiment can have a
more honourable name upon its flag than "Hatchie," and, to my
certain knowledge, no regiment can more justly and proudly
bear that name on its colours than the Sixth Texas Cavalry.

With kind regards, Colonel, I am truly yours,

(Signed)                         Dabney H. Maury.

Memphis, Tennessee, June 4, 1867.

General L. S. Ross,

Waco, Texas:

My Dear Sir—I am requested by General Forrest, who is completely immersed in business connected with a large railroad
contract in Arkansas, to acknowledge the receipt of your very
esteemed favour of the 21st *ult.*, and to return his, and my own,
sincere thanks for your report. You may very well suppose I
took great interest in, not only reading your summary of operations while with Forrest, but also in seeing, for the first time,
the high testimony General Maury bears to your old regiment
at Hatchie bridge. For, you will remember, I was with you, on
your staff, on that occasion, and have always taken some little
credit to myself for the assistance I was so fortunate as to be able
to render to your brigade that day.

I was the first to discover that Moore's Brigade, which we had
crossed the river to support, as also another command (Whitfield's Legion, I think), had both been scattered, or destroyed as
organisations, and that your small brigade, of less than 700 men,
was about to be assailed by Hulburt's whole army. I remember
that I gained this information from General Moore, whom I
accidentally met retiring from the front, all alone on the bank
of the river, and immediately communicated to you, with the
request of General Moore that you should 'fall back' across the
stream, or you would be overwhelmed in ten minutes, or less
time, by a force of at least 8,000 men; I remember that you refused, at first, to comply with Moore's request, and sent Captain
D. R. Gurley and myself to General Maury for orders, who,
upon ascertaining the facts, immediately dispatched you the

order to retire.

Then, at 'common time,' the brigade was moved by the left flank to the road leading to the bridge (without letting the men know, at first, that they were falling back), when the order to 'file left' was given, and the command brought off in good order, quietly and safely, with the exception of a portion of the extreme right, which, misunderstanding the first order, moved by the 'right flank' instead of the left, and so became separated, and near a hundred of them captured. Withdrawing to the east bank of the Hatchie River, and taking position on a little ridge two or three hundred yards distant, the brigade there made the gallant stand for several hours, to which General Maury so complimentarily alludes. With best regards to my friend Gurley, whom I shall always remember as one of the best and truest, and most efficient of men I ever knew,

I remain, my dear sir, very truly yours,

(Signed)                                                    J. A. Pryor.

But as the foregoing pages of this narrative deals with the services of Ross in the Confederate Army, it would be a useless repetition to repeat what has already been said, unless having a direct bearing upon General Ross individually, or tending to illustrate some trait of character.

The defeated Confederate Army retreated, *via* Holly Springs to Grenada, Mississippi, near which place the four Texas regiments were remounted, as already stated. Then came the Holly Springs raid, which forced Grant to retire to Memphis, Tennessee, thus delaying the Vicksburg catastrophe twelve months. Then the march to Tennessee, and the brilliant action at Thompson's Station, in which three thousand of the enemy were captured. Then the long and tedious march to Mississippi for the relief of beleaguered Vicksburg, and the innumerable affairs in the performance of this duty; the fall of Vicksburg and retreat to Jackson, on every foot of which road Ross' Brigade disputed stubbornly the advance of Sherman.

The services of Colonel Ross were fully appreciated by his superiors in rank, and he was placed in command of a brigade composed of the First Mississippi Cavalry and the Sixth Texas, and dispatched to the Tennessee valley, conducting a brilliant campaign, against vastly superior forces, by land and river. In testimony of the high appreciation in which they held Colonel Ross, the following testimonial of the officers of the First Mississippi Cavalry is adduced:

Camp First Mississippi Cavalry,<br>December 21, 1863.

Colonel L. S. Ross:

The officers of the First Mississippi Cavalry desiring to express their appreciation of you as an officer, have designated the undersigned as a committee to communicate their feelings.

It is with profound regret that they part with you as their Brigade Commander, and will cherish, with kind remembrance, your generous and courteous conduct toward them, and the gallant bearing you have ever displayed in leading them in battle. The service, with all its hardships and privations, has been rendered pleasant under your direction and leadership. They deplore the circumstances which render it necessary that they should be taken from your command, but feel confident that, in whatever field you may be called upon to serve, the country will know no better or more efficient officer. Our regret is shared by all the men of the regiment, and you carry with you their best wishes for your continued success.

In conclusion, allow us to say, we are proud to have served under you, and with your gallant Texans, and hope yours, and theirs, and our efforts in behalf of our bleeding country, will at length be crowned with success.

Very respectfully,

W. V. Lester, Captain Company K.<br>J. E. Turner, Captain Company I.<br>J. A. King, Captain Company G.

Lieutenant-General Stephen D. Lee wrote Mr. Seddon, the Secretary of War, October 2, 1863:

Colonel L. S. Ross is one of the best disciplinarians in the army, and has distinguished himself on many battlefields, and his promotion and assignment will increase the efficiency of *the most reliable troops under my command.*

General D. H. Maury wrote from Mobile, Alabama, October 6, 1863:

During the Battle of Hatchie, Colonel L. S. Ross commanded his brigade, and evinced such conspicuous gallantry, that, when called upon to report to the War Department the name of the officer who had been especially distinguished there, and at Corinth, I reported the name of Colonel L. S. Ross to General S. Cooper, Adjutant and Inspector-General of the Confederate States Army.

Hon. F. R. Lubbock, while a member of the President's staff at Richmond, Virginia, wrote General Ross:

I have learned, with pride and great satisfaction, of the good behaviour, and gallant conduct, and high-bearing of the Texas soldiers, and particularly of Ross' Brigade.

General W. H. Jackson, commanding Cavalry Division, wrote the Secretary of War, October 1 1863:

I regard Colonel L. S. Ross as one of the best disciplinarians, and one of the most gallant officers, in the 'Army of the West.'

General Joseph E. Johnston wrote the Secretary of War, October 3, 1863, urging the promotion of Colonel Ross.

All this was done positively without the solicitation of Colonel Ross, and, in point of fact, without his knowledge and consent. The first intimation that Ross had of the honour to be conferred upon him, was the reception of his commission as a Brigadier-General, in the presence of the enemy, before Yazoo City. The appointment sought the man, and there was no one amid all that galaxy of glory, who wore the "wreathed stars" during the stormy period of the war, more deserving the honour than Laurence Sullivan Ross.

We may merely mention the most salient features of the campaigns, henceforth, which, like the rounds of a ladder, bear us, step by step, to the end.

Sherman commenced his memorable march from Vicksburg to Meridian. Ross harassed his columns in front, rear, and flank incessantly, and retarded the Federal advance until the defeat of Smith's corps, by General Forrest, near West Point, caused Sherman to abandon the idea of marching to Mobile, as he subsequently did to Savannah. Ross was now dispatched, in post-haste, to the Yazoo valley, up which stream a Federal flotilla was ascending, accompanied by a land force of about 3,500 men.

The spirited Battles of Liverpool, Satartia, and Yazoo City, were fought, each resulting in a complete victory for Ross, who drove the Federals on board their transports, and, though protected by ironclad gunboats, drove them down the Yazoo and into Vicksburg. The fol-

lowing testimonial of the citizens of Yazoo City, to the services of
Ross and his brigade, is a volume in itself:

Yazoo City, February 6, 1864.

General L. S. Ross:

We, the undersigned, citizens of Yazoo City, do hereby tender
you, and your gallant command, our heartfelt thanks for the
noble manner in which you have repelled the enemy, though
far superior in numbers, thus saving us from the insults and
other indignities which they would have heaped upon us.
(Signed): W. H. Mangum, John M. Clark, S. H. Wilson, Alex.
Smith, James P. Thomas, Jr., M. P. Dent, R. M. Grail, H. B. Kidd,
Mark Berry, S. D. Hightower, F. M. Cassels, John Smith, D. Kear-
ney, R. C. Shepherd, W. L. Stamford, S. C. Goosey, Richard Stephens, S. T. Pierse, F. Barksdale, F. G. Stewart, —— Gibbs, Louis
Franklin, J. W. Barnett, C. Hollingsworth, Louis Rosenthral, A.
Asher, M. L. Enlich, John Hagman, Jacob Hagman, A. H. Mont-
gomery, Captain O. T. Plummer (Volunteer and Conscript Bu-
reau), Captain W. J. Blackburn (Volunteer and Conscript Bu-
reau), B. J. Harris, James Schmitt, W. Ragster, R. B. Powell, R.
R. Callahan, J. O. Dwyer, J. Bradley, C. Swann, Joseph Carr, J. W.
Campton, Samuel Goodwin, J. S. Wallace, Fred. Knabke, John
S. Murphy, —— Murphy, J. Mozer, John Reilly, James Carter,
James P. O'Reilley, H. C. Tyler, Thomas R. Smith, Hiram Har-
rison.

The brigade was ordered from the Yazoo section to re-enforce the
army of General Johnston, in Georgia. The engagements during this
campaign were of almost daily occurrence. Ross' Brigade, at times,
constituted a portion of the Confederate line in front of Sherman,
and, at other times, was engaged in repelling, fighting, and capturing
Federal raiders in the rear of General Johnston's army. In the advance
to Nashville, Ross and Armstrong were the eyes of Hood, and, in his
defeat and retreat, their two brigades absolutely saved the army from
annihilation. But, as has been aptly said, the tide of Confederate success reached its greatest height in Pickett's charge upon Cemetery
Heights, and Hood's ephemeral successes were but the spasmodic efforts that precede final dissolution.

The end came; and the commencement of the end dates from the
day that General Johnston inaugurated his ignoble retreat by retiring
from Dalton, Georgia. Had he assumed the offensive there, the Con-

federacy would have been spared the sad catastrophe that befell it.

It is not pleasant to contemplate these heroic men struggling against an iliad of woes. They had borne their banners on the highest waves of victory, and stood as conquerors on the Ohio itself. Now, footsore and weary, ragged, famished, after nine-tenths of their numbers had been offered as sacrifices upon the altar of duty, they stood contemplating the inevitable. The rest is known of all.

General Ross returned to his home, near Waco, and, with his interesting family, lived the quiet and honourable life of a farmer. Since his twentieth year, he had shared all the vicissitudes of a soldier's life. The golden morning of life had been spent, without the hope of fee or reward, in the arduous duties and dangers of the battlefield. He now sought repose, content to remain on

*The Sabine farm, amid contiguous hills,*
*Remote from honours and their kindred ills."*

But, in 1873, his friends called him from retirement by electing him Sheriff of McLennan County. In this position he remained several years, and so efficient were his services, that he was styled, by those who had opportunities for judging, "The model Sheriff of Texas!" Voluntarily retiring from office, he again sought the privacy of his country home. In 1875, he was elected a member of the Constitutional Convention that framed the present organic law of Texas. As tending to illustrate, in some degree, the part borne by General Ross, and the policies advocated by him in the prosecution of this grave duty, a few extracts are reproduced from the leading journals of the time. The Waco *Daily Telephone*, of November 8, 1877, in a rather hostile review of the Constitution, and especially of Article V. (the Judiciary), says:

> Judge Ballinger and General Ross protested against their action (the "Rutabagas"), but were overslaughed. . . . .Our readers will remember the unanswerable argument of General Ross against the reduction of the judges, salaries, and judicial districts, against which the "Rutabagas" opposed—not their arguments, but their votes.

The *State Gazette*, Colonel John D. Elliott, editor, said:

> We can never refer to the name of General Ross without feeling an inspiration of admiration scarcely ever equalled in our experience of life. He is one of nature's noblemen as artless and unostentatious as a child, as courageous and heroic as ever

bore the image of man, and as able as the ablest of the land. His record in the Constitutional Convention showed him as exalted a patriot and statesman as the man of letters and thorough representative of the people. He is eminently fitted for the highest trust of the Commonwealth. We know of no citizen of the State who would add greater lustre in her chief magistracy than General Sul Ross.

The following letter is from the pen of Colonel John Henry Brown, and appeared in the columns of the Dallas *Morning Call:*

*Another Richmond!—A Good Man for Governor—Enthusiastic Suggestion of General Sul Ross, of Waco.—*A soldier-boy on the frontier—a leader of Indian scouts under Van Dorn while yet a youth—the gallant boy captain who rescued Cynthia Ann Parker after twenty-five years captivity—a private soldier winning his way up to a Brigadier-Generalship—the hero of more than a hundred battles and fights—the modest and educated gentleman—for five years the model Sheriff of the State, and in the Constitutional Convention displaying the highest qualities of eloquence and enlightened statesmanship—why may not his thousands of friends present his name for the position of Chief Magistrate of the State he has so nobly, and ably, and disinterestedly served since he was thirteen years old? Why not? He has never intimated such a wish; but his friends claim the right to mention his name. Ask the people of the whole frontier ask the people of his large district—ask his neighbours—ask the thirty thousand ex-soldiers who know his deeds, and see what they all say. They will send up one grand shout for Sul Ross.

All of which the *Telephone* endorsed in the following language:

General Ross' sound, practical abilities, are unquestioned, and few men are more justly esteemed. We believe he would fill any position which he consents to accept, with ability, faithfulness, and dignity. We do not know, however, that he would consent to become an aspirant, at this time, for the gubernatorial office. We do know, however, that he will never intrigue or scheme for the position; and, if tendered the nomination, it will be a voluntary offering by the State at large, without reference to local or personal predilections and efforts. Under those circumstances, General Ross would make a Governor equal to any Texas ever had.

Such, in brief, is a hasty synopsis of the life of General L. S. Ross. The foregoing pages of this narrative attempt to elaborate some of the incidents in his career that won for himself the confidence of his superiors in rank, and for his brigade the encomium of all. Nothing like a complete history of Ross, or his brigade, is claimed here. At this late day, in the absence of all documentary material to use in the construction, that desideratum is impossible of attainment; and, with the conclusion drawing nigh, the author feels like exclaiming: The half has not been told; and the fragment here preserved falls far short of doing the subject justice! Probably, no general officer who commanded troops in the late war, drew them in closer sympathy to himself than General Ross.

Each man of his brigade regarded his dashing young chieftain as a personal friend. As Junot was prompt to resent a fancied insult to Napoleon, so would the troopers of Ross have drawn their sabres at any allusion disparaging to their idolised leader. Brave unto rashness himself—he had seven horses shot under him in the course of the war—yet he was solicitous of the welfare of his men, and all his plans of attack or defence contained, in an eminent degree, the element of prudence. Often, with his skeleton brigade, he seemed tempting the wrath of the Fates, and as risking all upon a single cast of the die; but no mission of danger ever appalled his men, for, following his dashing and seemingly reckless lead, they again and again plucked "the flower safety from the nettle danger."

In the disastrous retreat of Hood from Nashville, the brigades of Ross and Armstrong were the palladiums of hope to the discomfited army; and had it not been for their interposing shields, Hood's army, as an organisation, would have ceased to exist ere a passage of the Tennessee river could have been attained.

A characteristic letter from the general's pen will conclude this sketch of his life—a letter written in the expectation that no eye save the author's would ever scan its pages—as tending to illustrate somewhat those noble qualities of heart that so endeared him to his men. The noble sentiments expressed are characteristic of the man.

General Ross was recently elected to a seat in the State Senate, distancing his competitor by an unparalleled majority, and running two thousand votes ahead of his own party ticket. *Apropos* to General Ross' opposition to the "Judicial Article" of the State Constitution, it is gratifying to his friends to know that five years of experience has demonstrated his wisdom in pronouncing the article, on the floor of the Convention, "wholly inadequate to meet the wants of the great State of Texas, and that, as a system, it must prove in the end more expensive than the one sought to be displaced." As the Democratic party in convention at Dallas demands, through the "platform," an amendment to the Constitution to meet this particular want, a more emphatic and unqualified vindication of General Ross' course in the Constitutional Convention could not be framed.

Waco, Texas.

Victor M. Rose,
Victoria, Texas:

My Dear Friend—Your kind letter did not reach me promptly, but I hasten to assure you of my approval of the commendable work you design. You will probably remember that, during the war, Captain Dunn, whose health had failed, detailed to write a full and accurate history of the operations of the brigade, and I furnished him with all necessary data—orders, papers, etc.—so as to render his duty of easy compliance; but, unfortunately, he died in Alabama, and this information was received, together with that, that my trunk and papers entrusted to his care had fallen into the hands of the enemy.

In my trunk was found twenty stands of colours, and other trophies which we had captured from the Federals. My memory is too defective to be relied upon at this late day for much valuable information, but such as I can trust, I will gladly give you; and I feel warranted in saying, that Captain Gurley, and others of our comrades, will aid you in your noble work, which, I trust, you will not delay for the endorsement of anyone.

I was glad to hear from you. Indeed, every few days, by letters or calls from my noble, brave boys, am I assured that they remember me kindly. No churchman ever loved to tell his beads as I love to recount their valour and their loyalty in the discharge of a solemnly-conceived duty. Long after I was thoroughly satisfied they knew they were being called upon to follow a "will o' the wisp" to their utter discomfiture—naked, footsore, and famished as they were, yet, with heroic devotion, they met every peril unflinchingly, and encountered every hardship unmurmuringly. I hope steps will be taken soon to bring about a happy reunion of all those who are still living, and then we can take steps to honour and embalm the memory of the dead.

I would be pleased to have suggestions from any, or all, of our comrades everywhere, as to the practicability of getting up some kind of an organisation, and I am ready to concur in any plan devised. My health is not very good. I contracted a cold from exposure in the Mississippi swamp when we were crossing over those arms, and it eventually settled on my lungs, and from that time I have suffered much from bronchitis, and have often thought consumption would ensue. I am farming, and making enough to provide for the wants of myself and wife, and six children. Happily, my early training upon the frontier, among the early pioneers of Texas, inculcated no very extravagant desires. Please remember me to all my "boys," and tell them that if we are never permitted to meet *en masse* on this earth, when we "cross over the river" we shall enjoy a grand and glorious reunion, and have a long, long time to talk it all over.

Very truly your friend,
(Signed)                            L. S. Ross.

# Battle of the Wichita

Ross' faithful Indian scouts reported the discovery of a Comanche village near the Wichita mountains, and, immediately, Major Van Dora set the column in motion (including Ross' command), and, by a fatiguing forced march all night, came in the immediate vicinity of the village just at break of day. A reconnaissance showed that the wily Comanches were not apprehensive of an attack, and were sleeping in fancied security. The horses of the tribe were grazing near the outskirts of the village, and consisted of a *caballado* of about five hundred head. Major Van Dorn directed Captain Ross, at the head of his Indians, to "cut off" the horses, and drive them from the camp, which was effected speedily, and thus the Comanches were forced to fight on foot—a proceeding extremely harrowing to the proud warriors' feelings.

Just as the sun was peeping above the eastern horizon, Van Dorn charged the upper end of the village, while Ross' command, in conjunction with a detachment of United States Cavalry, charged the lower. The village was strung out along the banks of a branch for several hundred yards. The morning was very foggy, and, after a few moments of firing, the smoke and fog became so dense that objects at but a short distance could be distinguished only with great difficulty. The Comanches fought with absolute desperation, and contended for every advantage, as their women and children, and all their possessions, were in peril.

A few moments after the engagement became general, Ross discovered a number of Comanches running down to the branch, about one hundred and fifty yards from the village, and concluded that they were beating a retreat. Immediately, Ross, Lieutenant Van Camp, of the United States Army, Alexander, a "regular" soldier, and one Caddo

Indian, of Ross' command, ran to the point with the intention of intercepting them. Arriving, it was discovered that the fugitives were the women and children. In a moment, another posse of women and children came running immediately past the squad of Ross, who, discovering a little white girl among the number, made his Caddo Indian grab her as she was passing. The little pale-face—apparently about twelve years of age—was badly frightened at finding herself a captive to a strange Indian and stranger white men, and was hard to manage at first.

Ross now discovered, through the fog and smoke of battle, that a band of some twenty-five Comanche warriors had cut his small party off from communication with Van Dorn, and were bearing immediately down upon them. They shot Lieutenant Van Camp through the heart, killing him ere he could fire his double-barrelled shot-gun. Alexander, the United States cavalryman, was likewise shot down before he could fire his gun (a rifle). Ross was armed with a Sharpe's rifle, and attempted to fire upon the exultant red devils, but the cap snapped. "Mohee," a Comanche warrior, seized Alexander's rifle, and shot Ross down.

The indomitable young ranger fell upon the side on which his pistol was borne, and, though partially paralyzed by the shot, he turned himself, and was getting his pistol out, when "Mohee" drew his butcher-knife, and started toward his prostrate foe some fifteen feet away—with the evident design of stabbing and scalping him. He made but a few steps, however, when one of his companions cried out something in the Comanche tongue, which was a signal to the band, and they broke away in confusion. "Mohee" ran about twenty steps, when a wire-cartridge, containing nine buckshot, fired from a gun in the hands of Lieutenant James Majors (afterward a Confederate General), struck him between the shoulders, and he fell forward on his face, dead.

"Mohee" was an old acquaintance of Ross, as the latter had seen him frequently at his father's post on the frontier, and recognised him as soon as their eyes met. The faithful Caddo held on to the little girl throughout this desperate *melee*, and, strange to relate, neither were harmed. The Caddo, doubtless, owed his escape to the fact that the Comanches were fearful of wounding or killing the little girl. This whole scene transpired in a few moments, and Captain N. G. Evans' company of the Second United States Cavalry, had taken possession of the lower end of the Comanche village, and Major Van Dorn held the upper, and the Comanches were running into the hills and brush; not, however, before an infuriated Comanche shot the gallant Van Dorn with an arrow.

Van Dorn fell, and it was supposed that he was mortally wounded. In consequence of their wounds, the two chieftains were compelled to remain on the battle-ground five or six days. After the expiration of this time, Ross' Indians made a "litter, "after their fashion, borne between two gentle mules, and in it placed their heroic and beloved "boy Captain," and set out for the settlements at Fort Belknap. When this mode of conveyance would become too painful by reason of the rough, broken nature of the country, these brave Caddos—whose race and history are but synonyms of courage and fidelity—would vie with each other in bearing the burden upon their own shoulders.

At Camp Radziminski, occupied by United States forces, an ambulance was obtained, and the remainder of the journey made with comparative comfort. Major Van Dorn was also conveyed to Radziminski. He speedily recovered of his wounds, and soon made another brilliant campaign against the Comanches. Ross recovered sufficiently in a few weeks so as to be able to return to college at Florence, Alabama, where he completed his studies, and graduated in 1859.

The little girl captive—of whose parentage or history nothing could be ascertained, though strenuous efforts were made—was named by her benefactor, "*Lizzie* Ross," in honour of Miss *Lizzie* Tinsley, daughter of Dr. D. R. Tinsley, of Waco. The sentiments that prompted the chivalric ranger in this selection of a name, will soon be discovered to the reader.

The soldier, Alexander, recovered of his wound in the course of several months, but of the brave fellow's subsequent career, the author knows nothing.

General Ross, after the expiration of twenty-two years since the Battle of the Wichita, said to the author:

I shall never forget the feelings of horror that took possession of me when I saw the arrow sent clear up to the *feather* into the body and heart of the gallant young Van Camp, who, I think, belonged to the Engineers, and only accompanied Major Van Dorn in the capacity of a volunteer aid. I then thought but little of my own danger, but expected, of course, that my time had come to balance accounts.

Of Lizzie Ross (we will anticipate the thread of the narrative), it can be said that, in her career, is afforded a thorough verification of Lord Byron's saying: *"Truth is stranger than fiction!"* She was adopted by her brave and generous captor, properly reared and educated, and became a beautiful and accomplished woman. Here were sufficient romance and vicissitude, in the brief career of a little maiden, to have tuned the "roundelay's" of "troubadour and *mennesanger.*" A solitary lily, blooming amidst the wildest grasses of the desert plains.

A little Indian girl in all save the Caucasian's conscious stamp of superiority. Torn from home, perhaps, amid the heart-rending scenes of rapine, torture, and death. A stranger to race and lineage stranger even to the tongue in which a mother's lullaby was breathed. Affiliating with these wild Ishmaelites of the prairie—a Comanche in all things save the intuitive premonition *that she was not of them!* Finally, redeemed from a captivity worse than death by a knight entitled to rank, for all time in the history of Texas, *primus inter pares.*

Lizzie Ross accompanied General Ross' mother on a visit to the State of California, a few years since, and while there, became the wife of a wealthy merchant near Los Angeles, where she now resides, the queen of a happy household, surrounded by all things that render life attractive or desirable.

Such is the romantic story of Lizzie Ross a story that derives additional interest because of the fact of its absolute truth in all respects.

General Ross was united in marriage to Miss Lizzie Tinsley, of Waco. Mrs. Ross is a lady of sterling qualities of mind and heart, and, in all respects, a congenial companion of her heroic husband. The union has been blessed by six children; and now, in the midst of the peaceful quiet that surrounds his happy home, the general, doubtless, beguiles the tedium of ennui by recounting to his "young brigade" the exploits of his old. The latter are descending the hill of life toward the setting sun, in obedience to the distant sound of the final tattoo that comes from beyond the western hills; the former, lit by the aureole of his rising glories, are responding to the morning reveille with youth, and health, and hope.

May their paths be the paths of peace; and if the trade of war must be pursued, may it never be the tocsin of internecine strife that shall summon them to the field of carnage and death. No bloody chasm now divides the Grey and Blue! A reunited people commands the peace of sections! These are the tidings of great joy to the people of the American Union—one indissoluble whole of indestructible States! And so may it ever be, "For we be brethren!"

# Reminiscences of Camp Chase

Kilpatrick succeeded in getting away from Lovejoy Station with about thirty or forty of the Texas Brigade, among whom are now remembered: Captain Noble; Lieutenants Teague, Moon and West; Privates Crabtree, Pirtle, Nidever, Mapes, "Major" White, Reuben White, Fluellen, and Ware. The march of the prisoners to the lines of General Sherman was fatiguing in the extreme. The Confederates had been in the saddle for three consecutive days, during which time they had partaken of not one regular meal; and the Union troopers were almost as destitute of rations, though what little they had was generously divided with their famished prisoners. The prisoners were well treated by their captors. It was only the "home guard" who delighted in misusing these unfortunates of war, just as the professional politician on either side refuses even now to be placated. The men who confronted each other in battle were too brave to feel pleasure in inflicting pain on a prisoner.

The braves of Hancock, Custer, McClellan, and Rosecranz are not the men who have kept the "bloody shirt" waving; nor are the men of Joe Johnston, Beauregard, Maxy, and Ross, found among the impracticables, who, like his excellency, the late President Jeff. Davis, imagine the Confederacy still exists. General Sherman's convention with General Johnston expressed the sentiments of the soldiers on either side. Arriving at Sherman's quarters the prisoners were placed in the "bull-pen," and given a "square" meal of "hard-tack" and "sow-belly," as crackers and bacon were called by the Federals. In the "bull-pen" were a number of whining, canting, oath-seeking hypocrites and sycophants, who, with the characteristic zeal of new converts, employed their time in maligning everything connected with their suffering section, and in extolling the superior civilization of the North. The fiery and impetuous Crabtree could not brook this despicable servility, and he undertook to do battle, singly and alone, in vindication of the South.

A lively "scrimmage" was on the *tapis*, Crabtree knocking his opponents right and left, when the guard interposed on behalf of the new converts, whom every brave Unionist secretly despised. After a day or two spent here, the prisoners were placed on the cars and conveyed to Nashville. Here the forlorn fellows were placed in the yard of the penitentiary, and kept for several days, as General Wheeler was in the vicinity with a large force of cavalry, and a rescue was feared. Finally, by rail again, the prisoners were taken to Louisville, Kentucky. Upon entering the guard-house, each prisoner was required to deposit, in a large tub near the door, his pocket-knife, money, and whatever else of value he possessed. No account whatever was taken of the articles so confiscated, nor did the prisoners ever hear of their property again, or compensation for the same.

The journey from Kentucky's metropolis, through Cincinnati and Columbus, to Camp Chase, distant four miles from the capital of Ohio, was without incident, save the escape of Lieutenant A. J. West, of the Sixth Texas. Sometime before reaching Louisville, and while the cars were flying at the rate of forty miles an hour, the night being intensely dark, this daring young officer jumped from the train, and. strange to say, suffered no accident or injury from the rash leap. He made his way through the enemy's lines in safety to his own command.

Camp Chase was situated near the Sciota River, so said, for, during the author's sojourn of near nine months in those delectable quarters, he had no opportunity for observation beyond the prison walls. The "Camp" consisted of three "prisons," designated respectively, "No. 1," "No. 2," and "No. 3." In "No. 1" officers exclusively were confined, "No's 2 and 3 "accommodated the twenty or thirty thousand privates on hand a number sufficient to have averted the catastrophe at Petersburg. The "prisons" were enclosed by a plank-wall upwards of fifteen feet high. On the top of this wall a guard, consisting of about twenty "posts," was stationed, with doubtless another line on the outside below, as certainly a heavy "relief" was always immediately on hand. A slight ditch, or furrow, on the inside of the wall, and parallel with it, was the "dead-line," over which no "Reb" might venture, unless desirous of making himself the target of the vigilant guard.

The quarters the prisoners consisted of comfortable frame buildings in two rows, and fronting upon a common street. The houses were capable of containing near two hundred prisoners. Bunks in tiers of three formed the sleeping accommodations. Colonel W. P. Richardson commanded the post, and Lieutenant Sankey was Provost Marshal. The rations consisted of three crackers and about four ounces of white fish per day. Sometimes the bill of fare was varied by the issuance of beef and flour, but not in quantities exceeding the above estimate. In consequence of such short rations, the prisoners were constantly experiencing the pangs of hunger, and that some died absolutely of sheer starvation, the writer is indubitably certain. Three men occupied a bunk, and sometimes during the night one would die, when not unfrequently the remaining two would actually contend over the corpse for his rations and blankets.

Men here—many—lost all self-respect, and the worst passions of our nature predominated over the good. Though the prisoners were not allowed money, yet they were given "sutler's checks" in lieu, ranging in denominations from five to fifty cents. The sutler's shop abutted against the wall, and through a crevice, about three inches wide and six in length, a prisoner, blessed with the possession of these coveted checks, could purchase stationery, needles and thread, *gutta-percha* buttons, tobacco, and a few other immaterial articles.

Anything, however, in the nature of provisions or clothing was under the severest ban. Nothing eatable entered the prison walls save the meagre rations doled out to the half-famished men. Many of the prisoners, addicted to the use of tobacco, would occasionally sell one meal per day for five cents, with which to purchase a half-dozen chews of the weed. In this way a considerable trade sprang up, and several prisoners conducted quite a grocery business.

One, a Georgian, Waddell of name, earned quite a considerable little sum of money. The old skin-flint converted his bunk into a store, and here higgled with the starving wretches who brought their rations to exchange with him for a small piece of tobacco, or extolled the flavour of the same rations to some would-be purchaser who had the "sutler's checks" to pay for the luxury.

Robberies were not unfrequent, and an incorrigible Englishman—who was the subject of quite a voluminous correspondence between Lord Lyons and Mr. Seward—was frequently punished. This wretch was sometimes fastened to a cross, and his face laid directly under the spout of the pump, though the weather was bitter cold, and the water pumped into his face until respiration would be suspended. At other times, he was placed in a barrel having holes through which the arms protruded, and in this novel jacket he would be compelled to "mark time" in the snow for hours.

The author remembers meeting in prison No. 2, a young Illinoisan, who represented himself as the county judge at Paris, Illinois, imprisoned simply because he was accused of being a "copperhead." To add to the calamities of the wretched 'men, the small-pox broke out among them, and from twenty to thirty of the poor fellows were carried out in rude coffins each morning to the "silent camping-ground." Of the small company of Texans, Reuben White and Al. Nidever died.

An old Frenchman is remembered—they called him "Old Bragg," who had been blown up at Vicksburg with the gallant Third Louisiana Regiment, and captured. "Old Bragg" had one leg missing, one arm and one eye gone, and the poor old fellow's mind was sadly impaired. His whole thought was bent upon an exchange of prisoners, and each morning he would arise at daylight from his hard bunk and announce: "Boys, ze exchange he come today; zay tell me so last night!" and forthwith he would begin to pack up his scanty effects and hobble to the prison gate, where he would remain the greater portion of the day in expectation of being called to commence the glad journey to his sun-kissed Louisiana. This was his programme, without material variation, for several months. The poor old fellow finally died before the "exchange came," and sleeps in that silent camp, with thousands of his comrades, in the midst of a people who have no flowers to strew upon the rebel's grave.

It may be noted that quite an industry sprung up in the manufacture of gutta-percha rings and other trinkets, which went to swell the traffic of old Waddell.

About the only diversion afforded within the walls was in walking around the camp, and, thus engaged, could be seen thousands of aimless men, unless the desire to "kill time" be an aim, walking around and around the camp like tigers, bears, and lions in their cages.

The author cannot refrain from acknowledging the kindness of a fellow-prisoner, Mr. John D. Miller, of Victoria, Texas, who, though in a separate prison, managed to convey some of the desired checks to him. And, though lucre is not unwelcomed at any time, this certainly was the most heartily welcomed and thoroughly appreciated of any ever received, before or since.

Thus the winter passed. The spring came. Lincoln's brutal assassination startled the prisoners, and the surrender of Lee destroyed the last vestige of lingering hope. Applicants for the oath now became so numerous, and, as they were treated with such contempt by the "reb to the last," that it was deemed best to separate them, giving the rebs prison No. 3, and the "razor-backs," as the applicants for the oath were called, prison No. 2. About this time Colonel Hawkins, of Tennessee, gained access to prison No. 3, and made the boys a brief, but eloquent, "talk," concluding:

> Remain true to the cause of Dixie; and, if our worst fears are realised, we can be able to say with King Francis at Pavia, '*All is lost but honour.*'

This manly utterance was applauded by the ragged, half-starved patriots to the echo.

Finally, the "exchange came," though poor "Old Bragg" slept too soundly to hear the summons, and the prisoners were conveyed south in batches of 500. The squad in which the author left proceeded by rail to Cairo, and thence down the Mississippi River to New Orleans. At Cairo, the kind-hearted citizens vied with each other in their contributions to the necessities of the miserable Southerners.

Without disembarking at New Orleans at all, the prisoners were steamed back to Vicksburg, and here disembarked under the auspices of a negro guard. This was the most humiliating experience of the whole period of captivity. The noble ladies of Vicksburg interested themselves in ministering to the necessities of the Confederates. The Texans were especially indebted to Miss Nora Roach—whom to call an angel, is but to compliment the saintly host that ministers around the "great white throne." At Vicksburg, Ross' *miserables* were paroled, and soon *en route* for their Texan homes.

The Unionists, while heaping merited censure on the Confederate authorities for the maltreatment of Federal prisoners at Andersonville, and other Southern prisons, deny the charge of mistreatment of Confederate prisoners themselves. In support of what is here stated as being the rule at Camp Chase, from September, 1864, until May, 1865, the author prefers to any truthful Confederate there confined within the period specified. They could not have been treated worse and live, for many absolutely died of starvation. An exchange of prisoners was demanded in the interest of humanity.

The Washington administration refused to sign a cartel, because it would give the South what she most needed—men. The Confederacy was unable to properly feed her own soldiers in the field. The Washington administration were well advised of this fact, yet it allowed Union prisoners to die of ill-treatment, when one word pronounced by Lincoln and his advisers, would have freed them. Posterity will judge correctly who is responsible for the graves at Camp Chase, Camp Douglas, Rock Island, Andersonville, Richmond, and other pens North and South.

★★★★★★

Note. During the trying days in Camp Chase, there were some who never relaxed in their fealty to the South, and who never forgot that they were gentlemen. Among these it is a pleasure to name James Arnold, Sixth Texas Cavalry, now of Wartrace, Tennessee; James Crabtree, J. D. White, Perry Pirtle, William Fluellen, of the Third Texas Cavalry, and John D. Miller, of Victoria, Texas.

★★★★★★

*The South.*
*Victor M. Rose.*
*1.*
*She hath doff'd the weeds of her widowhood,*
*To resume the trappings of pride;*
*In the midst of the festive and gay she stood,*
*With the mien of a willing bride.*
*2*
*She hath smiled on the suit of a stranger knight*
*Whose progress admits of no pause;*
*But e'er in her heart a memorial light,*
*Burns on for the dear Lost Cause.*
*3*
*O, loyal and true in her heart of hearts,*
*As the fealty demanded above;*
*But the Union restored of segregate parts,*
*Must divide with the dead her love.*

The Lone Star Defenders

BATTLE FLAG OF THE THIRD TEXAS CAVALRY

# Contents

To
my comrades
Survivors of Ross' Brigade of Texas Cavalry
and
to our children and grandchildren
I affectionately dedicate
this Volume.

# Introduction

As my recollections of the war between the States, or the Confederate War, in which four of the best years of my life (May, 1861, to May, 1865) were given to the service of the Confederate States of America, are to be written at the earnest request of my children, and mainly for their gratification, it is, perhaps, proper to preface the recital by going back a few years in order to give a little family history.

I was born in what is now the suburbs of the town of Gurley in Madison County, Alabama, on the 9th day of November, 1834. My father, Samuel Boulds Barron, was born in South Carolina in 1793. His father, James Barron, as I understand, was a native of Ireland. My mother's maiden name was Martha Cotten, daughter of James Cotten, who was from Guilford County, North Carolina, and who was in the battle of Guilford Court House, at the age of sixteen. His future wife, Nancy Johnson, was then a young girl living in hearing of the battle at the Court House.

About the beginning of the past century, 1800, my Grandfather Cotten, with his wife, her brother Abner Johnson, and their relatives, Gideon and William Pillow, and their sister, Mrs. Dew, moved out from North Carolina into Tennessee, stopping in Davidson County, near Nashville. Later Abner Johnson and the Pillows settled in Maury County, near Columbia, and about the year 1808 my grandfather and his family came on to Madison County, Alabama, and settled at what has always been known as Cave Springs, about fifteen miles east or southeast from Huntsville. In the second war with Great Britain (the War of 1812) my Grandfather Cotten again answered the call to arms, and as a captain he served his country with notable gallantry.

It is like an almost forgotten dream, the recollection of my paternal grandmother and my maternal grandfather, for both of them died when I was a small child. My maternal grandmother, however, who lived to the age of eighty-seven years, I remember well. In my earliest recollection my father was a school-teacher, teaching at a village then called "The Section," afterwards "Lowsville," being now the town of Maysville, twelve miles east of Huntsville. He was well-educated and enjoyed the reputation of being an excellent teacher. He quit teaching, however, and settled on a small farm four miles east of Cave Springs, on what is known as the "Cove road," running from Huntsville to Bellefonte.

Here he died when I was about seven years of age, leaving my mother with five children: John Ashworth, a son by her first husband; my brother, William J. Barron, who now lives in Huntsville, Alabama; two sisters, Tabitha and Nancy Jane; and myself. About nine years later our mother died. In the meantime, our half-brother had arrived at man's estate and left home. Soon after our mother's death we sold the homestead, and each one went his or her way, as it were, the sisters living with our near-by relatives until they married. My brother and myself found employment in Huntsville and lived there. Our older sister and her husband came to Texas in about the year 1857, and settled first in Nacogdoches County. In the fall of 1859 I came to Texas, to bring my then widowed sister and her child to my sister already here. And so, as the old song went, "I am away here in Texas."

CHAPTER 1

# The Outbreak of the War

No, I am not going to write, or attempt to write, a history of the war, or even a detailed account of any campaign or battle in which I participated, but only mean to set forth the things which I witnessed or experienced myself in the four years of marching, camping, and fighting, as I can now recall them—only, or mainly, personal reminiscences. Incidentally I will give the names of my comrades of Company C, Third Texas Cavalry, and tell, so far as I can remember, what became of the individuals who composed the company. I will not dwell on the causes of the war or anything which has been so often and so well told relating thereto, but will merely state that I had always been very conservative in my feelings in political matters, and was so all through the exciting times just preceding the war while Abolitionism and Secession were so much discussed by our statesmen, orators, newspapers, and periodicals.

I had witnessed the Kansas troubles, which might be called a skirmish before the battle, with much interest and anxiety, and without losing faith in the ability and wisdom of our statesmen to settle the existing troubles without disrupting the government. But on my journey to Texas, as we glided down the Mississippi from Memphis to New Orleans, on board the *Lizzie Simmons*, a new and beautiful steamer, afterwards converted into a cotton-clad Confederate gunboat, we obtained New Orleans papers from an upriver boat. The papers contained an account of John Brown's raid on Harper's Ferry. I read this, and became a Secessionist. I saw, or thought I saw, that the storm was coming, that it was inevitable, and it seemed useless to shut my eyes longer to the fact.

The year 1860, my first in Texas, was a memorable one in several respects, not only to the newcomers but to the oldest inhabitant. The severest drouth ever known in eastern Texas prevailed until after the middle of August. It was the hottest summer ever known in Texas, the temperature in July running up to 112 degrees in the shade. It was a Presidential election year, and political excitement was intense. The Democrats were divided, while the Abolitionists had nominated Abraham Lincoln as their candidate for President, with a good prospect of electing him by a sectional vote. Several towns in Texas being almost destroyed by fire during the extreme heat of the summer, an impression became generally prevalent that Northern incendiaries were prowling through the State burning property and endeavouring to incite the negroes to insurrection.

The excitement, apprehension, unrest, and the vague fear of unseen danger pervading the minds of the people of Texas cannot be understood by persons who were not in the State at that time. The citizens organised patrol forces and armed men guarded the towns, day and night, for weeks. Every passing stranger was investigated and his credentials examined. The poor peddler, especially, was in imminent danger of being mobbed at any time on mere suspicion.

At the November election Abraham Lincoln was elected President. This was considered by the Secessionists as an overt act on the part of the North that would justify secession. I was out in the country when the news of the election came, and when, on my return, I rode into Rusk the Lone Star flag was floating over the court-house and Abraham Lincoln, in effigy, was hanging to the limb of a sweet gum tree that stood near the northwest corner of the court yard. From this time excitement ran high. Immediate steps were taken by the extreme Southern States to secede from the Union, an act that was consummated as soon as practicable by the assembling of State conventions and the passage of ordinances of secession. Now, too, volunteer companies began organising in order to be ready for the conflict which seemed to be inevitable.

We soon raised a company in Rusk for the purpose of drilling and placing ourselves in readiness for the first call for troops from Texas. We organised by electing General Joseph L. Hogg, father of Ex-Governor J. S. Hogg, as captain. The company was named "The Lone Star Defenders," for every company must needs have a name in those days. Early in 1861, however, when it appeared necessary to prepare for actual service, the company was reorganised and the gallant Frank M. Taylor made captain, as General Hogg was not expected to enter the army as captain. Several of the States had already seceded, the military posts in the South were being captured by the Confederates and Fort Sumter, in Charleston Harbour, was fired upon by our General Beauregard on the 12th day of April, 1861. The dogs of war were turned loose. War now became a stern reality, a war the magnitude of which no one then had any conception. President Lincoln's first call for volunteers was for ninety-day men, and the Confederate volunteers were mustered in for one year.

Having learned that Elkanah Greer, of Marshall, had been commissioned colonel and ordered to raise a regiment of Texas cavalry, we lost no time in reporting ourselves ready to make one company of the regiment, and soon received instructions to report at Dallas, on a certain day in June, when a regiment would be formed. So on Monday morning, June 10, in the year of our Lord, 1861, we were to leave, and did leave, Rusk for Dallas—and beyond, as the exigencies of the war might determine. The population of the town, men, women, and children, were on the streets, in tears, to bid us farewell. Even rough, hard-faced men whose appearance would lead one to believe they hadn't shed a tear since their boyhood, boo-hoo'd and were unable to speak the word "goodbye." This day of leave-taking was the saddest of the war to many of us.

After we had mounted our horses we assembled around the front of the old Thompson Hotel, which stood where the Acme Hotel now stands, when our old friend, General Hogg, standing on the front steps, delivered us a formal and a very tender farewell address. War was not unknown to him, for he had been a soldier in the early days of Texas, as well as a member of the Texas Congress in the days of the republic. He was a fine specimen of the best type of Southern manhood—tall, slender, straight as an Indian, and exceedingly dignified in his manner. As brave as "Old Hickory," he often reminded me of the pictures I had seen of General Jackson, and he certainly had many similar traits of character. We venerated, admired, and loved him, and he was warmly attached to the company. In his address he gave us much good advice, even to the details of mess duties and the treatment of our messmates. Among other things, he said:

> Don't ever jeer at or mock any of your comrades who cannot stand the fire of the enemy. Some of you, perhaps, will find yourselves unable to do so. Some men are thus constituted without knowing it, until they are tried. So you should be charitable towards such unfortunates.

Later I found these words of our old soldier friend to be true. This ceremony ended, we sadly moved off by twos, over the hill, and up the street leading into the Jacksonville road.

As we marched forward sadness was soon succeeded by merriment and good cheer. Some of the boys composed a little song, which was frequently sung by I. K. Frazer and others as we went marching on. It began:

*The Lone Star Defenders, a gallant little band,*
*On the tenth of June left their native land.*

Before leaving home we had spent two weeks in a camp of instruction, and learned something of the duties of camp life and the necessary art of rolling and unrolling our blankets. We camped the first night near Jorial Barnett's, between Jacksonville and Larissa. Two of the Barnett boys were going with us, and several from Larissa. When we reached Larissa next morning we there found a young man, Charley Watts, who was a bugler, and had been in the Federal Army, he said. He was willing and anxious to go with us, and we wanted him, as he was young and active, but he was afoot, and seemed to own nothing beyond his wearing apparel. So we appealed to the citizens, as a goodly number had gathered into the little village to see the soldiers pass, and in little more time than it takes to tell it, we had him rigged with horse, bridle, saddle, and blankets. Charley proved to be a fine bugler, the finest bugler I ever heard in either army, and he was a most gallant young fellow. We moved on, bidding farewell to Captain Taylor's noble and patriotic old mother, as we passed her residence.

Fearing we might be left out of the regiment, we dispatched Captain Taylor and one or two others well-mounted men to go ahead and secure and hold our place for us. The ladies of Cherokee County having presented us with a beautiful flag, this we unfurled and marched through the towns and villages along the way in great style and military pomp. At Kaufman we received quite an ovation. Arriving there about ten o'clock in the morning, we were met by a deputation of citizens, who invited us to dine at the hotel at the expense of the town. This was very reluctantly declined, for we were afraid of losing time. Poor fellows, we often regretted missing that good dinner, and we really had plenty of time, if we had only known it.

To show our appreciation of their hospitality we marched around the public square, displaying the flag and sounding the bugle. When we had arrived in front of a saloon we were halted and all invited to dismount and drink, without cost to us. We here spent perhaps an hour, during which time numbers of the boys entered stores to purchase small necessary articles, and in every instance pay was declined.

In due time we went into camp in a post oak grove two miles east of Dallas, a locality, by the way, which is now well within the city limits. And here we remained for some time.

Eight other organised companies were soon camped in different localities in the neighbourhood, but we were still one company short. However, as there were many men, including a large squad from Kaufman County, some from Cherokee and other counties, on the ground wishing to go with us, and who could not get into the organised companies because they were all full, they organised themselves into a tenth company, which completed the necessary number for the regiment.

We spent about four weeks in Dallas County, a delay caused in good part by the necessity of waiting for the arrival of a train from San Antonio carrying United States wagons and mules captured at that post by the Confederates. The time, however, was well spent in daily drills, in feeding, grazing and attending to our horses; and then, too, we were learning valuable lessons in camp life. While here we had plenty of rations for ourselves and plenty of forage for the horses.

The citizens of Dallas County, as far as we came in contact with them, were very kind to us. Our nearest neighbour was a German butcher by the name of Nusbauman. We used water from the well in his yard and were indebted to him and his family for many acts of kindness.

On one occasion Mrs. Nusbauman complained to Captain Taylor that one of his men had borrowed her shears to cut hair with, and would not bring them back. No, she did not know the name of the offender.

The captain then said, "*Madame*, do you know the man when you see him?"

"Oh, yes."

"Well, when he comes to draw water again you sprinkle flour on his back and I will find your shears."

In a few hours one of the men came out from the well with his back covered with flour—and the shears were promptly returned.

Our next nearest neighbours were a family named Sheppard, who lived a few hundred yards south of our camp, and whose kindness was unbounded. Their house was our hospital for the time we were in their vicinity, and the three young ladies of the family, Misses Jennie Wood, Maggie, and another, were unremitting in their attentions to the sick. On one damp, drizzly day when I had a chill they heard of it somehow, and in the afternoon two of them drove up in a buggy and called for me to go home with them, where I could be sheltered, as we yet had no tents. I went, of course, recovered in one day, convalesced in about three days, and reluctantly returned to camp. In an effort to do some washing for myself, I had lost a plain gold ring from my finger, a present from Miss Cattie Everett of Rusk, and Miss Jennie Wood Sheppard replaced it with one of her own. This ring was worn by me continually, not only durng the war, but for several years after its close.

I do not remember the date, but some day near the end of June "The Lone Star Defenders," that "gallant little band," were formally mustered into the service of the Confederate States of America, for one year. We were subjected to no physical examination, or other foolishness, but every fellow was taken for better or for worse, and no questions were asked, except the formal, "Do you solemnly swear," etc. The company was lettered "C," Greer's Regiment, Texas Cavalry— afterwards numbered and ever afterwards known as the Third Texas Cavalry. We were mustered in, officers and men, as follows:

Officers—Frank M. Taylor, captain; James J. A. Barker, first lieutenant; Frank M. Daniel, second lieutenant; James A. Jones, second lieutenant; Wallace M. Caldwell, orderly sergeant; John D. White, second sergeant; S. B. Barron, third sergeant; Tom Petree, fourth sergeant; William Pennington, first corporal; Thomas F. Woodall, second corporal; C. C. Acker, third corporal; P. C. Coupland, fourth corporal; Charles Watts, bugler; John A. Boyd, ensign.

Privates—Peter Acker, John B. Armstrong, David H. Allen, James M. Brittain, R. L. Barnett, James Barnett, Severe D. Box, A. A. Box, William P. Bowers, John W. Baker, C. C. Brigman, George F. Buxton, Jordan Bass, Carter Caldwell, William P. Crawley, A. G. Carmichael, A. M. Croft, James P. Chester, Leander W. Cole, James W. Cooper, William H. Carr, W. J. Davis, James E. Dillard, F. M. Dodson, John E. Dunn, O. M. Doty, H. H. Donoho, B. C. Donald, Stock Ewin, John J. Felps, I. K. Frazer, John Germany, Luther Grimes, E. M. Grimes, J. H. Gum, L. F. Grisham, W. L. Gammage, W. D. Herndon, J. R. Halbert, W. T. Harris, D. B. Harris, Thomas E. Hogg, John Honson, Warren H. Higginbotham, R. H. Hendon, William Hammett, James B. Hardgrave, Felix G. Hardgrave, R. L. Hood, William Hood, James Ivy, Thomas J. Johnson, J.

PETER F. ROSS
Major and Lieutenant-Colonel Sixth
Texas Cavalry

LIEUTENANT-COLONEL JILES S. BOGGESS
Third Texas Cavalry

H. Jones, John B. Long, Ben A. Long, George C. Long, R. C. Lawrence, John Lambert, J. B. Murphy, William P. Mosely, John Meyers, Harvey N. Milligan, W. C. McCain, G. A. McKee, W. W. McDugald,, Dan Mc-Caskill, Samuel W. Newberry, William A. Newton, George Noland, Baxter Newman, J. T. Park, T. A. Putnam, Lemon R. Peacock, W. T. Phillips, Lemuel H. Reed, T. W. Roberts, Cythe Robertson, Calvin M. Roark, John B. Reagan, A. B. Summers, John W. Smith, Cicero H. Smith, Rufus Smith, Sam E. Scott, J. R. Starr, James R. Taylor, Reuben G. Thompson, Dan H. Turney, Robert F. Woodall, Woodson O. Wade, F. M. Wade, E. S. Wallace, R. S. Wallace, John R. Watkins, C. C. Watkins, Joe L. Welch, Thomas H. Willson, N. J. Yates.

Total rank and file—112 men.

In addition to the above list of original members, the following named recruits were added to the company after we had lost several of our men by death and discharge:

A. J. Gray, Charles B. Harris, J. T. Halbert, John E. Jones, Wm. H. Kellum, W. S. Keahey, S. N. Keahey, J. D. Miller, T. L. Newman, T. L. Nosworthy, John W. Wade, Wyatt S. Williams, Eugene W. Williams.

Total—125 men enlisted in the company.

| | |
|---|---|
| Of these the killed numbered | 14 |
| Died of disease | 16 |
| Discharged | 31 |
| Commissioned officers resigned | 3 |
| Missing and never heard of | 2 |
| Deserted | 7 |
| Survived (commissioned and non-commissioned officers, 12; privates, 40) | 52 |
| | 125 |

Of these recruits, six, the first on the list, came to us in February and March, 1862; the next three joined us in April, 1862; the remaining four joined us in 1863, while we were in Mississippi.

The company consisted mainly of natives of the different Southern States, with a few native Texans. Aside from these we had Buxton, from the State of Maine; Milligan, from Indiana, and three foreigners, William Hood, an Englishman; John Dunn, Irish, and John Honson, a Swede. Milligan was a printer, and being too poor to buy his outfit when he joined us, he was furnished with horse and accoutrements by our friend, B. Miller, a German citizen of Rusk.

# CHAPTER 2

# Off for the Front

After the companies were mustered into the service the regiment was organised. Colonel Elkanah Greer was commissioned by the Confederate War Department. Walter P. Lane was elected lieutenant-colonel, and George W. Chilton, father of United States Senator Horace Chilton, was made major. M. D. Ecton, first lieutenant of Company B, was made adjutant, Captain ———— Harris, quartermaster, Jas. B. Armstrong, of Henderson, commissary, and our Dr. W. W. McDugald, surgeon.

Thus was organised the first regiment to leave the State of Texas, and one of the best regiments ever in the Confederate service. I would not say that it was the best regiment, as in my opinion the best regiment and the bravest man in the Confederate Army were hard to find. That is to say, no one regiment was entitled to be designated "the best regiment," as no one of our brave men could rightly be designated "the bravest man in the army." Napoleon called Marshal Ney *"the bravest of the brave,"* but no one could single out a Confederate soldier and truthfully say, "He is the bravest man in the army." It was unfortunately true that all our men were not brave and trustworthy, for we had men who were too cowardly to fight, and we had some men unprincipled enough to desert; but taken all in all, for gallantry and for fighting qualities under any and all circumstances, either in advance or retreat, the regiment deservedly stood in the front rank in all our campaigning.

The regiment was well officered, field staff, and line. Colonel Greer was a gallant man, but unfortunately his mind was too much bent on a brigadier's stars; Major Chilton, whenever an opportunity offered, showed himself to be brave and gallant; but Walter P. Lane, our lieutenant-colonel, was the life of the regiment during our first year's service. A more gallant man than he never wore a sword, bestrode a war horse, or led a regiment in battle. He was one of the heroes of San Jacinto, and a born soldier. In camps, in times when there was little or nothing to do, he was not overly popular with the men, but when the fighting time came he gained the admiration of everyone.

At last the long-looked-for train came—United States wagons drawn by six-mule teams, poor little Spanish or Mexican mules, driven by Mexicans. They brought us tents, camp kettles, mess pans and such things, and for arms, holster pistols. We were furnished with two wagons to the company and were given Sibley tents,—large round tents that would protect sixteen men with their arms and accoutrements,— a pair of holster pistols apiece, and a fair outfit of "cooking tricks." We were then formed into messes of sixteen men each, and each mess was provided with the Sibley tent, the officers being provided with wall tents. Fairly mounted, we were pretty well equipped now, our chief deficiency being the very poor condition of the mules and the lack of proper arms, for the men, in mustering, had gathered up shotguns, rifles, and any kind of gun obtainable at home, many of them being without a firearm of any kind.

A large number had had huge knives made in the blacksmith shops, with blade eighteen to twenty-four inches long, shaped something like a butcher's cleaver, keen-edged, with a stout handle, a weapon after the order of a Cuban machete. These were carried in leather scabbards, hung to the saddle, and with these deadly weapons the boys expected to ride through the ranks of the Federal armies and chop down the men right and left. Now, however, to this equipment were added the pair of holster pistols. These very large, brass-mounted, single-barrelled pistols—with barrels about a foot long—carried a large musket ball, and were suspended in holsters that fitted over the horn of the saddle, thus placing them in a convenient position for use. In addition to all this, every fellow carried a grass rope at least forty feet long and an iron stake pin. These latter were for staking out the horses to graze, and many was the untrained horse that paid dear for learning the art of "walking the rope," for an educated animal would never injure himself in the least.

All things being ready, we now started on our long march, accompanied by Captain J. J. Goode's battery, which had been organised at Dallas, to join General Ben McCulloch in northwestern Arkansas, where he, with what forces he had been able to gather, was guarding our Arkansas frontier. Leaving Dallas on the—day of July, we moved via McKinney and Sherman, crossing Red River at Colbert's ferry, thence by the overland mail route through the Indian Territory to Fort Smith, Ark., and beyond. We made moderate marches, the weather being very warm, and we then had no apparent reason for rapid movements.

When near McKinney we stopped two or three days. Here our man from the State of Maine began to give us trouble. When sober, Buxton was manageable and a useful man to the company, but when he was in liquor, which was any time he could get whisky, he was troublesome, quarrelsome, and dangerous, especially to citizens.

One afternoon Captain Taylor and myself rode into McKinney, where we found Buxton drunk and making trouble. The captain ordered him to camp, but he contumaciously refused to go. We managed to get him back to the rear of a livery stable, near a well, and Captain Taylor forced him down across a mound of fertilizer—holding him there. Then he ordered me to pour water on Buxton, which I did most copiously. I drew bucket after bucket of cold water from the well and poured it upon Buxton's prostrate, soldierly form, until he was thoroughly cooled and partially sobered, when the captain let him up and again ordered him to camp—and he went, cursing and swearing vengeance.

This man, after giving us a good deal of trouble from time to time until after the Battle of Elkhorn in the spring of 1862, was jailed in Fort Smith for shooting a citizen in the street, and here we left him and crossed the Mississippi River. He made his escape from jail and followed us to the State of Mississippi, when Lieutenant-Colonel Lane ordered him out of camp. He afterwards returned to Rusk, where he was killed one day by a gunshot wound, but by whom no one seemed to know.

We passed through Sherman early in the morning, and I stopped to have my horse shod, overtaking the command at Colbert's ferry in the afternoon, when they were crossing Red River. The day was fair, the weather dry and hot. The river, very low now, had high banks, and in riding down from the south side you came on to a wide sandbar extending to a narrow channel running against the north bank, where a small ferryboat was carrying the wagons and artillery across. A few yards above the ferry the river was easily fordable, so the horsemen had all crossed and gone into camp a mile beyond the river, as had most of the wagons. I rode to the other side and stopped on the north bank to watch operations.

All the wagons but one had been ferried over, and this last one had been driven down on the sandbar near the ferry landing, waiting for the boat's return, while two pieces of artillery were standing nearby on the sandbar. Suddenly I heard a roaring sound up the river, as if a wind storm was coming. I looked in that direction and saw a veritable flood rushing down like a mighty wave of the sea, roaring and foaming as it came. The driver of the team standing near the water saw it and instinctively began turning his team to drive out, but, realising that this would be impossible, he detached his mules and with his utmost efforts was only able to save the team, while every available man had to lend assistance in order to save the two pieces of artillery. In five minutes' time, perhaps, the water had risen fifteen to eighteen feet, and the banks were full of muddy, rushing water, and remained so as long as we were there. The wagon, which belonged to the quartermaster, was swept off by the tide and lost, with all its contents. It stood in its position until the water rose to the top of the cover, when it floated off.

After camping for the night, we moved on. As we were now in the Indian Territory, the young men were all on the look-out for the beautiful Indian girls of whom they had read so much, and I think some of them had waived the matter of engagement before leaving home until they could determine whether they would prefer marrying some of the pretty girls that were so numerous in this Indian country. We had not gone far on our march when we met a Chickasaw damsel. She was rather young in appearance, of medium height, black unkempt hair, black eyes, high cheekbones, and was bareheaded and bare-footed. Her dress was of some well-worn cotton fabric, of a colour hard to define, rather an earthy colour. In style it was of the extreme low neck and short kind, and a semi-bloomer. Of other wearing apparel it is unnecessary to speak, unless you wish a description of another Indian.

This one was too sensible to weight herself with a multiplicity of garments in July. She was a regular middle of the roader, as she stuck close to that part of the Territory strictly. As we were marching' by twos we separated and left her to that part of the highway which she seemed to like best. She continued her walk westwardly as we continued our march eastwardly, turning her head right and left, to see what manner of white soldiers the Confederate Government was sending out. This gave all an opportunity to glimpse at her charms. Modestly she walked along without speaking to any of us, as we had never been introduced to her. Only one time did I hear her speak a word, and that was apparently to herself. As Lieutenant Daniel passed her with his long sabre rattling, she exclaimed, in good English: "*Pretty white man!*—got big knife!"

As we went marching on the conversation became more general; that is, more was said about the beautiful country, the rich lands and fine cattle, and not so much about beautiful Indian girls. But every fellow kept his eye to the front, expecting we would meet scores of girls, perhaps hundreds, but all were disappointed, as this was the only full-blooded Indian we met in the highway from Colbert's ferry to Fort Smith. The fact is, the Indians shun white people who travel the main road. Away out in the prairie some two hundred yards you will find Indian trails running parallel with the road, and the Indians keep to these trails to avoid meeting the whites. If they chance to live in a hut near the road you find no opening toward the road, and, if approached, they will deny that they can speak English, when, in fact, they speak it readily and plainly.

One day I came up with one of our teamsters in trouble. He needed an axe to cut down a sapling, so I galloped back to an Indian's hut nearby, and as there was no enclosure, rode around to the door. The Indian came out and I asked him to lend me an axe a few minutes. He shook his head and said, "Me no intender," again and again, and this was the only word I could get out of him until I dismounted and picked up the axe, which was lying on the ground near the door. He then began, in good English, to beg me not to take his axe. I carried it to the teamster, however, but returned it to the Indian in a few minutes.

There are, or were then, people of mixed blood living along the road in good houses and in good style, where travellers could find entertainment. Numbers of these had small Confederate flags flying over the front gateposts—and all seemed to be loyal to our cause. Two young Choctaws joined one of our companies and went with us, one of them remaining with us during the war, and an excellent soldier he was, too.

At Boggy Depot the ladies presented us with a beautiful flag, which was carried until it was many times pierced with bullets, the staff shot in two, and the flag itself torn into shreds. Arriving at Big Blue River, we lost one or two horses in crossing, by drowning. But finally we reached Fort Smith, on a Saturday, remaining there until Monday morning.

While in the Choctaw Nation our men had the opportunity of attending an Indian war dance, and added to their fitness for soldiers by learning the warwhoop, which many of them were soon able to give just as real Indians do.

Fort Smith, a city of no mean proportions, is situated on the south bank of the Arkansas River, very near the line of the Indian Territory. Another good town, Van Buren, is situated on the north bank of the river, five miles below Fort Smith. While we were at Fort Smith orders came from General McCulloch, then in southwest Missouri, to cut loose from all encumbrances and hasten to his assistance as rapidly as possible, as a battle was imminent. Consequently, leaving all trains, baggage, artillery, all sick and disabled men and horses to follow us as best they could, we left on Monday morning in the lightest possible marching order, for a forced march into Missouri. Our road led across Boston Mountain, through Fayetteville and Cassville, on towards Springfield.

Crossing the river at Van Buren, we began the march over the long, hot, dry, and fearfully dusty road. As we passed through Van Buren I heard "Dixie" for the first time, played by a brass band. Some of the boys obtained the words of the song, and then the singers gave us "Dixie" morning, noon, and night, and sometimes between meals. This march taxed my physical endurance to the utmost, and in the evening, when orders came to break ranks and camp, I sometimes felt as if I could not march one mile farther. The first or orderly sergeant and second sergeant having been left behind with the train, the orderly sergeant's duties fell upon me, which involved looking after forage and rations, and other offices, after the day's march.

On Saturday noon we were at Cassville, Mo. That night we marched nearly all night, lying down in a stubble field awhile before daylight, where we slept two or three hours. About ten o'clock Sunday morning, tired, dusty, hungry, and sleepy, we went into camp in the neighbourhood of General McCulloch's headquarters, in a grove of timber near a beautiful, clear, little stream. The first thing we did was to look after something to eat for ourselves and horses, as we had had no food since passing Cassville, and only a very light lunch then. The next thing was to go in bathing, and wash our clothes, as we had had no change, and then to get some longed-for sleep. In the meantime, Colonel Greer had gone up to General McCulloch's headquarters to report our arrival.

I was not present at the interview, but I imagine it ran something like this, as they knew each other well. Colonel Greer would say: "Hello, General! How do you do, sir? Well, I am here to inform you that I am on the ground, here in the enemy's country, with my regiment of Texas cavalry, eleven hundred strong, well mounted and armed to the teeth with United States holster pistols, a good many chop knives, and several double-barrelled shotguns. Send Lyons word to turn out his Dutch regulars, Kansas jayhawkers and Missouri home guards, and we'll clean 'em up and drive 'em from the State of Missouri."

"Very well, very well, Colonel; go back and order your men to cook up three days' rations, get all the ammunition they can scrape up in the neighbourhood, and be in their saddles at eleven o'clock tonight, and I will have them at Dug Springs at daylight tomorrow morning and turn them loose on the gentlemen you speak of."

Anyway, whatever the interview was, we had barely stretched out our weary limbs and folded our arms to sleep when the sergeant-major, that fellow that so often brings bad news, came tripping along through the encampment, hurrying from one company's headquarters to another, saying: "Captain, it's General McCulloch's order that you have your men cook up three days' rations, distribute all the ammunition they can get and be in their saddles, ready to march on the enemy, at eleven o'clock tonight."

Sleep? Oh, no! Where's the man who said he was sleepy? Cook three days' rations? Oh, my! And not a cooking vessel in the regiment! But never mind about that, it's a soldier's duty to obey orders without asking questions. I drew and distributed the flour and meat, and left the men to do the cooking while I looked after the ammunition. Here the men learned to roll out biscuit dough about the size and shape of a snake, coil it around a ramrod or a small wooden stick, and bake it before the fire.

This Sunday afternoon and night, August 4, was a busy time in our camp. Some were cooking the rations, some writing letters, some one thing, and some another; all were busy until orders came to saddle up. We were camped on the main Springfield road, and General Lyon, with his army, was at Dug Springs, a few miles farther up the same road. We were to march at eleven o'clock and attack him at daylight Monday morning. There already had been some skirmishing between our outposts and his scouts. We had never been in battle, and we were nervous, restless, sleepless for the remainder of the day and night after receiving the orders.

Some of the things that occurred during the afternoon and night

212

would have been ludicrous had not the whole occasion been so serious. In my efforts to obtain and distribute all the ammunition I could procure I was around among the men from mess to mess during all this busy time. Scores of letters were being written by firelight to loved ones at home, said letters running something like this:

Camp ———, Mo., Aug. 4, 1861.

My Dear ———:

We arrived at General McCulloch's headquarters about 10 a. m. today, tired, dusty, hungry, and sleepy, after a long, forced march from Fort Smith, Ark. We are now preparing for our first battle. We are under orders to march at eleven o'clock to attack General Lyon's army at daylight in the morning. All the boys are busy cooking up three days' rations. I am very well. If I survive tomorrow's battle I will write a postscript, giving you the result. Otherwise this will be mailed to you as it is.

Yours affectionately,

——— ———

Numbers of the boys said to me: "Now, Barron, if I am killed tomorrow please mail this letter for me." One said: "Barron, here is my gold watch. Take it, and if I am killed tomorrow please send it to my mother." Another said: "Barron, here is a gold ring. Please take care of it, and if I am killed tomorrow I want you to send it to my sister." Another one said: "Barron, if I am killed tomorrow I want you to send this back to my father." At last it became funny to me that each seemed to believe in the probability of his being killed the next day, and were making nuncupative wills, naming me as executor in every case, without seeming to think of the possibility of *my* being killed. During the remainder of our four years' service, with all the fighting we had to do, I never again witnessed similar preparations for battle.

# CHAPTER 3

# Our First Battle

Well, eleven o'clock came, we mounted our horses and rode out on the road to Dug Springs, under orders to move very quietly, and to observe the strictest silence—and, when necessary, we were not even to talk above a whisper. The night was dark and we moved very slowly. About three o'clock in the morning an orderly came down the column carrying a long sheet of white muslin, tearing off narrow strips, and handing them to the men, one of which each man was required to tie around his left arm. From our slow, silent movement I felt as if we were in a funeral procession, and the white sheet reminded me of a winding sheet for the dead. As we were not uniformed these strips were intended as a mark of the Confederate soldiers, so we might avoid killing our own men in the heat and confusion of battle.

At daylight we were halted and informed that General Lyon's forces had withdrawn from Dug Springs. After some little delay our army moved on in the direction of Springfield, infantry and artillery in the road and the cavalry on the flank,—that is, we horsemen took the brush and marched parallel with the road, in order to guard against ambush and surprises. We moved slowly in this manner nearly all day without coming up with the enemy—at noon we took a short rest, and dinner, and here many of us consumed the last of our three days' rations.

Along in the afternoon, as we were considerably ahead of the infantry, we filed into the road and were moving slowly along, when suddenly we heard firing in our rear. Of course every one supposed the infantry had come up with the enemy and they were fighting. We were immediately halted, and Lieutenant-Colonel Lane came galloping back down the column shouting, "Turn your horses around, men, and go like h—l the other way." Instantly the column was reversed, and the next minute we were following Colonel Lane at full speed. For two or three miles we ran our tired horses down the dusty road, only to learn that some of the infantry, who had stopped to camp, were firing off their guns simply to unload them.

We then retraced our steps and moved on up the road to Wilson's Creek, nine miles from Springfield, and camped on the ground that was to be our first battlefield.

We came to the premises of a Mr. Sharp, situated on the right hand or east side of the road. Just beyond his house, down the hill, the creek crossed the road and ran down through his place, back of his house and lot. On the left hand or west side of the road were rough hills covered with black jack trees, rocks, and considerable underbrush. Before coming to his dwelling we passed through his lot gates down in the rear of his barn and premises, and camped in a strip of small timber growing along the creek. In the same enclosure, in front and south of us, was a wide, uncultivated field, with a gradual upgrade all the way to the timber back of the field. Here we lived on our meagre rations for several days. In the meantime, the whole army then in Missouri, including General Sterling Price's command, was concentrated in the immediate vicinity.

One day during the week we heard that a company of Missouri home guards, well-armed, were at Little York, a small village six or seven miles west from our camps. Now, the home guards were Northern sympathisers, so one afternoon our company and another of the regiment, by permission, marched to Little York on a raid, intending to capture the company and secure their arms. We charged into the town, but the enemy we sought was not there, and we could find but four or five supposed members of the company. Anyway, we chased and captured every man in town who ran from us, including the surgeon of the command, who was mounted on a good horse, being the only man mounted in the company. Several of the boys had a chase after him, capturing his horse, which was awarded to John B. Long, who, however, did not enjoy his ownership very long, for the animal was killed in our first battle. We then searched for arms, but found none.

In one of the storehouses we found a large lot of pig lead, estimated at 15,000 pounds. This we confiscated for the use of the Confederate Army. In order to move it, we pressed into service the only two wagons we could find with teams, but so overloaded one of them that the wheels broke down when we started off. We then carried the lead on our horses,—except what we thought could be hauled in the remaining wagon,—out some distance and hid it in a thicket of hazelnut bushes. We then, with our prisoners and the one wagon, returned to camp. When the prisoners were marched up to regimental headquarters Lieutenant-Colonel Lane said, "Turn them out of the lines and let them go. I would rather fight them than feed them."

This raiding party of two companies that made the descent upon Little York was commanded by Captain Taylor, and the raid resulted, substantially, as I have stated. Nevertheless, even the next day wild, exaggerated stories of the affair were told, and believed by many members of our own regiment as well as other portions of the army, and in Victor Rose's *History of Ross's Brigade*, the following version of the little exploit may be read:

> Captain Frank Taylor, of Company C, made a gallant dash into a detachment guarding a train loaded with supplies for Lyon, routing the detachment, taking a number of prisoners, and capturing the entire train.

And "the historian" was a member of Company A, Third Texas Cavalry! From this language one would infer that Captain Taylor, alone and unaided, had captured a supply train with its escort!

On Friday, August 9, the determination was reached to move on Springfield and attack General Lyon. We received orders to cook rations, have our horses saddled and be ready to march at nine o'clock p. m. At nine o'clock we were ready to mount, but by this time a slight rain was falling, and the night was very dark and threatening. We "stood to horse," as it were, all night, waiting for orders that never came. The infantry, also under similar orders, slept on their arms. Of course our men, becoming weary with standing and waiting, lay down at the feet of their horses, reins in hand, and slept. Daylight found some of the men up, starting little fires to prepare coffee for breakfast, while the majority were sleeping on the ground, and numbers of our horses, having slipped their reins from the hands of the sleeping soldiers, were grazing in the field in front of the camp.

Captain Taylor had ridden up to regimental headquarters to ask for instructions or orders, when the enemy opened fire upon us with a battery stationed in the timber just back of the field in our front, and the shells came crashing through the small timber above our heads. And as if this were a signal, almost instantly another battery opened fire on General Price's camp. Who was responsible for the blunder that made it possible for us to be thus surprised in camp, I cannot say. It was said that the pickets were ordered in, in view of our moving, at nine o'clock the night before, and were not sent out again; but this was afterwards denied. If we had any pickets on duty they were certainly very inefficient. But there is no time now to inquire of the whys and wherefores.

Captain Taylor now came galloping back, shouting: "Mount your horses and get into line!" There was a hustling for loose horses, a rapid mounting and very soon the regiment was in line by companies in the open field in front of the camps. It was my duty now to "form the company," the same as if we were going out to drill; that is, beginning on the right, I rode down the line requiring each man to call out his number, counting, one, two, three, four; one, two, three, four, until the left was reached. This gave every man his place for the day, and every man was required to keep his place. If ordered to march by twos, the horses were wheeled to the right, number 2 forming on the right of number 1; if order, to for fours, numbers 3 and 4 moved rapidly up on the right of numbers 1 and 2, and so on. This being done in the face of the aforesaid battery, with no undue haste, was quite a trying ordeal to new troops who had never before been under fire, but the men stood it admirably.

As soon as we were formed we moved out by twos, with orders to cross the Springfield road to the hills beyond, where General Ben McCulloch's infantry, consisting of the noble Third Louisiana and the Arkansas troops, some three thousand in all, were hotly engaged with General Lyon's command. General Lyon was personally in front of General Sterling Price's army of Missouri State Guards, being personally in command of one wing of the Federal Army (three brigades), and Sigel, who was senior colonel, commanded the other wing (one brigade). General McCulloch was in command of the Confederate troops and General Price of the Missourians.

We moved out through Mr. Sharp's premises as we had come in, but coming to the road we were delayed by the moving trains and the hundreds of unarmed men who were along with General Price's army, rushing in great haste from the battlefield. The road being so completely filled with the mass of moving trains and men rushing pell-mell southward, it cost us a heroic effort to make our way across. In this movement the rear battalion of the regiment, under Major Chilton, was cut off from us, and while they performed good service during part of the day, we saw no more of them until the battle ended.

By the time we crossed the road the battle had become general, and the fire of both artillery and musketry was constant and terrific. The morning was bright and clear and the weather excessively warm, and as we had been rushed into battle without having time to get breakfast or to fill our canteens, we consequently suffered from both hunger and thirst. After crossing the road, we moved up just in the rear of our line of infantry, and for five hours or more were thus held in reserve, slowly moving up in column as the infantry lines surged to the left, while the brave Louisiana and Arkansas troops stood their ground manfully against the heavy fire of musketry and artillery.

As our position was farther down the hill than that occupied by the line of infantry, we were in no very great danger, as the enemy's shot and shell usually passed over us, but, nevertheless, during the whole time the shots were passing very unpleasantly near our heads, with some damage, too, as a number of the men were wounded about the head. One member of Company C was clipped across the back of the neck with a minie ball. After hours of a most stubborn contest our infantry showed some signs of wavering. Colonel Greer at this critical moment led us up rapidly past their extreme left,—had us wheel into line, and then ordered us to charge the enemy's infantry in our front. With a yell all along the line, a yell largely mixed with the Indian war-whoop, we dashed down that rough, rocky hillside at a full gallop right into the face of that solid line of well-armed and disciplined infantry.

It was evidently a great surprise to them, for though they emptied their guns at us, we moved so rapidly that they had no time to reload, and broke their lines and fled in confusion. The battery that had been playing on our infantry all day was now suddenly turned upon us, otherwise we could have ridden their infantry down and killed or captured many of them, but we were halted, and moved out by the left flank from under the fire of their battery. Their guns were now limbered up and moved off, and their whole command was soon in full retreat towards Springfield. During the engagement General Nathaniel Lyon had been killed, and the battle, after about seven hours' hard fighting, was at an end. The field was ours.

Thus ended our first battle. Would to God it had been our last, and the last of the war! General McCulloch called it "The Battle of Oak Hill." but the Federals called it "The Battle of Wilson's Creek."

This first battle was interesting to me in many ways. I had been reading of them since my childhood and looking at pictures of battlefields during and after the conflict, but to see a battle in progress, to hear the deafening roar of artillery, and the terrible, ceaseless rattle of musketry; to see the rapid movements of troops, hear the shouts of men engaged in mortal combat, and to realise the sensation of being a participant, and then after hours of doubtful contest to see the enemy fleeing from the field—all this was grand and terrible. But while there is a grandeur in a battle, there are many horrors, and unfortunately the horrors are wide-spread—they go home to the wives, fathers, mothers, and sisters of the slain.

After the battle was over we were slowly moving in column across the field unmolested, but being fired on by some of the enemy's sharpshooters, who were keeping up a desultory fire at long range, when young Mr. Willie, son of Judge A. H. Willie, a member of Company A, which was in advance of us, came riding up the column, passing us. I was riding with Captain Taylor at the head of our company, and just as Willie was passing us a ball from one of the sharpshooters' rifles struck him in the left temple, and killed him. But for his position the ball would have struck me in another instant.

After all the Federals capable of locomotion had left the field, we were moved up the road on which Sigel had retreated, as far as a mill some five miles away, where we had ample witness of the execution done by our cavalry—dead men in blue were strewn along the road in a horrible manner. On returning, late in the afternoon, we were ordered back to the camp we had left in the morning. As we had witnessed the grandeur of the battle, Felps and myself concluded to ride over the field and see some of its horrors. So we rode leisurely over the field and reviewed the numerous dead, both men and horses, and the few wounded who had not been carried to the field hospitals. General Lyon's body had been placed in an ambulance by order of General McCulloch, and was on its way to Springfield, where it was left at the house of Colonel Phelps. His horse lay dead on the field, and every lock of his grey mane and tail was clipped off by our men and carried off as souvenirs.

Further on we found one poor old Missouri home guard who was wounded. He had dragged himself up against a black jack tree and was waiting patiently for some chance of being cared for. We halted and were speaking to him, when one of his neighbours, a Southern sympathiser, came up, recognised him and began to abuse him in a shameful manner. "Oh, you d——d old scoundrel," he said, "if you had been where you ought to have been, you wouldn't be in the fix you are in now." They were both elderly men, and evidently lived only a few miles away, as the Southerner had had time to come from his home to see the result of the battle.

I felt tempted to shoot the old coward, and thus put them on an equality, and let them quarrel it out. But as it seemed enough men had been shot for one day, we could only shame him and tell him that if he had had the manliness to take up his gun and fight for what he thought was right, as his neighbour had done, he would not be there to curse and abuse a helpless and wounded man, and that he should not insult him or abuse him any more while we were there. We continued our ride until satisfied for that time, and for all time, so far as I was concerned, with viewing a battlefield just after the battle, unless duty demands it.

Our train came up at night, bringing us, oh, so many letters from our post office at Fort Smith, but the day's doings, the fatigue, hunger, thirst, heat, and excitement had overcome me so completely that I opened not a letter until the morning. Reckoning up the day's casualties in Company C, we found four men and fifteen horses had been shot; Leander W. Cole was mortally wounded, and died in Springfield a few days later; J. E. Dillard was shot in the leg and in allusion to his long-leggedness it was said he was shot two and one half feet below the knee and one and one half feet above the ankle; T. Wiley Roberts was slightly wounded in the back of the head, and P. C. Coupland slightly wounded.

Some of the horses were killed and others wounded. Roger Q. Mills and Dr. —— Malloy, two citizens of Corsicana, were with us in this battle, having overtaken us on the march, and remained with us until it was over, then returning home. Roger Q. Mills was afterwards colonel of the Tenth Texas Infantry. Dr. Malloy was captain of a company, and fell while gallantly fighting at the head of his company in one of the battles west of the Mississippi River.

I will not attempt to give the number of troops engaged, as the official reports of the battle written by the officers in command fail to settle that question. General Price reported that he had 5221 effective men with 15 pieces of artillery. General McCulloch's brigade has been estimated at 4000 men, with no artillery, and this officer's conclusion was that the enemy had 9000 to 10,000 men, and that the forces of the two armies were about equal. The Federal officers in their reports greatly exaggerated our strength, and, I think, greatly underestimated theirs, especially so since, General Lyon being killed, it devolved upon the subordinates to make the reports.

Major S. D. Sturgis, who commanded one of Lyon's brigades, says their 3700 men attacked an army of 23,000 rebels under Price and McCulloch, that their loss in killed, wounded, and missing was 1235, and he supposed the rebel loss was 3000. Major J. M. Schofield, General Lyon's adjutant, says their 5000 men attacked the rebel army of 20,000. General Fremont, afterwards, in congratulating the army on their splendid conduct in this battle, says their 4300 men met the rebel army of 20,000. They give the organisation of their army without giving the numbers. General Lyon had four brigades, consisting, as they report, of six regiments, three battalions, seven companies, 200 Missouri home guards and three batteries of artillery, many of their troops being regulars.

Their army came against us in two columns. General Lyon, with three brigades and two batteries, Totten's six pieces, and Dubois, with four, came down the Springfield road and attacked our main army in front. Colonel Franz Sigel, with one brigade and one light battery, marched down to the left, or east of the road and into our rear, and attacked the cavalry camp with his artillery, as has already been stated.

Poor Sigel! it would be sufficient to describe his disastrous defeat to merely repeat their official reports. But I would only say that his battery was lost and his command scattered and driven from the field in utter confusion and demoralization in the early part of the day and that it was followed some five miles by our cavalry and badly cut up, he himself escaping capture narrowly by abandoning his carriage and colours and taking to a cornfield. It was said by the Federals that he reached Springfield with one man before the battle was ended. But the forces led by the brave and gallant Lyon fought bravely. The losses are given officially as follows: Federals: killed, 223; wounded, 721; missing, 291. Total, 1235. Confederates: killed, 265; wounded, 800; missing, 30. Total, 1095.

# CHAPTER 4

# The War in Missouri

A battle—or danger—will often develop some characteristics that nothing else will bring out.

One, Gum, was a shabby little man, mounted on a shabby little mustang pony; in fact, his horse was so shabby that he would tie him, while we were at Dallas, away off in the brush in a ravine and carry his forage half a mile to feed him rather than have him laughed at. Gum was a Missourian, and got into the company somehow, with his fiddle, and aside from his fiddling he was of little use in camps. During the time we were kept slowly moving along in the rear of our infantry, engaged mainly in the unprofitable business of dodging balls and shells that were constantly whizzing near our heads, Captain Taylor was very anxious that his company should act well under fire and would frequently glance back, saying: "Keep your places, men." Gum, however, was out of place so often he finally became personal, "Keep in your place, Gum."

At this Gum broke ranks and came trotting up on his little pony, looking like a monkey with a red cap on, for, having lost his hat, he had tied a red cotton handkerchief around his head. When opposite the captain he reined up, and with a trembling frame and in a quivering voice, almost crying, he said: "Captain, I can't keep my place. I am a coward, and I can't help it."

Captain Taylor said, sympathetically: "Very well, Gum; go where you please."

It so happened that a few days later we passed his father's house, near Mount Vernon, and the captain allowed him to stop and remain with his father. And thus he was discharged. At this stage of the war we had no army regulations, no "red tape" in our business. If a captain saw fit to discharge one of his men he told him to go, and he went

222

without reference to army headquarters or the War Department. I met Gum in November, fleeing from the wrath of the home guards, as a man who had been in the Confederate Army could not live in safety in Missouri.

One of our men, in the morning when I was forming the company, was so agitated that it was a difficult matter to get him to call his number. During the day a ball cut a gash about skin deep and two inches in length across the back of his neck, just at the edge of his hair. As a result of this we were two years in getting this man under fire again, though he would not make an honest confession like Gum, but would manage in some mysterious way to keep out of danger. When at last we succeeded in getting him in battle at Thompson's Station in 1863, he ran his iron ramrod through the palm of his right hand and went to the rear. Rather than risk himself in another engagement he deserted, in the fall of that year, and went into the Federal breastworks in front of Vicksburg and surrendered. This man was named Wiley Roberts.

Captain Hale, of Company D, was rather roughhewn, but a brave, patriotic old man, having not the least patience with a thief, a coward, or a braggart. While he had some of the bravest men in his company that any army could boast of, he had one or two, at least, that were not among these, as the two stalwart bullies who were exceedingly boastful of their prowess, of the ease with which Southern men could whip Northerners, five to one being about as little odds as they cared to meet. This type of braggart was no novelty, for every soldier had heard that kind of talk at the beginning of the war. While we were moving out in the morning when Sigel's battery was firing and Captain Hale was coolly riding along at the head of his company, these two men came riding rapidly up, one hand holding their reins while the other was pressed across the stomach, as if they were in great misery, saying, when they sighted their commander: "Captain Hale, where must we go? we are sick."

Captain Hale looked around without uttering a word for a moment, his countenance speaking more indignation than language could express. At last he said, in his characteristic, emphatic manner: "Go to h—l, you d——d cowards! You were the only two fighting men I had until now we are in a battle, and you're both sick. I don't care when you go."

Other incidents could be given where men in the regiment were tried and found wanting, but the great majority were brave and gallant men who never shirked duty or flinched from danger.

An instance of the opposite character may be told of Joe Welch. Joe was a blacksmith, almost a giant in stature. Roughly guessing, I would say he was six feet two inches in height, weighing about 240 pounds, broad-shouldered, raw-boned, with muscles that would laugh at a sledge. Joe had incurred the contempt of the company by acting in a very cowardly manner, as they thought, in one or two little personal affairs before we reached Missouri. But when we went into battle Joe was there, as unconcerned and cool, apparently, as if he was only going into his shop to do a day's work; and when we made our charge down that rough hillside when the enemy's bullets were coming as thick as hailstones, one of Joe's pistols jolted out of its holster and fell to the ground. Joe reined in his horse, deliberately dismounted, recovered the pistol, remounted, and rapidly moved up to his place in the ranks. Those who witnessed the coolness and apparent disregard of danger with which he performed this little feat felt their contempt suddenly converted into admiration.

Another one of our men was found wanting, but through no fault of his own, as he was faithful as far as able. This was William Hood. Hood was an Englishman, quite small, considerably advanced in years, destitute of physical endurance and totally unfit for the hardships of a soldier's life. He was an old-womanish kind of a man, good for cooking, washing dishes, scouring tin plates, and keeping everything nice around the mess headquarters, but was unsuited for any other part of a soldier's duty. Hood strayed off from us somehow during the day, and for some part of the day was a prisoner, losing his horse, but managed to get back to camp afoot at night, very much depressed in spirits.

The next morning, he was very proud to discover his horse grazing out in the field two or three hundred yards from the camp. He almost flew to him, but found he was wounded. He came back to Captain Taylor with a very sad countenance, and said: "Captain Taylor, me little 'orse is wounded right were the 'air girth goes on 'im." The wound was only slight and as soon as the little 'orse was in proper traveling condition little Hood was discharged and allowed to return home.

As already stated, we returned late in the evening to the camp we had left in the morning to rest and sleep for the night, for after the excitement of the day was over bodily fatigue was very much in evidence. Our train came up about nightfall, but as I was very tired, and our only chance for lights was in building up little brush fires, the opening of my letters was postponed until the bright Sunday morning, August 11, especially as my mail packet was quite bulky. One large envelope from Huntsville, Ala., contained a letter and an exquisite little Confederate flag some ten or twelve inches long. This was from a valued young lady friend who, in the letter, gave me much good advice, among other things warning me against being shot in the back. And I never was.

During the day the command marched into Springfield, to find that the Federal Army had pushed forward Saturday night. They had retreated to Rolla, the terminus of the railroad, and thence returned to St. Louis, leaving us for a long time in undisputed possession of southwest Missouri, where we had but little to do for three months but gather forage and care for our horses and teams and perform the routine duties incident to a permanent camp.

From Springfield we moved out west a few miles, camping for a few days at a large spring called Cave Spring. Here several of our men were discharged and returned home. Among them James R. Taylor, brother of Captain, subsequently Colonel, Taylor of the Seventeenth Texas Cavalry, who was killed at the Battle of Mansfield, La.

Southwest Missouri is a splendid country, abounding in rich lands, fine springs of pure water, and this year, 1861, an abundant crop of corn, oats, hay, and such staples had been raised. Nevertheless, a very unhappy state of things existed there during the war, for the population was very much divided in sentiment and sympathy—some being for the North and some for the South, and the antagonism between the factions was very bitter. Indeed, so intense had the feeling run, the man of one side seemed to long to see his neighbour of the other side looted and his property destroyed. Men of Southern sympathy have stealthily crept into our camps at midnight and in whispers told us where some Union men were to be found in the neighbourhood, evidently wishing and expecting that we would raid them and kill or capture, rob, plunder or do them damage in some terrible manner.

Such reporters seemed to be disappointed when we would tell them that we were not there to make war on citizens, and the Union men themselves seemed to think we were ready to do violence to all who were not loyal to the Southern Confederacy. When we chanced to go to one of their houses for forage, as frequently happened, we could never see the man of the house, unless we caught a glimpse of him as he was running to some place to hide, and no assurance to his family that we would not in any manner mistreat him would overcome the deep conviction that we would. This bitter feeling and animosity among the citizens grew to such intensity, as the war advanced, that life became a misery to the citizen of Missouri.

We moved around leisurely over the country from place to place, foraging and feeding a few days here and a few days there, and in the early days of September, passing by way of Mount Vernon and Carthage, we found ourselves at Scott's Mill, on Cowskin River, near the border of the Cherokee Nation. At Mount Vernon we witnessed a farce enacted by Company D. Dan Dupree was their first lieutenant, and a very nice, worthy fellow he was, too, but some of his men fell out with him about some trivial matter, and petitioned him to resign, which he did. Captain Hale, supposing possibly they might also be opposed to him, and too diffident to say so, he resigned too, and the other officers followed suit, even down to the fourth and last corporal, and for the time the company was without an officer, either commissioned or non-commissioned.

At this early stage of the war, for an officer to resign was a very simple and easy thing. He had only to say publicly to his company, "I resign," and it was so. The company was now formed line to prepare for the election of officers, and the mode of procedure was as follows: The candidates would stand a few paces in front of the line, their back to the men. The men were then instructed to declare their choice, by standing behind him, one behind the other, and when all votes were counted the result was declared. The outcome on this occasion was that Captain Hale and all the old officers were re-elected, except Dupree. Later in the year members of Company A petitioned their captain to resign, but he respectfully declined, and though many of his men were very indignant, we heard no more of petitioning officers to resign.

While we were camped on the beautiful little Cowskin River measles attacked our men, and we moved up to Carthage, where we remained about eight weeks, during which time we passed through a terrible scourge of measles and typhoid fever. As a result, Company C lost five men, including Captain Taylor. Fortunately, we were in a high, healthy country, and met in Carthage a warm-hearted, generous people. In addition to our competent and efficient surgeon and his assistant during this affliction, we had a number of good physicians, privates in the regiment, who rendered all the assistance in their power in caring for the sick. The court house was appropriated as a hospital, and, soon filled to its capacity, the generous citizens received the sick men into their houses and had them cared for there. How many of the regiment were sick at one time I do not know, but there were a great many; the number of dead I never knew. Our surgeon went from house to house visiting and prescribing for the sick both day and night, until it seemed sometimes as if he could not make another round.

The day after we reached Carthage I was taken down with a severe case of measles, and glided easily into a case of typhoid fever. Dr. McDugald went personally to find a home for me, and had me conveyed to the residence of Mr. John J. Scott, a merchant and farmer, where for seven weeks I wasted away with the fever, during all of which time I was as kindly and tenderly cared for by Mrs. Scott as if I had been one of her family; and her little girl Olympia, then about eleven years old, was as kind and attentive to me as a little sister could have been. My messmate and chum, Thomas J. Johnson, remained with me to wait on me day and night during the entire time, and Dr. McDugald, and also Dr. Dan Shaw, of Rusk County, were unremitting in their attention. A. B. Summers took charge of my horse, and gave him better attention than he did his own. Captain Taylor was also very low at the same time, and was taken care of at the house of Colonel Ward. The fever had left me and I had been able to sit up in a rocking chair by the fire a little while at a time for a few days, when General Fremont, who had been placed in command of the Federal Army in Missouri, began a movement from Springfield in the direction of Fayetteville, Ark., and we were suddenly ordered away from Carthage.

All the available transportation had to be used to remove the sick, who were taken to Scott's Mill. A buggy being procured for Captain Taylor and myself, our horses were hitched to it and, with the assistance of Tom Johnson and John A. Boyd, we moved out, following the march of the command into Arkansas. The command moved south, *via* Neosho and Pineville, and dropped down on Sugar Creek, near Cross Hollows, confronting General Fremont, who soon retired to Springfield, and never returned. At Sugar Creek we stole Ben A. Long out of camp, and made our way to Fayetteville, where we stopped at the house of Martin D. Frazier, by whose family we were most hospitably treated. Here Captain Taylor relapsed, and died.

Captain Francis Marion Taylor was a noble, brave, and patriotic man, and we were all much grieved at his death. He had been at death's door in Carthage, and Dr. McDugald then thought he was going to die, telling him so, but he rallied, and when we left there he was much stronger than I was, being able to drive, while that would have been impossible with me. When he relapsed he did not seem to have much hope of recovering, and after the surgeon, at his own request, had told him his illness would terminate fatally, he talked very freely of his approaching death. He had two little children, a mother, and a mother-in-law, Mrs. Wiggins, all of whom he loved very much, and said he loved his mother-in-law as much as he loved his mother. He gave me messages for them, placed everything he had with him (his horse, gold watch, gold rings, sword, and his trunk of clothes) in my charge, with specific instructions as to whom to give them—his mother, his mother-in-law and his two little children.

I continued to improve, but recovered very slowly indeed, and remained in Fayetteville until the early days of December. The regiment was ordered to go into winter quarters at the mouth of Frog Bayou, on the north bank of the Arkansas River, twelve miles below Van Buren, and when they had passed through Fayetteville on their way to the designated point, I followed, as I was now able to ride on horseback. Cabins were soon erected for the men and stalls for the horses, and here the main command was at home for the winter. I was furloughed until March 1, but as the weather was fine I remained in the camp for two weeks before starting on the long home journey to Rusk. Many other convalescents were furloughed at this time, so finally, in company with Dr. W. L. Gammage, who, by the way, had been made surgeon of an Arkansas regiment, and two or three members of Company F who lived in Cherokee County, I started to Rusk, reaching the end of my journey just before Christmas.

My first night in Cherokee County was spent at the home of Captain Taylor's noble mother, near Larissa, where I delivered her son's last messages to her, and told her of his last days. The next day I went on to Rusk and delivered the messages, horse, watch, etc., to the mother-in-law and children. Mr. Wiggins's family offered me a home for the winter, and as I had greatly improved and the winter was exceedingly mild, I spent the time very pleasantly until ready to return to the army. Among other things I brought home the ball that killed Leander Cole, and sent it to his mother.

## CHAPTER 5

# The War in Missouri—Continued

In the latter part of February, 1862, I left Rusk in company with Tom Hogg, John Germany, and perhaps one or two more of our furloughed men, for our winter quarters on the Arkansas River. We crossed Red River and took the road running along the line between Arkansas and the Indian Territory to Fort Smith. After crossing Red River, we began meeting refugees from Missouri and north Arkansas, on their way to Texas, who told us that our army was moving northward, and a battle was expected very soon. This caused us to push on more rapidly, as we were due to return March 1, and were anxious to be in our places with the command. When we reached Van Buren we learned that our whole army was in motion, that a battle was imminent and might occur any day.

By this time the weather had grown quite cold, and leaving Van Buren at 9 a. m., we had to cross Boston Mountain, facing a north wind blowing snow in our faces all day. Nevertheless, we slept fifty miles from there that night, camping with some commissary wagons on the road, a few miles from Fayetteville. Here we learned that the army was camped along the road between there and Fayetteville. The next morning, we started on at a brisk gait, but before we could pass the infantry they were filing into the road. We took to the brush and galloped our horses about six miles and overtook the Third Texas, which was in the advance, now passing out of the northern suburbs of Fayetteville, and found Company C in the advance guard on the Bentonville road.

We advanced slowly that day, without coming in contact with the enemy, and camped that night at Elm Springs, where the snow fell on us all night. Of course we had no tents, but slept on the ground without shelter. This seemed pretty tough to a fellow who, except for a few fine days in December, had not spent a day in camp since September, during all that time occupying warm, comfortable rooms. Up to this time I had never learned to sleep with my head covered, but finding it now necessary, I would first cover my head and face to keep the snow out, stand that as long as I could, then throw the blanket off, when the snow would flutter down in my face, chilling me so that I could not sleep. So between the two unpleasant conditions I was unable to get any rest at all.

Sometime before daybreak we saddled up and moved on, the snow being three or four inches deep, and early in the morning we passed the burning fires of the Federal pickets. By nine o'clock the storm had passed, the sun shining brightly, and about ten o'clock we came in sight of Bentonville, a distance said to be two miles. We could plainly see the Federal troops moving about the streets, their bright guns glistening in the sunshine, afterwards ascertained to have been Sigel's column of General Curtis' army. We were drawn up in line and ordered to prepare for a charge.

To illustrate what a magic influence an order to charge upon the enemy has, how it sends the sluggish blood rushing through the veins and livens up the new forces, I will say that while we were standing in line preparing to charge those fellows, I was so benumbed with cold that I could not cap my pistols. I tried ever so hard to do so, but had my life depended upon it I could not have succeeded. We were thrown into columns of fours and ordered to charge, which we did at a brisk gallop, and before we had gone exceeding one-half mile I had perfect use of my hands, was comfortably warm, and did not suffer in the least with cold at any time during the rest of the day.

We charged into the town, but the enemy had all moved out. I suppose it was the rear of the command that we had seen moving out. That afternoon we were ambushed by a strong force, and were fired on in the right flank from a steep, rough hill. We were ordered to charge, which order we attempted to obey by wheeling and charging in line up a hill so steep and rough that only a goat could have made any progress, only to find our line broken into the utmost confusion and under a murderous fire of infantry and artillery from an invisible enemy behind rocks and trees. In the confusion I recognised the order "dismount and fall into line! "I dismounted, but when I fell into what I supposed was going to be the line I found Lieutenant J. E. Dillard and J. B. Murphy, "us three, and no more." While glancing back I saw the regiment was charging around on horseback, while the captains of companies were shouting orders to their men in the vain endeavour to get them into some kind of shape.

In the meantime, the bullets were coming thick around us three dismounted men, knocking the bark from the hickory trees in our vicinity into our faces in a lively manner. Finally concluding we could do no good without support, we returned to our horses, mounted, and joined the confusion, and soon managed to move out of range of the enemy's guns. Brave old Captain Hale, very much chagrined and mortified by this affair, considered the regiment disgraced, and said as much in very emphatic, but not very choice, English.

I do not remember the precise language he used, but he was quoted as saying: "This here regiment are disgraced forever! I'd 'a' rather died right thar than to a give airy inch!" I do not know how many men we lost in this affair, but Vic. Rose says ten killed and twenty wounded. I remember that Joe Welch was wounded in the thigh, but I do not remember any other casualty in Company C. This was reckoned as the first day of the three days' Battle of Elkhorn Tavern, or Pea Ridge.

General Earl Van Dorn had taken command of the entire army on March 2, and conducted the remainder of the campaign to its close. General Price's division consisted of the Missouri troops. General McCulloch was placed in command of the infantry of his old division, consisting of the Third Louisiana, commanded by Colonel Louis Hebert (pronounced Hebair), and the Arkansas infantry, and General James McIntosh, who had just been promoted to brigadier-general, commanded the cavalry. Brigadier-General Samuel R. Curtis, who commanded the Federal Army in our front, was concentrating his forces near Elkhorn Tavern and Pea Ridge, near the Arkansas and Missouri line.

After the ambush and skirmish alluded to above, General Sigel moved on northward with his command and we moved on in the same direction, and near nightfall camped by the roadside. Here, as we had neither food for man nor forage for beast, I started out to procure a feed of corn for my horse, if possible, riding west from camp, perhaps five miles, before I succeeded. For a while at first I searched corncribs, but finding them all empty I began searching under the beds, and succeeded in obtaining fifteen or twenty ears. Part of this I fed to my horse, part of it I ate myself, and carried part of it on for the next night.

We were now near the enemy. Leaving camp about two hours before daylight, we made a detour to the left, passed the enemy's right flank, and were in his rear near Pea Ridge. General Price, accompanied by General Van Dorn, passed around his left and gained his rear near Elkhorn Tavern, where General Van Dorn established his headquarters. About 10.30 a. m. we heard General Price's guns, as he began the attack. Our cavalry was moving in a southeasterly direction toward the position of General Sigel's command, and near Leetown, in columns of fours, abreast, the Third Texas on the right, then the Sixth and Ninth Texas, Brook's Arkansas battalion, and a battalion of Choctaw Indians, forming in all, five columns. Passing slowly through an open field, a Federal light battery, some five hundred or six hundred yards to our right, supported by the Third Iowa Cavalry, opened fire upon our flank, killing one or two of our horses with the first shot.

The battery was in plain view, being inside of a yard surrounding a little log cabin enclosed with a rail fence three or four feet high. Just at this time one of General McCulloch's batteries, passing us on its way to the front, was halted, the Third Texas was moved up in front of it, and were ordered to remain and protect it. Lieutenant-Colonel Walter P. Lane rode out to the front, facing the enemy's battery, and calling to Charley Watts, he said: "Come here, Charley, and blow the charge until you are black in the face."

With Watts by his side blowing the charge with all his might, Lane struck a gallop, when the other four columns wheeled and followed him, the Texans yelling in the usual style and the Indians repeating the warwhoop, dashing across the field in handsome style. The Federal cavalry charged out and met them, when a brisk fire ensued for a few minutes; but, scarcely checking their gait, they brushed the cavalry, the Third Iowa, aside as if it was chaff, charged on in face of the battery, over the little rail fence, and were in possession of the guns in less time than it takes to tell the story.

In this little affair twenty-five of the Third Iowa Cavalry were killed and a battery captured, but I do not know how many of the gunners were killed. The Choctaws, true to their instinct, when they found the dead on the field, began scalping them, but were soon stopped, as such savagery could not be tolerated in civilized warfare. Still a great deal was said by the Federal officers and newspapers about the scalping of a few of these men, and it was reported that some bodies were otherwise mutilated. Colonel Cyrus Bussey of the Third Iowa certified that he found twenty-five of his men dead on the field, and that eight of these had been scalped.

General McCulloch's infantry and artillery soon attacked General

Sigel's command in our front, and the engagement became general all along the line. The roar of artillery and the rattle of musketry were terrific all day until dark, with no decisive advantage gained on either side. The Third Texas was moved up behind Pea Ridge, dismounted, and placed in line of battle just behind the crest of the ridge, to support our infantry, a few hundred yards in front of us, with orders not to abandon the ridge under any circumstances. Here we remained until late in the afternoon without further orders, in no particular danger except from the shells from the enemy's artillery that came over the ridge and fell around us pretty constantly.

Generals McCulloch and McIntosh had both been killed early in the day, and Colonel Louis Hebert, who was senior colonel and next in rank, had been captured. All this was unknown to us, and also unknown to General Van Dorn, who was with General Price near Elkhorn Tavern, two or three miles east of our position. Late in the afternoon Colonel Greer sent a courier in search of General McIntosh or General McCulloch, to ask for instructions, or orders, and the sad tidings came back that they were both killed; nor could Colonel Hebert be found.

The firing ceased at night, but we remained on the field, uncertain as to the proper thing to do, until a courier who had been sent to General Van Dorn returned about 2 a. m., with orders for all the forces to move around to General Price's position. When this was accomplished it was near daylight, and we had spent the night without sleep, without rations, and without water. General Curtis, perhaps discovering our movement, was also concentrating his forces in General Price's front.

The Confederates made an attack on the enemy early in the morning, and for an hour or two the firing was brisk and spirited, but as our men were starved out and their ammunition about exhausted, they were ordered to cease firing. As the Federals also ceased firing, the forces were withdrawn quietly and in an orderly manner from the field, and we moved off to the south, moving east of General Curtis, having passed entirely around his army.

The number of forces engaged in this battle were not definitely given. General Van Dorn in his report stated that he had less than 14,000 men, and estimated the Federal force at from 17,000 to 24,000, computing our loss at 600 killed and wounded and 200 prisoners, a total of 800. General Curtis reported that his forces engaged consisted of about 10,500 infantry and cavalry, with 49 pieces of artillery, and his statement of losses, killed, wounded, and missing adds up a total of 1384. The future historian, the man who is so often spoken of, is going to have a tough time if he undertakes to record the truths of the war. When commanding officers will give some facts and then round up their official reports with fiction, conflicts will arise that, it appears to me, can never be reconciled. A private soldier or a subordinate officer who participates in a battle can tell little about it beyond what comes under his personal observation, which is not a great deal, but he is apt to remember that little very distinctly.

In reference to the close of the battle, General Curtis among other things said: "Our guns continued sometime after the rebel fire ceased and the rebels had gone down into the deep caverns through which they had begun their precipitate flight. Finally, our firing ceased." Speaking of the pursuit he says:

General Sigel also followed in this pursuit towards Keetsville . . . General Sigel followed some miles north towards Keetsville, firing on the retreating force that ran that way.

Then adds:

The main force took the Huntsville road which is directly south.

This is true. Now, I dare say, there never was a more quiet, orderly, and uninterrupted retreat from a battlefield. The Third Texas was ordered to cover the retreat, and in order to do this properly we took an elevated position on the battlefield, where we had to remain until our entire army moved off and everybody else was on the march and out of the way. The army moved out, not precipitately, but in a leisurely way, not through "deep caverns," but over high ground in plain view of the surrounding country. Company C was ordered to take the position of rear guard, in rear of the regiment.

The regiment finally moved out, Company C waiting until it had gone some distance, when the company filed into the road and moved off. And then James E. Dillard and the writer of this remained on the field until the entire Confederate army was out of sight. During all this time not a Federal gun was fired, not a Federal soldier came in view. Nor were we molested during the entire day or night, although we moved in a leisurely way all day, and at night Company C was on picket duty in the rear until midnight.

Keetsville is a town in Missouri north of the battlefield. Sigel, it was stated, "followed some miles north towards Keetsville, firing on the retreating force that ran that way." There were about twenty-four pieces of our artillery that got into the Keetsville road through mistake; they were without an escort, entirely unprotected. After we had gone about three days' march, leaving Huntsville to our left and Fayetteville to the right, the Third Texas was sent in search of this artillery, and, after marching all night and until noon next day, passing through Huntsville, we met them, and escorted them in. They had not been fired on or molested in the least. The Federal officers, however, were not chargeable with all the inaccuracies that crept into official reports.

General Van Dorn in his report of this campaign, says:

On the 6th we left Elm Springs for Bentonville. . . . . I therefore endeavoured to reach Bentonville, eleven miles distant, by rapid march, but the troops moved so slowly that it was 11 a. m. before the leading division (Price's)—reached the village, and we had the mortification to see Sigel's division, 7000 strong, leaving it as we entered.

Now, as I have already stated, the Third Texas was in advance, and we saw Sigel leaving Bentonville long before 11 a. m., and Price's division never saw them in Bentonville nor anywhere else that day. General Curtis reported that two of his divisions had just reached his position, near Pea Ridge, when word came to him that General Sigel, who had been left behind with a detachment of one regiment, was about to be surrounded by a "vastly superior force," when these two divisions marched rapidly back and with infantry and artillery checked the rebel advance, losing twenty-five men killed and wounded. So this was the force that ambushed us, and according to this account, Sigel moved out of Bentonville in the morning with one regiment, instead of 7000 men. So the reader of history will never know just how much of fiction he is getting along with the "history."

Leaving the battlefield in the manner stated, we moved very slowly all day. In fact, fatigue, loss of sleep, and hunger had rendered a rapid movement impossible with the infantry. Our men were so starved that they would have devoured almost anything. During the day I saw some of the infantry men shoot down a hog by the side of the road, and, cutting off pieces of the meat, march on eating the raw bloody pork without bread or salt. The country through which we were marching was a poor, mountainous district, almost destitute of anything for the inhabitants to subsist upon, to say nothing of feeding an army. Stock of any kind appeared to be remarkably scarce. J. E. Dillard managed to get a small razor-back pig, that would weigh perhaps twenty-five pounds, strapped it on behind his saddle and thus carried it all day. When we were relieved of picket duty and went into camp at midnight, he cut it up and divided it among the men. I drew a shoulder-blade, with perhaps as much as four ounces of meat on it. This I broiled and ate without salt or bread.

We continued the march southward, passing ten or twelve miles east of Fayetteville. About the fourth day we had been resting, and the commissary force was out hustling for something to eat, but before we got any rations the Third Texas was suddenly ordered to mount immediately and go in search of our missing artillery. This was in the afternoon, perhaps four o'clock. Moving in a northeasterly direction, we marched all night on to the headwaters of White River, where that stream is a mere creek, and I do not think it would be an exaggeration to say that we crossed it twenty times during the night. About 10 a. m. we passed through Huntsville, county seat of Madison County, a small town having the appearance of being destitute of everything.

By this time the matter of food had become a very serious question, and we appeared to be in much greater danger of dying from starvation in the mountains of northern Arkansas than by the enemy's bullets. Our belts had been tightened until there was no relief in that, and, as if to enhance my own personal suffering, the tantalizing fact occurred to me that I was treading my native heath, so to speak, for I am a native of Madison County, and Huntsville had been my home for years, where to enjoy three squares a day had been an unbroken habit of years. But today I was literally starving in the town of Huntsville, County of Madison, aforesaid, and not a friendly face could I see, nor could a morsel of bread be procured for love or patriotism. Passing onward two or three miles, and having learned that the guns were coming, we rested, and privately made details to scour the country and beg for a little food "for sick and wounded men."

Tom Johnson went out for our mess, and the sorrowful tales that were told in behalf of the poor sick and wounded soldiers we were hauling along in ambulances, with nothing with which to feed them, would have melted a heart of stone. The ruse was a success, as the details came in at night with divers small contributions made from scant stores for "the poor sick and wounded men," which were ravenously consumed by the well ones. The artillery shortly afterwards came up and was escorted by us to the command. Camping that night a few miles from Huntsville, the artillery had taken the wrong road as it left the battlefield, had gone up into Missouri, and had had a long circuitous drive through the mountains, but otherwise they were all right.

After we returned with the guns, the army moved on southward. When we were again in motion, as there was no further apprehension of being followed by the enemy, hunger having nearly destroyed my respect for discipline, I left the column by a byroad leading eastwardly, determined to find something to eat. This proved a more difficult errand than I had expected, for the mountaineers were very poor and apparently almost destitute of supplies. I had travelled twelve or fifteen miles when I rode down the mountain into a little valley, at the head of Frog Bayou, coming to a good log house owned and occupied by a Mr. Jones, formerly of Jackson County, Alabama, and a brother of Hosea, Allen, William, and Jesse Jones, good and true men, all of whom I knew.

If he had been my uncle I could not have been prouder to find him. Here I got a good square meal for myself and horse, seasoned with a good hearty welcome. This good, true old man was afterwards murdered, as I learned, for his loyalty to the Confederate cause. After enjoying my dinner and a rest, I proceeded on my way, intending to rejoin the command that evening; but, missing the road they were on, I met the regiment at our old winter quarters. Thus about the middle of March the Third Texas Cavalry was again housed in the huts we had erected on the bank of the Arkansas River. I do not know the casualties of the regiment, but as far as I remember Company C had only one man, Jos. Welsh, wounded, and one man, Orderly Sergeant W. M. Caldwell, captured. But as the prisoners were exchanged, our captured men soon returned to us.

Thus ended a short campaign which involved much suffering to me, as well as others, and was the beginning of trouble which nearly cost me my life, a trouble which was not fully recovered from until the following winter. When I was taken with measles in Missouri, the disease affected my bowels, and they became ulcerated, and all through the long spell of typhoid fever and the very slow convalescence this trouble was very hard to control. When I left Rusk to return to the army I was apparently well, but having been comfortably housed all winter was not in proper condition to enter such a campaign at this season of the year. Before leaving winter quarters the men were ordered to prepare ten days' rations, and when we overtook the command at Fayetteville they had been out nearly that length of time,

CAPTAIN D. R. GURLEY
Sixth Texas Cavalry, A. A. G. Ross' Brigade

FRANK M. TAYLOR
First Captain of Company C, Third Texas Cavalry

and rations were already growing scarce. We furloughed men and a number of recruits who had accompanied us to join the command were not here to draw or prepare rations, and our only chance for a living was to share rations with our comrades, who were as liberal and generous as they could be, but they were not able to do much.

From the time I overtook the command until we got back to winter quarters was about ten days, and the few days we were in winter quarters were spent in preparing to cross the Mississippi River. For the first four or five days I managed to procure, on an average, about one biscuit per day; for the other five days we were fortunate to get anything at all to eat, and usually got nothing. We were in the snow for two days and nights, and in a cold, drenching rain one night. On the 7th it was impossible to get a drink of water, to say nothing of food and sleep, and from the time the firing began in the morning until the next morning we could get no water, although we were intensely thirsty. While at winter quarters I had a chill, and started down grade in health, a decline in physical condition that continued until I was apparently nearly dead.

In December parts of our cavalry regiments went with Colonel James McIntosh into the Indian Territory to suppress Hopothlaohola, an ex-chief of the Creek Nation, who, with a considerable band of disaffected followers, was making trouble, and part of the Third Texas went on this expedition. They had a battle with the Indians in the mountains on the headwaters of Chustenala Creek, defeated and scattered the warriors, captured their squaws, ponies, and negroes, scattering them so effectually that we had no further trouble with them.

# CHAPTER 6

# The Siege of Corinth

Captain Frank M. Taylor having died. First Lieutenant J. J. A. Barker was promoted to captain and Private James E. Dillard was promoted to second lieutenant. After remaining at our winter quarters for a few days, resting and feeding up, we started on our long eastward journey, leaving the wounded and sick in charge of Dr. I. K. Frazer. We moved down on the north side of the Arkansas River, stopping two or three days opposite Little Rock. During our stay here I availed myself of the opportunity of seeing the capital of the State. From Little Rock we crossed the country to Duvall's Bluff on White River, where the men were requested to dismount, send their horses back to Texas, and go afoot for a time. This they agreed to without a murmur, on the promise that, at a proper time, we should be remounted.

On this march from Arkansas River to White River we crossed grand prairie, and, though I had often heard of these great stretches of dead level country, had never seen them. I do not know the distance that we marched in this grand prairie, but it was a good many miles, as we entered it early in the morning one day and had to camp in it that night, and for almost the whole distance water stood on the ground to the depth of about two or three inches, and it was a difficult matter to find dry ground enough to camp on at night.

Men haying been detailed to take our horses back to Texas, the animals were prepared for the journey, each detailed man having to manage a number of horses; and to do this they tied the reins of one horse to the tail of another, each man riding one horse and guiding the leader of the others, strung out in pairs behind him. As they were recrossing the grand prairie the buffalo-gnats attacked the horses, stampeding them and scattering them for many miles over the country, and were with much difficulty recaptured.

We waited several days at Duvall's Bluff for transportation to Memphis, Tenn., on our way to Corinth, Miss. General Joseph L. Hogg, who had been commissioned brigadier-general, accompanied by his staff, came to us here, with orders to take command of a brigade, including the Third Texas Cavalry at Memphis. General Hogg's staff was composed of civilians who had never seen service in the army, and this proved to be an unfortunate time of the year for men not inured to camp life to go into active service. His staff consisted of William T. Long, quartermaster; Daniel P. Irby, commissary; H. H. Rogers, of Jefferson, usually called General Rogers, ordnance officer; in addition, there were E. C. Williams, John T. Decherd, and H. S, Newland.

After several days' waiting a steamboat came up the river, landing at the Bluff, and we were crowded upon it for our journey down White River into the Mississippi and up to Memphis, and it was hard to realise that the booming, navigable river we were now on was the same stream we had forded so many times in the mountains of northern Arkansas on the night we went in search of our lost artillery. When we got on the Mississippi we found it very high, numbers of houses along the banks being surrounded by water up to the front doorsteps, where numerous small skiffs could be seen moored. These skiffs furnished the residents their only means of going from house to house.

Arriving at Memphis, we marched away up Poplar Street to the suburbs, and camped in a grove, where we remained several days, spending the time in preparation for the move to Corinth, Miss. Here General Hogg took formal command of his brigade, and, having told me that he wanted Tom Johnson and myself at his headquarters, he had us detailed,—Tom to the ordnance department and me in the quartermaster's department, while John A. Boyd was detailed to work in the commissary department.

Word having finally come for us to proceed to Corinth, we were crowded into a train on the Memphis & Charleston Railroad, *en route* to that city. On this train, as conductor, I found my former friend and schoolmate, William Wingo. The trip to Corinth was a very slow and tedious one, the train being loaded down with troops and supplies, and unfortunately had lost so much time it had to be run very carefully and make numerous stops. In consequence of this, some of our over-suspicious "patriots" went to General Hogg and implied that the enemy had forces but a short distance north of us and that the slow running and the many stoppages of the train was done evidently through treachery, and that the plan apparently was to give the enemy an opportunity to capture the train with the men and munitions on board.

I had been riding on a rear platform, conversing with Mr. Wingo, when I proceeded to General Hogg's coach, and found him considerably excited. In answer to my inquiry he told me what had been intimated and said the suggestion, he thought, was a plausible one, and that he had about determined to order the train forward at all hazards. He was rather an irritable man, and his suspicions were easily aroused. I endeavoured to quiet him, and did so for a time, by explaining the situation, and pointed out the danger we would be in of colliding with some other train unless the utmost caution was used, as was being done; and finally told him that I had known the conductor since he was a small boy, had gone to school with him, and was sure there was no treachery in him.

It was not a great while, however, before others came around with similar evil suspicions, until the general was wrought up to such a pitch that he peremptorily ordered the train run through to Corinth, regardless of consequences, else some dire calamity would overtake every person in charge of it. Well, we made the rest of the journey in very good time, at the risk of many lives, but fortunately without accident. For this our friend and new brigadier-general was on the next day ordered under arrest by General Beauregard. But nothing more ever came of it.

After dragging along for more than thirty hours over a distance ordinarily made in six or seven, we finally disembarked, in the middle of the night, on the north side of the railroad, about two miles west of Corinth. So here we were, without horses, to confront new conditions, under new commanders, constrained to learn the art of war in a different arm of the service, and to drill, to march, and fight as infantry.

The next morning after our arrival I mounted the quartermaster's horse, and rode into town, which was my duty as the quartermaster's right-hand man, to procure forage for our stock—that is, for the regimental and brigade headquarters horses, artillery horses and the wagon teams. I found the road leading from our camp to town almost impassable owing to the mud, impassable even for a good horse and rider, and utterly and absolutely impassable for a wagon at all, as the best team we had could not have drawn an empty wagon over the road.

I found Corinth all aglitter with brass buttons and gold lace, the beautiful Confederate uniform being much in evidence everywhere. I never had seen anything like it before.

The Battle of Shiloh had been fought while we were on the steamer between Duvall's Bluff and Memphis, General Albert Sidney Johnston had been killed, and the army under General Beauregard had fallen back to Corinth, and the town was literally alive with officers and soldiers. There were more headquarters, more sentinels, and more red tape here than I had ever dreamed of. I had not seen uniformed officers or men west of the Mississippi River, and had known nothing of red tape in the army. Knowing nothing of the organisation of the army beyond our own brigade, I had everything to learn in reference to the proper quartermaster, forage master, and master of transportation, as I must needs have railroad transportation for my forage.

So beginning at the top, I made my way to General Beauregard's headquarters; from there I was directed to division headquarters; thence to a quartermaster; and from one quartermaster to another, until I had about done the town—and finally found the right man. One lesson learned not to be gone over. Finding there was no difficulty in getting forage delivered in Corinth, I had now to hunt up the master of transportation and satisfy him of the impossibility of hauling it on wagons. Owing to the immense business just then crowding the railroad and the scarcity of rolling stock, it was really a difficult matter to get the transportation; but by dint of perseverance in the best persuasive efforts I could bring to bear, I succeeded in having one day's rations sent out by rail. The next day the same thing as to transportation had to be gone over, and the next, and the next, and each succeeding day it became more difficult to accomplish, until a day came when it was impossible to get the forage hauled out at all.

I rode back to camp and notified the battery and the different headquarters that I would issue forage in Corinth, which would have to be brought out on horseback. All accepted the situation cheerfully except Rogers, who didn't seem to like me, and I suppose it was because I called him *Mr.* Rogers, instead of General Rogers, as others did. He went directly to General Hogg and said: "I think that fellow Barron should be required to have the forage hauled out."

General Hogg said:

I do not think you should say a word, sir; you have been trying for a week to get a carload of ammunition brought out and have failed. This is the first day Barron has failed to get the forage brought out; if you want your horses to have corn, send your servant in after it.

I had no further trouble with Mr. Rogers.

I cannot remember exactly the time we spent at Corinth. It was from the time of our landing there until about the 29th day of May, say six or seven weeks; but to measure time by the suffering and indescribable horrors of that never-to-be-forgotten siege, it would seem not less than six or seven months. From the effects of malaria, bad water, and other combinations of disease-producing causes, our friends from home soon began to fall sick, and, becoming discouraged, the staff officers began to resign and leave the service. Rogers, I believe, was the first to go. He was soon followed by the quartermaster and commissary, and soon all the gentlemen named as coming to the front with General Hogg we're gone, except John T. Decherd, who had been made quartermaster in place of William T. Long, resigned. I bought Long's horse and rigging, and Decherd and myself continued to run that department for a time, and Tom Johnson was made ordnance officer in place of Rogers, resigned. General Hogg, being stricken down with disease, was removed to the house of a citizen two or three miles in the country, where he was nursed by his faithful servant Bob, General W. L. Cabell meantime being placed in command of the brigade. General Hogg died a few days later—on the day of the Battle of Farmington.

The following "pathetic story of Civil War times "having been published in the Nashville (Tenn.) *Banner, Youth's Companion,* Jacksonville (Tex.) *Reformer,* and perhaps many other papers, I insert it here in order to give its correction a sort of permanent standing:

### A Soldier's Grave

A pathetic story of Civil War times is related to the older people of Chester County in the western part of Tennessee by the recent death of ex-Governor James S. Hogg of Texas. Some days after the battle of Shiloh, one of the decisive and bloody engagements of the war, fought on April 6-7, 1862, a lone and wounded Confederate soldier made his way to a log cabin located in the woods four miles west of Corinth, Miss., and begged for shelter and food. The man was weak from hunger and loss of blood, and had evidently been wandering through the woods of the sparsely settled section for several days after the battle.

The occupants of the cottage had little to give, but divided this little with the soldier. They took the man in and administered to his wants as best they could with their limited resources. They were unable to secure medical attention, and the soldier, already emaciated from the lack of food and proper attention, gradually grew weaker and weaker until he died. Realising his approaching end, the soldier requested that his body be buried in the wood near the house, and marked with a simple slab bearing his name, "General J. L. Hogg, Rusk, Texas."

The request was complied with, and in the years that passed the family which had so nobly cared for this stranger moved away, the grave became overgrown with wild weeds, and all that was left to mark the soldier's resting-place was the rough slab. This rotted by degrees, but was reverently replaced by some passer-by, and in this way the grave was kept marked; but it is doubtful if the few people who chanced to pass that way and see the slab ever gave a thought to the identity of the occupant of the grave, until after the election of Hon. James S. Hogg to the governor-ship of the State of Texas. Then someone of Chester County who had seen the grave wrote Governor Hogg concerning the dead soldier. In a short time, a letter was received, stating that the soldier was Governor Hogg's father, and that he entered the Confederate army when the war first broke out, and had never been heard of by relatives or friends.

After more correspondence Governor Hogg caused the grave to be enclosed by a neat iron fence, and erected a handsome plain marble shaft over the grave. This monument bears the same simple inscription which marked the rough slab which had stood over the grave of one of the South's heroic dead.

Conceding the truth of the statement that General J. L. Hogg, of Rusk, Texas, died at a private house four miles west of Corinth, Miss., in the spring of 1862, was buried nearby, and that his grave has been properly marked by his son, ex-Governor James S. Hogg, not a word of truth remains in the story, the remainder being fiction pure and simple, and the same may be refuted by a simple relation of the facts and circumstances of General Hogg's brief service in the Confederate army and his untimely death—facts that may easily be verified by the most creditable witnesses.

Joseph L. Hogg was appointed brigadier-general by the Confederate War Department in February, 1862. When his commission came he was ordered to report for duty at Memphis, Tenn., where he would be assigned to the command of a brigade of Texas troops. After the Battle of Elkhorn, a number of Texas regiments were ordered to cross the Mississippi River, among them the Third and Tenth Texas Cavalry—Company C of the Third and Company I of the Tenth were made up at Rusk. General Hogg's oldest son, Thomas E. Hogg, was a private in Company C, and these two regiments formed part of the brigade.

General Hogg met the Third Texas at Duvall's Bluff on White River, where we dismounted, sent horses home, and went by steamer to Memphis, accompanied by General Hogg. (The Battle of Shiloh was fought while we were on this trip.) After the delay incident to the formation of the brigade, getting up necessary supplies, etc., we were transported by rail, in command of General Hogg, to Corinth, or rather we were dumped off on the side of the railroad some two or three miles west of that town. Here General Hogg remained in command of his brigade until he was taken sick and removed by the assistance of our very efficient surgeon, Dr. Wallace McDugald, attended by his negro body servant, Bob ———, than whom a more devoted, a more faithful and trustworthy slave never belonged to any man.

General Hogg was taken to a private house some two miles west of our camp, where he had every necessary attention until his death. The faithful Bob was with him all the time. Dr. McDugald turned his other sick over to young Dr. Frazer, his assistant, and spent the most of his time with the general,—was with him when he died,—giving to him during his illness every medical care known to the science of his profession.

Thomas E. Hogg also was frequently with his father—was there when he passed away. I visited General Hogg only once during his illness, some two or three days before his death. I was kept very busy during this time, and owing to a change in our camps I had to ride six or seven miles to see him, and only found one opportunity of doing so. I found him as comfortably situated as could be expected for a soldier away from home, and receiving every necessary attention.

I will state that General Hogg came to us neatly dressed in citizen's clothes—never having had an opportunity of procuring his uniform, so that in fact he never wore the Confederate grey. He was not wounded, was not under fire of the enemy; neither was his brigade, until the Battle of Farmington, which occurred the day that General Hogg died. After his death and after the army was reorganised, "for three years or during the war," Dr. McDugald,—who afterwards married General Hogg's daughter,—Dr. I. K. Frazer, Thomas J. Johnson, one of the General's staff, Thomas E. Hogg, and the ever-faithful Bob all came home, and of course related minutely to the widow, the two daughters, and the three minor boys, John Lewis, and James Stephen, all the circumstances of the sickness, the lamented death and burial of the husband and father, Brigadier-General Joseph Louis Hogg.

Our camp was moved to a point about three miles east of Corinth. Decherd, the quartermaster, resigned and W. F. Rapley was appointed quartermaster by General Cabell. The rate at which our men fell sick was remarkable, as well as appalling, and distressing in the extreme. The water we had to drink was bad, very bad, and the rations none of the best. The former we procured by digging for it; the earth around Corinth being very light and porous, holding water like a sponge. When we first went there the ground was full of water, and by digging a hole two feet deep we could dip up plenty of a mean, milky-looking fluid; but as the season advanced the water sank, so we dug deeper, and continued to go down, until by the latter part of May our water holes were from eight to twelve feet deep, still affording the same miserable water. My horse would not drink a drop of the water the men had to use, and if I failed to ride him to a small running branch some two miles away he would go without drinking. The rations consisted mainly of flour, made into poor camp biscuit, and the most unpalatable pickled beef.

As fared General Hogg and his staff, so fared all the new troops who saw their first service at Corinth. While many of the old troops were taken sick, it was much worse with the new. We had one or two new Texas regiments come into our brigade, whose first morning report showed 1200 men able for duty; two weeks from that day they could not muster more than 200 men able to carry a musket to the front. The sick men were shipped in carload lots down the Mobile & Ohio Railroad, some dying on the trains, and hundreds of others succumbing at the different towns and stations where they were put off along down that road south of Corinth. It seemed impossible for the surgeons and their assistants properly to care for the number of sick on their hands.

Day after day as I passed the Mobile & Ohio depot, I saw scores of the poor sick fellows on the platform waiting to be hauled off. On the day we left Corinth I passed Booneville, a station ten miles below Corinth, and here were perhaps fifty sick men lying in the shade of the trees and bushes. One of the attendants with whom I was acquainted told me he had just returned from a tramp of two or three miles, after water for a wounded man. At every house he came to the well buckets had been taken off and hid, and he finally had to fill his canteen with brackish pond water. Why these sick men had been put off here in the woods, when the station was the only house in sight, where they could not even get a drink of water, I do not know. The mere recollection of those scenes causes a shudder to this day. I was told that two dead men were lying on the platform at Booneville, and a Federal scouting party burned the station during the day. If it was true, they were cremated.

As for myself, I was sick, but was on duty all the time. I performed all the active duties of the brigade quartermaster, being compelled to go to Corinth and back from one to three times daily, looking after forage and other supplies; carried all orders and instructions to the regimental quartermasters; superintended the moving of the trains whenever and wherever they had to be moved; and, in fact, almost lived in my saddle. But, with the exception of two or three nights spent with the troops at the front, when the day's duties were over, I was comfortably situated at headquarters, having a good wall tent, a cot, and camp-stool, and was kindly treated by General Cabell and the members of his staff. Dr. S. J. Lewis of Rusk was our brigade surgeon, and did everything he could for my comfort and, had I been well, my position would have been as pleasant as I could have desired in the army, as my duties mainly involved active horseback exercise, while my personal surroundings were very agreeable.

Nevertheless, I lost my appetite so completely that I was unable to eat any of the rations that were issued to the army. I could no more eat one of our biscuits than I could have eaten a stone, and as for the beef, I could as easily have swallowed a piece of skunk. The mere sight of it was nauseating. Had I not been at headquarters doubtless I would have starved to death, since there we were able to get a ham or something else extra occasionally, and I managed to eat, but barely enough to keep soul and body together. Dr. Lewis saw me wasting away from day to day, and advised me to take a discharge—and quit the service; but this I declined to do. I paid General Hogg a short visit one afternoon during his illness, and another afternoon I rode over to Colonel Bedford Forrest's camp, to see my brother and some other Huntsville, Ala., friends. I found that my brother had gone, on sick leave, with Wallace Drake, one of his comrades, to some of Drake's relatives, down the railroad. With these exceptions I was not away from my post at any time. I must have gained some reputation for efficiency, as the quartermaster of our Arkansas regiment offered to give me half his salary if I would assist him in his office.

All the time we were at Corinth Major-General Halleck, with a large army, was moving forward from Pittsburgh Landing, on the Tennessee River, near the Shiloh battlefield, by regular approaches. That is, he would construct line after line of entrenchments, each successive line being a little nearer to us. Hence our troops were often turned out and marched rapidly to the front, in expectation of a pitched battle that was never fought, sometimes being out twenty-four hours. On one occasion an active movement was made to Farmington in an effort to cut off a division of the enemy that had ventured across Hatchie River, and the move was so nearly successful that the enemy, to escape, had to abandon all their camp equipage. On one of the days when our troops were rushing to the front in expectation of a battle, I came up with an old patriot marching along through the heat and dust under an umbrella, while a stout negro boy walking by his side carried his gun. This was the only man I saw during the war that carried an umbrella to fight under. As the battle failed to come off that day, I had no opportunity of learning how he would have manipulated the umbrella and gun in an engagement.

After General Hogg's death and the promotion of Colonel Louis Hebert to brigadier-general, the Third Texas was transferred to Hebert's brigade, and I was temporarily separated from it. On May 8 our year's enlistment having expired, the men re-enlisted for three years, or during the war, and the regiment was reorganised by the election of regimental and company officers, when all the commissioned officers not promoted in some way returned to Texas. Captain Robert H. Cumby, of Henderson, was elected colonel, Captain H. P. Mabry, of Jefferson, lieutenant-colonel, and our Captain J. J. A. Barker, major. James A. Jones was elected captain of Company C, John Germany, first lieutenant, William H. Carr and R. L. Hood, second lieutenants. I was not present at the election. Dr. Dan Shaw, of Rusk County, was made surgeon of the regiment.

Finally, on May 28, we received orders to strike tents and have the trains ready to move. General Cabell came to my tent and advised me to go to the hospital, but I insisted that I could make it away from there on horseback. The next morning the trains were ordered out. Dr. Lewis, having procured about eight ounces of whisky for me, I mounted my horse and followed, resting frequently, and using the stimulant. About noon I bought a glass of buttermilk and a small piece of corn bread, for which I paid one dollar. This I enjoyed more than all the food I had tasted for several weeks.

On the day of the evacuation of Corinth, May 29, the Third Texas, being on outpost, was attacked by the enemy in force, and had quite a sharp battle with them in a dense thicket of black jack brush, but charged and gallantly repulsed them. Our new colonel and lieutenant-colonel not being able for service, Major Barker had asked our old Lieutenant-Colonel Lane to remain with us for the time, so the regiment was commanded by him and Major Barker. The regiment sustained considerable loss in this affair, in killed and wounded. Among the killed was my friend, the gallant young Major J. J. A. Barker; our orderly sergeant, Wallace Caldwell, was mortally wounded, and John Lambert disabled, so that he was never fit for service again.

For the gallant conduct of the regiment on this occasion, General Beauregard issued a special order complimenting the Third Texas, and specially designating a young man by the name of Smith, from Rusk County. Smith in the charge through the brush found himself with an empty gun confronting a Federal with loaded musket a few feet from him. The Federal threw his gun down on him and ordered him to surrender. Smith told him he would see him in Hades first, and turned to move off when the fellow fired, missed his body, but cut one of his arms off above the elbow, with a buck and ball cartridge. This was the kind of pluck that General Beauregard admired.

★★★★★★

Headquarters West'n Dep't.
Baldwin. June 4, 1862.

General Order No. 62:

The general commanding takes great pleasure in calling the attention of the army to the brave, skilful and gallant conduct of Lieut. Col. Lane, of the Third Regt. Texas Dismounted Cavalry, who with two hundred and forty-six men, on the 29th *ult.*, charged a largely superior force of the enemy, drove him from his position, and forced him to leave a number of his dead and wounded on the field. The conduct of this brave regiment is worthy of all honour and imitation. In this affair, Private J. N. Smith was particularly distinguished for brave and gallant conduct in the discharge of his duty, and was severely wounded. To him, on some future occasion, will be awarded a suitable "Badge of Honour."

By command of Gen'l Beauregard.

(Signed):                                    George W. Brent, Acting Chief of Staff.

Private J. N. Smith, Third Texas Dismounted Cavalry.

Official copy. M. M. Kimmell, Maj. & A. A. G.

★★★★★★

On that day the entire army was withdrawn and moved out from Corinth and vicinity. The manner and complete success of this movement of General Beauregard's has been very highly complimented by military critics.

CHAPTER 7

# Battle of Iuka

In the early days of June our command halted and went into camp near Tupelo, Miss., where it remained for several weeks. Here, as I was physically unfit for service, I voluntarily abandoned my place at General Cabell's headquarters and returned to my own regiment. Obtaining, without difficulty, a thirty days' furlough, I called on Dr. Shaw for medicine, but he informed me that he had nothing but opium, which would do me no good. But he added, "You need a tonic; if you could only get some whisky, that would soon set you up." Mounting my horse, I went down into Pontotoc County, and, finding a good-looking farmhouse away from the public roads, I engaged board with Mr. Dunn, the proprietor, for myself and horse for thirty days. Mr. Dunn told me of a distillery away down somewhere below the town of Pontotoc, and finding a convalescent in the neighbourhood I sent him on my horse to look for it, with the result that he brought me back four canteens of "tonic."

Now Mr. Dunn's family consisted of that clever elderly gentleman, his wife, and a handsome, intelligent daughter, presumably about twenty years of age. I soon realised that I had been very fortunate in the selection of a boarding house and that my lot for the next thirty days had been cast in a pleasant place, for every necessary attention was cheerfully shown me by each member of the family. They had lost a son and brother, who had wasted away with consumption, and in my dilapidated and emaciated condition they said I favoured him, so they were constantly reminded of a loved one who had gone to his grave in about the same manner I seemed to be going, and they felt almost as if they were ministering to the wants of one of the family. They lived in a comfortable house, and everything I saw indicated a happy, well-to-do family.

Their table, spread three times a day, was all that could be desired. We had corn bread, fresh milk and butter, fresh eggs, last year's yam potatoes, a plentiful supply of garden vegetables and other good things, everything brought on the table being well prepared. At first I had little or no appetite, but thanks to Miss Dunn's treatment, it soon began to improve. She, using the "tonic," gave me an egg-nog just before each meal, and, blackberries being plentiful, she gave me blackberries in every form, including pies and cordial, all of which, for one in my condition, was the best possible treatment.

So I improved and gained strength, not rapidly, but steadily, and though the thirty days was not as much time as I needed for a complete convalescence, it was all I had asked for. Mr. Dunn manifested a great deal of interest in my welfare; he did not think I could recover my health in the service, and urged me most earnestly to go back to camp, get a discharge, and go to Cooper's Well, a health resort down in Mississippi, and I was almost compelled to promise him I would do so, when in truth I had no such intention. The thirty days having expired, I bade farewell to these good people who had taken in a stranger and so kindly cared for him, and returned to camp, not strong or well by any means, but improved, especially in the matter of an appetite.

Going up to regimental headquarters upon my return to the command I let out my horse for his board, procured a rifle and at once reported to our company commander for duty. The strictest military discipline was maintained by General Louis Hebert in every particular, and one day's duty was very much like the duties of every other day, with a variation for Sunday. Of course the same men did not have the same duties to perform every day, as guard duty and fatigue duty were regulated by details made from the alphabetical rolls of the companies, but the same round of duties came every day in the week. At reveille we must promptly rise, dress, and hurry out into line for roll call; then breakfast. After breakfast guard-mounting for the ensuing twenty-four hours, these guards walking their posts day and night, two hours on and four hours off.

Before noon there were two hours' drill for all men not on guard or some other special duty; then dinner. In the afternoon it was clean up camps, clean guns, dress parade at sundown; then supper, to bed at taps. On Sunday no drill, but, instead, we had to go out for a review, which was worse, as the men had to don all their armour, the officers button up their uniforms to the chin, buckle on their swords, and all march about two miles away through the dust and heat to an old field, march around a circle at least a mile in circumference, and back to camps. All that, including the halting and waiting, usually took up the time until about noon.

With the understanding and agreement that I would be excused from the drill ground when I broke down, and when on guard be allowed to rest when I had walked my post as long as I could, I went on duty as a well man. For quite a while I was compelled to leave the drill ground before the expiration of the two hours, and when I found I could not walk my post through the two hours some one of my comrades usually took my place. It was necessary for me to muster all my courage to do this kind of soldiering, but the exertion demanded of me and the exercise so improved my condition that soon I no longer had to be excused from any part of my duties. We had men in the command afflicted with chronic diarrhoea who, yielding to the enervating influence of the disease, would lie down and die, and that was what I determined to avoid if I could.

Among other bugle calls we had "the sick call." Soon after breakfast every morning this, the most doleful of all the calls, was sounded, when the sick would march up and line themselves in front of the surgeon's tent for medical advice and treatment. Our surgeon, Dr. Dan Shaw, was a character worthy of being affectionately remembered by all the members of the Third Texas Cavalry. He was a fine physician, and I had fallen in love with him while he was a private soldier because he so generously exerted his best skill in assisting Dr. McDugald to save my life at Carthage, Mo. He was a plain, unassuming, jolly old fellow, brave, patriotic, and full of good impulses. He was the man who indignantly declined an appointment as surgeon soon after the battle of Oak Hills, preferring to remain a private in "Company B, Greer's Texas regiment," to being surgeon of an Arkansas regiment.

Knowing that he had no medicine except opium, I would go up some mornings, through curiosity, to hear his prescriptions for the various ailments that he had to encounter. He would walk out with an old jack-knife in his hand, and conveniently located just behind him could be seen a lump of opium as big as a cannonball. Beginning at the head of the line he would say to the first one: "Well, sir, what is the matter with you?"

"I don't know, doctor; I've got a pain in my back, a hurting in my stomach, or a misery in my head, or I had a chill last night."

"Let me see your tongue. How's your bowels?" "He would then turn around and vigorously attack the lump of opium with his knife, and roll out from two to four pills to the man, remarking to each of his waiting patients: "There, take one of these every two hours." Thus he would go, down the line to the end, and in it all there was little variation—none to speak of except in the answers of the individuals, the number of pills, or the manner of taking. And what else could he do? He had told me frankly that he had nothing in his tent that would do me any good, but these men had to have medicine.

For water at Tupelo we dug wells, each company a well, using a sweep to draw it. In this hilly portion of the State good water could be obtained by digging from twenty to twenty-five feet.

From the time of the reorganisation at Corinth up to the middle of July Company C had lost a number of men. Some, as McDugald and Dillard, were commissioned officers, and did not re-enlist; some were discharged on applications, and others under the conscription law then in force, a law exempting all men under eighteen and over forty-five years of age. Among those discharged I remember the two Ackers, Croft, I. K. Frazer, Tom Hogg, Tom Johnson, W. A. Newton, William Pennington, and R. G. Thompson, all of whom returned to Texas except William Pennington, who remained with us a considerable time, notwithstanding his discharge. In the regimental officers several changes had been made. After the death of Major Barker, Captain Jiles S. Boggess, of Company B, from Henderson, was promoted to major; Colonel R. H. Cumby resigned, and Lieutenant-Colonel Mabry was made colonel. J. S. Boggess, Lieutenant-Colonel, and Captain A. B. Stone, of Company A, from Marshall, promoted to major.

About the first of August we moved up the railroad to Saltillo, about fifteen miles north of Tupelo, established camps, dug wells, and remained about three weeks. Here the Fortieth (?) or Mississippi regiment joined the brigade. This was a new regiment, just out from home, and it seemed to us, from the amount of luggage they had, that they had brought about all their household goods along. This regiment is remembered for these distinct peculiarities. Aside from the weight and bulk of its baggage they had the tallest man and the largest boy in the army, and the colonel used a camel to carry his private baggage. The tall man was rather slender, and looked to be seven feet high; the boy was sixteen or eighteen years old, and weighed more than three hundred pounds.

The brigade now consisted of the Third Texas, Whitfield's Texas Legion, the Third Louisiana, the Fourteenth and Seventeenth Arkansas, and the Fortieth Mississippi. (Of this last I am not positive, but believe I am correct). The army here, commanded by General Price, was composed of two divisions commanded by Generals Little and D. H. Maury. Many of the troops that came out of Corinth with General Beauregard had gone with General Bragg into Kentucky. At the end of three weeks we moved farther up the railroad to Baldwin. Here we dug more wells, and it was my fortune to be on the second day's detail that dug our company well. The first detail went down some eight feet, about as deep as they could throw the earth out. The next morning four of us, including C. C. Watkins and myself, the two weakest men, physically, in the company, were detailed to continue the digging. We arranged means for drawing the earth out, and began work, two at the time, one to dig and one to draw.

At quitting time in the evening we had it down twenty-one feet, and had plenty of water. But we were not to remain long at Baldwin, as preparations for moving on Iuka were soon begun. As commissary supplies were gathered in for the approaching campaign they were stored in the freight department of the depot. One R. M. Tevis, of Galveston, was acting as commissary of subsistence, and Charlie Dunn, of Shreveport, was his assistant. They occupied a small room, the station agent's office, in the building during the day. A good many fatigue men were usually about the place during the day, to handle the stuff that was brought in.

One day, while I was on the platform, a country wagon drove up. Tevis and Dunn seemed to have expected its arrival, as they were soon out looking after the unloading. Among the rest was a barrel, a well-hooped, forty-gallon barrel, and instead of being sent in with the other stores it was hurriedly rolled into the private office of the commissary. This proved to be a barrel of peach brandy. Now, peach brandy was "contraband." The character and contents of the barrel were shrewdly guessed by the bystanders as it was hurried into its hiding-place, and its locality, after it had been stowed away, was clearly observed and mental note made thereof. The depot building was located at the north end of a cut and was elevated fully three feet above the ground, platforms and all.

The Third Texas was camped along on the east side of the cut, say one hundred yards below the depot. The supplies were guarded day and night, the guards walking their beats, around on the platform. The next morning the guards were seen pacing the beats all right enough, but in the bottom of that barrel was an auger hole, and there was an auger hole through the depot floor, but there was not a gill of brandy in the barrel. At dress parade that morning it was unnecessary to call in an expert to determine that the brandy, when it leaked out, had come down the railroad cut. The two gentlemen most vitally interested in this occurrence dared not make complaint, but bore their sad bereavement in profound silence, and no one else ever mentioned it.

This brief stay at Baldwin terminated our summer vacation and our study of Hardie's infantry tactics. The constant all-summer drilling and the strict discipline we had been subjected to had rendered our dismounted cavalry the most efficient troops in the army, as they were good in either infantry or cavalry service, as was afterwards abundantly proved.

All things being ready, the march to Iuka was begun under General Price, with his two divisions. Up to this time the only infantry marching I had done, beyond drilling and reviews, was the two moves, Tupelo to Sattillo and Sattillo to Baldwin. As we were furnished transportation for cooking utensils only, the men had to carry all their worldly effects themselves and the knapsack must contain all clothing, combs, brushes, writing material and all else the soldier had or wished to carry, in addition to his gun, his cartridge box with forty rounds of ammunition, his cap box, haversack, and canteen. The weather was extremely hot, and the roads dry and fearfully dusty.

While I had been on full duty for some time I was very lean, physically weak, and far from being well, and starting out to make a march of several days, loaded down as I was, I had some misgivings as to my ability to make it; but I did not hesitate to try. As the object of the expedition was to move on Iuka and capture the force there before General Grant could reinforce them from Corinth, a few miles west of that place, the troops were moved rapidly as practicable, the trains being left behind to follow on at their leisure. Unfortunately for me, I was on guard duty the last night before reaching our destination, and as we moved on soon after midnight I got no sleep.

Next morning after daylight, being within six or seven miles of Iuka, the Third Texas and Third Louisiana were placed in front, with orders to march at quick time into Iuka. Now, literally, this means thirty inches at a step and 116 steps per minute; practically it meant for us to get over that piece of road as rapidly as our tired legs could carry us. To keep up with this march was the supreme effort of the expedition on my part. I do not think I could have kept up if Lieutenant Germany had not relieved me of my gun for three or four miles of the distance. We found the town clear of troops, but had come so near surprising them that they had to abandon all their commissary stores, as they did not have time to either remove or destroy them. At the end of the march my strength was exhausted, and my vitality nearly so. The excitement being at an end, I collapsed, as it were, and as soon as we went into camp I fell down on the ground in the shade of a tree where I slept in a kind of stupor until nearly midnight.

We remained about a week in and around Iuka, in line of battle nearly all the time, expecting an attack by forces from Corinth; and as it was uncertain by which one of three roads they would come, we were hurried out on first one road and then another.

One afternoon we were hurriedly moved out a mile or two on what proved to be a false alarm, and were allowed to return to camps. On returning we found a poor soldier lying in our company camp with a fearful hole in his head, where a buck and ball cartridge had gone through it. A musket was lying near him, and we could only suppose he was behind in starting on the march, and had killed himself accidentally.

On the night of September 18 we marched out about four miles on the Corinth road, leading west, and lay in line of battle until about 4 p. m. the next day, when a courier came in great haste, with the information that the enemy was advancing on the Bay Springs road from the south, with only a company of our cavalry in front of them. We had then to double quick back about three miles in order to get into the road they were on. We found them among the hills about one and a half miles from the town, a strong force of infantry, with nine or ten pieces of artillery, and occupying a strong position of their own selection. We formed on another hill in plain view of them, a little valley intervening between the two lines.

Our fighting force consisted of General Little's division of two brigades, Hebert's, and a brigade of Alabama and Mississippi troops commanded by Colonel John D. Martin, and the Clark battery of four guns, Hebert's brigade in front of their centre, with two of Martin's regiments on our right and two on our left. We began a skirmish fire, and kept it up until our battery was in position, when we began a rapid fire with canister shot. We then advanced in double line of battle, slowly at first, down the hill on which we had formed, across the little valley and began the ascent of the hill on which the enemy was posted, General W. S. Rosecrans in command. As we ascended the hill we came in range of our own artillery, and the guns had to be silenced. The entire Federal artillery fire was soon turned on us, using grape and canister shot, and as their battery was directly in front of the Third Texas, their grape shot and musketry fire soon began to play havoc with our people, four of our men, the two files just to my right, being killed.

We charged the battery, and with desperate fighting took nine pieces and one caisson. The horses hitched to the caisson tried to run off, but we shot them down and took it, the brave defenders standing nobly to their posts until they were nearly all shot down around their guns,—one poor fellow being found lying near his gun, with his ramrod grasped in both hands, as if he were in the act of ramming down a cartridge when he was killed. The infantry fought stubbornly, but after we captured their guns we drove them back step by step, about six hundred yards, when darkness put an end to a battle that had lasted a little more than two and a half hours, the lines being within two hundred yards of each other.

I cannot give the number of Federal troops engaged in the battle, but General Rosecrans, in giving his casualties, enumerates eighteen regiments of infantry, three of cavalry, one detached company, and four batteries of artillery. The cavalry was not in the engagement, and I think he had but two batteries engaged. One of these, the Eleventh Ohio Light Battery, lost its guns and fifty-four men.

The total Federal loss, reported, was 790, including killed, wounded, and missing. Hebert's brigade, that did the main fighting, was composed of six regiments, reporting 1774 for duty, and lost 63 killed, 305 wounded, and 40 missing; total, 408. Colonel Martin had four regiments (1405 men), and lost 22 killed and 95 wounded; total, 117. We had two batteries with us, the Clark battery and the St. Louis battery, but they only fired a few shots. The Third Texas had 388 men, and lost 22 killed and 74 wounded; total, 96. Company C lost W. P. Bowers, Carter Caldwell, W. P. Crawley, and W. T. Harris killed; and J. J. Felps severely wounded.

Crawley had a belt of gold around his waist, but only four or five of us knew this, and I presume, of course, it was buried with him. General Maury's division was not engaged. General Henry Little, our division commander, was killed. Lieutenant Odell, of the Third Texas, who was acting regimental commissary and who was mounted on my horse, was killed, and the horse was also killed. Colonels Mabry and Whitfield, and, I believe, all our other colonels were wounded.

The captured artillery was drawn by hand into town that night, where the guns were left next morning, after being spiked, as we had no spare horses to pull them away. Spiking guns means that round steel files were driven hard into the touch-holes, giving the enemy the trouble of drilling these out before the guns can be of any use again. As General Ord was marching rapidly with a strong force from Corinth to reinforce General Rosecrans, General Price concluded to retreat. Putting the trains in the road some time before daylight, early in the morning the troops marched out southward, leaving our wounded men in Iuka and sending a detail back to bury the dead. As General Hebert's brigade had stood the brunt of the battle the evening before, we were put in front and, to clear the road for the other troops, we had to move at double quick time for six miles.

This used me up, and I obtained permission to go as I pleased, which enabled me to outgo the command and to rest occasionally while they were coming up. We made a march of twenty-five miles that day on our way back to Baldwin. But oh, how my feet were blistered! They felt as if I had my shoes filled with hot embers. Late in the afternoon, when I was away ahead of the command I came to Bay Springs. This little village stands on a bluff of a wide, deep creek, and is crossed by a long, high bridge.

At this time, when the creek was low, the bridge was at least twenty-five feet above the mud and water below. I climbed down under the bluff, just below the bridge, to a spring, where I slaked my thirst, bathed my burning feet and sat there resting and watching the wagons cross the bridge.

Presently a six-mule team, pulling a wagon heavily loaded with ammunition in boxes, was driven onto the bridge, and as it was moving slowly along one of the hind wheels, the right one, ran so close to the edge that the end of the bridge flooring crumbled off and let the wheel down. Gradually this wheel kept sliding until the other hind wheel was off. This let the ammunition go to the bottom of the creek, followed by the wagon bed. Soon off came one fore wheel. This pulled off the other one, then the wagon tongue tripped the off-wheel mule and he dangled by the side of the bridge, and soon pulled the saddle mule off, and this process gradually went on, until the last mule started, and as he fell off his hamestring caught on the end of the bridge flooring, and for an instant the whole outfit of wagon and six mules hung by the hamestring, when it broke and down went the wagon and the six mules atop of it. The driver had seen the danger in time to make his escape.

We soon arrived at Baldwin, our starting point. Our wounded

left at Iuka fell into the hands of the enemy and were kindly treated and well cared for. The good women of the town and surrounding country came to their rescue nobly, and they received every necessary attention.

# CHAPTER 8

# Battle of Corinth

Captain Dunn, of Company F, was one of our badly wounded men, one of his legs having been broken by a grape shot. Captain Dunn was a unique character. He was a lawyer by profession, a very bright fellow, and lived at Athens, Tex. The first I ever knew of him he came to Rusk just before the war, to deliver an address to a Sunday-school convention. He was a very small man. In fact, so diminutive in stature that he was almost a dwarf. He was a brave, gallant soldier, a companionable, pleasant associate, and much of a wag. He was a great lover of fun, so much so that he would sacrifice comfort and convenience and risk his reputation in order to perpetrate a joke.

The ladies who came to nurse and care for our wounded soldiers at Iuka were like other women in one particular respect, at least,—they were desirous to know whether the soldiers were married or single, religious or otherwise, and if religious, their church relationship, denominational preferences and so on, and would converse with the boys with a view of learning these particulars. The usual questions were put to Captain Dunn by one of these self-sacrificing attendants. He made no effort to deny that he was married and, with some hesitation, frankly acknowledged that he was a member of the church of the Latter Day Saints, usually called Mormons, which was enough information for one interview. With the exclamation, "Why, you a Mormon!" the woman retired.

In whispers she soon imparted to all the other ladies who visited the hospital the astounding information that one of the Texas soldiers was a Mormon. They were incredulous, but after being vehemently assured by the interviewer that she had it from his own lips, some believed it was true, while others believed it was a joke or a mistake. To settle the question, they appointed a committee of discreet ladies to ascertain the truth of the matter, and the committee promptly waited upon Captain Dunn. Without loss of time in preliminaries, the spokeswoman of the committee said: "Captain Dunn, we have heard that you are a Mormon and have come to you, as a committee, to learn the truth of the matter. Are you a Mormon?"

"Yes, madam," said Captain Dunn.

"Have you more than one wife?"

"Yes," said Captain Dunn, "I have four wives."

"Captain Dunn, don't you think it awful wrong? Don't you think it's monstrous to be a Mormon?"

"No, madam," said Dunn, "that's my religion, the religion I was brought up in from childhood. All of my regiment are Mormons. All of them that are married have two or more wives. The colonel has six; some have four, and some five, just as they may feel able to take care of them."

A meeting of the ladies was then called, an indignation meeting, and indignation was expressed in unmeasured terms. The very idea! that they had scraped lint, torn their best garments into bandages, had cooked and brought soups and all the delicacies they could prepare to the hospital—done all they could, even to the offering up their prayers, for a detestable Mormon, with four wives! It was unanimously resolved that it could be done no longer. From that good hour, in passing through the hospital ministering to the wants of all the other wounded, they gave Dunn not even as much as a look, to say nothing of smiles, cups of cold water, soups, cakes, pies, and other more substantial comforts.

This neglect of Captain Dunn was eventually noticed by the other soldiers, talked of, and regretted by them and its cause inquired into. They earnestly interceded with the ladies in his behalf, and urged them that whatever Captain Dunn's faults might be, he was a brave Confederate soldier, and had been severely wounded in an attempt to defend their homes, that he was suffering greatly from his wounds; that if he was a Mormon he was a human being, and for humanity's sake he deserved some attention and sympathy, and should not be allowed to die through neglect. This argument finally prevailed, the resolution was rescinded, and the captain fared well for the rest of the time, even better than he had before the matter came up.

One day one of the ladies asked Captain Dunn how it happened that he got his leg so badly crushed. In the most serious manner he said to her: "Well, madam, I am captain of a company, and when we got into the battle the Yankees began shooting cannonballs at us, and to protect my men I got out in front of them and would catch the cannonballs as they came and throw them back at the Yankees; but when the battle grew real hot they came so fast I couldn't catch all of them, and one of them broke my leg."

As soon as our men thought they were able to travel they were paroled and allowed to go free. When Captain Dunn was paroled he went to Texas for a rest, until he supposed he might be exchanged. On his return, he was traveling through Arkansas when a woman on the train asked him where he was going? He replied, "Madam, I am going to Richmond in the interest of the women of Texas. I am going to make an effort to induce the Confederate congress, in view of the great number of men that are being killed in the war, to pass a law providing that every man, after the war ends, shall have two wives."

When paroling our people their paroles were filled out by a Federal officer and presented to them for their signatures. The majority of the men cared little about the form, but only of the fact that they were to be allowed to go free until they were exchanged. But when they came to Colonel Mabry he read the parole over very carefully. He was described as H. P. Mabry, a colonel in the "so-called Confederate States Army."

Mabry shook his head and said, "Sir, can you not leave out that 'so-called'?" He was informed that it could not be done. "Then," said the colonel, "I will not sign it."

"In that case," said the officer, "you will have to go to prison."

"Well," Mabry replied, "I will go to prison and stay there until I rot before I will sign a parole with that 'so-called Confederate States' in it."

Captain Lee, of the Third Texas, was of the same way of thinking, and they both went to prison and remained there until they were exchanged, being sent to some prison in Illinois. Some months after they were exchanged and came back to us we captured some prisoners one day. One of them inquired if the Third Texas was there, and was told that it was. "Then," said he, "take me to Colonel Mabry or Captain Lee, and I'll be all right."

This man was a "copperhead" whose acquaintance they had made while in prison. He didn't want to serve in the army against us, but had been drafted in, and was glad of an opportunity of changing his uniform.

At Baldwin about two days was spent in preparation for a march to Ripley, there to join General Van Dorn's command for a move on Corinth. I was on fatigue duty while at Baldwin, and had no time to recuperate after the hard campaign to Iuka and back, having been on guard duty the night before arriving at Ripley. We camped at that town one night and started next morning, September 29, 1862, for Corinth, General Van Dorn in command. On that morning I found myself with a fever, and feeling unequal to a regular march I obtained permission to march at will, and found Lieutenant R. L. Hood and F. M. Dodson in the same condition and having a like permit. We joined our forces and moved up the hot, dusty road about six miles.

Being weary, foot-sore, and sick, we turned into the woods, lay down and went to sleep under some oak trees and did not wake until the beef cattle were passing us in the afternoon. This meant that we had slept until the entire army was ahead of us—cavalry, infantry, artillery, and wagon train. We moved on until night without overtaking our command. Nearing the village of Ruckersville it occurred to me that many years ago this had been the post office of Peter Cotten, my mother's brother. Stopping at a house to make inquiries, I learned that Willis Cook, his son-in-law, lived only three-quarters of a mile west of the village. We turned in that direction, and soon found the place without difficulty. My call at the gate was answered by my uncle at the front door.

I recognised his voice, although I had not heard it since I was a small boy. Going into the house I made myself known to him and his daughter, Mrs. Crook, and received a cordial welcome, such a welcome as made me and my comrades feel perfectly at home. My good cousin, Tabitha, whose husband, Willis Crook, was in the cavalry service, and in the army then on its way to Corinth, soon had a splendid supper ready for us and in due time offered us a nice bed. We begged out of occupying the beds, however, and with their permission stretched our weary limbs under a shade tree in the yard and enjoyed a good night's sleep.

Next morning one or two of the party had chills, and we rested for the day. We soon learned that a Federal cavalry command had dropped in behind our army, and so we were cut off. Had we gone on in the morning we would probably have been captured during the day. Learning how we could find parallel roads leading in the direction we wished to go, late in the evening we started, travelled a few miles and slept in the woods. The next morning, we moved on until ten o'clock, and meeting a ten-year-old boy on a pony in a lane, we asked him if he knew where we could get something to eat. He said there was a potato patch right over there in the field. We asked him to whom it belonged, and he answered: "It belongs to my uncle; but he is laying out in the brush to keep out of the army;" and told us that his uncle lived up on the hill a short distance ahead of us.

We did not go into the potato patch, but went up to the uncle's house. The house was a fairly good one, and in the front were two good-sized rooms with a wide, open hall. As we marched up to the rail fence in front of the house a woman came out into the hall, and we could see that the very looks of us aggravated and annoyed her. By way of getting acquainted with her, Dodson said: "Madam, have you got any water?"

In a sharp, cracked voice, she answered: "I reckon I have. If I hain't, I would be in a mighty bad fix!"

Having it understood that Dodson was to do the talking, we marched in and helped ourselves to a drink of water each, from a bucket setting on a shelf in the hall. During the next few minutes' silence of the most profound sort prevailed. We stood there as if waiting to be invited to sit down and rest, but instead of inviting us to seats she stood scowling on us as if she was wishing us in Davy Jones' locker or some similar place. Hood and myself finally moved a little towards the front of the hall, and the following dialogue took place between Dodson and the woman: Dodson: "Madam, we are soldiers and are tired and hungry. We have been marching hard, and last night we slept in the woods and haven't had anything to eat. Could we get a little something here?"

"No, you can't. I don't feed none of your sort. You are just goin' about over the country eatin' up what people's got, and a-doin' no good."

"Why, madam, we are fighting for the country."

"Yes, you are fightin' to keep the niggers from bein' freed, and they've just as much right to be free as you have."

"Oh, no, madam; the Bible says they shall be slaves as long as they live."

"The Bible don't say no sech a thing."

"Oh, yes, it does," said Dodson, gently; "let me have your Bible and I'll show it to you."

"I hain't got no Bible."

"Madam, where is your husband?"

"That's none of your business, sir!"

266

"Is he about the house, madam?"

"No, he ain't."

"Is he in the army, madam?"

"No, he ain't. If you *must* know, he's gone off to keep from bein' tuk to Ripley and sold for twenty-five dollars."

"Why, madam, is he a nigger?"

"No, he ain't a nigger; he's just as white as you air, sir."

"Well, madam, I didn't know that they sold white men in Mississippi."

"No, you don't know what your own people's a-doin'."

During the conversation I kept my eye on the lowest place in the fence. What she said about being sold for twenty-five dollars was in allusion to a reward of that amount offered by the conscript authorities for able-bodied men who were hiding in the brush to keep out of the army.

That night we lodged with a good old Confederate who treated us the best he could. Next morning Dodson bought a pony from him, which we used as a pack-horse to carry our luggage. We then moved much easier. Late in the evening we crossed Hatchie River on the bridge over which the army had passed on its way to Corinth. Here we found Adam's Brigade and Whitfield's Legion guarding the bridge, that it might be used in the event of the army's being compelled to retreat. This bridge was only a short distance south of the Memphis & Charleston Railroad, and a few miles west of Corinth. We took the railroad and followed it nearly all night, turning off to sleep a little while before daylight. Early in the morning we struck across into the main-travelled road, and pushed on in an effort to rejoin our command.

About nine or ten o'clock we came to a house, and determined to try for some breakfast, as we were quite hungry. We afterwards learned that a poor old couple occupied the house. Walking up to the front door we asked the old lady if we could get some breakfast, telling her we had been out all night and were hungry, and so on, the usual talk. She very readily said, yes, if we would wait until she could prepare it. She then invited us to come in and be seated, and said she would have the meal ready in a few minutes.

In a little while she came back and invited us in to breakfast in a little side room used for a kitchen and dining-room. As we started in I was in front, and as we entered the little dining-room and came in sight of the table she began to apologise because she was unable to give us anything more. I glanced at the table and saw a small, thin hoe-cake of corn bread and a few small slices of bacon, "only this and nothing more." I asked her if that was all she had. She answered that it was. Then I said, "Where are you going to get more when that is gone?" She did not know. Not doubting the truth of her statements, I said: "Madam, while we are hungry and do not know when we will get anything to eat, we could not take all you have. While we are just as thankful to you as if you had given us a bountiful breakfast, we are soldiers, and can manage to get something to eat somewhere, and will leave this for you and your husband," and we bade her goodbye without sitting down to the table or tasting her scanty offering.

This poor old woman, who must have been sixty or more years old, had said, without a murmur and without hesitation or excuse, that she would prepare us some breakfast, and gone about it as cheerfully as if she had had an abundance, cooking us all the provisions she had, and only regretted she could not do more for us,—this, too, when not knowing where she would get any more for herself.

After leaving this humble abode we soon began to meet troops, ambulances, and so on, and from them we learned that our army was falling back. Instead of going farther we stopped on the roadside and waited for our command. Noticing a squad of soldiers out some distance from the road engaged apparently about something unusual, my curiosity led me out to where they were. To my surprise I found they were Madison County, Alabama, men, most of whom I knew. They were burying a poor fellow by the name of Murry, whom I had known for years, and who lived out near Maysville. They had rolled him up in his blanket and were letting him down into a shallow grave when I approached, and they told me that some of the boys that I knew were wounded—in a wagon just across the road.

I soon found my old friends, John M. Hunter and Peter Beasley, of Huntsville, Ala., in a common, rough road-wagon. Poor Hunter! he was being hauled over the long, rough road only that he might die among his friends, which he did in a few days. Beasley was not dangerously wounded.

We soon after joined our command and marched westward toward Hatchie bridge. But long before we got there Generals Ord and Hurlbut had come down from Bolivar, Tenn., with a heavy force of fresh troops, had driven our guards away, and were in undisputed possession of the crossing. Whitfield's Legion had been on the west side and had been so closely crowded, with such a heavy fire concentrated on the bridge, that they had to take to the water to make their escape.

Here was a problem confronting General Van Dorn, a problem which must be speedily solved, otherwise a dire calamity awaited his whole army. These two divisions of fresh troops were in front of an army of tired, hungry, worn-out Confederates, with General Grant's victorious army only a few miles in our rear. What was called the boneyard road ran some miles south of us and crossed the river on a bridge at Crum's Mill; but this bridge, as a precautionary measure, had just been burned, and even now its framework was still aflame. The route we were on led west from Corinth parallel with, and but a little south of, the Memphis & Charleston Railroad, crossing Hatchie only a short distance south of Pocahontas.

After crossing the river, we would turn south on the main Ripley road, and this road ran parallel with the river, passing not far, three or four miles perhaps, west of Crum's Mill, so that a force might move rapidly from Corinth, on the boneyard road, cross at Crum's Mill and strike us in the flank and possibly capture our trains. Hence the precaution of burning this bridge. Everything of our army, whether on wheels, on foot, or on horseback, was now between Ord and Hurlbut in front and Grant and Rosecrans in the rear, without a crossing on Hatchie. The trains were parked, with a view, as I was told at the time, to burning them, leaving the troops to get out as they could, and we already had visions of swimming the stream. Personally I was wondering how much of my luggage I could get over with, and whether or not I could make it with a dry gun and cartridge box. General Price, in this dilemma, undertook to get the trains out, and he succeeded notably.

We had a pretty heavy skirmish with the forces at the bridge, with infantry and artillery, but only to divert attention from the trains as they moved out to gain the boneyard road. General Price went to the mill and, pulling down the gable end, cast it on the mill dam, and thus made a temporary bridge over which the trains and artillery were driven. Then that gallant old man, who had just proved himself to be as much at home acting as chief wagon master as when commanding his army corps, sat on his horse at the end of his unique bridge nearly all night, hurrying the wagons and artillery across. On the west bank of the stream he kept a bonfire alight, which threw a flickering glare across the bridge. As each teamster drove on to the east end of the queer bridge he would slow up his team and peer through the dim light for the proper and safe route. Just as he would slow up one could hear the loud, distinct voice of "Old Pap" shouting: "Drive up there! Drive up! Drive up! Drive up!" And thus it continued until every wheel had rolled across to the west side of the Hatchie.

After we left the vicinity of the bridge and after the skirmishing ceased, there was no time for order in marching, unless it was with the rear-guard; no time to wait for the trains to stretch out into the road and to follow it then in twos. We fell into the road pell-mell, and moved in any style we wished to, in among the wagons, or any way just so we moved along and kept out of the way of those behind us. During the afternoon, in the middle of the road, I stumbled upon a small pile of corn meal, half a gallon, maybe, that had sifted out of a commissary wagon, and gathered part of it into my haversack, mixed with a little dirt. I crossed the bridge away along, I suppose, about 11 p. m., after which I stopped and watched General Price's manoeuvres and the crossing of the wagons until after midnight.

In the meantime, I hunted around and found an old castaway tin cup, dipped up some river water and made up some dough, and then spreading it out on a board, I laid it on General Price's fire until it was partially cooked. Surely it was the most delicious piece of bread I have ever tasted, even to this day.

When a good portion of the Third Texas had come up we moved on into the Ripley road and were sent northward for a mile or two, where we lay in line of battle in ambush, near the road until the trains had all passed.

After daylight we moved on towards Ripley, being again permitted to march at will, as we had marched the night before. Approaching Ruckersville my heart turned again toward my good cousin, Tabitha Crook. Taking little David Allen with me, I made haste to find her home. Arriving there a short time before dinner, I said to her, "Cousin, I am powerful hungry."

"Oh, yes," she said, "I know you are, Willis came by home last night, nearly starved to death."

Soon we were invited into her dining-room and sat down to a dinner fit for a king. Here I met her brother, George Cotten, whom I had never seen before. After dinner Mrs. Crook insisted that we rest awhile, which we did, and presently she brought in our haversacks filled up, pressed down, and running over with the most palatable cooked rations, such as fine, light biscuits, baked sweet potatoes, and such things, and my mess rejoiced that night that I had good kins-people in that particular part of Mississippi, as our camp rations that night were beef without bread.

We then moved on to Holly Springs and rested for some days, after a fatiguing and disastrous campaign, which cost us the loss of many brave soldiers, and lost General Van Dorn his command, as he was superseded by General J. C. Pemberton.

The Battle of Corinth was fought October 3 and 4, 1862. I do not know the number of troops engaged, but our loss was heavy. According to General Van Dorn our loss was: Killed, 594; wounded, 2162; missing, 2102. Total, 4858. The enemy reported: Killed, 355; wounded, 2841; missing, 319. Total, 3515. But if General Rosecrans stated the truth, our loss was much greater than General Van Dorn gave, as he (General R.) stated that they buried 1423 of our dead, which I think is erroneous. Company C lost our captain, James A. Jones, mortally wounded; John B. Long and L. F. Grisham, captured. As Captain Jones could not be carried off the field, Long remained with him and was taken prisoner, being allowed to remain with Captain Jones until he died. They were sent to Louisville, Ky., and then to Memphis, Tenn., where Captain Jones lingered for three months or more. After his death, Long, aided by some good women of Memphis, made his escape and returned to us.

It was at the Battle of Corinth that the gallant William P. Rogers, colonel of the Second Texas Infantry, fell in such a manner, and under such circumstances, as to win the admiration of both friend and foe. Even General Rosecrans, in his official report, complimented him very highly. The Federals buried him with military honours. It was at Corinth, too, that Colonel L. S. Ross, with the aid of his superb regiment, the Sixth Texas Cavalry, won his brigadier-general's commission.

The evening before reaching Holly Springs we had what in Texas would be called a wet norther. Crawling in a gin-house I slept on the cotton seed, and when we reached Holly Springs I had flux, with which I suffered very severely for several days, as the surgeon had no medicine that would relieve me in the least. In a few days we moved south to Lumpkin's Mill, where we met our horses and were remounted, the Third, Sixth, Ninth and Whitfield's Legion composing the cavalry brigade, which organisation was never changed. The army was soon falling back again, and continued to do so until it reached Grenada, on the south bank of Yalabusha River.

As we were now in the cavalry service we did the outpost duty for the army north of the Yalabusha.

JOHN GERMANY
Fourth and last Captain Company C, Third Texas Cavalry

JESSE W. WYNNE
Captain Company B, Third Texas Cavalry

# CHAPTER 9

# Holly Springs Raid

Winter weather came on us very early for the climate, snow having fallen to the depth of two or three inches before the middle of October, while the forests were still green, and the weather was intensely cold all during the fall months. While in this part of the field we had to be active and vigilant without having much fighting to do, and we enjoyed life fairly well.

General Washburn was sent out from Memphis with a force, estimated to be 10,000 men, and crossing Cold Water he came in our direction. The brigade in command of Lieutenant-Colonel John S. Griffith, of the Sixth Texas, moved up northwest to the little town of Oakland to meet him. Starting in the afternoon we marched through a cold rain which benumbed us so that many of us were unable to tie our horses when we stopped to camp at night. Next morning, we passed through Oakland about ten o'clock and met the enemy a mile or two beyond and had a lively little engagement with them, lasting, perhaps, half an hour, in which our men captured a baby cannon, somewhat larger than a pocket derringer.

As we advanced in the morning, Major John H. Broocks, of the Legion, commanded the advance guard composed of a squadron of which our company was a part. About a half mile out of the little town, when we came to where the road forked, he halted and ordered me to take five men and go on the left-hand road a half or three-fourths of a mile, get a good position for observation, and remain there until he ordered me away. We went on and took our position, the main force moving on the right-hand road. Very soon they met the enemy and got into an engagement with them across a field nearly opposite our position. After a while the firing having ceased, we heard our bugle sound the retreat, heard the brigade move out, and soon the Federals advanced until they had passed the forks of the road, when a battery began throwing shells at us. But no orders came from Major Broocks. Our position becoming untenable, and knowing we had been forgotten, and being unable to regain the road, we struck due south through the woods and rode all night, in order to rejoin the command. Finding it next morning, Major Broocks was profuse in his apologies for having forgotten us.

In the fight at Oakland we had about ten men wounded, Chaplain R. W. Thompson, of the Legion, voluntarily remaining to take care of them and dress their wounds. He had gotten them into a house and was very busy dressing the injury of one of them when a Federal soldier, with a musket in his hand, walked in and purposed making him a prisoner. Mr. Thompson was very indignant and stormed at the fellow in such a manner as to intimidate him, and he walked out and left him, and Thompson went on with his duties. Presently he was again accosted, and straightening himself up, he looked around to confront an officer and gaze into the muzzle of a cocked revolver.

The officer asked, "Who are you?"

"I am a Confederate soldier," said Thompson.

"Then," said the officer, "I guess I'll take you up to General Washburn's quarters."

"I guess you will not," replied Thompson.

"Well, but I guess I will," said the officer.

By this time Thompson was very indignant and said: "Sir, just take that pistol off me for half a minute and I'll show you whether I will go or not."

"But," said the officer, "I am not going to do that, and to avoid trouble, I guess you had better come on with me."

So Rev. Mr. Thompson went, and was soon introduced to the general, who said to him, "To what command do you belong, sir?"

Thompson answered, "I belong to a Texas cavalry brigade."

"Are you an officer or private?" inquired the general.

"I am a chaplain," said Thompson.

"You are a d—— d rough chaplain," said the general.

"Yes," replied the chaplain, "and you would say I was a d—— d rough fighter if you were to meet me on a battlefield with a musket in my hands."

"How many men have you in your command, sir?" asked the general, meaning the force he had just met.

Mr. Thompson replied, "We have enough to fight, and we have

enough to run, and we use our discretion as to which we do."

The general stamped his foot in anger and repeated the question, and got the same answer. "You insolent fellow!" said the general, stamping his foot again.

"Now," said Thompson in return, "let me say to you, General, that if you wish to gain any information in regard to our forces that will do you any good, you are interrogating the wrong man."

"Take this insolent fellow out of my presence and place him under guard!" said the general. This order was obeyed, when a crowd soon began to gather around Thompson, growing larger and larger all the time and looking so vicious that Thompson was actually afraid they were going to mob him. Casting his eyes around he saw an officer, and, beckoning to him, the officer made his way through the crowd and soon dispersed it. Thompson's "insolence" cost him a long march— from there to the bank of the Mississippi River, where they released him, with blistered feet, to make his way back to his command.

Mr. Thompson was indiscreet, perhaps, in his manner, which was, no doubt, detrimental to himself; but he felt conscious that they had no right to detain him as a prisoner, or to interfere with his duties, and their manner irritated him. He was a good, whole-souled man, bold and fearless, and the best chaplain I knew in the army. What I could say about army chaplains, so far as my observation went, would not be flattering and, perhaps, had better be unsaid. But the Rev. R. W. Thompson, as chaplain of Whitfield's Texas Legion, was a success, and he was with us in adversity as well as in prosperity. When at leisure he preached to us and prayed for us; when in battle he was with the infirmary corps, bearing the wounded from the field, or assisting the surgeons in dressing their wounds and ministering to their wants. We all loved him, and thank God he was spared to do noble work for his Master and his church for many years after the Civil War was over, and I believe he is still living.

This Oakland affair occurred December S, 1862. We had 1264 cavalry with a battery of four guns. Brigadier-General C. C. Washburn had 2500 men and two batteries. The engagement lasted about fifty minutes.

In the meantime, General Grant had organised a fine army of about 75,000 men, including infantry, artillery, and cavalry, and was slowly moving down the Mississippi Central Railway. His front had reached as far south as Coffeeville, his objective point being Vicksburg, and he intended to co-operate with the river forces in taking that Confederate stronghold. General Pemberton's small army was gradually falling back before him. As the general depot of Federal supplies was at Holly Springs, and to destroy Grant's supplies might turn him back, or at least would cripple him more than the best fighting we could do in his front, this was determined on.

General Earl Van Dorn, who was known to be a fine cavalry officer, was just then without a command. Lieutenant-Colonel John S. Griffith, commanding a brigade, joined by the officers of the regiments composing the brigade, about the 5th of December petitioned General Pemberton to organise a cavalry raid, to be commanded by General Van Dorn, for the purpose of penetrating General Grant's rear, with the idea of making an effort to destroy the supplies at Holly Springs, and to do any other possible injury to the enemy. In due time the raid was organised. We took Holly Springs, captured the guards, destroyed the supplies, and General Grant was compelled to abandon his campaign.

From this time General Van Dorn commanded us until his untimely death at the hands of an assassin. A more gallant soldier than Earl Van Dorn was not to be found, and as a cavalry commander I do not believe he had a superior in either army. What I may say about this, however, here or elsewhere, I know is of little worth, as most people have formed and expressed an opinion—some in favour of Forrest, some Stuart, and some Joe Wheeler; but any man who was with us on this expedition and at other times, and who watched General Van Dorn's manoeuvres closely, studied his stratagems and noted the complete success of all his movements, would have to admit that he was a master of the art of war in this line of the service. At the head of an infantry column he moved too rapidly, too many of his overmarched men failed to get into his battles; but place him in front of good men well mounted, and he stood at the head of the class of fine cavalry commanders.

With three brigades, ours, General W. H. Jackson's and Colonel McCulloch's, aggregating about 3500 men in light marching order, without artillery, we moved from the vicinity of Grenada early after dark, about the 18th of December, and marched rapidly all night. We passed through Pontotoc next day, when the good ladies stood on the street with dishes and baskets filled with all manner of good things to eat, which we grabbed in our hands as we passed rapidly through the town. After passing Pontotoc a command of Federal cavalry dropped in on our rear, fired a few shots and picked up some of our men who had dropped behind. Among those picked up was our Indiana man, Harvey N. Milligan. Somehow the boys had come to doubt Milligan's loyalty, and suspected that he had fallen behind purposely to allow himself to be captured. When the rear was fired on the colonel commanding the rear regiment sent a courier up to notify General Van Dorn. The fellow came up the column in a brisk gallop. Now, to pass from the rear to the front of a column of 3500 cavalry rapidly marching by twos is quite a feat, but he finally reached General Van Dorn, and with a military salute he said: "General, Colonel ———— sent me to inform you that the Yankees have fired on his rear!"

"Are they in the rear?" inquired the general.

"Yes, sir," answered the courier.

"Well, you go back," said the general, "and tell Colonel ———— that that is exactly where I want them."

It was interesting to note how adroitly he managed to keep in our rear on the entire expedition all their forces that attempted in any way to interfere with our movements. Their scouts were, of course, watching us to determine, if possible, our destination.

In going north from Pontotoc, General Van Dorn, instead of taking the Holly Springs road, passing east of that place, headed his command towards Bolivar, Tenn. Their conclusion then was, of course, that we were aiming to attack Bolivar. Stopping long enough at night to feed, we mounted our horses and by a quiet movement were placed on roads leading into Holly Springs, dividing the command into two columns, so as to strike the town by two roads. We moved slowly and very quietly during the night, and while we were moving directly towards the town guards were placed at the houses we passed lest some citizen might be treacherous enough to inform the enemy of our movements. The road our column was on was a rough, unworked, and little used one.

At the first appearance of dawn, being perhaps three miles from town, we struck a gallop and, meeting no opposition, we were soon pouring into the infantry camps near the railroad depot, situated in the eastern suburbs. The infantry came running out of the tents in their night clothes, holding up their hands and surrendered without firing a gun. Our other column encountered the mounted cavalry pickets, and had a little fight with them, but they soon galloped out of town, and on this bright, frosty morning of December 20, a. d. 1862, the town, with its immense stores of army supplies, was ours. Standing on the track near the depot was a long train of box cars loaded with rations and clothing only waiting for steam enough to pull out for the front. This was burned as it stood. Leaving the Legion to guard the prisoners until they could be paroled, the Third Texas galloped on uptown. The people, as soon as it was known that we were Confederates, were wild with joy.

Women came running out of their houses, to their front gates as we passed, in their night robes, their long hair streaming behind and fluttering in the frosty morning air, shouting and clapping their hands, forgetting everything except the fact that the Confederates were in Holly Springs! On every hand could be heard shouts—"Hurrah for Jeff Davis! Hurrah for Van Dorn! Hurrah for the Confederacy!"

A mere glance at the stores—heaps upon heaps of clothing, blankets, provisions, arms, ammunition, medicines, and hospital supplies for the winter, all for the use and comfort of a vast army—was overwhelming to us. We had never seen anything like it before. The depot, the depot buildings, the machine shops, the roundhouse, and every available space that could be used was packed full, and scores of the largest houses uptown were in use for the same purpose, while a great number of bales of cotton were piled up around the court-house yard. One large brick livery stable on the public square was packed full, as high as they could be stacked, with new, unopened cases of carbines and Colt's army six-shooters, and a large brick house nearby was packed full of artillery ammunition.

For about ten hours, say from 6 a. m. to 4 p. m., we laboured destroying, burning, this property, and in order to do this effectually we had to burn a good many houses. Riding out in the afternoon, to the yard where the wagons were being cut down and burned, I found numbers of mules and horses running at large, some of our men turning their lean horses loose and taking big fat captured horses instead. Just then it occurred to me that I had no horse of my own in Mississippi, my mount having been killed at Iuka. John B. Long being in prison when the horses came, I was using his. Now, if I only had some way of taking one of these horses out. Starting back uptown, puzzling over this problem, I met a negro boy coming out of a side street, and hailed him. In answer to my inquiries he said his name was Jake, and belonged to Mr. ——— down at Toby Tubby's ferry on the Tallahatchie.

"What are you doing here?" I inquired.

"Dese Yankees has bin had me prisoner."

After a little further colloquy, he readily agreed to go with me.

"'Cause," said he, "you-all done whipped de Yankees now. Dey bin braggin' all de time how dey could whip de rebels so fast, and when you all come in here dis mornin' dey went runnin' everywhere, looking back to see if de rebels was comin'. I done see how it is now. I don't want nothin' more to do with dese Yankees. I'se bin hid under de floor all day."

I took one of the abandoned horses, procured a mule for Jake to ride, with saddle, bridle and halter, and taking the outfit uptown said to Jake: "Now, when we start you fall in with the other negroes, in the rear, and keep right up, and when we camp you inquire for Company C, Third Texas Cavalry—and hold on to the horse at all hazards."

I had no further trouble with Jake. He carried my instructions out all right. About 4 p. m., having finished our day's work, we moved out of the northeast part of the town, and looking back we saw the Federal cavalry coming in from the southwest.

In this raid we captured about 1500 prisoners, according to General Van Dorn, and General Grant said the same. They were commanded by Colonel R. C. Murphy of the Eighth Wisconsin Infantry. Poor Murphy! he was peremptorily dismissed from the service without even a court martial. General Grant estimated their loss in supplies destroyed at $400,000, while General Van Dorn's estimate was $1,500,000. Doubtless one was too low and the other one too high. We marched out a few miles and camped for the night, and all the evening we could hear the artillery cartridges exploding in the burning buildings.

The next day early we were on the march northward. That morning when I awoke I felt a presentiment that if we had to fight during that day I would be wounded, and no effort of mine was sufficient to remove the impression, even for a moment. As the weather was quite cold, visions of the horrors of going to prison in midwinter troubled me, since a wound that would put me past riding my horse would mean that I would be left to fall into the enemy's hands.

Near noon we came to Davis' Mill, near the Tennessee line, not far from Lagrange, Tenn., where we made an effort to destroy a railroad bridge and trestle on Wolfe River. It was guarded by 250 troops, commanded by Colonel William H. Morgan of the Twenty-Fifth Indiana Infantry. We were fooling about this place three hours perhaps, and it was late before I understood the meaning of our manoeuvres. Our brigade was dismounted, double-quicked here and double-quicked there, double-quicked back to our horses, remounted, galloped off to another place, double-quicked again somewhere else and back to our horses. Then, remounting, we took another gallop and double-quicked again to the only tangible thing I saw during the day, and that was to charge a blockhouse or stockade.

The enemy was in what they called a blockhouse, constructed by taking an old sawmill as a foundation and piling up cotton bales and cross-ties, and throwing up some earthworks. Approaching this by a wagon road we came to a bridge across a slough perhaps two hundred yards from their fort. We met their first bullets here, as part of their fire could be concentrated on this bridge. Crossing a little river bottom, entirely open except for a few large white oak trees, we came to a bridge across Wolfe River about seventy yards from their works. To charge in column across this bridge under their concentrated fire was the only chance to get to them, but coming to this bridge we found that the floor was all gone, leaving only three stringers about ten inches square, more or less, on which we could cross. Running along the bank up the river to the right was a levee some three feet high.

The men in front, five or six impetuous fellows, running on to the stringers, one of them fell as he started across, and the others crossed the river. When I reached the bridge the command was deploying behind the levee without attempting to cross. I remained near the bridge. By this time, I was more fatigued, I thought, than I had ever been, with the perspiration streaming off my face, cold as the day was. Here we kept up a fire at the smoke of the enemy's guns, as we could not see anything else, until a courier could find General Van Dorn, inform him of the situation and ascertain his wishes as to the advisability of our attempting to cross the river. Anxious to know what had become of the men that went onto the bridge, I rose up and looked over the levee. One of them had been killed and was lying in the edge of the water, and the others were crouched under the opposite bank of the river out of immediate danger.

While this observation only required a moment of time and a moment's exposure above the levee, I distinctly felt a minie ball fan my right cheek. While I had not doubted for a moment that I was going to be shot somewhere sometime during the day, this narrow escape of having a minie ball plough through my cheek was very unpleasant. The thought of the ugly scar such a wound would leave flashed into my mind, and wondering where I was to be wounded I settled down behind the levee and continued firing my Sharps' rifle without exposing myself. Finally, we were ordered to fall back.

As soon as we were on our feet, and while crossing the little bottom, we would again be exposed to the enemy's fire, so the command fell back at double-quick. I rose and started, and, looking around, I saw Lieutenant Germany fall, and turned back to assist him, supposing he was shot; but as I approached him he jumped up and passed me, laughing, having merely stumbled and fallen. This threw me behind everybody. I soon found I was so fatigued that I could not double-quick at all, so I slowed up into an ordinary walk. The command, in the meantime, to avoid the fire that could be concentrated on the slough bridge, had flanked off to the left some distance above, and crossed on chunks and logs that had fallen in the slough.

Very soon I was the only target for the men in the blockhouse, and they shot at me for sheer amusement. At last a ball struck me on the right thigh. Thinking it was broken, I stopped, bearing all my weight on my left foot, and, selecting a large white oak nearby, intending, if I could not walk to manage somehow to pull myself behind this to shield myself, I waited for "something to turn up." Soon learning, however, that my thigh was not broken, I moved on. Rather than lose time in going up to where the command had crossed and run the risk of being left behind, supposing that on reaching the horses they would mount and move off, I determined to cross on the bridge, which I did in a slow walk, and am sure there was no less than a hundred shots fired at me.

Somehow I felt that I was not going to be shot more than once that day, so even after I got across the bridge and lay down to drink out of a little pool of water in the road, their bullets spattered water in my face. I managed to get off with the command, and while my wound was slight it bled freely and caused me a good deal of pain, as I had to ride constantly for several days, and was unable to dismount to fight any more on this trip.

We camped not far from Davis' Mill, and crossed the Memphis & Charleston Railroad early next morning, cutting the telegraph wires, tearing up the track, burning cross-ties, and bending and twisting the rails. Leaving, we struck a gallop towards Sommerville, Tenn., and galloped nearly all day. Entering Sommerville unexpectedly, we created a little consternation. There was a Union mass meeting in the town, and, there being no thought that there was a Confederate soldier in a hundred miles of them, they were having an enthusiastic time. Some of the old gentlemen, pretty boozy on good Union whisky, stood on the streets and gazed at us with open mouths. I heard one old fellow yell out, "Hurrah for Sommerville!" Another one standing near him yelled out, "Oh, d——n Sommerville to h—l; I say hurrah for the soldiers!"

The good ladies, however, when they learned who we were, began bringing whatever they had to eat, handing it to us as we passed along. Camping a few miles out, next morning we took the road leading to Jackson, Tenn., a road which passes west of Bolivar. In the afternoon, however, we changed our course, traveling by roads leading eastward, and camped several miles north of Bolivar.

Next morning, December 24, by making demonstrations against Bolivar, General Van Dorn induced the enemy to gather all his forces in the vicinity for its defence, including 1500 cavalry under Colonel Grierson, sent by General Grant in pursuit of us. We moved down a main road leading into Bolivar from the north, formed fours, driving in their cavalry scouts and infantry pickets to the very suburbs of the town, where the column was turned to the right through alleys, by-ways, and vacant lots until we were south of the town, when moving quietly out southward, we thus again had all our opposition in our rear. Moving down the railroad seven miles, Middleburg was attacked. As our troops dismounted and formed a line, Ed. Lewis, of Company B, was killed. I remained mounted, with the horses. The command moved up into the town and found the enemy in a brick house with portholes, through which they fired. This was not taken. Of Company C, A. A. Box was killed here. After staying for two hours, perhaps, we moved off just as the enemy's cavalry from Bolivar came up and fired on our rear.

The next point threatened was Corinth, in order to concentrate the forces in that neighbourhood. Leaving Middleburg, we passed through Purdy, took the Corinth road, and moved briskly until night, went into camp, fed, and slept until 1 a. m., when we saddled up, mended up the camp-fires and moved through neighbourhood roads, into the Ripley road. Reaching Ripley at noon we rested, fed, and ate our Christmas dinner. In about two hours we moved out, and look-ing back we could see the enemy's cavalry from Corinth entering the town. They fired a piece of artillery at us, but as they were in our rear we paid no attention to them. Crossing the Tallahatchie at Rocky Ford we camped on the banks of the stream. Here General Van Dorn waited for the enemy until noon the next day, but Colonel Grierson, who was pretending to follow us, never put in an appearance. In the afternoon we moved to Pontotoc and camped there that night in a terrible drenching rain. We then moved leisurely back into our lines, with "no one to molest us or make us afraid."

# CHAPTER 10

# The Engagement at Thompson's Station

"The Holly Springs raid," never to be forgotten by the participants therein, having now become a matter of history, we rested for a time. January, 1863, came, and with it a great deal of rain, making mud very abundant and the roads very bad. During one of these cold rainy days, who should come pulling through the mud nearly half a leg deep, but the "aforesaid Harvey N. Milligan, late of Indiana." He had made his escape from the enemy, and, minus his horse, had made his way back to us through the rain and mud afoot. "I told you Milligan was all right," was a remark now frequently to be heard. A day or two after this, word came around that there were a half dozen horses at regimental headquarters to be drawn for by the companies. I went up to represent Company C, and drawing first choice, I selected a horse and gave him to Milligan. During that same year he deserted on that very horse, and rode him into the Federal lines.

My boy Jake having brought my horse out of the enemy's lines, of course I expected he would wish to return home, and I proposed to give him the mule and let him go to his master. But no, he begged me to allow him to stay with me, to feed and attend to my horse, do my mess duties and such work. Of course I could not drive him off. This boy, eighteen or nineteen years old, perhaps, became a splendid servant, and as much devoted to me, apparently, as if I had raised him. Some months after this we were passing through Columbus, Miss., one day, and his owner, happening to be there, saw him, arrested him and sent him home. When I heard of it that night of course I supposed I would never see Jake any more, but to my surprise he came back in a short time, mounted on a splendid mule. When I started back to Texas in February, 1865, Jake was anxious to go with me, but I gave him a horse and saddle, and told him to take care of himself.

The severe horseback service we had had since the Battle of Corinth, and our diet, principally sweet potatoes, had restored my health completely, my wound had healed, and I was in good condition to do cavalry service. At this time, too, I was detailed to work in the regimental quartermaster's department. We were ordered to middle Tennessee, and started through the cold mud. My present position put me with the trains on a march, and we had a great time pulling through the mud, and in some places we found it almost impassable. Crossing the Tennessee River, a short distance below the foot of Mussell Shoals we struck the turnpike at Pulaski, Tenn., proceeding thence to Columbia, and then, crossing Duck River a few miles below that place, we moved up and took position near Springhill in front of Franklin, and about thirteen miles south of that place.

One evening soon after we went into camp on the turnpike some ten miles below Columbia, two men rode into the camp inquiring for me. I soon learned that it was my brother, accompanied by "Pony" Pillow, who had come for me to go with them to Colonel Billy Pillow's, who lived on a turnpike three or four miles west from the one we were on. Obtaining permission, I then accompanied them. My brother had been sick for some time, and had been cared for by the Pillows, first by Granville Pillow's family and then by Colonel Billy's family. He had now recovered and was about ready to return to his command, which was on the right wing of General Bragg's army, while we were camped on the extreme left.

I found Colonel Billy Pillow to be a man of ninety-four years, remarkably stout and robust for a man of his age. His family consisted of a widowed daughter, Mrs. Smith, who had a son in the army; his son, "Pony" Pillow; and his wife. This old gentleman was a cousin to my grandmother Cotten, and had moved with her family and his from North Carolina when they were all young people. They told me of my grandmother's brother, Abner Johnson, who had lived in this neighbourhood a great many years, and died at the age of 104 years. The next day we visited Colonel Pillow's sister, Mrs. Dew, a bright, brisk little body, aged ninety-two years, and the day following we spent the day at Granville Pillow's. Granville Pillow was a brother of General Gideon J. Pillow, and nephew of Colonel Billy.

He was not at home, but we were welcomed and well entertained by Mrs. Pillow and her charming young married daughter, whose husband was in the army. Mrs. Pillow inquired to what command I belonged, and when I told her I belonged to a Texas command, she asked me if I was an officer or private? When I told her I was a private, she said it was a remarkable fact that she had never been able to find an officer from Texas, and that the most genteel, polite and well-bred soldier she had met during the war was a Texas private. She added that while Forrest's command had camped on her premises for several weeks, and many of them had come into her yard and into her house, she never had found a private soldier among them. This was in keeping with the "taffy" that was continually given the Texas soldiers as long as we were in Tennessee.

In the afternoon, bidding my brother farewell, I left him, overtaking my command, as it had finished crossing Duck River and was camped on the north bank.

Franklin is situated on the south bank of Big Harpeth River, being fortified on the hills north of the river overlooking the town. General Van Dorn established his headquarters at Spring Hill, about thirteen miles south of Franklin, on the Franklin and Columbia turnpike. Brigadier-General W. H. Jackson was assigned to duty as commander of a division composed of Whitfield's Texas brigade and Frank C. Armstrong's brigade. Many of the Texas boys were very indignant, at first, that General Jackson, a Tennessean, should be placed over them— so much so that they hanged him in effigy. He was sensible enough to pay no attention to this, but went on treating us so kindly and considerately that we all learned to respect him and like him very much.

Sometime in the early part of this year, 1863, Colonels J. W. Whitfield and Frank C. Armstrong were appointed brigadier-generals. Near the end of February, I think, John B. Long returned to us, and reported the death of our captain, James A. Jones, having remained with him until he died in Memphis, after which J. B. made his escape. First Lieutenant John Germany now being promoted to captain, and Second Lieutenant W. H. Carr promoted to first lieutenant, this left a vacancy in the officers, which was filled by my election by the company as second lieutenant. So I gave up my position with the quartermaster and returned to the company, quitting the most pleasant place I had ever had in the army, for Captain E. P. Hill, our quartermaster, was one of the best and most agreeable of men, my duties were light, and my messmates and associates at headquarters good, jolly fellows.

Our duties in front of Franklin were quite active, as we had several important roads leading southward to guard, and frequent skirmishes occurred, as the pickets usually stood in sight of each other on the hills that were crossed by the turnpike roads, especially on the main Columbian pike. In addition to the Columbia pike, running directly south from Franklin, there was Carter's Creek pike, leading southwest, and the Lewisburg pike, leading southeast. Still no considerable fighting was done until the 4th day of March, which culminated in the Battle of Thompson Station on the 5th. On the 4th, Colonel John Coburn of the Thirty-Third Indiana Volunteers was ordered out by General Gilbert, with a force of nearly 3000 men, including infantry, cavalry, and about six pieces of artillery, to proceed to Spring Hill and ascertain what was there.

About four miles from Franklin they were met by a portion of General Van Dorn's command, and pretty heavy skirmishing resulted, when both armies fell back and camped for the night. Our forces retired to Thompson's Station, nine miles south of Franklin, and went into camp south of a range of hills running across the pike just south of the station. This is a very hilly country, and the Nashville & Decatur Railroad runs through a little valley between two ranges of hills, and the station is in the valley a short distance west of Columbia pike.

On the morning of the 5th the enemy was found to be advancing again, and leaving our horses behind the hill, we crossed over to the north side, and near a church just south of the station we were formed behind a stone fence—that is, Whitfield's brigade, other troops to our right and left, our artillery being posted to our right on the hill near the pike. The enemy advanced to the range of hills north of the station, on which was a cedar brake. From our position back to the hill and cedar brake was an open field with an upgrade about half a mile wide, the station, with its few small buildings, standing in between the lines, but much nearer to us. The Federal artillery was posted, part on each side of the pike, directly in front of ours, and the batteries soon began playing on each other.

Colonel Coburn, not seeing our line of dismounted men behind the stone fence, ordered two of his infantry regiments to charge and take our batteries, and they came sweeping across the field for that purpose. When they came to within a short distance of our front, Whitfield's brigade leaped over the fence, and, joined by the Third Arkansas, of Armstrong's brigade, charged them, and soon drove them back across the open field, back to the hill and cedar brake, their starting point. Here they rallied, and being re-enforced they drove our forces back to the station and stone fence, where, taking advantage of the houses and stone fence, our forces rallied and, being joined by the remainder of General Armstrong's brigade, drove them back again. This attack and repulse occurred three successive times.

In the meantime, General Forrest, with two regiments of his brigade, had been ordered to move around to the right and gain their rear, and as they retired to their hill and cedar brake the third time, Forrest opened fire on their rear, and they threw down their guns and surrendered—that is, those that were still upon the field. Their artillery, cavalry, and one regiment of infantry had already left.

The engagement lasted about five hours, say from 10 a. m. to 3 p. m. Our loss was 56 killed, 289 wounded, and 12 missing; total, 357. The enemy's loss was 48 killed, 247 wounded, and 1151 captured; total, 1446. Among the captured were seventy-five officers, including Colonel Coburn, the commander, and Major W. R. Shafter, of the Nineteenth Michigan, who is now Major-General, and one of the heroes of the Spanish-American War.

★★★★★★

Since the above was written Major-General William Rufus Shafter had been placed upon the retired list. In the fall of 1906 he was stricken with pneumonia, near Bakersfield, Cal., where he died November 12, after a short illness.

★★★★★★

Company C lost Beecher Donald, mortally wounded. Among the killed of the Third Texas of my acquaintances I remember Drew Polk (alias "Redland Bully"), of Company E, and Sergeant Moses Wyndham, a friend of mine, of Company A. From the day of the Oak Hill battle up to this day we had never been able to get T. Wiley Roberts into even a skirmish, but to-day he was kept close in hand and carried into the battle, but ran his ramrod through his right hand and went to the rear as related in this chronicle. Among the losses was Colonel S. G. Earle, of the Third Arkansas, killed; and my friend H. C. Cleaver, an officer in the same regiment, was wounded. Rev. B. T. Crouch of Mississippi, a chaplain, was killed while acting as aide-de-camp to General Jackson. Captain Broocks, brother of Lieutenant-Colonel John H. Broocks, was also killed.

The dwelling houses in the vicinity of Thompson's Station were situated in the surrounding hills overlooking the battlefield, but out of danger, and from these houses a number of ladies witnessed the battle. When they saw the enemy being driven back they would clap their hands and shout, but when our forces were being driven back they would hide their eyes and cry. Thus they were alternately shouting and crying all day, until they saw nearly twelve hundred of the enemy marched out and lined up as prisoners, and then they were permanently happy.

Here we lost the beautiful flag presented to us in the Indian Territory, the staff being shot in two, while in close proximity to the enemy. The bearer picked it up, but as he had to make his escape through a plum thicket the flag was torn into narrow ribbons and left hanging on the bushes.

General Van Dorn had four brigades under his command at this time—Forrest's brigade of four regiments and a battalion, Martin's brigade of two regiments, Armstrong's brigade of two regiments, one battalion, and one squadron, and Whitfield's brigade of four Texas regiments. All these participated, more or less, in the battle, but as Jackson's division was in the centre the brunt of the battle fell on them, as the losses will show. Whitfield lost 170 men, Armstrong, 115, Forrest, 69, and Martin, 3.

General Gordon Granger took command at Franklin immediately after the Battle of Thompson Station. He and General Van Dorn were said to be classmates at West Point, and good friends personally, but it seemed that they made strenuous efforts to overreach or to outgeneral each other.

About March 8 another expedition was sent out by the enemy apparently for the purpose of driving us out of the neighbourhood. Skirmishing began on the Columbia and Lewisburg pikes, some three or four miles south of Franklin, and was continued on the Columbia road for about three days, until we fell back across Rutherford Creek and took a strong position behind a range of hills south of the creek, destroying the bridges. In the meantime, heavy rains were falling, the creek rising so that General Granger's forces were delayed about two days in their efforts to cross, and all that could be done was to skirmish across the creek. Duck River, just behind us, rose so high and ran so swift, that pontoon bridges could not be maintained across it.

A battle could not be risked with only a small ferryboat in such a stream. Still the skirmishing went on, until the trains and artillery were ferried across, when, leaving skirmishers on the hill to deceive the enemy, we moved up the river through cedar brakes to White's bridge, twenty miles, crossed to the south side of the river, and when the enemy crossed Rutherford Creek they found no rebels in their front. We moved down through Columbia, and five or six miles down the Mount Pleasant turnpike and went into camp.

"Pony" Pillow's wife had been kind enough to knit me a pair of fine yarn gauntlets, and having heard that we had crossed Duck River, she sent them to me, by her husband, who came up soon after we struck camp. While he was there I was ordered to take a squad of men whose horses needed shoes, go into the country and press one or two blacksmith shops, and run them for the purpose of having a lot of shoeing done. I got my men and went home with Pillow, took charge of shops in the neighbourhood, and was kept on duty there about eight days, staying with my old grand-cousin's family every night. I enjoyed this opportunity of talking with the old gentleman very much, as he had known my maternal grandparents when they were all children in Guilford County, North Carolina, before the Revolutionary War. He, himself, had been a soldier for eight years of his life, and had been shot through the body with a musket ball. In these war times he loved to talk about his exploits as a soldier. While I was there he mounted his horse and rode several miles through the neighbourhood, to the tanyard and the shoe shop, to procure leather and have a pair of boots made for his grandson, who was in the army.

The work of shoeing the horses having been completed, and Duck River having subsided, we crossed back to the north side again, taking up our old position near Spring Hill, and resumed our picketing and skirmishing with General Granger's forces. It is unnecessary, even if it were possible, to allude to all these skirmishes. The picket post on Carter's Creek pike, eight miles from Franklin, was regarded as important for some reason, and an entire regiment from our brigade was kept there. One regiment for one week and then another regiment for the next, and were sent there with strict orders to have horses saddled and everything in readiness for action at daybreak in the morning. The Third Texas had been on the post for a week, and was relieved by the Legion under Lieutenant-Colonel Broocks.

The Legion had been there two or three days, and had grown a little careless, as nothing unusual had ever happened to any of the other regiments while on duty there. Just at daybreak one morning in the latter part of April Granger's cavalry came charging in upon them and completely surprised them in their camps, before they were even up, and captured men, horses, mules, wagons, cooking utensils—everything. Colonel Broocks and some of his men made their escape, some on foot and some on horseback, but more than a hundred were captured, their wagons cut down and burned, their cooking utensils broken up, and their camp completely devastated. One of the escaped men came at full speed to our camps, some three miles away, and as quick as possible we were in our saddles and galloping towards the scene of the disaster—but we were too late. We galloped for miles over the hills in an effort to overtake the enemy and recapture our friends, but failed.

We all felt a keen sympathy for Colonel Broocks and his men, for no officer in the army would have felt more mortification at such an occurrence than the brave, gallant John H. Broocks. It was said that he was so haunted by the sounds and scenes of the capture of his regiment that he was almost like one demented, and that for days and days afterwards he would sit away off alone on some log, with his head down, muttering, "Halt! you d——d rebel, halt!"

At one time during April General Van Dorn, with a goodly number of his command, made a demonstration upon Franklin, drove in all their outposts, and, selecting the Twenty-Eighth Mississippi Cavalry and leading it himself, he charged into the heart of the town.

The night following the race we made after the Broocks' captors, my horse fell sick and became unfit for service. In consequence I was ordered to send him to the pasture in charge of the command, a few miles below Columbia, and take command of "the sick, lame, and lazy camp" on Rutherford Creek, a temporary camp made up of slightly disabled men, and men with disabled horses or without horses. I was on duty here two weeks, with about as little to do as could be imagined. It was while I was on duty here that General Van Dorn's death occurred at his headquarters at Spring Hill. He was assassinated by one Dr. Peters, who was actuated by an insane jealousy.

Dr. Peters was an elderly man, with a pretty young wife; General Van Dorn was a gay, dashing cavalier. Dr. Peters was in the general's office when he came in from breakfast, and asked the general to sign a pass permitting him to pass through the picket lines. As General Van Dorn was writing his signature to the paper, Dr. Peters stood behind him. When Van Dorn had given the last stroke with the pen, the doctor shot him in the back of the head, and, having his horse ready saddled, he mounted and galloped up to our pickets, passed through, and made his escape. As soon as the crime was known a number of the general's escort mounted their horses and gave chase, but they were too late to stop the doctor. In a few days after this very sad occurrence General Jackson's division was ordered to Mississippi by rapid marches, and about the middle of May we reluctantly bade *adieu* to this beautiful, picturesque middle Tennessee.

# CHAPTER 11

# The Surrender of Vicksburg

I now disbanded my important command on Rutherford Creek, and telling my men that every fellow must take care of himself, I joined the movement towards Mississippi. Leaving in the afternoon, we camped on the north bank of Duck River opposite Columbia. That night while walking into a deep gully I sprained an ankle very badly. Next morning my foot and ankle were so swollen I could not wear my boot, so I exchanged it for an old rusty brogan shoe found in an ambulance, and shipped all my luggage in the ambulance. I made my way to the pasture eight miles below, mounted my horse and joined the command.

Before reaching camp that night my horse was taken with a peculiar lameness in one of his hind legs. Next morning soon after starting he became lame again, and grew rapidly worse, so much so that I fell behind, being unable to keep up. Soon I had to dismount and lead him, driving him and urging him along in every possible way, spending the day in that manner, and walking most of the time. In the afternoon I saw that contingent called stragglers. One man rode up and said to me, "Hello, Barron! you are gone up for a horse. You'll have to have another. Have you got any money?"

"Not much," I replied.

Pulling out a one-hundred-dollar bill, he said: "Here, take this; it will do you some good."

During the afternoon another, and after a while still another passed me, saying and doing precisely the same thing. Crossing Elk River just before dark, I stopped to spend the night at the first house on the road. The next morning my horse was dead. I had expected to trade him, but now I was completely afoot, encumbered with my rigging, fifteen miles behind the command, which had gone on the Athens, Ala., road.

After visiting the lot, I went back to breakfast, feeling that I was a good many miles from home, but not particularly daunted. I had all the time believed that a soldier who volunteered in the Confederate army in good faith and was honestly doing his duty would come out of all kinds of difficulties in good shape. After breakfast I watched the road until noon. At last a man of our brigade came along leading a horse, and I inquired to whom he belonged.

"One of the boys that was sent to the hospital."

I then explained to him my situation.

"All right," said he, "you take this pony, find you a horse, and leave the pony with the wagon train when you come to it."

"The pony" was a shabby little long-haired mustang with one hip bone knocked down, but I was mounted for the time.

It was now Saturday afternoon. I was only thirty miles from Huntsville and might find a horse there, so it occurred to me, but I had no desire to go there at this time. In the condition circumstances had placed me, I only wished to procure a horse suitable for my necessities and follow my command. I mounted the mustang and took the Huntsville road, inquiring for horses along the way. I stayed all night at Madison Cross roads, and was not recognised by the man at whose house I spent the night, although I had been acquainted with him for several years. I went out next morning, Sunday as it was, and examined and priced one or two horses in the neighbourhood, but found I could not pay for one even if I had fancied him, which I did not.

So I continued my course towards Huntsville, jogging along very slowly on my borrowed horse, as the weather was quite warm. When within two or three miles of town I left the Pulaski road and turned in through some byways to the residence of Mr. Tate Lowry, a friend of mine who lived near the Meridianville pike, a mile or two out of town. I rode up to his place about noon, just as he had returned from church. He extended me a very cordial welcome to his house, which was only occupied by himself, his good old mother, and little boy. We soon had a good dinner.

Out in the office I enjoyed a short sleep, a bath, and began dressing myself, Mr. Lowry coming in and placing his entire wardrobe at my service. I was soon inside of a nice white shirt and had a pair of brand new low-quartered calfskin shoes on my feet. He then brought me a black broadcloth frock coat, but there I drew the line. Having a neat grey flannel overshirt, I donned that, buckled on my belt and felt somewhat genteel. As there were to be religious services at the

Cumberland church in the afternoon, we agreed to go into town. We walked in, however, as I had no disposition to show the mustang to my friends in town, and when we arrived at the church we found the congregation assembled and services in progress. I went quietly in and seated myself well back in the church, and when the services ended everybody, male and female, came up to shake hands, all glad to see me, among them my home folks, Mrs. Powers ("Aunt Tullie"), and Miss Aggie Scott, her niece.

I accompanied them home, and met Mr. W. H. Powers, with whom I had lived and worked for several years, and who was my best friend. I found it a delightful experience to be here after an absence of more than three and half years. Of course I explained to them why I was in Huntsville and how I became lame. On Monday morning Mr. Powers called me in the parlour alone, and said to me, "Do you need any money?"

"That depends," I said, "on the amount a horse is going to cost me."

"Well," he said, "if you need any, let me know, and at any time that you need any money, and can communicate with me, you can get all the Confederate money you need."

During the day our L. H. Reed came in from the command, bringing me a leave of absence to answer my purpose while away from the command.

Here I met my friend (Rev. Lieutenant-Colonel W. D. Chadick), who said to me upon learning my purpose in this neighbourhood: "I have a good horse I bought very cheap, to give my old horse time to recover from a wound. He is about well now, and as I cannot keep two horses you can have him for what he cost me."

"How much was that?"

"Three hundred dollars."

"All right," said I, "the three one hundred dollar bills are yours, and the horse is mine."

This animal was a splendid sorrel, rather above medium size, about seven years old, sound as a dollar, and a horse of a good gaits. When I had gone forty miles from Huntsville one thousand dollars of the same currency would not have bought him. On Tuesday I had him well shod, mounting him the next morning, and while I was sorely tempted to remain longer, I started for Mississippi. I really had a very bad ankle, and could have called on an army surgeon and procured an extension of my leave and spent a few days more in this delightful way, but hoping to be well enough to perform the duties that came to my lot by the time I reached the command, I pulled myself away.

I went out and got the pony, left the borrowed articles of clothing, and crossing Tennessee River at Brown's Ferry, I laid in corn enough before I left the valley to carry me across the mountains where forage was scarce. I strapped it on the pony and made good time to Columbus, Miss. Here I was detained several hours by Captain Rice, the post commander, much against my will. He claimed that he was ordered by General Jackson, in case he found an officer in the rear of the command, to detain him until he gathered up a lot of stragglers, who were to be placed in charge of the officer, to be brought up to the command. After worrying me several hours, he turned me over a squad of men, and I started out with them. As soon as I crossed the Tombigbee River I turned them all loose, and told them I hoped they would go to their commands; as for me, I was going to mine, and I was not going to allow a squad of men to detain me for an instant.

I passed through Canton about dark one evening, and learning what road the command was probably on, having left my pony as per instructions, I rode into our camp just at midnight. The next morning, we moved to Mechanicsburg, loaded, capped, and formed fours, expecting to meet the enemy, which, however, did not prove to be the case. I therefore was able to be at my post by the time the first prospect of a fight occurred.

On my way down one day, I passed where the command had camped on a small creek, and noticing several dead mules I inquired into the cause, and was told they were killed from eating "Sneeze weed," a poisonous plant that grows in middle and southern Mississippi. I learned to identify it, and as we had several horses killed by it afterwards, I was very careful when we camped, to pull up every sprig of it within reach of my horse.

On the long march from Spring Hill, Tenn., to Canton, Miss., Company C had the misfortune to lose four men—Dunn, Putnum, and Scott deserted, and McCain was mysteriously missing, and never heard of by us again.

General U. S. Grant had swung round with a large army through Jackson, Miss., fought a battle with General Pemberton at Raymond and another at Baker's Creek, Champion Hill, where General Pemberton was driven back, having General Loring's division and twenty pieces of his artillery cut off. Pemberton was compelled to fall back across Big Black River at Edward's Depot into Vicksburg with the remainder of his army, and General Grant had thrown his army completely around Vicksburg on the land side, and that city was besieged. We were sent down here to hover around the besieging army, to see that they "'have deyselves, and keep off our grass."

The large gunboats in the river, above and below, with their heavy ordnance were bombarding the city. These huge guns could be heard for many miles away, from early morning until night. When I first heard them I inquired the distance to Vicksburg, and was told it was a hundred miles. During the siege we had active service, driving in foraging parties, picketing, scouting, and occasionally skirmishing with the enemy.

About the first of July we drove the enemy's pickets from Messenger's Ferry, on Big Black River, and held that crossing until the 5th. Vicksburg was surrendered on the 4th, and on the evening of the 5th our pickets were driven from the ferry by a large force under General Sherman, who began crossing the river and moving east. General Joseph E. Johnston was in command of our army outside of Vicksburg, and at the time the city was surrendered he was down on Big Black, with his forces and a train loaded with pontoons—everything indicating his intention to attempt a cut through the enemy's line to relieve General Pemberton. As soon as the surrender occurred General Johnston began falling back towards Jackson, and we fought the advancing enemy several days while he was making this retrogressive movement. We fought them daily, from early in the morning until late in the afternoon, holding them in check, though some days they advanced several miles and others only two or three, owing to the nature of the ground and the more or less favourable position afforded us.

This detention gave General Johnston time to move his trains and infantry back at leisure and to get his army in position in front of Jackson. Finally falling back to Jackson, we passed through our infantry lines in front of the city and took our position on the extreme right wing of our army, beyond the northern suburbs of the city. Jackson, it may be well to state, is located on the west bank of Pearl River. General Sherman's right wing rested on Pearl River south of the city, and his lines extended in a semicircle around the west of the city. Here we fought more or less for about a week, with some pretty severe engagements, directly in front of the city. In passing through the northern portion of the city to the position assigned to us we passed the State Lunatic Asylum.

After we formed a line and everything was quiet, there being no enemy in our front, Joe Guthery, of Company B, sauntered out and reconnoitred a little and upon his return he approached Captain Jesse Wynne and said: "Captain, you ought to see General Johnston's fortifications down by the asylum. He's got a great big swiege gun planted there that demands the whole country around."

One afternoon our works were assaulted by a brigade of General Lauman's division, who were almost annihilated. For this move he was promptly superseded, as it was claimed he acted without orders. After some heavy fighting in front of the city I chanced to pass our field hospital where the surgeons were at work, and just behind the hospital I looked into an old barrel about the size of a potato barrel and discovered it was nearly full of stumps of arms and legs, bloody and maimed, just as they had fallen under the knife and saw. This to me was so ghastly a sight that I never remember it without a shudder.

As we had heretofore been dismounting to fight, I had not had an opportunity of trying my new horse under fire until now. We had a long line of skirmishers in extension of our line to the right in front of us and three or four hundred yards from a line of the enemy's skirmishers. They were in the brush not exposed to view, so a desultory fire was kept up all along the line. I was sent up the line to deliver some orders to our men, and as I had to ride up the entire line and back, the enemy's skirmishers soon began firing at me, and kept it up until I made the round trip, the minie balls constantly clipping the bushes very near me and my horse. This completely demoralised him, and he would jump as high and as far as he possibly could every time he heard them. Some horses seem to love a battle, while others are almost unmanageable under fire. The first horse I rode in the army was lazy and had to be spurred along ordinarily, but when we were going into a battle and the firing began he would champ the bits, pull on the bridle, and want to move up.

After some four days in front we were sent to the rear of Sherman's army, where we captured a few wagons and ambulances and destroyed some cotton, and upon returning encountered the enemy's cavalry at Canton. While we were on this enterprise General Johnston had retired from Jackson and fallen back to Brandon, and General Sherman, after a few days, returned to Vicksburg. Our brigade now moved out into Rankin County for a rest. Here orders were issued for thirty-day furloughs to one officer and three men of the company. As Lieutenant Hood was away on sick leave, I proposed to Lieutenant Carr that we would concede Captain Germany the first leave. No, he would not do that; he was as much entitled to it as Captain Germany.

"All right," said I; "then we'll draw for it, and I will be sure to get it."

The drawing turned out as I had prophesied, and I presented the furlough to Captain Germany. The furloughs those days had a clause, written in red ink, "provided he shall not enter the enemy's lines," and that meant that in our case our men should not go to Texas.

In this "Siege of Jackson," as General Sherman called it (July 10-16, 1863), the enemy's reported losses in killed, wounded and missing numbered 1122. I am unable to give our losses, but in the assaults they made we lost very few men. General Sherman had three army corps on this expedition.

Our rest near Pelahatchie Depot was of short duration, as we were soon ordered back to guard the country near Vicksburg on the Big Black and Yazoo Rivers, with headquarters at Bolton Station. During Sherman's occupation of Jackson, he had destroyed miles of railroad track, bridges, and depots, and had also destroyed rolling stock, including passenger cars, flat cars, and locomotives. Now in August a force of their cavalry came out from Memphis and undertook to steal all the rolling stock on the Mississippi Central Railroad. They came down about as far as Vaughan's Station and gathered up the rolling stock, including a number of first-class locomotives, intending to run them into Memphis or Grand Junction.

We were sent after them and had a lively race. As they were about twenty-four hours ahead of us they would have succeeded, doubtless, had not someone burned a bridge across a small creek opposite Kosciusko. As may be imagined, we gave them no time to repair the bridge. We moved about a hundred miles in two days, with no feed for men or horses except green corn from the fields.

Reaching Durant very late at night in a drenching rain we were turned loose to hunt shelter in the dark as best we could, and we had a great time getting into vacant houses, under sheds, awnings, in stables or any available place that we might save our ammunition. At Old Shongolo, near Vaiden, the good ladies had prepared a splendid picnic dinner for us, but as we could not stop to partake of it they lined up on each side of the column as we passed, with waiters loaded with chicken, ham, biscuit, cake, pies, and other tempting viands and the men helped themselves as they passed, without halting.

One evening we stopped just before night to feed, for the horses were hot and tired, and our men hungry and in need of sleep. The horses were hastily attended to, that we might get some sleep, as we were to remain here until midnight, then resume the march. At starting time, I found my horse foundered. Groping my way through the darkness to General Whitfield's headquarters, I told him I could not go on, for my horse was foundered.

"Old Bob's in the same fix," he said. "Cross Big Black River as soon as you can, and go back to the wagon train, and tell that fellow that has got old Bob to take good care of him."

As the command moved off I started in the opposite direction. I had only gone a short distance when I came up with Lieutenant Barkley of the Legion, in the same sad condition. After daylight we stopped to breakfast at a house on the road, then crossed the Big Black, and, as our horses grew worse, we made a short day's travel and spent the night with Mr. Fullylove, a generous old gentleman. Next morning the horses travelled still worse. About 10 a. m. we came to the residence of Hon. Mr. Blunt, of Attalah County, and decided that, with the permission of the family, we would remain here until morning.

Consulting Mrs. Blunt, she said: "Mr. Blunt is not at home. The only persons with me are my daughter and a young lady visiting us; but if I knew you were gentlemen I would not turn you off."

We told her we were Texans, and claimed to be gentlemen—and we remained there until the next morning. After caring for our horses we were invited into the parlour or sitting-room and introduced to the young ladies. The visitor was Miss Hattie Savage, who lived only a few miles away. Soon the usual interrogatory was propounded. "Are you gentlemen married?"

Barclay answered: "Yes, I am married. I have a wife and baby at home," and exhibited the little one's picture.

I told them I was not so fortunate as to be married. Soon we had a good dinner and spent quite a pleasant day. The next morning, with many thanks for the generous hospitality we had enjoyed, we said goodbye to the three ladies.

I found that my horse's condition grew constantly worse, so that now he could scarcely get along at all. After traveling about three miles we came to the house of Mr. Leftwich Ayres, who proved to be a very excellent man. Seeing the condition of our horses, he invited us to remain with him until morning, which we did. At this time and ever afterward I received only kind and generous treatment from all the members of this family, which consisted of Mr. Ayres, his wife and her grown daughter, Miss Joe Andrews. A Mr. Richburg owned and operated a tanyard and boot shop near the Ayres place. I visited his shop and left my measure for a pair of boots, and found Mr. Richburg to be a most excellent man. He made me several pairs of boots afterwards. Next morning Mr. Ayres said to me: "Your horse cannot travel. Old Arkansaw is the only horse I have; take him and ride him, and I will take care of your horse until he is well." I accepted the proposition, and Barclay and myself returned to our commands.

General Whitfield followed the Federals to Duck Hill, near Grenada, without overtaking them, and returned to Canton, and to Big Black and Yazoo Rivers.

When I supposed from the lapse of time that my horse had recovered, I obtained permission and went after him. Reaching Mr. Ayres' home about ten o'clock one morning, he met me at the gate and told me that my horse was about well, that he had just turned him out for the first time to graze. I immediately felt uneasy, and being anxious to see him we walked around his enclosure and soon found him; but as soon as I came near him I saw the effects of the deadly sneeze weed, and in spite of all we could do for him in a few hours he was dead. Mr. Ayres was very much grieved and said, "I would not have had your horse die at my house under the circumstances for a thousand dollars. There's old Arkansaw; take him and make the best you can of him—ride him, trade him off, or anything." I therefore returned to the command on Old Arkansaw, a pretty good old one-eyed horse.

It is not possible now to remember all the movements made by us during the next two or three months, the number of foraging parties we drove back or the number of skirmishes with the enemy. As I have said I returned to the command mounted on Old Arkansaw, but did not keep him long, as I traded him for a pony, and traded the pony for a mule, a splendid young mule, good under the saddle, but not the kind of a mount I desired. Awaiting for a favourable time, I obtained leave to go to Huntsville, where I could obtain money to buy another horse. I soon made the distance over the long road at the rate of forty miles per day on my mule.

Passing through Tuscaloosa one morning, after a travel of thirty-two miles, I put up with Mr. Moses McMath, father-in-law of General Joseph L. Hogg. Here I found General L. P. Walker, our first Secretary of War, who had started to Huntsville. We travelled together as far as Blountsville, he relating to me many interesting facts about the early days of the Confederate army, and here we learned that a division of

Federal cavalry was then in Madison County.

At Warrenton, in Marshall County, I met Hop Beard, son of Arthur Beard, who had lost one of his hands in Forrest's cavalry, and had a horse which he was now willing to sell. From Warrenton I went to Lewis' Ferry on Tennessee River, fifteen miles below Huntsville. Here I found my half-brother, J. J. Ashworth. Crossing the river at this place I went up on the Triana road as far as William Matkin's, about seven miles from Huntsville. Here I found Miss Aggie Scott, of the household of my friend, W. H. Powers, and was advised that it was unsafe to go to town. I therefore sent a message to Mr. Powers by Dr. Leftwich, who lived in the neighbourhood, and he brought me seven hundred dollars. With this I returned to Warrenton and purchased a splendid black horse of Mr. Beard, really the best horse for the service that I had owned. I called him Black Prince.

With the horse and mule, I returned to Mississippi. I had met several Huntsville people at Warrenton, among them my friend Tate Lowry. He insisted that when I got back to Noxubee County, Mississippi, that I stop and rest at his plantation. I reached there about ten o'clock one rainy day, and remained there until next morning. I found his overseer a clever, agreeable man, and the plantation a very valuable property, and was shown the fine stock and everything of interest on the place. Noticing a long row of very high rail pens filled with corn, I remarked on the fine crop of corn he had made. "Oh," said he, "that is only the tax in kind where I throw every tenth load for the Government."

And that was really only one-tenth of his crop! Our government claimed one-tenth of all produce, which was called "tax in kind."

As I passed through Macon I was offered five hundred dollars for my mule, but I had determined to carry it back and give it to Mr. Ayres in place of Old Arkansaw. I rode up to Mr. Ayres' house about three o'clock in the afternoon, presented him with the mule, and remained there until morning. While there Mrs. Ayres gave me enough of the prettiest grey jeans I ever saw, spun and woven by her own hands, to make a suit of clothes. I sent to Mobile and paid eighty-five dollars for trimming, such as buttons, gold lace, etc., and had a tailor make me a uniform of which I justly felt proud.

In September, perhaps it was, General Whitfield, on account of failing health, was transferred to the trans-Mississippi department, and the Rev. R. W. Thompson, the Legion's brave chaplain, also left us and recrossed the Mississippi. The brigade was commanded alternately by

Colonel H. P. Mabry, of the Third Texas, and Colonel D. W. Jones, of the Ninth, until Colonel L. S. Ross, of the Sixth Texas, was appointed brigadier-general and took permanent command of us, and the brigade was ever after known as Ross' Brigade. Colonel Mabry was given command of a Mississippi brigade and sent down on the river below Vicksburg.

Early in December we attempted to capture a foraging party that came out from Vicksburg. Starting early in the night, Colonel Jones was sent with the Ninth Texas around to intercept them by coming into the road they were on hear the outside breastworks. The command moved slowly until morning, when coming near the enemy we gave chase, galloping ten miles close at their heels. When they passed the point Colonel Jones was trying to reach he was in sight. We ran them through the outer breastworks and heard their drums beat the long roll. When we turned about to retire two of our men, Milligan and Roberts, fell back and entered the enemy's breastworks and surrendered.

## CHAPTER 12

# Battle at Yazoo City

The early days of January, 1864, found us floundering through the swamps in an effort to deliver to the trans-Mississippi department a lot of small arms, rifles, and bayonets. General Stephen D. Lee, commander of the cavalry in our department, wrote General Ross that there had been two or three unsuccessful efforts to put two thousand stands of arms across the Mississippi, and asking whether he thought his command could put them over. General Ross replied, "We will try." So the brigade started with several wagons loaded with the arms and a battery of four pieces. This January proved to be the coldest month of the war, and for downright acute suffering from exposure and privation probably no month of our campaigning equalled this.

We crossed Yazoo River at Murdock's ferry, and pretty soon were in Sunflower Swamp, about eight miles across. A slow rain was falling and the weather very threatening. With all the teams we had and all the oxen that could be procured in the vicinity, an all-day's job, we reached Sunflower with one lone piece of artillery, every other wheeled vehicle being hopelessly bogged down in the swamp from two to five miles in our rear. While the command was crossing the river a blizzard swooped down upon us. By the time we reached a camp two miles beyond, icicles were hanging from our horses, and everything we possessed that was damp was freezing. The cold continued to increase, next morning everything was frozen stiff, and it would have been possible to skate on the ponds near the camps. In this state of affairs General Ross said to us: "What shall we do, give up the expedition or take these guns on our horses and carry them through?"

The boys said: "Carry them through." We mounted and rode back to the river, left the horses on the bank and crossed in a ferryboat, where ensued a grand race for the wagons across the rough, frozen

302

ground and ice, for on a fellow's speed depended the distance he would have to go for the load of guns he was to carry back to the horses. Warren Higginbothom, an athletic messmate of mine, passed me, and I asked him to save me some guns at the first wagon, which he did, and I returned to camp with other fortunate ones; but some of them were late in the night returning. So we remained in the same camp for another night. Many of the men were thinly clad and poorly shod for such a trip in the bitter cold weather, I myself being clad in a thin homespun grey jean jacket, without an overcoat; and having hung my gloves before the fire to dry and gotten them burned to a crisp, I was barehanded as well.

The next morning every man, including General Ross himself, took his quota of the guns, usually four apiece, and started to Gaines' ferry, on the Mississippi, about fifty miles distant. Passing through Bogue Folio Swamp about seven miles, crossing the stream of that name and passing through the Deer Creek country, the garden spot of Mississippi, we came to within about three miles of the river and camped in a dry cypress swamp. As the river was closely patrolled by gunboats our aim was to cross the guns over at night. As no craft that a man could cross the river in was allowed to remain in the river, we found a small flatboat and dragged it with oxen over the frozen ground to the river, walking with loads of guns to meet it. The river here was running south and the cold north wind was coming down stream in almost a gale. The water was low and we approached it on a wide sandbar.

Having slid the boat into the water, John B. Long, Nathan Gregg, of Company A, Si James, the Choctaw, and one other of the command volunteered to row it over. After it was well loaded with guns the boat was pushed off, but the strong wind drifted them down the river some distance, and, returning, they drifted down still farther, so that it was nine o'clock next morning when they returned to camp, with their clothes from their waists down covered with a sheet of ice so thick that they could not sit down. The first gunboat that passed destroyed the little flat. We then built another small boat, but before we could get it ready for use all the eddy portion of the river near the bank was frozen over and the current a mass of floating ice, so that it was impossible to cross in such a craft at night.

Procuring two skiffs in addition to the boat, we crossed the remainder of the guns over in daylight, pushing through the floating ice with poles, the guns being delivered to Colonel Harrison's command on the west bank of the river. For the days and nights, we were engaged in crossing these guns we lived on fresh pork found in the woods, eating this without salt, and a little corn parched in the ashes of our fires. The weather continued to grow colder, until the ice was four inches thick on the ponds. The guns being disposed of, the piece of artillery was run down to the bank of the river, when soon a small transport came steaming up the river. It was given one or two shots, when it blew a signal of distress and steamed to the opposite shore and landed, and was soon towed off by a large boat going up the river. With some of our men barefooted and many of them more or less frostbitten we returned to Deer Creek, where we could get rations and forage.

As for forage there were thousands of acres of fine corn ungathered, and we only had to go into the fields and gather what we wanted. The Federals had carried off the able-bodied negroes, and the corn was still in the fields, and along the creek and through the farms there were thousands and thousands of wild ducks. I am sure I saw more ducks at one glance than I had seen all my life before. We retraced our steps through the swamps and the canebrakes and recrossed the Yazoo River in time to meet a fleet of twelve transports, loaded with white and black troops, escorted by two gunboats, ascending that river, evidently making for Yazoo City.

The Third Texas was sent out to meet a detachment of the enemy moving up the Mechanicsburg and Yazoo City road, and drove them back towards Vicksburg, the rest of the brigade, in the meantime, fighting the river force at Satartia and Liverpool. The Third rejoined the brigade at Liverpool, but being unable to prevent the passage of the enemy, we moved rapidly up the river and beat them to Yazoo City. Placing our artillery in some earthworks thrown up by Confederates in the early part of the war, we formed a line of riflemen down at the water's edge. The fleet soon came steaming up the river, and when the front gunboat came opposite to us the battery began playing upon it, while the rifles kept their portholes closed so that they could not reply. It was not long before they abandoned the effort to land, dropped back and were soon out of sight down the river. Later in the day, from the smoke, we could see that they were steaming up Sunflower River, west of us.

When the people of Yazoo City saw that we had saved their town from occupation by negro troops, their gratitude knew no bounds, and this gratitude was shown practically by as great a hospitality as was

CAPTAIN H. L. TAYLOR
Commander Ross' Brigade Scouts

LEONIDAS CARTWRIGHT
Company E, Third Texas Cavalry; Member of Taylor's Scouts, Ross' Brigade

ever extended by any people to a command of Confederate soldiers. In the evening a squadron, including Company C, was left on picket below the city for the night, at the point occupied during the day, while the command moved out on the Benton road to camp. To the pickets during the evening the •citizens sent out cooked provisions of the nicest and most substantial character, sufficient to have lasted them for a week.

The next morning the brigade returned and as everything remained quiet, with no prospect of an early return of the enemy's fleet, I rode uptown to take a view of the city. Numbers of others had done the same, and as the hour of noon approached we began to get invitations to dinner. Meeting a little white boy, he would accost you thus: "Mr. Soldier, Mamma says come and eat dinner with her." Next a little negro boy would run up and say: "Mr. Soldier, Mistis say come and eat dinner with her." And this manner of invitation was met on every corner, and between the corners. I finally accepted an invitation to dine with the family of Congressman Barksdale.

We were not allowed to enjoy the hospitality of this grateful city long on this visit, as General Sherman, who had planned a march to the sea, moved eastwardly out from Vicksburg, with a formidable force of infantry and artillery, and we were ordered to follow him. This we did, and kept his infantry closed up and his men from straggling. His cavalry, moving out from Memphis, was to form a junction with his main force at Meridian. Reaching that place, he halted, and we camped in the pine wood three or four miles north of the town. General Forrest was between us and the enemy's cavalry, and our object was to prevent a junction, thus defeating the purpose of the expedition, and if Forrest was unable to drive the cavalry back we were to go to his assistance—that is, Jackson's division was to do this.

One very cold, cloudy evening near sundown I was ordered to report to General Ross, mounted. When I reached headquarters I received verbal orders to proceed to Macon with the least possible delay, take charge of some couriers already there, use the telegraph, ascertain General Forrest's movements, and report from time to time by courier. The distance to Macon was, say, forty-five or fifty miles, and the way led mainly through forests, with a few houses on the road. Clad in my grey jean jacket, without overcoat or gloves, but well mounted and armed, I started, alone. Soon after dark a light snow began to fall and continued all night. About midnight I reached DeKalb, the county seat of Kemper County, where I spent half an hour in an effort to rouse somebody who could put me on the road to Macon. At daylight I was several miles from my destination. Stopping at a house for breakfast I lay down before the fire and slept while it was being prepared, and after breakfast finished my journey.

Approaching Macon from the south I crossed Noxubee River, spanned by a splendid covered bridge, and noticed that it was so filled with tinder that it easily might be fired if the Federal troops should come in sight. As I rode into the town and halted to make some inquiries, quite a number of citizens gathered around me to learn who I was, and ask for the news. One sympathetic old gentleman, seeing that my hands were bare and cold, stepped up and presented me with a pair of gloves. I found that the citizens were scared and excited, as they were situated between Sherman and his cavalry. I endeavoured to allay their uneasiness, and advised them not to burn the bridge, even if the enemy should appear, as that would only cause a temporary delay, and would be a serious loss to the town and country. From this they concluded I was a spy in the interest of the enemy, as I learned later, and for a day or two my every movement was closely watched.

I now put up my horse, found my couriers, repaired to the telegraph office, and informed the operator of my instructions. I spent most of the time in the telegraph office, when late at night the operator told me of the suspicion that I was a spy, and that he had cleared it up by asking General Jackson over the wires who I was. After this, while on this duty, I was treated with great kindness.

General Jackson now moved up to re-enforce General Forrest, and I rejoined the command as it passed Macon. We moved up as far as Starkville, but, learning that the enemy's cavalry had been driven back, we returned to the vicinity of Meridian. As was expected, General Sherman began falling back towards Vicksburg, we following him. Arriving at Canton, Sherman, taking an escort, returned to Vicksburg, leaving his army to follow in command of General MacPherson. Under his command the Federal Army moved without straggling and without further depredations. We learned from this improved condition of army discipline to respect MacPherson, and regretted to learn of his being killed in battle in front of Atlanta in July.

It was as the enemy returned on this trip that a battalion of Federal cavalry passed through Kosciusko, and their commander played a practical joke on the Union merchants there. These merchants, when they learned the Federals were coming, closed their doors and met them in the outskirts of town, and were loud in their assertions of loyalty to the Union. The officer asked them if they had done anything for the Union they loved so much.

"No," said they, "we have had no opportunity of doing anything, being surrounded by rebels as we are."

"Well," said the officer, "we'll see. Maybe I can give you a chance to do a little something for the Union."

Moving on uptown he found the rebels with open doors, and, in riding round, he would ask them why they had not closed up. They answered that they were so-called rebels, and were at the mercy of him and his men, and if their houses were to be plundered they did not wish the doors broken, and so they would offer no resistance. He placed guards in all the open doors, with instructions to permit no one to enter; then turning to his men, he told them if they could find anything they wanted in the houses that were closed, to help themselves, which they did. And thus an opportunity was given the "loyal" proprietors to do something for the Union.

Ross' brigade returned to Benton on the 28th of February, and was in the act of going into camps at Ponds, four miles down the plank road towards Yazoo City, when a squadron of negro cavalry from the city came in sight. General Ross ordered detachments of the Sixth and Ninth Texas to charge them. The negroes after the first fire broke in disorder and ran for dear life. The negro troops, a short time previous to this, had caught and murdered two of the Sixth Texas, and as these fellows were generally mounted on mules very few of them got back inside the breastworks, these few being mostly the white officers, who were better mounted than the negroes. Among the killed along the road was found a negro that belonged to Charley Butts, of Company B, he having run away to join the First Mississippi Coloured Cavalry.

On the evening of March 4 Brigadier-General Richardson, with his brigade of West Tennessee Cavalry, joined General Ross for the purpose of assisting in driving the enemy from Yazoo City, which is situated on the east bank of Yazoo River. The city with its surroundings was occupied by a force of about 2000 white and negro troops, commanded by Colonel James H. Coats, supported by three gunboats. About eight o'clock on the morning of March 5, 1864, the city was attacked by Ross' and Richardson's brigades, Brigadier-General L. S. Ross in command. Our fighting strength was about 1300 men, with two or three batteries; but as we dismounted to fight, taking out the horse-holders, every fourth man, this would reduce our fighting strength to about 1000 men.

The enemy had the advantage of several redoubts and rifle-pits, the main central redoubt being situated on the plank road leading from Benton to Yazoo City. We fought them nearly all day, and at times the fighting was terrific. With the Third Texas in advance we drove in their pickets and took possession of all the redoubts but the larger central one. This one was in command of Major George C. McKee, of the Eleventh Illinois Regiment with nine companies: about four companies of the Eighth Louisiana negro regiment; Major Cook, with part of his First Mississippi negro cavalry, the same that had murdered the two Sixth Texas men; and one piece of artillery. The Third and Ninth Texas and Fourteenth Tennessee cavalry found themselves confronting this redoubt. Two of our batteries were placed so as to obtain an enfilading fire at easy range, and threw many shells into the redoubt, but failed to drive the enemy out.

In the meantime, General Richardson, with the rest of his brigade, the Sixth Texas and the Legion, drove the remainder of the enemy's forces entirely through the city to the protection of their gunboats, and gained possession of the entire place except one or two brick warehouses near the bank of the river, behind which their troops had huddled near the gunboats. The Sixth Texas and Legion took position on the plank road in rear of the large redoubt, and thus at four o'clock in the afternoon we had it entirely surrounded, we being in front some 150 yards distant. At this juncture General Ross sent Major McKee a flag of truce and demanded an unconditional surrender. The firing ceased and the matter was parleyed over for some time. The first message was verbal, and Major McKee declined to receive it unless it was in writing.

It was then sent in writing, and from the movements we could see, we thought they were preparing to surrender. But they refused, owing perhaps to the fact that General Ross declined to recognise the negro troops as soldiers; and how they would have fared at the hands of an incensed brigade of Texas troops after they had murdered two of our men in cold blood was not pleasant to contemplate. As for the negro troops,—well, for some time the fighting was under the black flag— no quarter being asked or given. Retaliation is one of the horrors of war, when the innocent are often sacrificed for the inhuman crimes of the mean and bloodthirsty.

The parley in reference to surrendering being at an end, little more firing was indulged in, as both parties seemed to have grown tired of shooting at each other. The troops were under the impression that we were to assault the redoubt, but instead of doing so we quietly retired just before nightfall, and returned to our camp on the Benton road. This was explained by General Ross in his report in this way:

> To have taken the place by assault would have cost us the loss of many men, more, we concluded, than the good that would result from the capture of the enemy would justify.

Our loss in this engagement was: Ross' brigade, 3 killed and 24 wounded; Richardson's brigade, 2 killed and 27 wounded; total, 56. The enemy reported: 31 killed, 121 wounded, and 31 missing; total, 183.

Among our severely wounded was John B. Long, of Company C. Early in the day, ten o'clock perhaps, he was shot down on the skirmish line and was carried off the field and the word came down the line: "John B. Long is killed.—John B. Long is killed." This was heard with many regrets, as he was a favourite soldier in the command. This report was regarded as true by all of us at the front, until we returned to our camp. The next morning, I found him in Benton, wounded in the head; unconscious, but not dead, and he is not dead to this day (August, 1899). The next morning all the enemy's forces left Yazoo City, and again Ross' brigade was regarded as an aggregation of great heroes by these good people.

One morning while we were camped in this neighbourhood, one of the boys came to me with an invitation to visit a lady residing between our camps and Benton. She wished to see me because I had lived in Huntsville, Ala. When I called I found Mrs. Walker, daughter-in-law of General L. P. Walker, of Huntsville. She was a beautiful young woman, bright, educated and refined, easy and self-possessed in manner, and a great talker. She lived with her parents, Mr. and Mrs. Simpson, her husband being in the army. Mrs. Walker was an enthusiastic friend of the brigade, and would not admit that they had ever done anything wrong, and contended that, inasmuch as they had defended the city and county so gallantly, anything they needed or wanted belonged to them, and the taking it without leave was not theft. And this was the sentiment of many of these people.

For the remaining days of March, we occupied practically the same territory we had been guarding from the fall of Vicksburg. On or about the last of March General Ross sent Colonel Dudley W. Jones, in command of the Third and Ninth Texas regiments, to attack the outpost of the force at Snyder's Bluff, destroy Yankee plantations, etc.,

etc. I did not accompany this expedition, I am sure, as I have no recollection of being with it; nor do I now remember why I did not do so. The Yankee plantations alluded to were farms that had been taken possession of by Northern adventurers, and were being worked under the shadow of the Federal army by slaves belonging to the citizens. Cotton being high, they expected to avail themselves of confiscated plantations and slaves to make fortunes raising cotton. Colonel Jones captured and destroyed at least one such plantation, captured one hundred mules, some negroes, and also burned their quarters.

Early in April we started east, with the ultimate purpose of joining General Joseph E. Johnston's forces in Georgia, moving by easy marches. There was some dissatisfaction among the men on account of heading our column toward the rising sun, as they had been promised furloughs on the first opportunity, and this looked like an indefinite postponement of the promised boon. Arriving at Columbus, Miss., we rested, and here Lieutenant-General Leonidas Polk, then commanding the department, made a speech to the brigade, alluding to the fact that they had been promised furloughs, postponed from time to time, and assured us that as soon as the present emergency ended Ross' brigade should be furloughed. He assured the men that he had the utmost confidence in their bravery and patriotism, and though it had been hinted to him, he said, that if he allowed these Texans to cross the Mississippi River they would never return, he entertained no such opinion of them.

We now moved from Columbus to Tuscaloosa, Ala., the former capital of that grand old State. The good people of this beautiful little city on the banks of the Black Warrior had never before seen an organised command of soldiers, except the volunteer companies that had been organised here and left the city and vicinity, and their terror and apprehensions when they learned that a brigade of Texans had arrived was amusing. They would not have been in the least surprised if we had looted the town in twenty-four hours after reaching it. As we remained here several days, and went in and out of the city in a quiet orderly manner, they soon got over their fears.

There were numbers of refugees here from Huntsville, Florence, and other north Alabama towns, and some of us found acquaintances, especially General Ross and his adjutant-general, Davis R. Gurley, who had been in college at Florence. During our stay the ladies gave several nice parties for the benefit of the brigade. While we were here a great many fish were being caught in a trap above the city, and the men would sometimes go at night in skiffs up to the trap and get the fish. On one occasion Lieutenant Cavin, Harvey Gregg, and a man named Gray, of Company A, went up, and getting their boat into a whirlpool, it was capsized and the men thrown out into the cold water, with overcoats and pistols on. Gregg and Gray were drowned and Cavin was barely able to get out alive. After several days we moved some miles south of the city, where forage was more convenient.

In the meantime, General Loring, with his division, had come on from Mississippi. Receiving an invitation through Captain Gurley to attend a party given by a Florence lady to him and General Ross, I went up and spent two or three days in the city. While there I visited my friends in Loring's division, and also visited the State Lunatic Asylum, where I found in one of the inmates, Button Robinson, of Huntsville, a boy I had known for years. I also attended a drill of the cadets at the university. Friends of the two young men that were drowned had been here dragging the river for their bodies for some days, and finally they got one of General Loring's batteries to fire blank cartridges into the water, and their bodies rose to the surface, when they were taken out and buried.

The mountainous country lying north of Tuscaloosa and south of the Tennessee valley was at this time infested with Tories, deserters, "bushwhackers," and all manner of bad characters, and it was reported that the Tories in Marion County were in open resistance. So on the morning of the 19th of April Colonel D. W. Jones, of the Ninth, was sent with detachments of the Sixth and Ninth Texas and a squadron from the Third, under Captain Lee, amounting in all to about 300 men, up into that county to operate against these Tories. On the same morning I was ordered to take fifteen men of Company C and accompany Lieutenant DeSauls, of the Engineers' Corps, from Tuscaloosa, up the Byler road to Decatur, on the Tennessee River, and return by way of the old Robertson road, leading through Moulton and Jasper to the starting point, for the purpose of tracing out those roads to complete a military map then in preparation.

Applying to the quartermaster and commissary for subsistence for my men and horses, I was instructed to collect "tax in kind." We moved out in advance of Colonel Jones' command. Our duties on this expedition necessitated our stopping at every house on the road to obtain the numbers of the lands,—that is, the section, township, and the range,—ascertain the quarter section on which the house stood, learn the names of all creeks, note all cross roads, etc., etc. I subsisted the men and horses on tax in kind, which I had to explain to the poor people in the mountains, as they had never heard of the law. There was not much produced in this country, and there were so many lawless characters in the mountains that the tax collectors were afraid to attempt to collect the impost.

The people offered me no resistance, however, and to make the burden as light as possible I would collect a little from one and a little from another. I had the horses guarded every night, but really had no trouble. I met with one misfortune, much deplored by me, and that was the killing of James Ivey by Luther Grimes, but under circumstances that attached no blame to Grimes in the eyes of those who saw the occurrence, as Ivey made the attack and shot Grimes first, inflicting a scalp wound on the top of his head. I reported the facts when I reached the command, and there was never any investigation ordered.

## CHAPTER 13

# Under Fire for One Hundred Days

We reached General Roddy's headquarters near Decatur, on Saturday, and rested until Monday noon. Starting back, we passed through Moulton, were caught in a cold rain, sheltered our horses under a gin-shed, and slept in the cotton seed without forage or rations. Next morning, I instructed the men to find breakfast for themselves and horses, and meet me at Mr. Walker's, down on the road. Taking DeSauls and one or two others, I went on to Mr. Walker's, a well-to-do man, who owned a mill, where I hoped to get breakfast and some rations and forage to carry us across the mountain. Arriving at Walker's, he came out to the gate and I asked him first about forage and rations to take with us, and he said we could get them. Leaving DeSauls to question him about his land, I sought the lady of the house to arrange for breakfast. I found her very willing to feed us, as we were from eastern Texas, and knew of her father, who lived in Rusk County.

Now DeSauls was a resident of New Orleans, was dressed in a Confederate grey jacket and cap, and wore a pair of corduroy trousers. Soon after the lady left the front room to have breakfast prepared, DeSauls came in with a fearful frown on his face and said to me: "Barron, don't you think that d——d old scoundrel called me a Yankee?"

"Oh," said I, "I guess he was joking."

Just at this time Mr. Walker came up, looking about as mad as DeSauls, and said, "No, I am not joking. I believe you are all Yankees; look at them corduroy breeches! There hasn't been a piece of corduroy in the South since the war began, without a Yankee wore it."

I treated the matter as a joke at first, until finding that the old gentleman was in dead earnest, I undertook to convince him that he was wrong, but found it no easy matter. Finally, I asked him the distance to Huntsville? Forty miles. Then through my familiarity with the people and country in and around Huntsville I satisfied him that he was wrong, and then we were treated kindly by him and his family.

After leaving Tennessee valley we passed through the most desolate country I ever saw. For more than a day's march I found but one or two houses inhabited, and passing through the county seat of Winston County I was unable to find any person to tell me the road to Jasper. Arriving at Tuscaloosa I learned that Colonel Jones had returned and that the brigade had gone to Georgia, and I followed it, passing through Elyton, Blountsville, Talledega, and Blue Mountain. Camping one night at Blountsville, I met my friend Bluford M. Faris, formerly of Huntsville. Arriving at Talledega, I determined to spend one day, Saturday, there in order to have some shoeing done. This was conscript headquarters for a large area of country, with a major commanding, and there was post-quartermaster, commissary, a provost marshal, and all the pomp and circumstance of a military post. I thought at one time I would have some trouble, but fortunately I came out all right.

In the first place I camped in a grove of timber convenient to water, but soon received a message from the commander that I had camped near his residence, and would I move somewhere else? He did not want men to depredate upon his premises. I replied that I would make good every depredation my men committed, and that it was not convenient for me to move. I was busy for some time in procuring rations, forage, and an order for horseshoeing, and about the time I had these matters arranged I got a message requesting me to come to the provost marshal's office.

On my way I saw my men out in line of battle near the courthouse, with guns loaded and capped. Calling one of them to me, I learned that one or two of them had gone into the provost's office and he had cursed them as d——d stragglers belonging to a straggling brigade, and they gave him back some rough words, whereupon he had threatened to arrest them, and they were waiting to be arrested. Coming to the office I found the man in charge was a deputy. Introducing myself, I inquired what he wanted. He said some of my men had been to his office and cursed him, and he had threatened to arrest them and wished to know if I could control them.

I told him I could control them as easily as I could control that many little children, but if he wished to arrest any of them, the men were just out there and he might send his men out to attempt it—if he could. I asked him what provocation he had offered, and made him acknowledge that he had called them "stragglers." I then told him they were not stragglers, but good soldiers and, besides, they were all gentlemen, and if he had not first insulted them they would have treated him in a gentlemanly way; that if he wished to deal with them to proceed, otherwise I would take charge of them. Oh, no, he did not wish to have any trouble. If I was willing for my men to take a drink, I had his permission, and the poor fellow was more than willing to turn the "stragglers" over to me. I called them all up, accompanied them to a saloon, and told them that those who wished it could take a drink. We then went about our business without further trouble.

From Talladega I proceeded to Blue Mountain, intending to go from there to Rome, but learning that our army was gradually falling back, and being unable to learn its position or when I could safely calculate on striking it in the flank, I turned my course southward, passed through Carrolton, crossed the Chattahoochee River, followed the river up to Campbellton, recrossed it and found my command fighting near new New Hope church on the —— day of May, 1864.

A detailed account of this campaign would make a large volume, and of course cannot be undertaken in these brief recollections. Our division of cavalry reached Rome, Ga., about the middle of May, and fought the Federal advance the same day, and then for one hundred days were under fire, with the exception that on two occasions we were ordered to follow cavalry raids sent to our rear. But for this brief respite we were under constant fire for this period, each day and every day. We were assigned a position on the extreme left of General J. E. Johnston's army, a position occupied by us during the entire campaigning, while General Joe Wheeler's cavalry was on the extreme right.

To give one day's duty is practically to give the duties of many other days. We always fought on foot. Sometimes behind breastworks, sometimes not, sometimes confronting infantry and sometimes cavalry. We would be up, have our horses equipped, form a line, detail horse-holders, and march to the front by daybreak, and take our position on the fighting line. About nine o'clock our cooked rations, consisting of one small pone of corn bread and three-eighths of a pound of bacon, was distributed to each man as we stood or lay in line of battle. While these rations would not have made a good hearty breakfast, they had to last us twenty-four hours. The skirmishing might be light or heavy, we might charge the enemy's works in our front, or we might be charged by them. Usually the musket-firing, and often artillery-firing, would be kept up until night, when leaving a skirmish line at the front, we would retire to our horses. We often changed position after night, which involved night marching, always changing in a retrograde movement. Sometimes the fighting would become terrific, for at times General Sherman would attack our whole line, miles and miles in length, and, under General Johnston these attacks were made with heavy loss to Sherman's army. Particularly was this the case in front of Big Kenesaw, Little Kenesaw, and Lost Mountain.

In this campaign the cavalry service was much harder than the infantry service. When night came on the infantry could fall down and sleep all night unless they had to change their position, while the cavalry were burdened with their horses. Marching back to our horses we hustled for all the forage the Government could furnish us, which was usually about one quart of shelled corn, and we were compelled to supplement this with something else, whatever we could find; sometimes it was oats, often green crab grass from the fields, and later, green fodder or pea vines. Often this gathering of horse feed lasted until ten or eleven o'clock, when the horses would be stripped and we could sleep, provided we were not to move.

Early in June it began to rain, and continued raining day and night for about twenty-five days, until the country was so boggy that it was almost impossible to move artillery or cavalry outside of the beaten roads. Sometimes when the rain was pouring down in torrents the enemy would be throwing shrapnels at us, and hundreds, perhaps thousands, of them without exploding, plunged into the soft earth and are doubtless there yet. During the rainy season there was a great deal of thunder and lightning, and artillery duels would occur either day or night, and sometimes it was difficult to distinguish between the thunder of heaven and the thunder of cannon and bursting shells.

On one of those very rainy days we were in some timber south of a farm, while the enemy was in the timber north of it, only a few hundred yards distant, and had been firing at us in a pretty lively manner. General Ross sent for me and told me to go ascertain how far the enemy's line extended beyond our left. I mounted my horse and rode off, conning over in my mind the perplexing question as to how I was to gain the desired information, as the enemy in the thick woods could not be seen, and I could think of no other method than to ride into the field in view of their skirmishers, draw their fire and move on until the end of their line was apparent.

Accordingly, I rode into the open field and moved along some distance without being shot at; looking across the field near the opposite fence, I fancied I saw a line of skirmishers just inside of it, and tried in vain to attract their attention at long range. I rode back and forth, getting nearer to them all the time, until I got close enough to discover that the fancied pickets were black stumps, an illusion occasioned by the fact that a man in dark blue uniform on a rainy day looks black at a distance of two or three hundred yards. I was then worse puzzled than at first, for to go back and tell General Ross that I could not learn anything about their lines would never do. After a little hesitation I threw down the fence and rode into the thick undergrowth, expecting every minute to meet a volley of bullets. Going on some little distance I heard the word "Halt!" I halted, and was soon gratified to learn that I was confronting a small Confederate scouting party. Informing them of my object, they proposed showing me what I was looking for, and I was therefore able to return and report to my general, sound in body and much easier in mind.

During this long rainy spell, we rarely slept two nights on the same ground and never had a dry blanket to sleep on. On the 3d day of July we fought General Schofield's Corps nearly all day, fighting and falling back (as they were pushing down a road leading to Sand Town, a crossing on the Chattahoochee River), passing through a line of breastworks on the crest of a ridge crossing the road at right angles, erected and occupied by the Georgia Militia, about the middle of the afternoon. As we passed into the breastworks one of our men was killed by a long-range ball. The militia had never been under fire and had never seen a man killed before. We were instructed to form a line immediately in their rear and rest, and to support them if the enemy should come; but beyond throwing a few shells over the works and skirmishing at long range, we had no farther trouble with the enemy that afternoon.

Our men were very much amused at the sayings and doings of the militia at this time, but subsequently the Georgia militia were commanded by General G. W. Smith, an experienced officer, and after this they acted very gallantly in battle. They retired at night and we, leaving skirmishers in the works, went into camp. The next morning the Third Texas went into these breastworks, and while Captain Germany and myself were out in front deploying skirmishers he was severely wounded just below the knee, and was unfit for duty for several months.

General Schofield's Corps advanced in solid line of battle, and were allowed to take the works while we fell back a short distance into the timber and heard them give three cheers for Abe Lincoln, three cheers for General Sherman and three cheers for General Schofield! We then fought them again back through the timber until we came to a lane leading between farms across a little valley nearly a mile wide. On the hill beyond was our infantry in breastworks, and just beyond the breastworks was the narrow river bottom and Sand Town crossing, and down in this little bottom were our horses. As we entered the lane the enemy ran a battery up to the edge of the timber and shelled us every step of the way as we pulled through the long lane, tired and dusty, about noon, that hot 4th of July. Passing through the breastworks we mounted our horses in a shower of shells and crossed the river. Here we rested for twenty-four hours.

I went into Atlanta on the morning of the 5th, and skirmishing across the river again began in the afternoon. Here for some days we had a comparatively easy time, only picketing and skirmishing across the river. As this seemed void of results, the men on the north and south side of the river would agree upon a truce and go in bathing together. They would discuss the pending race for President between Lincoln and McClellan. The Confederates would trade tobacco for molasses and exchange newspapers, and when the truce was at an end each side would resume its respective position, and the firing would be renewed.

There continued to be more or less fighting north of the river until July 9, when General Johnston fell back into the defences immediately in front of Atlanta. General Sherman's army also crossed the river and confronted General Johnston's lines near the city. On or about the 19th General Johnston was superseded by General John B. Hood, and then began a series of hard battles around Atlanta, which were continued on the 20th, 21st, 22d, and other days, in which the losses on both sides were heavy. The Federal general, James B. MacPherson, was killed on the 22d. On the 28th was fought the battle of Ezra Church. On this day Companies C and D of the Third Texas were on picket in front of our command, and in the afternoon were driven back by overwhelming numbers, John B. Armstrong being slightly wounded and R. H. Henden very severely wounded.

We were soon met with orders to mount and move out to Owl Rock church on the Campbellton and Atlanta road, to assist Colonel Harrison, who was understood to be contending with General Mc-Cook's division of cavalry. General McCook had crossed the river near Rivertown, not far from Campbellton, for the purpose of raiding in our rear, and General Stoneman, with another division, had simultaneously moved out around the right wing of our army. The purpose was for these two commands to co-operate and destroy the railroad in our rear. General Wheeler's cavalry was sent after Stoneman. As General McCook had at least twelve hours the start of us we were unable to overtake him until afternoon of the next day. In the meantime, before daylight, he struck the wagon train belonging to our division, burned ninety-two wagons and captured the teamsters, blacksmiths, the chaplain of the Third Texas, and the inevitable squad that managed under all circumstances to stay with the train.

We came up with McCook's command near Lovejoy Station, which is on the railroad thirty miles below Atlanta. We learned with joy that General Wheeler had overtaken Stoneman, captured him and a large portion of his command, and was able to come with a portion of his troops to assist in the operations against McCook. McCook now abandoned all effort to destroy railroad property, and began a retreat in order to get back into the Federal lines. We followed him until night when, as we had been in our saddles twenty-eight hours, we stopped, fed on green corn and rested a few hours. Sometime before daylight next morning we mounted and moved on briskly. Early in the day we came close upon the enemy's rear and pressed them all day, during which time we passed scores of their horses, which from sheer exhaustion had been abandoned. Many of our horses, too, had become so jaded that they were unable to keep up.

About the middle of the afternoon, when near Newnan, the Federals stopped to give us battle. They had chosen a position in a dense skirt of timber back of some farms near the Chattahoochee River bottom, and here followed a battle which I could not describe if I would. I can only tell what the Third Texas did and sum up the general result. We were moved rapidly into the timber and ordered to dismount to fight. As many of our men were behind, instead of detailing the usual number of horse-holders, we tied the horses, leaving two men of the company to watch them.

Almost immediately we were ordered into line, and before we could be properly formed were ordered to charge, through an undergrowth so dense that we could only see a few paces in any direction. As I was moving to my place in line I passed John Watkins, who was to remain with the horses, and on a sudden impulse I snatched his Sharpe's carbine and a half dozen cartridges. On we went in the charge, whooping and running, stooping and creeping, as best we could through the tangled brush. I had seen no enemy in our front, but supposed they must be in the brush or beyond it. Lieutenant Sim Terrell, of Company F, and myself had got in advance of the regiment, as it was impossible to maintain a line in the brush, Terrell only a few paces to my right. Terrell was an ideal soldier, courageous, cool, and self-possessed in battle.

Seeing him stop I did likewise, casting my eyes to the front, and there, less than twenty-five yards from me, stood a fine specimen of a Federal soldier, behind a black jack tree, some fifteen inches in diameter, with his seven-shooting Spencer rifle resting against the tree, coolly and deliberately taking aim at me. Only his face, right shoulder, and part of his right breast were exposed. I could see his eyes and his features plainly, and have always thought that I looked at least two feet down his gun barrel. As quick as thought I threw up the carbine and fired at his face. He fired almost at the same instant and missed me. Of course I missed him, as I expected I would, but my shot had the desired effect of diverting his aim and it evidently saved my life.

Directly in front of Terrell was another man, whom Terrell shot in the arm with his pistol. The Federals both turned around and were in the act of retreating when two or three of Terrell's men came up and in less time than it takes to tell it two dead bodies lay face downwards where, a moment before, two brave soldiers had stood. I walked up to the one who had confronted me, examined his gun, and found he had fired his last cartridge at me. Somehow I could not feel glad to see these two brave fellows killed. Their whole line had fallen back, demoralised by the racket we had made, while these two had bravely stood at their posts. I have often wondered what became of their remains, lying away out in the brush thicket, as it was not likely that their comrades ever looked after them. And did their friends and kindred at home ever learn their fate?

We moved forward in pursuit of the line of dismounted men we had charged, and came in sight of them only to see them retreating across a field. Returning to our horses we saw them stampeding, as Colonel Jim Brownlow, with his regiment of East Tennesseans, had gotten among them, appropriated a few of the best ones, stampeded some, while the rest remained as we had left them. We charged and drove them away from the horses and they charged us three times in succession in return, but each time were repulsed, though in these charges one or two of the best horses in the regiment were killed under Federal riders. These men were, however, only making a desperate effort to escape, and were endeavouring to break through our lines for that purpose, as by this time General McCook's command was surrounded and he had told his officers to get out the best they could.

In consequence his army had become demoralised and badly scattered in their effort to escape. The prisoners they had captured, their ambulances, and all heavy baggage were abandoned, everything forgotten except the desire to return to their own lines. General Stoneman had started out with 5000 men and General E. M. McCook had 4000. Their object was to meet at Lovejoy Station, on the Macon Railroad, destroy the road, proceed to Macon and Andersonville and release the Federal prisoners confined at those two places. This engagement lasted about two hours, at the end of which we were badly mixed and scattered in the brush, many of the Confederates as well as Federals not knowing where their commands were. General Ross summed up the success of his brigade on this expedition as follows: Captured, 587, including two brigade commanders, with their staffs; colours of the Eighth Iowa and Second Indiana; eleven ambulances, and two pieces of artillery. General Wheeler's men also captured many prisoners.

Our loss on the expedition was 5 killed and 27 wounded. Among the wounded I remember the gallant Lieutenant Tom Towles, of the Third. The command now returned to its position in General Hood's line of battle, the prisoners being sent to Newnan, while I was ordered to take a sufficient guard to take care of them until transportation could be procured to send them to Andersonville. I had about 1250 enlisted men and 35 officers, who were kept here for several days. I confined them in a large brick warehouse, separating the officers from the privates by putting the officers in two rooms used for offices at the warehouse. I made them as comfortable as I could, and fed them well. I would turn the officers out every day into the front porch or vestibule of the warehouse, where they could get fresh air. They were quite a lively lot of fellows, except one old man, Colonel Harrison, I believe, of the Eighth Iowa. They appreciated my kindness and made me quite a number of small presents when the time came for them to leave.

This Newnan affair occurred July 30, 1864. General Hood had apparently grown tired of assaulting the lines in our front, and resumed the defensive. Our duties, until the 18th of August, were about the same as they had been formerly—heavy picketing and daily skirmishing. The casualties, however, were continually depleting our ranks: the dead were wrapped in their blankets and buried; the badly wounded sent to the hospitals in Atlanta, while the slightly wounded were sent off to take care of themselves; in other words, were given an indefinite furlough to go where they pleased, so that a slight wound became a boon greatly to be prized. Many returned to Mississippi to be cared for by some friend or acquaintance, while some remained in Georgia.

# CHAPTER 14

# Kilpatrick's Raid

On the night of August 18 Ross' brigade was bivouacked a short distance east of the road leading from Sand Town, on the Chattahoochee River, to Fairburn, on the West Point Railroad, eighteen miles west of Atlanta, thence to Jonesboro, on the Macon Railroad, some twenty miles south of Atlanta. This latter was the only railroad we then had which was of any material value to us, and we knew that General Sherman was anxious to destroy it, as an unsuccessful effort in that direction had been made only a few days previous.

We had a strong picket on the Sand Town and Fairburn road, and, as all was quiet in front, we "*laid us down to sleep,*" and, perchance, to dream—of home, of the independence of the Confederate States, and all that was most dear to us. It was one of those times of fair promises, to the weary soldier, of a solid night's rest, so often and so rudely broken. Scarcely had we straightened out our weary limbs and folded our arms to sleep, when we were aroused by the shrill notes of the bugle sounding "boots and saddles." Our pickets were being driven in rapidly, and before we were in our saddles General Judson Kilpatrick, with a force of five thousand cavalry, with artillery, ambulances, pack mules and all else that goes to constitute a first-class cavalry raiding force, had passed our flank and was moving steadily down the Fairburn road. The Third Texas were directed to move out first and gain their front, to be followed by the other regiments of the brigade.

For the remainder of the night we moved as best we could down such roads as we could find parallel to Kilpatrick's line of march—so near, in fact, that we could distinctly hear the clatter of their horses' hoofs, the rumbling of their artillery, and the familiar rattle of sabres and canteens. Soon after daylight we came in sight of his column crossing the railroad at Fairburn, charged into it and cut it in two for the time. They halted, formed a line of battle, and we detained them in skirmishing until we managed to effect our object,—the gaining their front,—and during the day, until late in the afternoon, detained them as much as possible on their march.

Below Fairburn Kilpatrick's main column took the Jonesboro road, while a small column took the road leading to Fayetteville, a town about ten miles west of Jonesboro. Ross' brigade, continuing in front of the main column and that of Armstrong, followed the Fayetteville road. Just before night we passed through Jonesboro, which is ten or twelve miles from Fairburn, and allowed Kilpatrick to occupy the town for the night. Ross' brigade occupied a position south of the town near the railroad, while Armstrong was west; General Ferguson, whose brigade was numerically stronger than either of the others, being directed to go out on a road leading east. As we afterwards learned, they failed to find their road, or got lost, and, so far as I remember, were not heard from for a day or two. Thus posted, or intended to be posted, the understanding and agreement was that we should make a triangular attack on Kilpatrick at daylight the next morning.

Our brigade moved on time and marched into the town, only to learn that, with the exception of a few stragglers who had overslept themselves, not a Federal soldier was to be found. The brigade followed them eastwardly from Jonesboro, and in due time came up with their rear-guard at breakfast behind some railworks near Lee's Mill, and from this time until along in the afternoon we had a pretty warm time with their rear. They were moving on a road that intersects the McDonough and Love joy road, and when they struck this road they turned in the direction of Lovejoy Station.

We finally came up with the main force ensconced behind some heavy railworks on a hill near a farmhouse a short distance east of the station. We had to approach them, after leaving the timber, through a lane probably three-quarters of a mile in length. The farm was mostly uncultivated, and had been divided into three fields by two cross-fences, built of rails running at right angles with the lane, and these were thrown right and left to admit of the free passage of cavalry. In the eastern cross fence, however, a length some twenty or thirty yards, and but a few rails high, was left standing, when a ditch or ravine running along on the west side was too deep to be safely crossed by cavalry. In this lane the command dismounted, leaving the horses in the hands of holders, and deployed in line in the open field, to the left or south side of the lane, and a section of Croft's Georgia battery was placed on an elevation to the right of the lane.

I had been sent back to Lee's Mill to hurry up a detail left to bury one of our dead, so was behind when the line was formed. Having, on the day we fought McCook, picked up a mule for my boy Jake to ride, I now had him leading my horse to rest his back, while I rode the mule. I rode up and gave my rein to a horse-holder, and was hurrying on to join the line when they charged the railworks, and when I got up with them they had begun to fall back. The brigade, not having more than four hundred men for duty, was little more than a skirmish line. During the day General Hood had managed to place General Reynolds' Arkansas brigade at Lovejoy Station, which fact Kilpatrick had discovered, and while we were showing our weakness in an open field on one side, General Reynolds managed to keep his men under cover of timber on the other.

Thus Kilpatrick found himself between an unknown infantry force in front and a skirmish-line of dismounted cavalry and a section of artillery in his rear. He concluded to get out of this situation—and he succeeded. Being repulsed in the charge on the railworks, by a heavy fire of artillery and small arms, we fell back and re-formed our line behind the first cross fence. Three regiments of the enemy then rapidly moved out from behind their works, the Fourth United States, Fourth Michigan, and Seventh Pennsylvania, and charged with sabres, in columns of fours, the three columns abreast. As they came on us at a sweeping gallop, with their bright sabres glittering, it was a grand display. And Ross' brigade was there and then literally run over, trampled underfoot, and, apparently annihilated.

Just before the charge they had shelled our horses in the lane, which, consequently, had been moved back into the timber. What could we do under the circumstances? If we had had time to hold a council of war and had deliberated over the matter ever so long, we would probably have acted just as we did; that is, acted upon the instinct of self-preservation, rather than upon judgment. No order was heard; not a word spoken; every officer and every man took in the whole situation at a glance: no one asked or gave advice: no one waited for orders. The line was maintained intact for a few seconds, the men emptying their pieces at the heads of the columns. This created a momentary flutter without checking their speed, and on they came in fine style. There was no time for reloading, and every one instinctively started for the horses a mile in the rear, a half mile of open field behind us, and all of us much fatigued with the active duties performed on the sultry summer day.

Being very much fatigued myself and never being fleet of foot, I outran only two men in the brigade, Lieutenant W. H. Carr, of Company C, and W. S. Coleman, of Company A, of the Third Texas, who were both captured, and I kept up with only two others, Captain Noble and Lieutenant Soap, also of the Third Texas. We three came to the ravine already described, at the same instant. Soap dropped into it, Noble jumped over and squatted in the sage grass in the corner of the fence. I instantly leaped the ravine and the rail fence, and had gone perhaps ten or fifteen steps when the clatter of horses' hoofs became painfully distinct, and "Surrender, sir!" rang in my ear like thunder.

Now, I had had no thought of the necessity of surrendering, as I had fondly hoped and believed I would escape. Halting, I looked up to ascertain whether these words were addressed to me, and instantly discovered that the column directly in my wake was dividing, two and two, to cross the ravine, coming together again just in front of me, so that I was completely surrounded. This was an emergency. As I looked up my eyes met those of a stalwart rider as he stood up in his stirrups, his drawn sabre glittering just over my head; and, as I hesitated, he added in a kind tone: "That's all I ask of you, sir." I had a rifle in my hand which had belonged to one of our men who had been killed near me during the day. Without speaking a word, I dropped this on the ground in token of my assent. "All right," said he, as he spurred his horse to overtake some of the other men.

Just at this time our artillery began throwing shells across the charging columns, and the first one exploded immediately above our heads, the pieces falling promiscuously around in my neighbourhood, creating some consternation in their ranks. Taking advantage of this, I placed my left hand above my hip, as if struck, and fell as long a fall as I could towards the centre of the little space between the columns, imitating as best I could the action of a mortally wounded man,— carefully falling on my right side to hide my pistol, which I still had on. Here I lay, as dead to all outward appearances as any soldier that fell during the war, and remained in this position without moving a muscle, until the field was clear of all of Kilpatrick's men who were able to leave it.

To play the role of a dead man for a couple of hours and then make my escape may sound like a joke to the inexperienced, and it was really a practical joke on the raiders; but to me, to lie thus exposed on the bare ground, with a column of hostile cavalry passing on either side all the time, and so near me that I could distinctly hear any ordinary conversation, was far from enjoyable.

I am no stranger to the hardships of a soldier's life; I have endured the coldest weather with scant clothing, marched day after day and night after night without food or sleep; have been exposed to cold, hunger, inclement weather and fatigue until the power of endurance was well-nigh exhausted, but never did I find anything quite so tedious and trying as playing dead. I had no idea of time, except that I knew that I had not lain there all night. The first shell our men threw after I fell came near killing me, as a large piece ploughed up the ground near enough to my back to throw dirt all over me. Their ammunition, however, was soon exhausted, the guns abandoned, and that danger at an end.

As things grew more quiet the awful fear seized me that my ruse would be discovered and I be abused for my deception, and driven up and carried to prison. This fear haunted me until the last. Now, to add to the discomfort of my situation, it began to rain, and never in my life had I felt such a rain. When in my fall I struck the ground my hat had dropped off, and this terrible rain beat down in my face until the flesh was sore. But to move an arm or leg, or to turn my face over for protection was to give my case completely away, and involved, as I felt, the humiliation of a prison life; than which nothing in the bounds of probability in my life as a Confederate soldier was so horrible, in which there was but one grain of consolation, and that was that I would see my brother and other friends who had been on Johnson's Island for some months.

The last danger encountered was when some dismounted men came near driving some pack mules over me. Finally, everything became so quiet that I ventured to raise my head, very slowly and cautiously at first, and as not a man could be seen I finally rose to my feet. Walking up to a wounded Pennsylvania cavalryman I held a short conversation with him. Surveying the now deserted field, so lately the scene of such activity, and supposing as I did that Ross' brigade as an organisation was broken up and destroyed, I was much distressed. I was left alone and afoot, and never expected to see my horse or mule any more, which in fact I never did, as Kilpatrick's cavalry, after charging through the field, had turned into the road and stampeded our horses.

I now started out over the field in the hope of picking up enough plunder to fit myself for service in some portion of the army. In this I succeeded beyond my expectation, as I found a pretty good, completely rigged horse, only slightly wounded, and a pack-mule with pack intact, and I soon loaded the mule well with saddles, bridles, halters, blankets, and oil cloths. Among other things I picked up a Sharp's carbine, which I recognised as belonging to a messmate. While I was casting about in my mind as to what command I would join, I heard the brigade bugle sounding the assembly! Sweeter music never was heard by me. Mounting my newly-acquired horse and leading my pack-mule, I proceeded in the direction from which the bugle notes came, and on the highest elevation in the field, on the opposite side of the lane, I found General Ross and the bugler. I told my experience, and heard our gallant brigadier's laughable story of his escape. I sat on my new horse and looked over the field as the bugle continued to sound the assembly occasionally, and was rejoiced to see so many of our men straggling in from different directions, coming apparently out of the ground, some of them bringing up prisoners, one of whom was so drunk that he didn't know he was a prisoner until the next morning.

Near night we went into camp with the remnant collected, and the men continued coming in during the night and during all the next day. To say that we were crestfallen and heartily ashamed of being run over is to put it mildly; but we were not so badly damaged, after all. The horse-holders, when the horses stampeded, had turned as many as they could out of the road and saved them. But as for me, I had suffered almost a total loss, including the fine sword that John B. Long had presented me at Thompson's Station, and which I had tied on my saddle. My faithful Jake came in next morning, and although he could not save my horse, he had saved himself, his little McCook mule and some of my soldier clothes. My pack-mule and surplus rigging I now distributed among those who seemed to need them most.

Including officers, we had eighty-four or eighty-five men captured, and only sixteen or eighteen of these were carried to Northern prisons. Among them were seven officers, including my friend Captain Noble, who was carried to Johnson's Island, and messed with my brother until the close of the war. Captain Noble had an eye for resemblances. When he first saw my brother he walked up to him and said, "I never saw you before, but I will bet your name is Barron, and I know your brother well."

The other prisoners who escaped that night and returned to us next day included my friend Lieutenant Soap, who brought in a prisoner, and Luther Grimes, owner of the Sharp's carbine, already mentioned, who had an ugly sabre wound in the head. I remember only two men of the Third Texas who were killed during the day—William Kellum of Company C, near Lee's Mill; and John Hendricks, of Company B, in the charge on the railworks. These two men had managed to keep on details from one to two years, being brought to the front under orders to cut down all details to increase the fighting strength, and they were both killed on the field the first day they were under the enemy's fire.

Among the wounded was Captain S. S. Johnson, of Company K, Third Texas, gunshot wound, while a number of the men were pretty badly hacked with sabres. Next day General Ross went up to General Hood's headquarters and said to him: "General, I got my brigade run over yesterday."

General Hood replied, "General Ross, you have lost nothing by that, sir. If others who should have been there had been near enough to the enemy to be run over, your men would not have been run over."

This greatly relieved our feelings, and the matter became only an incident of the campaign, and on the 22nd day of August Ross' brigade was back in its position ready for duty.

# CHAPTER 15

# Union Soldier's Account of Kilpatrick's Raid

After the war ended I made a friend of Robert M. Wilson of Illinois, who served in the Fourth United States Cavalry, and he kindly wrote out and sent me his account of this raid, and by way of parenthesis I here insert it, as it may be of interest.

The following is an account of the Kilpatrick raid, made in August, 1864, written partly from memory and partly from a letter written August 28, 1864, by Captain Robert Burns, acting assistant adjutant-general of the First Brigade, Second Cavalry Division, I acting as orderly for him part of the time on the raid. I was detailed at brigade headquarters as a scout during the Atlanta campaign and until General Wilson took our regiment as his escort. On the 17th of August, 1864, at one o'clock, a. m., ours and Colonel Long's Brigade (the First and Second), of Second Cavalry Division, all under the command of Colonel Minty, left our camp on Peach Tree Creek, on the left of our army northeast of Atlanta, at seven o'clock next morning; reported to General Kilpatrick at Sand Town on the right of our army, having during the night passed from one end or flank of our army to the other.

We remained at Sand Town until sundown of the 18th, when we started out to cut the enemy's communications south of Atlanta. Two other expeditions, Stoneman's and McCook's, well equipped, before this had been ruined in attempting the same thing. We, however, imagined we were made of sterner stuff, and started off in good spirits. The command consisted of Third

Cavalry Division (Kilpatrick's), under Colonel Murray, about 2700 men, and two brigades of our division (the Second), under command of Colonel Minty, about 2700 men also—the whole commanded by Kilpatrick (or Kill Cavalry, as we always called him).

Away we went, Third Division in advance. The night was a beautiful moonlight one, and we would have enjoyed it more if we had not been up all the night preceding. We did not go more than three miles before we ran into the enemy's pickets, when we had to go more slowly, driving them before us, dismounting to feel the woods on both sides, etc., etc. Consequently, it was morning when we reached the Atlanta & West Point Railroad near Fairburn. At Red Oak we had torn up about half a mile of the track when the rear battalion of Seventh Pennsylvania Cavalry was suddenly attacked by a force of dismounted men and artillery. Just back of where our column was struck were the ambulances, the darkies leading officers' horses, pack-mules, etc., etc. Several shells dropped among them, and they thought the kingdom had come, sure. The Fourth United States Cavalry, being in rear of the ambulances, soon drove the enemy away. All this time the head of the column kept moving on, as time was precious and we could not stop for slight scrimmages.

General Kilpatrick, not being satisfied with the progress made by his advance, ordered our brigades to take the front and Murray the rear. (We had learned before starting that it was expected we, our division, would do all the fighting.) Long's brigade, in advance, had not gone more than half a mile when he found a strong force of the enemy in his front. He had to dismount his men to drive the enemy from the rail barricades they had made, but he would find them in the same position half a mile farther on. Long kept his men dismounted, having number four lead the horses. I was close up with the advance with Colonel Minty. We drove the enemy steadily but slowly back, until we came to the valley through which Flint River runs, when they were reinforced by Ferguson's brigade of cavalry (we had been fighting Ross' brigade thus far), and opened on us sharply with artillery when we commenced descending the hill, the shells and bullets rattling lively around us.

Two guns of our battery—we had with us four guns of Chicago Board of Trade which belonged to our division, and Murray had with him four guns of the Eleventh Wisconsin Battery—were soon brought up and succeeded in silencing the enemy's artillery, the first striking an artilleryman and blowing him to pieces. Our division were then all dismounted and moved forward at the double-quick under fire of our eight guns, and drove the enemy clear through Jonesboro, crossing the bridge on the stringer. Our brigade (First) had the advance, being nearly all deployed as skirmishers.

We then seized the railroad for which we had started, and we commenced to smash things generally. The track was torn up for about two miles, the depot and public buildings burned, and destruction was let loose. While this was going on the enemy returned to the attack, and our division was sent to meet them, the Third Division turning the rails. The enemy were driven southward and we were pushed that way, to shove them farther back. Before was darkness and death, behind the burning buildings and smoking ruins, and now it also began to thunder, lightning, and pour down rain in torrents.

All this time General Kilpatrick had one of his bands behind us playing "Yankee Doodle "and other patriotic airs. It appeared as if defeat was coming, for we could hear the whistle of the cars in front of us and knew that the enemy were being reinforced from below. We then determined to flank them, so about midnight our brigade, followed by the Third Division, moved in a southeasterly direction about seven miles, Long's brigade being left to cover the rear.

When seven miles out we stopped to feed, close to 6 a. m., about a mile from Murray's Division, but were little protected, as both hills were cleared and the valley had but few trees in it. Our brigade was ordered to mount and move forward when Colonel Long's brigade was attacked by the cavalry that followed us from Jonesboro. The enemy's forces consisted of the brigades of Ross, Ferguson, and Armstrong, about 4500 men. Our brigade moved on and turned sharply to the right, in a southwesterly direction, to strike the railroad again about eight miles below Jonesboro. I stayed on the hill with Captain Burns, for a short time, to witness the skirmishing between Long and the enemy. From where we were all our manoeuvres could be distinctly seen, as also the enemy, who would advance upon our men, only to be driven back. It was a beautiful sight. 'By

Heaven, it was a noble sight to see—by one who had no friend or brother there.'

Captain Burns, myself following, now galloped off to overtake our brigade, which we soon did. Colonel Long had orders to follow as quickly as possible, Colonel Murray to come after. We (our brigade) pushed for Lovejoy Station. When within a mile and a half of the railroad we halted for the rest of the command to join us. About a mile from the railroad the road forks, the two prongs striking the railroad about a half a mile apart. A few hundred feet in front of and parallel to the railroad another road ran. The Fourth Michigan was sent by the right-hand road to the railroad, which it reached without any trouble; the rest of the brigade took the left-hand prong of the road, having for the last mile or two been driving off about a dozen cavalrymen. As we neared the railroad the firing became hotter and hotter. The Seventh Pennsylvania Cavalry was dismounted and sent forward to the woods—one battalion, four companies, of it had been advance guard. Hotter grew the firing, and the horses of the advance who had dismounted came hurrying back.

The Fourth United States (Regulars) were then dismounted and sent in. Captain Burns was sent back to hurry up two of Long's regiments, but before this could be done the Seventh Pennsylvania and Fourth Regulars were driven from the woods in some confusion. We had run on a brigade of infantry who were lying in the woods behind barricades at the side of the railroad, and a force of the enemy was also pushed in on the right, where the Fourth Michigan were at work. Long's brigade was put in position to check the advancing Confederates, and our battery brought up, as the woods in front and on our left were swarming with the enemy, and the Fourth Regulars and Seventh Pennsylvania were placed in support of the battery. Poor fellows, they were badly cut up!

One of Long's regiments was formed near the fork of the road, the Fourth Michigan was being placed there, and the enemy tried again and again to take our battery. It fought magnificently, and the guns were made to radiate in all directions and did splendid work, our men supporting them well. One of the guns, by the rebound, had broken its trail off short, so that it could not be drawn from the field. When the rest of the pieces had been withdrawn Colonel Minty called for men to draw

334

off the piece by hand. Captain Burns took about twenty men of the Fourth Michigan Cavalry down and helped pull it off, though the enemy were very close to us. While this was taking place, heavy firing was heard in our rear, for the cavalry with which we had been fighting had followed us, and had us in a pretty tight box, as follows: a brigade of infantry in our front and partly on our left; a division moving on our right and but a short distance off; three brigades of cavalry in our rear. Stoneman and McCook threw up the sponge under like circumstances. We decided we must leave the railroad alone, and crush the enemy's cavalry, and consequently withdrew from fighting the infantry, who now became very quiet, probably expecting to soon take us all in.

The command was faced to the rear as follows: Our brigade was formed on the right hand side of the road, each regiment in columns of fours (four men abreast); the Fourth Regulars on the left; Fourth Michigan centre; Seventh Pennsylvania on the right, Long's brigade formed in close columns with regimental front, that is, each regiment formed in line, the men side by side, boot to boot, thus:

MINTY'S BRIGADE

| FOURTH U. S. | FOURTH MICH. | SEVENTH PENN. |
| --- | --- | --- |
| o o o o | o o o o | o o o o |
| o o o o | o o o o | o o o o |
| o o o o | o o o o | o o o o |
| o o o o | o o o o | o o o o |
| o o o o | o o o o | o o o o |

LONG'S BRIGADE

FIRST OHIO

o o o o o o o o o o o o o o o o o o

THIRD OHIO

o o o o o o o o o o o o o o o o o o o

FOURTH OHIO

o o o o o o o o o o o o o o o o o o o

The last regiment was deployed in rear of the others so as to take in a large space of ground and pick up prisoners and trophies. You see, we were to break through the enemy, smashing them, and Long was to sweep over the ground and pick them up. This was soon determined on, for there was no time to lose.

335

A few of our men were in front of us, dismounted, skirmishing with the enemy, and they were told to throw down the fence where they were. The enemy all this time was keeping them engaged as much as possible, while a large force of them were building rail barricades. We were formed just below the brow of the hill, skirmishers on the crest of it, the enemy's artillery to our left and front playing over us, and bullets and shells flying thick over our heads. We drew sabre, trotted until we came to the crest of the hill and then started at a gallop. Down the hill we went, the enemy turning canister upon us, while the bullets whistled fiercely, and the battery away on our right threw shells. We leaped fences, ditches, barricades, and were among them, the artillery being very hot at this time.

You could almost feel the balls as they passed by. The Fourth Michigan and Seventh Pennsylvania went straight forward to the woods, the field over which they passed being at least a half a mile wide, with three fences, one partially built barricade, and a number of ditches and gullies, some very wide and deep. Of course many of the men were dismounted, and upon reaching the woods they (our men) could not move fast, and they turned to the right and joined the main column in the road about one and a half miles from the start. The Fourth Regulars (my regiment, as I joined it when the charge was ordered) could not keep parallel with the rest of the brigade on account of high fences in our front, and seeing an opening in the fence we turned to the left, and struck out on the main road, coming upon the enemy in the road near their battery, and sending them flying.

We were soon among the led horses of the dismounted men in their rear and among the ambulances, and a perfect stampede took place, riderless horses and ambulances being scattered in all directions, we in the midst of them, shooting and cutting madly. A part of our regiment, with some of the Fourth Michigan and Seventh Pennsylvania, dashed at the battery, drove the men from the pieces, and captured three of the guns. Private William Bailey, a young Tennessean from near McMinnville, who belonged to Fourth Michigan Cavalry (he was associated with me at headquarters as scout), shot the captain. We brought away the guns, and the charge continued for about two miles, when we halted for the command to close up. Colonel Long's brigade did not charge in line as it was intended, for, finding that the ground was impracticable, it formed in column and followed the Fourth Regulars. Colonel Murray's command, instead of sweeping all to the left, as we supposed they would do, turned to the right and followed Long. Had Murray done what was expected, both sides of the road would have been cleaned out.

Immediately after the charge and while we were pushing through the woods it commenced to rain, and poured in torrents. The command was now started for McDonough, but before the whole of it had moved off, Long's brigade, which had been moved to cover the rear, was fiercely attacked by the infantry of the enemy. Colonel Long fought them for about two hours, when, his ammunition giving out, he was obliged to retire. (Here Long was wounded twice.) The Fourth Michigan and Seventh Pennsylvania were formed in the rear, Long behind rail barricades which had been hastily thrown up. The Fourth United States Regulars being out of ammunition were sent on to McDonough, where the Ninety-Second Illinois Mounted Infantry divided ammunition with some of us near this town. One of Long's regiments assisted the Fourth Michigan and Seventh Pennsylvania. Long passed his men through when the enemy came on us. Then we had it hot and heavy, the enemy charging several times, but were repulsed.

All this fighting here was done dismounted, and was for the purpose of holding back the enemy until our main column could get out of the way. Our battery (three pieces) during this fight burst one gun and wedged another, getting a shell part way down it, so it could not be moved either way, so we had one gun only, but that was used with effect, the enemy meanwhile playing their artillery into our columns all along the road. You see our two brigades had to do all the fighting, lead the charge, and cover the retreat. As soon as our men had passed on about a mile, our rear-guard followed, and we were not molested again. We pushed slowly on to McDonough, crossed Walnut Creek, and near morning lay down in the mud for sleep. How tired we were I cannot tell, and men would tumble prone from their horses, and it was next to impossible to awaken them.

Frequently two or three men would fall asleep upon their horses, who would stop, and the whole column behind them would naturally do the same, too, supposing that there was obstruction ahead. Hundreds of men were sometimes asleep in that way upon their horses in the mud for an hour or so at a time. During this time, I fell asleep for about two hours, and awoke drenched to the skin, for it was raining, and fearfully dark and very disagreeable. About two o'clock we found a place to stop. I never before that knew what fatigue meant, for I had not slept a wink for the nights of the 17th, 18th, 19th, and 20th until the morning (about 2 a. m.) of the 21st, except what I had when riding along. We had had but three meals, and but little time to eat them, had fought seven pretty hard fights, besides skirmishing, etc., etc. At daybreak the next morning we started on again. At Cotton River the bridge was gone, the stream much swollen by rain, so that it could not be forded and the horses were obliged to swim it.

As the current was very swift, we had a terrible time crossing it. We, our brigade, lost one man and about sixty horses drowned here, and nearly all our pack-mules also. We could not get the wagon with the two disabled guns across at all, and rumour said they were buried here, and the site marked as the graves of two soldiers of the Fourth United States Cavalry. It was terrible to see the poor wounded carried across, some fastened on horses, while others were taken over in ambulances.

We all finally got over, but if the enemy had pushed us here most of the command would have been captured. We were now nearly all out of am munition, and many an anxious glance I gave to the rear, it being a relief when all were over. We then crossed South River bridge, burning all the bridges for ten miles each side, and camped that night at Lithonia. The next day we returned to our camp at Peach Tree Creek, having made a complete circuit of the two armies of Hood and Sherman. We did not do all we hoped we could when we started, but *we did all we could*. Notwithstanding what we had suffered, General Sherman was much dissatisfied with us, expecting more from us than lay in our power (or his either) to accomplish.

In the above narrative I have drawn very largely from a letter written August 28, 1864, by Captain Burns (as stated before), printed in a work called *Minty and the Cavalry*, though about all I have written occurred under my own observation. We captured three stands of colours claimed to belong to the Third

G. A. McKee
Private Company C, Third Texas Cavalry

Lieutenant S. B. Barron
Third Texas Cavalry Photo 1882

Texas Cavalry, Zachariah Rangers, and Benjamin's Infantry. Our aggregate loss in First and Second Brigades, killed, wounded, and missing, was 14 officers, 192 men."

Robert M. Wilson,<br>Company M, Fourth United States Cavalry.

★★★★★★

If the Third Texas colours were captured by them, they were found in an ambulance, as we did not have the flag unfurled on this expedition.

It will be noted here that the aggregate loss of 206 men is only the loss of one division, not including Kilpatrick's Division and the two batteries.

★★★★★★

# CHAPTER 16

# Close of the Atlanta Campaign

General Sherman had been impatient and dissatisfied that his cavalry was unable to destroy the Macon or Brunswick Railroad, and now changed his tactics. He had been in front of Atlanta, since General Hood had been in command, a period of about five weeks., In a few days after Kilpatrick's return, he began withdrawing his forces from the front of that beleaguered city, crossed to the north side of the Chattahoochee, marched his main force down to Sand Town, recrossed the river, and moved directly on Jonesboro, some twenty miles below Atlanta.

I do not believe, and never have believed, that General Hood understood this manoeuvre until it was too late to save even his stores, arms, and ammunition in Atlanta. His infantry scouts, it was understood and believed at the time, watched the enemy's movements, to the point of their crossing to the north side of the Chattahoochee, and reported that they were retreating, while our cavalry scouts reported that they were recrossing at Sand Town, in heavy force in our front.

We, that is, our cavalry, began fighting the head of their column as soon as they crossed the river, and fought them for detention and delay, as best we could, all the way to the Flint River Crossing near Jonesboro, just as we had fought Kilpatrick's force a few days before. General Hood, being advised that a heavy force of infantry and artillery was moving on Jonesboro, sent a portion of his army down there, and they fought the enemy most gallantly, but it seemed to me that our army should have been in their front long before they crossed Flint River. As it was, General Sherman threw his army across the railroad, on the first day of September, between us and Atlanta, and, while the fighting was terrific, we were unable to drive them off.

A terrible battle, in which there were no breastworks, was fought late in the evening, and General Cleburne's division was cut in two, for the first time during the war, when General Govan of his division was captured and Colonel Govan killed. We were in line, dismounted, just on General Cleburne's right, forming a mere skirmish line, in order to cover the enemy's front. The welcome shades of night soon gathered around us, and the fighting ceased when the opposing lines were almost together. I was on picket two or three hundred yards back of the enemy's line until one or two o'clock in the morning. All this time they were felling timber and strengthening their position for the fighting they expected in the morning. During the evening Lieutenant-Colonel Berry of the Ninth Texas Cavalry was killed.

Soon after midnight a courier from General Hood passed us and informed us that Atlanta was given up. As soon as he reached our headquarters a courier was sent to order us to fall back. And thus ended the last battle of the long campaign about Atlanta, a campaign involving continuous fighting for three and a half months.

Very soon after General Hood's courier passed us we began to hear the artillery ammunition exploding in Atlanta. All was burned that could not be carried away on the march, as we now had no railroad transportation. After burning the arms, ammunition, and stores that could not be transported, General Hood moved out with his army, and the Federals took undisputed possession of the city the next day. General Hood, after burning his supplies, had moved out during the night eastwardly and by a circuitous march joined his other forces near Lovejoy Station. General Sherman soon abandoned Jonesboro, moved his army into and around Atlanta and two tired armies rested. Sherman reported his loss in this campaign at 34,514, quite a large army in itself.

Our army settled down for the time being near Jonesboro, Ross' brigade doing outpost duty. The ranks of the brigade had become very much depleted by the losses in killed, wounded, and captured during the Atlanta campaign, and the companies were temporarily consolidated. This caused the regiments of the brigade, except the Third Texas, to have on hand a number of supernumerary company officers. The Third having more officers in prisons and hospitals than the others, only had about enough officers after consolidation. These officers, with consent of the commanders, agreed to organise themselves into a scouting party. I had permission to join them, and as this offered some recreation, or at least a diversion, I did so, being the only member from the Third. They were all gallant and experienced officers and jovial companionable fellows.

We organised by selecting Captain H. W. Wade of the Sixth Texas commander. I cannot now recall all of them, but among them were Captains O. P. Preston, Reuben Simpson, Cook, and Broughton, and Lieutenants W. J. Swain, Thompson Morris, W. W. McClathie, Bridges, and Park. We were joined by the gallant Captain Reams, of Missouri, whose command had surrendered at the fall of Vicksburg, and who, having gone to Missouri to recruit his command, was captured and imprisoned, but had escaped into Canada, and from there made his way back to General Hood's army. We were sent on duty in the country lying north of the West Point Railroad and south of the Chattahoochee River, west and northwest of Atlanta—this being a large scope of country not occupied by either army and liable to be depredated upon by the enemy. Campbellton, the county seat of Campbell County, was a town of some importance situated on the south bank of the Chattahoochee River, some thirty miles northwestwardly from Atlanta. The Federal outpost in this direction was twelve or fifteen miles out from the city.

Our duties were performed for several weeks without incident worthy of mention. We were sometimes in the territory over which we had fought during the summer, and a more desolate country I never saw; not a domestic animal or fowl, and scarcely a bird, could be seen; the woods, where we had fed our horses shelled corn, had grown up in green corn more than knee high, and there were no animals to crop it down; the fences had all been torn down to build barricades, and the crops had been without cultivation or protection since the early summer; the corn had made small ears and the sorghum had grown up into little trifling stalks, and the people who lived hereabouts were subsisting on corn bread made of grated meal and syrup made in the crudest manner. Oh, the devastation and horrors of war! They must be seen to be realised.

One morning we met Lieutenant Bob Lee, with his scouts, and it was agreed that we would spend the day together on a trip towards the river between Campbellton and Sherman's outpost. Bob Lee was a fine scout, a member of the Ninth Texas Cavalry who had been promoted from the ranks to first lieutenant for his efficiency. Lee's scouts numbered twenty, while we numbered twenty-one, all well-armed with Colt's revolvers and well mounted. On our way we picked up Pem Jarvis, of Company K, Third Texas, who was glad to join us. Pem had the only gun in the company, and no pistol.

We moved north by any road or trail found to lead to the right direction, until about noon, when we struck the rear of a farm lying in a little valley. Along the opposite ridge ran the "ridge road" from Atlanta to Campbellton, probably half a mile distant. Near the road, in a strip of timber, stood a farmhouse. Near the house we heard a gun fire and a hog squeal. Throwing down the fence we rode in and moved across cautiously, so as not to be seen from the house. Passing out through a pair of draw-bars, three or four of the men galloped up to the house and into the yard, where they found two Federal soldiers in the act of dressing a hog they had just killed. From them we learned that a party of about sixty cavalrymen, in charge of an officer, and having with them two four-mule wagons, had just passed, going in the direction of Campbellton.

We started off, leaving the hog killers in charge of two of our men, and filed into the road. At the first house on the road, supposed to be Dr. Hornsby's, two ladies were in the act of mounting their horses at the gate. They were crying, and told us that some Yankee soldiers had passed there and insulted them, and that they were going to headquarters to ask for protection. They estimated the number at about sixty, with two wagons. This was about five miles from Campbellton.

We sent two of our scouts ahead to look for them, as there is also a road from Campbellton to Atlanta called the river road. If they returned by the ridge road we would meet them, if by the river road we would miss them. The scouts were to ascertain this matter and report. We moved on to within about two miles of the town and formed a line in the brush, a few steps south of the road and parallel with it, where, with bridles and pistols well in hand, we patiently waited the return of our scouts. The road from our position, towards town as far as we could see it, ran on a rough down grade and was lined with thick black jack brush. From here it was impossible for a horseman to get into the river road without going into town. The intention was, if they came our way, to wait until their column came up in our front and charge them in flank.

In due time we heard our scouts coming at a gallop, and looking up we saw they were being pursued by two Federals. One of the Federals reined up and stopped before he got in our front, while the other rode along nearly the entire front of our line, fired his gun at our scouts, cussed the d——d rebels, then stopped, and stood as if waiting for the column, which was then slowly moving up the hill. We could hear them driving milch cows, which they had taken from citizens, and accompanied by wagons loaded with the fruits of their day's robbery, such as tobacco, chickens, and turkeys. The fellow in our front furnished such a tempting target that one of our men fired, and the Federal dropped from his horse. This was sufficient to spoil the ambush, and we instantly spurred our horses into the road, gave a loud yell, and charged at full speed down the rough road, into the head of their column.

As we approached them they seemed almost to forget the use of their seven-shooting rifles in an effort to reverse their column, and before they could accomplish this we were in among them, and they ran for dear life back to gain the river road. We went along with them to town, and they fired back at us vigorously, and powder burned some of our men in the face, but no one of our men received as much as a scratch. We were better armed for such a contest than they were, for though they had good rifles, their pistols were few, while we carried from two to four Colt's revolvers apiece.

Jarvis' horse became unmanageable in the excitement and ran under some black jack, and knocked Jarvis' gun out of his hand and plunged in among the enemy, passing by several of them while Jarvis had nothing to defend himself with. Some of them were in the act of shooting him in the back, but invariably Bob Lee or someone else would save him by shooting his assailant in the back of the head. The foremost and best mounted men, about twenty in number, with one wagon, got through the town. We followed them a few hundred yards and turned back. We had twelve prisoners unhurt, and going back over the road we found fourteen dead and fifteen wounded. We had in our possession one wagon and team, thirty or forty rifles, a few pistols, and a number of horses with their rigging.

As I was going back on the road I came to an elderly wounded man just outside of the road. I reined up my horse, and as I did so he reached out a trembling hand, in which he held a greasy leather pocketbook, and said: "Here, take this, but please don't kill me." I told him to put up his pocketbook; that I would neither take that nor his life; that I only wanted his arms.

The slightly wounded men, who would likely be able to fight again very soon, we put into the wagon, and mounting the unhurt ones on the captured horses we paired off with them, and thus started for our own lines. I rode with one of the prisoners, who was quite a talkative fellow. Upon asking him why it was that so many of their men refused to surrender, and allowed themselves to be shot, he said:

"Our officers have told us that Ross's brigade never shows prisoners any quarter, but will rob and murder them; and we knew it was Ross's brigade as soon as you yelled that way."

I told him that was a great slander on the brigade; that no men would treat prisoners more kindly; that sometimes we were hard up for clothes and would take an overcoat, or blanket, or something of the kind from a fellow that was well supplied.

"Oh," said he, "that's nothing; we do that."

I then said to him: "I believe your boots will fit me, and these brogans of mine will do you just as well at Andersonville."

He said, "All right," and instantly he dismounted and pulled his boots off. We traded, and I had a good pair of kip boots that fit me, and he had brogan shoes, and was apparently happy. He asked me how it was that we were so much better mounted than they were. I explained that we furnished our own horses, and we must keep them or go to the infantry, and that made our men good horse-masters; while the United States Government furnished them with horses and they knew that when they rode one to death they would get another.

We continued our scouting duties in the same section of country until the early days of October, when General Hood moved around in General Sherman's rear, and began destroying his communications, capturing supplies and provisions. Sherman moved out of Atlanta and followed Hood until the latter came to the vicinity of Rome. General Hood unwilling to risk a battle in the open field, crossed the Coosa River, moving by way of Gadsden, Ala., towards Guntersville on the Tennessee River. When General Sherman discovered this movement he turned back towards Atlanta, devastating the country and despoiling the citizens as he went.

With General Hood's movement across the Coosa River he began his last campaign, and the last campaign for the Army of the Tennessee. His intention was to cross the Tennessee at Guntersville and march on Nashville, but he changed his mind and moved down the river to near Decatur, Tuscumbia, and Florence, Ross's brigade being in front of Decatur, then occupied by the Federals. General Sherman returning to Atlanta, that city was burned, and leaving the smoking ruins behind him, he entered upon his grand march to the sea, with none of General Hood's army, save General Wheeler's cavalry to molest him in his work of devastation.

A day or two after we got to Decatur General Ross ordered our scouting party back up the river to ascertain, if we could, what the enemy was doing in the rear of that place. We moved up on the south side of the river and stopped between Triana and Whitesburg. These towns were garrisoned and the river patrolled by gunboats. We remained in this neighbourhood without any further instructions for some weeks. Here I found my half-brother, J. J. Ashworth, who lived on the south bank of the river about fifteen miles from Huntsville, and about three miles above Triana.

In this neighbourhood were a number of my acquaintances from Madison County, refugeeing, as Huntsville, Brownsboro, and other towns were also garrisoned by the enemy. Several of us crossed the river afoot and remained some days in Madison County. But for the negroes we could have had a pleasant time, as every negro in the country was a spy who would run to report anything that looked suspicious to them, to one of the near-by garrisons, so we dared not allow them to see us. I knew the white people, and knew that they were loyal to our cause, but they could not allow their own negroes to know that they did anything for us, so that we, and they, too, had to be exceedingly careful.

In crossing the river, we had to watch for gunboats, make the passage during the night in a canoe, which must be drawn out and hidden, else the first passing gunboat would destroy it. Some three miles north of the river, in the bottom, lived Alexander Penland, a Presbyterian minister, a true and loyal friend to the Confederacy, and three or four miles further on, towards Huntsville, lived William Lanier, Burwell Lanier and William Matkins, the two latter on the Huntsville and Triana road. Dr. William Leftwich also lived in the same neighbourhood. All were good, trustworthy men, whom I knew well.

Since some of them had taken the non-combatant's oath they were allowed to go in and out of town at will, and from them I could learn of any movements along the M. & C. Railroad. We crossed the river after night, and being in possession of Mr. Penland's countersign, we found our way to his house, late at night, after the household was all asleep. I went to a certain front window, tapped lightly and whistled like a partridge.

Soon Mr. Penland thrust his head out and in a whisper inquired who we were and what was wanted. I explained to him briefly, and retired to a brush thicket nearby, where early next morning he brought us cooked provisions. In order to do this, he had to get up and cook for us himself before any of his negroes were awake. The next night we slept in William Lanier's farm and were fed by him in the same way. We crossed the Triana road and went to the top of a small mountain, from which we could see Huntsville. A rainy season set in and we found shelter in Burwell Lanier's gin-house, where he fed us. When we thought of recrossing the Tennessee we found that Indian Creek, which we had to cross, was outrageously high, spreading away out over the bottom. We spent a good part of an afternoon in constructing a raft by tying logs together with vines to enable us to cross that night. Just east of William Lanier's farm there was a large negro quarter, where idle and vicious negroes were in the habit of congregating, and inasmuch as their system of espionage upon the white people of the neighbourhood was very annoying, upon the suggestion of some of our friends we determined to raid this place before we left, carry off some of these meddlesome blacks and send them to some government works in south Alabama.

Accordingly, after dark we visited the quarter under the guise of recruiting officers from Whitesburg, told them we had been fighting for their freedom for about three years, and the time had now come for them to help us, and we had come for every able-bodied man to go with us to Whitesburg and join the army. I had our men call me Brown, for fear some of them might know me. It was laughable to hear the various excuses rendered for not going into the service. A lot of Confederate conscripts could not have thought up more physical ailments. We finally gathered up six that we decided were able for service, promising they should have a medical examination, and if they were really unfit for service they would be excused. Among them was a powerful, large, muscular black fellow that belonged to Jink Jordan. He had joined the army and, tiring of his job, was now a deserter, and we could see that he was greatly scared and very much opposed to going with us.

Upon leaving the negro houses we went through the field and the woods directly to our raft on the creek and had a great time getting across. The clouds were thick, it was intensely dark, and our means of crossing very poor. We had to make a number of trips, as we could only float three or four men, including the two that used the poles, at one time. In the confusion and darkness two of the prisoners had escaped, and two had just crossed, including the big deserter, when it became my duty to guard them with a short Enfield rifle belonging to one of the men. Having their hands tied with a cord and then tied together back to back, I was not uneasy about keeping them, but before I realised what they were doing they had slipped their hands through the cord and were running through the brush.

When the big deserter had gone some twelve or fifteen steps I shot him. He fell at the fire of the gun, but before I could get to him he scrambled up and went crashing through the brush like a stampeding ox. I learned afterwards that he went into Huntsville to a hospital for treatment, and that the ball had gone through the muscle of his arm and ploughed into his breast, but not deep enough to be fatal. We finally reached the bank of the river about one or two o'clock in the morning, with two of our prisoners. We then had to hoot like an owl until someone on the other side should wake up, and, hearing the signal, would bring us a canoe, which was finally done, and we crossed over in safety.

We crossed the river several times during our stay in the neighbourhood, particularly one very cold night, when several of us passed over, at the request of Mr. Penland, to transfer his pork to the south side. He had killed a lot of hogs, and was afraid the meat might be taken from him, or that he would be ordered out of the Federal lines as others had been, and he wished to place it in the hands of a friend south of the river for safety. We managed to get an old rickety canoe opposite his place, and crossed early in the night, and again played the role of Federal soldiers, as no one on his place but himself must know our real mission. Mrs. Penland had known me from childhood, but as she had lost her mind I did not fear recognition, and while Nancy, their negro woman, also had known me, she failed to recognise me, as I was Mr. Brown of the Federal Army.

We marched up and called for the man of the house, and when Mr. Penland came forward we told him we were rather short of rations down in Triana, and were out looking for meat, and wished to know if he had any. He acknowledged that he had just killed some meat, but only enough for his family use, and had none to spare. We were bound to have meat, and agreed to leave him one hog, and then yoked up a pair of oxen and hitched them to a wagon. While we were in the smokehouse preparing to take the meat out, Mr. Penland's two little girls, about nine and eleven, came crying around us, and in a most pitiful manner begged us not to take all of papa's meat; and poor Mrs. Penland came to the door and said: "Men, please don't take my little boy's pony."

When we had hauled all the meat to the river bank and returned the wagon, it was nearly midnight, and we compelled the woman Nancy to get up and prepare us a warm supper. After supper we returned to the river and floated the hogs across in our old canoe.

At this time my brother's son, George Ashworth, a gallant boy about sixteen years old, who had taken his father's place in General Roddy's command, was at home on furlough. One day a thief, believed to be a straggler from General Wheeler's command, took his horse from a lot some distance from the house, and carried him off. Lieutenant McClatchie and myself mounted a pony and a mule of my brother's and attempted to overtake him. We followed him as far as Atlanta, but failed to catch him, and then went into the city and viewed the wreck that Sherman had left behind him: thirty-six hundred houses were in ruins, including the best part of the city. This was Saturday, and being tired we went down to the neighbourhood of Jonesboro and remained with some of McClatchie's acquaintances until Monday morning. We were hospitably entertained at the home of Colonel Tidwell, and enjoyed a quiet rest in the company of Miss Mattie Tidwell and Miss Eva Camp.

One evening we passed through the town of Cave Springs, a locality with which I had become familiar while we were campaigning here. On the road we were to travel, at the first house after leaving town, two or three miles out, there lived a tall dignified old gentleman and his handsome young married daughter whose husband was in the army. They lived in a large two-story house, and a large commodious barn, with all other necessary out houses for comfort and convenience, had stood on his premises when I was there before—the barn filled to overflowing with wheat, oats, and corn.

Just across the road in front of the house, and stretching across the valley, was his large productive farm, covered with a heavy crop of ungathered corn. While this was the condition, I had come to this house at night, traveling in the same direction, and talked myself almost hoarse without being able to procure from this old gentleman a single ear of corn for my horse or a morsel of food for myself, although he knew I must go eight miles to the next house on the road. I didn't ask, nor did I wish, to enter his house, but only wanted a feed of corn and a little bread and meat. As we approached the house McClatchie proposed halting, to stay all night—provided we could. I related my earlier experience, but we stopped nevertheless.

Upon seeing us halt, the old gentleman came stepping down to the gate and spoke very kindly, and we asked him if we could spend the night with him. He said such accommodations as he could offer us we would be welcome to, adding:

I have no stables for your horses. Sherman's army passed this way and burned my barn, with its contents, my stables, and in fact carried off or destroyed everything I had to eat or feed on, and left me and my daughter without a mouthful of anything to eat. They carried every hog, every fowl, and every pound of meat, and even rolled my syrup out of the cellar, knocked the heads out of the barrels and poured the syrup out on the ground, but I will do the best I can for you.

His daughter, too, was very hospitable. At the supper table she detailed all the horrors of Sherman's visit, and the distressful condition they were left in, how they had to go to a neighbour's to borrow a few ears of corn to grate them for bread, and concluded by saying:

But as long as I have a piece of bread I will divide it with a Confederate soldier.

After supper she invited us into the parlour, where she had a nice piano and treated us to music. Verily "our friends, the enemy," had converted one family!

# CHAPTER 17

# My Last Battle

Haden Pryor, who lived eight miles west on the same road, was a whole-souled, big-hearted old gentleman, who also had a large place and plenty of everything to live on, and whose hospitality towards a Confederate soldier was unbounded. His boys were in the army in Virginia, and he and his wife were at home alone. I had stayed with him while hunting a blacksmith shop, and found that a tired Confederate soldier was more than welcome to his home. Lonely, and impatient for the war to close, that his gallant boys might come home, he would sit out on his front veranda and play solitaire, and was glad to see a soldier come, and sorry to see him leave. He had a nephew in our regiment that I knew and liked, and I had fallen in love with this old gentleman. Next morning McClatchie and I, when we came to his house, called to pay him our respects and to tell him goodbye.

This neighbourhood, or rather the neighbourhood just south of this, and a considerable scope of country lying along the western border of Georgia and the eastern border of Alabama, was infested with a class of the meanest white men on earth—Tories and deserters, men too cowardly to fight in either army, but mean and unscrupulous enough to do anything. We knew they were there, but while our army was in the neighbourhood they were never seen. Since the armies had left they were growing bolder, and we were told at Mr. Pryor's that morning about some of their thievery and robbery.

Providence protected us that day. Here were two roads, one to the left and one to the right, and we could follow one or the other and reach our destination in the same number of miles. The matter was left to me, and, without thinking of danger, I selected the right-hand road. On that day the left-hand road was waylaid by a band of these infamous characters and every Confederate soldier who attempted to pass the road was robbed of horse, arms, and everything of any value, and one or two of them murdered. These soldiers had been left behind slightly wounded or sick, and were on their way to overtake their commands. One of the murdered ones belonged to Ross's brigade.

Since the war I have heard, from a reliable source, a tragic story of this Pryor family, which, if told in detail, would sound like fiction. It seems that in the spring of 1865 a band of these cut-throats, eight in number, rode up to Haden Pryor's gate and without provocation shot him while he was standing in his front yard in presence of his wife; as he turned and was in the act of returning to his house he fell in his front veranda, a corpse. This was a few days after General Lee's surrender. His oldest son, John, and a younger one, with eight or ten other Confederates, on their way home that night came within eight or ten miles of their homes, when, tired and footsore, they lay down to rest until morning.

John Pryor, haunted by a strange presentiment, could not sleep, and determined he would quietly leave the camp and go on to his father's house. While he was dressing one of the others woke and said: "Hello, John, what are you up to?"

"I am going home," said John.

"Wait a minute," said the other, "and I'll go too."

From that one by one they all roused up and were soon on the road again. Arriving at home, John Pryor found his father a bloody corpse and his mother a widow. His mother told him how it all happened, and gave him the names of his father's murderers. The next day the funeral took place, and the noble father who had so patiently waited and longed for the return of his soldier boys was laid under the sod.

Over his father's grave John Pryor made a vow that he would not engage in any business whatever as long as one of his father's murderers was alive, and starting out upon his fixed purpose he killed one or two of them before the gang became alarmed. The rest now became panic-stricken and fled the country, hiding in different States. John hunted them constantly and relentlessly for weeks and months, until the weeks grew into years, and as he found them they were sent to their final account, one by one, until finally he found the last and least guilty one in Travis County, Texas, a few miles from Austin. It was in the spring of the year, and the man was ploughing when John walked into the field where he was. Seeing John coming and recognising him, he stopped his horse and, waiting until he was within a few steps of him, he said, "John, I know what you have come for; but I will ask you to let me go to the house and tell my wife and children goodbye."

John consented, and they went to the house, where were the innocent wife and two small children in a comfortable little home. The husband and father then said: "John, I never hurt your father; I didn't want those fellows to kill him, and told them not to do it."

"I remember that my mother told me something about this," replied John, "and said you were the only one who said a word against the murder of my father; and now I will retract my vow as to you, and leave you with your wife and children."

Now feeling that he had fulfilled his mission, Pryor returned to his home, and devoting his attention to business became a prosperous and successful man.

As we continued our way back to north Alabama, crossing Black Creek, we came to the residence of Mrs. Sansom. Here we stopped under pretence of lighting our pipes, and remained for an hour, merely to get a look at the young heroine, Miss Emily Sansom, the young girl who rode behind General Forrest and piloted him to a ford on the creek where he was in hot pursuit of Colonel Straight and his men. This story of Emily Sansom's heroism has been published so often that most people art; familiar with it. She now lives, a widow, in Upshur County, Texas. (Since this was written, this Southern heroine has passed to that bourne from which no traveller returns).

We pushed on to our former headquarters on the Tennessee River, to find that our people had been gone ever so long. General Hood had crossed the river about the last of November, Decatur, Huntsville, Triana, and Whitesburg had all been evacuated by the enemy, and our army was in middle Tennessee. Our scouts, as we afterwards learned, had crossed the river, passed through Huntsville and moved up to the vicinity of Shelbyville. Our command had participated in the fighting on the advance into Tennessee, had been in the battle of Franklin, and was then sent to Murfreesboro.

McClatchie and myself crossed the river and spent the night at the home of our friend, Rev. Alexander Penland. Next day we went into Huntsville, and while waiting for our horses to be shod I had time to see a number of my friends, among them Miss Aggie Scott, from whom I learned that my old friend, W. H. Powers, and his wife, were sojourning in New London, Conn. We went out in the evening and spent the night at the home of Mr. William Matkin, a few miles down the Triana road. Late at night Rev. Lieutenant-Colonel William D.

Chadick came to Mr. Matkin's, afoot, tired and somewhat excited, and informed us that a division of Federal cavalry had entered Huntsville that afternoon. He had been at home with his family, and told an interesting story of his escape. He had left his home, gone across lots, and reaching the Female seminary lot, had hidden under the floor of the seminary until nightfall, when he had made his way through back lots and fields until he was well out of town. He then found his way around to the Triana road and here he was.

General McCook was in command of the forces that had come in so unexpectedly, and learning that Colonel Chadick was at home, showed great anxiety to capture him, so much so that he visited his home in person. Finding Mrs. Chadick there, he interrogated her as to the whereabouts of her husband. She told him that Colonel Chadick was not at home. He seemed incredulous, and cross-questioned her closely, when something in her tone or her favour led him to change the conversation, and he said to her: "Madam, where are you from?"

She answered, "I am from Steubenville, Ohio."

"I am also from Steubenville, Ohio. What was your maiden name?"

She answered, "My maiden name was Cook."

"Were you Miss Jane Cook? "said he.

She answered, "I was."

Then said he: "Do you remember, many years ago, one Sunday morning, when you were on your way to Sunday school, that some little boys were cutting up in the street near the Episcopal church and a policeman was about to take them up when you interceded in their behalf and he let them off?"

She answered, "I do."

"I was one of those boys," said he, "and now, madam, I am ready to do anything in my power for your protection and comfort."

Guards were placed at her gates, and not a soldier allowed to enter the premises while General McCook's command remained there.

Colonel Chadick was well known to me, he having been pastor of the Cumberland Presbyterian church in Huntsville for several years while I lived there. He first entered the army as chaplain of the Fourth Alabama Infantry, and was with that famous regiment in the first battle of Manassas. He was afterwards made major of an Alabama battalion, of which Nick Davis was lieutenant-colonel, later consolidated with Coltart's battalion, to become the Fiftieth Alabama Infantry, when John G. Coltart became colonel and William D. Chadick lieutenant-colonel. At this time, he had an idea of raising a new regiment of cavalry, and wished me to return and raise a company for the regiment or else take a position on his staff, but we were now too near the end.

McClatchie and myself started out next morning and went up the Huntsville road a short distance, when we came in sight of a small party of Federal cavalry in the act of turning back. We took a road that led us into the Athens road at John N. Drake's place, where we learned that another party had come out there, and turned back. We then made our way directly to Pulaski, Tenn., on towards Columbia, and found the division on the Columbia pike hotly engaged with the enemy, who was pushing General Hood's retreat. Our rear-guard was commanded by General Forrest, and consisted of his own cavalry, Jackson's cavalry division, and about fifteen hundred infantry, under Major-General Walthal. The infantry were trans-Mississippi troops, including Vector's and Granberry's brigades.

General Hood's main army was retreating by different roads towards Bainbridge, where we were to cross the Tennessee River. Jackson's division of cavalry and the infantry of the rear-guard were on the main road, while General Forrest's cavalry was protecting other roads. We were uncomfortably crowded on the turnpike, but we left it at Pulaski, crossed Richland Creek on a bridge, and fired the bridge. The Federals soon came up and extinguished the fire, however, and then came pouring across the bridge, but as it was now late in the afternoon they did not attack any more for the day.

The next morning General Forrest selected a favourable position in the hills a few miles below Pulaski, masked his batteries, and formed his infantry in ambush, and, when the enemy came on us, attacked them with artillery, infantry, and cavalry, and after a sharp little battle drove them back handsomely, with some loss, capturing one piece of artillery and taught them that in the hills it was imprudent to rush upon an enemy recklessly. For the remainder of that day we were permitted to move quietly down the road unmolested.

That night one of General Frank Armstrong's Mississippi cavalry regiments was left on picket, and we moved on a mile or two and camped by the roadside. Just after daylight the next morning our Mississippi regiments came clattering in, closely pursued by the enemy's cavalry. We hastily formed a line across the road and checked the enemy, and then moved on to Sugar Creek and formed another ambush. There was a dense fog along the creek, such as I never saw in the interior. Our infantry were formed along the creek bank just above the crossing, and the cavalry in column of fours in the road forty or fifty yards back from the ford of the creek, and thus, in the fog, we were as completely concealed as if midnight darkness had prevailed. The infantry remained perfectly quiet until the head of the enemy's column was in the act of crossing the creek, when suddenly, with a yell they plunged through the creek and charged them. This threw the head of their column into confusion, when our cavalry charged them in column at a gallop, and pressed them back two or three miles. *And this was the last fight I was ever in!*

# CHAPTER 18

# Ross' Report of Brigade's Last Campaign

Headquarters Ross' Brigade, J. C. D.
Corinth, Miss., Jan. 12, 1865.

Captain:

I have the honour to submit the following report of the part performed by my brigade in the late campaign into Middle Tennessee.

First, however, and by way of introduction, it is proper to premise that we bore a full share in the arduous duties required of the cavalry in the Georgia campaign, and were particularly active during the operations of the army upon the enemy's line of communication.

October 24, in compliance with orders from division commander, I withdrew from my position near Cave Springs, Ga., crossed the Coosa River at Gadsden the day following, and by rapid marches arrived in front of Decatur, Ala., on the evening of the 29th. Was here halted to observe the movements of the enemy while the army rested at Tuscumbia. On the morning of November 8 a strong reconnoitring party, consisting of three regiments of infantry and one of cavalry, coming out from Decatur on the Courtland road, was promptly met, and after a sharp skirmish driven back with some loss.

The next day, being relieved by a portion of General Roddy's command, we retired down the valley to Town Creek and rested until the 18th, when we were ordered across the river at Florence, and moving at once to the front of the army, took position with the other cavalry commands on Shoal Creek. November 21, all things being ready for the advance, we were ordered forward, following in the rear of Armstrong's Brigade. The effective fighting strength of my command at this time was as follows: Third Regiment Texas Cavalry, 218; Sixth

Regiment Texas Cavalry, 218; Ninth Regiment Texas Cavalry, 110; Twenty-seventh Regiment Texas Cavalry, 140; making a total of 686. With this small force we joined the advance into Tennessee, strong in heart and resolved to make up in zeal and courage what was wanting in numbers.

The day after crossing Shoal Creek, General Armstrong, having still the advance, came up with Federal cavalry at Lawrenceburg. The fighting was chiefly with artillery, Captain Young's battery being freely used, and to good effect. About sunset the enemy withdrew in the direction of Pulaski. Early the next morning I was ordered to take the advance and move out on the Pulaski road. About twelve miles from Lawrenceburg we came upon the Federal pickets and drove them in. The Third Texas now dismounted and with two squadrons from the Twenty-seventh Texas moved forward and attacked the enemy, forcing him from his successive positions and following him up so vigorously as to compel the precipitate abandonment of his camps and all his forage.

The next day, having still the advance, when within five miles of Pulaski, we changed direction to the left, following the route taken by the enemy in his retreat the evening before, and arriving about noon in sight of the little village, Campbellsville, I found a large force of cavalry, which proved to be Hatch's division, drawn up to resist us. Lieutenant-Colonel Boggess was ordered promptly to dismount his regiment, the Third Texas, and move it to the front. Young's battery was hurried up from the rear, placed in position and, supported by the Sixth Texas (Colonel Jack Wharton, commanding), commenced shelling the enemy's lines. In the meanwhile, the Ninth Texas and the Legion were drawn up in column, in the field to the right of the wood, to be used as circumstances might require. These dispositions completed, I watched with interest the effect of the shelling from our battery, and very soon discovered from the movements of the enemy, an intention to withdraw, whereupon, believing this to be the proper movement, I ordered everything forward.

The Ninth Texas and Legion, led by their respective commanders, Colonel Jones and Lieutenant-Colonel Whitfield, rushed forward at a gallop, and passing through the village, fell upon the enemy's moving squadrons with such irresistible force as to scatter them in every direction, pursuing and capturing numbers of prisoners, horses, equipment, small arms, accoutrements, and four (4) stands of colours. The enemy made no effort to regain the field from which he had been driven, but while endeavouring to withdraw his broken and discomfited squadrons was attacked vigorously in flank by a portion of General Armstrong's brigade, and his rout made complete. The last of his forces, in full flight, disappeared in the direction of Lynville about sunset, and we saw no more of them south of Duck River. Our loss in the fight at Campbellsville was only five (5) men wounded, while our captures (I found upon investigation) summed up to be eighty-four (84) prisoners, and all their horses, equipments, and small arms, four (4) stands of colours and sixty-five (65) beef cattle. Without further opposition we arrived the next day in front of Columbia, and took the position assigned us on the Chapel Hill pike.

November 26, we remained in front of the enemy's works, skirmishing freely and keeping up a lively demonstration. On the morning of the 27th, being relieved by the infantry, we were ordered over to Shelbyville pike, and camped the following night on Fountain Creek. Crossing Duck River, the next morning, at the mill, nine miles above Columbia, we were directed thence to the right (on the Shelbyville road), and when near the Lewisburg and Franklin pike, again encountered the Federal cavalry. A spirited engagement ensued, begun by the Third Texas, which being detached to attack a train of wagons moving in the direction of Franklin, succeeded in reaching the pike, but was there met by a superior force of Yankees and driven back. Seeing this, I had Colonel Hawkins to hurry his regiment (the Legion) to the assistance of the Third, and ordered a charge, which was made in gallant style, and resulted in forcing the Yankees from the field in confusion, and with the loss of several prisoners and the colours of the Seventh Ohio Cavalry.

In the meanwhile, Colonel Wharton, with the Sixth Texas, charged into the pike to the right of where the Third and Legion were engaged, capturing an entire company of the Seventh Ohio Cavalry, three (3) stands of colours, several wagons loaded with ordnances, and a considerable number of horses, with their equipments. The Ninth Texas (Colonel Jones), having been detached early in the evening to guard the road leading to our right, with the exception of a slight skirmish with the enemy's pickets, in which several prisoners were taken, was not otherwise engaged during the evening. It was now after night and very dark. The enemy had disappeared from our front in direction of Franklin, but before establishing camps it was thought prudent to ascertain if any force had been cut off and yet remained between us and the river. Colonel Hawkins was therefore ordered up the pike with his regiment to reconnoitre, and had proceeded but a short distance before he was met by a brigade of Federal cavalry. An exciting fight ensued, lasting about half an hour, when the enemy, having much the larger force, succeeded in passing by us, receiving as he did so a severe fire into his flanks. This ceased the operations for the day, and we were allowed to bivouac, well pleased with the prospect of rest, after so much fatiguing exercise.

At Hunts cross roads the next day, when the other commands of cavalry took the left and moved upon Spring Hill, my brigade was advanced upon the road to Franklin. Afterwards, in obedience to orders of the division commander, we turned towards Thompson's Station, being now in rear of the Federal army, which still held its position on Rutherford's Creek. The Yankee cavalry, completely whipped, had disappeared in the direction of Franklin, and did not again show itself that day. When near Thompson's Station I discovered a few wagons moving on the pike, and sent Colonel Jones, with the Ninth and Legion, to intercept and capture them.

At the same time the Sixth and Third Texas were drawn up in line, and a squadron from the latter dispatched to destroy the depot. Colonel Jones was partially successful, capturing and destroying one wagon and securing the team. He then charged a train of cars which came up from the direction of Franklin, when the engineer becoming frightened, cut the engine loose and ran off southward. The train, thus freed, began to retrograde, and in spite of the obstructions thrown in its way and the efforts of the men to stop it, rolled back under the guns of a blockhouse and was saved. The guard, however, and all the men on the train were forced to jump off, and became our prisoners. I now had the railroad bridge destroyed, in consequence of which the engine that escaped from us, and another, became the prizes of our army the next day.

In the meantime, the enemy at the depot, observing the approach of the squadron from the Third Texas, set fire to all of his valuables, including a train of cars loaded with ordnance, and evacuated the place. Having accomplished all that could be effected in the station, we withdrew late in the evening, dropping back to the left of Spring Hill and halted until I could communicate with the division commander. About midnight I received the order directing me to again "Strike the pike" and attack the enemy's train, then in full retreat to Franklin; moved out at once to obey the order, guided by an officer of General Forrest's staff who knew the country.

When within half a mile of the pike I dismounted three (3) of my regiments, leaving the Ninth Texas mounted to guard their horses, and cautiously advancing on foot, got within one hundred yards of the enemy's train without being discovered. The Legion (Colonel Hawkins commanding) having the advance, fronted into line, fired a well-directed volley, killing several Yankees and mules, and rushed forward with a yell, producing among the teamsters and wagon guards a perfect stampede. The Yankees lost thirty-nine (39) wagons, some of which were destroyed, and others abandoned for the want of the teams, which we brought off. Remaining in possession of the pike for half an hour, we withdrew upon the approach of several bodies of infantry, which coming up in opposite directions, by mistake got to shooting into each other, and fired several volleys before finding out their error.

Having remounted our horses, we remained on the hill overlooking the pike until daylight, and saw the Yankee army in full retreat. While this was passing a regiment of cavalry appearing in the open field in our front was charged by the Sixth Texas, completely routed and driven to his infantry column. Soon after this we again pushed forward, keeping parallel with the pike, upon which our infantry was moving, crossed Harpeth River in the evening, about three miles above Franklin, only a small force of the enemy appearing to dispute the passage. Half a mile from the river we came upon a regiment of Yankee cavalry drawn up in line.

This the Ninth Texas at once charged and routed, but was met by a larger force, and in turn compelled to give back, the enemy following in close pursuit. The Third Texas now rushed forward, checked the advancing squadrons of the Yankees, and then hurled them back, broken and disorganised, capturing several prisoners and driving the others back upon their heavier lines. The gallant bearing of the men and officers of the Third and Ninth Texas on this occasion is deserving of special commendation, and it affords me much gratification to record to the honour of these noble regiments that charges made by them at Harpeth River have never been, and cannot be, surpassed by cavalry of any nation. By the charge of the Third Texas we gained possession of an eminence overlooking the enemy's position and held it until late in the evening, when discovering an intention on the part of the Yankee commander to advance his entire force, and being without any support, I withdrew to the south side of the river again.

Very soon the enemy advanced his whole line, but finding we had recrossed the river again, retreated, and during the night withdrew, from our front. The next day we moved forward, arrived in front of Nashville December 3, and took position on the Nolensville pike three miles from the city. Just in our front was a line of works, and wishing to ascertain what force occupied them, I had two squadrons of the Sixth Texas to dismount, deploy as skirmishers, and advance. We found the works held only by the enemy's skirmishers, who withdrew upon our approach. After this, being relieved by our infantry, we returned to the rear with orders to cook up rations.

On the morning of December 5 the brigade was ordered to Lavergne; found there a small force of infantry, which took refuge inside the fort, and after slight resistance surrendered upon demand of the division commander. Moving thence to Murfreesboro, where within a few miles of the city the enemy's pickets were encountered, and after a stubborn resistance driven back by the Sixth and Third Texas, dismounted. A few days after this Major-General Forrest invested Murfreesboro with his cavalry and one (1) division of infantry. The duty assigned my brigade being to guard all the approaches to the city, from the Salem to the Woodbury pike inclusive, was very severe for so small a force, and almost every day there was heavy skirmishing on some portion of our line.

December 15, a train of cars from Stevenson, heavily laden with supplies for the garrison at Murfreesboro, was attacked about seven miles south of the city, and although guarded by a regiment of infantry, two hundred strong, was captured and burned. The train was loaded with sugar, coffee, hard bread, and bacon, and carried full two hundred thousand rations. The men guarding it fought desperately for about an hour, having a strong position in a cut of the railroad, but were finally routed by a most gallant charge of the Sixth Texas, supported by the Third Texas, and 150 of them captured. The others escaped to blockhouses nearby. The next day, in consequence of the reverses to our arms at Nashville, we were withdrawn from the front of Murfreesboro, ordered across to Triana, and thence to Columbia, crossing Duck River in the evening of the 18th.

December 24, while being in the rear of our army, the enemy charged my rear-guard at Lynville, with a heavy force, and threatened to break over all opposition, when the Sixth Texas hastily forming, met and hurled them back, administering a most wholesome check to their ardour. At the moment this occurred our columns were all in motion, and it was of the utmost importance to break the charge of the enemy on our rear. Too much credit, therefore, cannot be given the Sixth Texas, for gallant bearing on this occasion. Had it failed to check the enemy, my brigade, and probably the entire division, taken at disadvantage, might have suffered severely. At Richland Creek, when the cavalry took position later in the day, I was assigned a position on the right of the railroad, and in front of the creek.

Soon afterwards, however, the enemy moving as if to cross above the bridge, I was withdrawn to the south side of the creek and took position on the hill near the railroad, skirmishing with the enemy in my front, holding him in check until our forces had all crossed the creek. We were then ordered to withdraw, and passing through Pulaski, again crossed Richland Creek and camped near Mr. Carter's for the night. The next day my brigade, alternating with General Armstrong in bringing up the rear, had frequent skirmishes with the enemy's advance. Nine miles from Pulaski, when the infantry halted and formed, I was ordered on the right. Soon after this the enemy made a strong effort to turn our right flank, but failed, and was driven back. About the same time the infantry charged and captured his artillery, administering such an effectual check that he did not again show himself that day.

This done, we retired leisurely, and after night bivouacked on Sugar Creek. Early the following morning the Yankees, still not satisfied, made their appearance, and our infantry again made dispositions to receive them. Reynolds' and Ector's brigades took position, and immediately in their rear I had the Legion and Ninth Texas drawn up in column of fours to charge, if an opportunity should occur. The fog was very dense and the enemy therefore approached very cautiously. When near enough to be seen, the infantry fired a volley and charged.

At the same time the Legion and Ninth Texas were ordered forward, and passing through our infantry, crossed the creek in the face of a terrible fire, overthrew all opposition on the further side, and pursued the thoroughly routed foe near a mile, capturing twelve (12) prisoners and as many horses, besides killing numbers of others. The force opposed to us here was completely whipped,—proved from the statements of the prisoners to be Hammond's brigade of cavalry. After this the Yankees did not again show themselves, and without further interruption we recrossed the Tennessee River at Bainbridge on the evening of the 27th of December.

Our entire loss during the campaign sums up as follows:

| COMMAND | KILLED | | WOUNDED | | CAPTURED | | AGGREGATE |
|---|---|---|---|---|---|---|---|
| | OFFICERS | EN. MEN | OFFICERS | EN. MEN | OFFICERS | EN. MEN | |
| Third Texas Cavalry. | | 2 | 3 | 22 | 1 | 2 | 30 |
| Sixth Texas Cavalry. | | 6 | 3 | 19 | | 1 | 29 |
| Ninth Texas Cavalry. | | 4 | | 17 | | 1 | 22 |
| Texas Legion........ | | | | 6 | | | 6 |
| Total.......... | | 12 | 6 | 64 | 1 | 4 | 87 |

We captured on the trip and brought off five hundred and fifty (550) prisoners, as shown by the records of my provost-marshal, nine (9) stands of colours, several hundred horses and their equipments, and overcoats and blankets sufficient to supply my command. We destroyed, besides, two trains of cars, loaded, one with ordnance, and the other with commissary stores; forty or fifty wagons and mules; and much other valuable property belonging to the Federal Army. My brigade returned from Tennessee with horses very much jaded, but otherwise in no worse condition than when it started, its morale not in the least affected nor impaired by the evident demoralization which prevailed to a considerable extent throughout the larger portion of the army.

Before closing my report, I desire to record an acknowledgment of grateful obligations to the gallant officers and brave men whom I have the honour to command. Entering upon the campaign poorly clad and ill- prepared for undergoing its hardships, these worthy votaries of freedom nevertheless bore themselves bravely, and I did not hear a murmur, nor witness the least reluctance in the discharge of duty, however unpleasant. All did well, and to this I attribute in a great measure the unparalleled success which attended all our efforts during the campaign.

To Colonel D. W. Jones, Colonel E. R. Hawkins, Colonel Jack Wharton, Lieutenant-Colonel J. S. Boggess, who commanded their respective regiments; and Lieutenant-Colonel P. F. Ross and Major S. B. Wilson, Sixth Texas; Lieutenant-Colonel J. T. Whitfield and Major B. H. Nosworthy, of Legion; Major A. B. Stone, Third Texas; and Major H. C. Dial, Ninth Texas; also Captains Gurly, Plummer, Killough and Preston; Lieutenants Alexander and Sykes; members of my staff: I feel especially indebted for earnest, zealous, and efficient co-operation. These officers upon many trying occasions acquitted themselves with honour, and it affords me pleasure to be able to commend to the favourable notice of the Brigadier-General commanding.

I have the honour to be, Captain, very resp't,

Your obedient Servant,

Official:                                                    L. S. Ross,

A. A. G. "59"                                        Brig. Gen'l., J. C.

# CHAPTER 19

# The End of the War

Although we moved in a very leisurely manner in order to give General Hood a chance to put a pontoon bridge across Tennessee River and cross his infantry, artillery, and wagon trains, the enemy never came in sight of us again.

Our Christmas was spent on this march. The weather was quite cold and many of our poor soldiers had to march over frozen ground barefooted. Between the 25th day of December, 1864, and the 1st day of January, 1865, everything had crossed to the south side of the river, during a little more than a month having seen much hard service, severe fighting, and demoralizing disaster. We continued to move leisurely southward. The main army moved to Tupelo, Miss., while our command moved to Egypt Station on the Mobile & Ohio Railroad. After crossing the river General Ross detailed Captain H. W. Wade, of the Sixth Texas, Lieutenant Thompson Morris, of the Legion, and myself as a permanent brigade court-martial.

Egypt Station is situated in one of the richest of the black land districts. Corn was abundant, and we remained there several days, during which time it rained almost incessantly, but the court-martial procured quarters in a house and was able to keep out of the black mud, which was very trying on the men in camp. Being scarce of transportation for baggage when we started to Georgia, the officers' trunks and valises, containing all their best clothes, were left in Mississippi in charge of a detail of two men, afterwards reduced to one. While we were moving out of Tennessee the baggage was run up to a small station on the Mobile & Ohio Railroad, and just before we reached it a small scouting party of the enemy's cavalry swooped down, fired the station, and all our good clothes went up in smoke. In fact, this and Kilpatrick's raid left me with almost "nothing to wear."

Leaving Egypt, we moved slowly back to our old stamping-ground in the Yazoo country. We camped one night some seventy-five miles north of Kosciusko, and in the morning, before the command was ready to move, about 180 men from the brigade, including several from Company C, Third Texas, mounted their horses and moved out, without leave, and started for the west side of the Mississippi River. They had organised what they were pleased to call an "owl train," a term of no significance worth explaining. It meant that they had become demoralized and impatient for the promised furlough, and had determined to go home without leave.

It was a source of great regret to see numbers of men who had been good soldiers for fully three and a half years thus defiantly quit the command with which they had so faithfully served, but not a harsh word was said to them, nor was effort made to stop them. Whether they would have returned or not, I do not know; perhaps many of them would, but circumstances were such that they never did. To this day many of them, perhaps all, live in constant regret that they were induced to take this one false step when we were so near the end.

On the same morning Lieutenant William H. Carr and myself obtained permission to go ahead of the command, to have some boots made, and started for Mr. Richburg's shop. A little after night the second day we reached the house of Mr. Savage, and obtained permission to spend the night. Soon after we were seated by a splendid blazing fire, his daughter, Miss Hattie, whom I had met at Mr. Blunt's about eighteen months before, came into the room. She recognised me very readily, and was apparently glad to meet me again. As there was to be a wedding at their house in about three days, she very cordially invited us to attend, which we agreed to do, provided we remained in the neighbourhood that long. We hurried on to Richburg's shop, ordered our boots, which he promised to make right away—that is, in about three days.

We then went to the home of my friends, the Ayres family, and made that our home for the time being. The wedding was attended by us, in company with Miss Andrews, the step-daughter, and our boots were finished just in time to enable us to join the wedding party at the dinner given the next day in Kosciusko, ten miles on our way. Here we dined, after which, bidding farewell to our friends and acquaintances, we hastened on to overtake our command.

Unexpectedly, a little later, we were favoured with an order to furlough one-half of the command, officers and men, it being my fortune to be of the "one-half." Selecting and sending up the names of those to be furloughed, writing up and returning the papers, consumed time, so that it was February before we were ready to start to Texas. Lieutenant-Colonel Jiles S. Boggess, of the Third Texas, being the ranking field officer to go, was to be nominally in charge of the furloughed men, and as he lived in Henderson, my expectation was to go home with him; but it turned out otherwise.

The day for starting was agreed on, leaving Colonel Boggess to bring my papers and meet me at Murdock's ferry on Yazoo River. I left camp the day before and went up to the home of John F. Williams and spent the night. John F. Williams had been sheriff of Cherokee County, Texas, in an early day, but had moved back to Mississippi. His two sons had joined our company, but Wyatt, the older one, being physically disqualified, had been discharged. He was anxious to come to his grandfather in Marshall, Texas, and I loaned him a horse on which to make the trip; and, declining to bring my boy Jake on so long a ride, to return so soon (as I then believed), I gave him a horse and saddle and told him to take care of himself.

Starting next morning with Wyatt Williams, I came on to Lexington and spent the night at the residence of our "Aunt Emma Hays." Mrs. Hays was one of the noblest women we met in Mississippi, a great friend to Ross's brigade collectively, and a special friend to a good many of us individually. Her good old mother, Mrs. West, was there. She had lived in Marion, Ala., and was strongly attached to persons of my name there, and would always insist that I favoured them, and was related to them; and the good, kind-hearted creature would do all she could for me and seemed to regret that she could not do more. These two kindly ladies furnished me luncheon enough to have lasted me, individually, almost to Rusk.

The next day we rode in the rain all day to Murdoch's ferry, where, as we arrived after dark, it required a good deal of yelling and waiting to get a boat to cross in. Finally, we stopped at Colonel Murdock's gate and, although his house appeared to be full of soldiers, we were welcome. Murdock was the big-hearted man who, when the brigade camped on his premises for a day and night, refused to sell the man sweet potatoes, but said: "Go back and tell the boys to come up to the house and get as many as they want."

I had made the acquaintance of Mrs. Murdock and her sister, Miss Ford, of Louisiana, who was visiting her, at Lexington some months previous. I found Captain Sid Johnson, of Tyler, was at Mrs. Murdock's home. Mrs. Murdock whispered to me and said: "Supper will soon be ready for the company, but I wish you and Captain Johnson to wait and eat with the family." This we did, and afterwards were invited into the parlour, and pleasantly entertained by the ladies, Mrs. Murdock the while urging me to remain and spend my leave of absence with them instead of going to Texas.

In the meantime, the rain continued to pour down, and increased in violence, continuing all next day and the next night. While the others all pushed on except Williams and myself, I remained there until afternoon. About noon Colonel Boggess reined up at the gate long enough to say "Come ahead," and rode off in a torrent of rain, and the next time I saw him he was in Henderson, his home. Finally, Williams and I started, intending to cross Sunflower Swamp and Sunflower River that evening, but soon found the whole country was overflowed, and losing much valuable time in trying to cross a creek without swimming it we had to lay out in the swamp that night. We cut a lot of cane for our horses to stand on, and piled a lot up by an old tree, and on that we sat down all night in the rain.

Next morning by swimming a large creek we reached Sunflower River, found it bank full, the ferryboat on the west side, and the ferryman gone. By going down the river three or four miles we found a farm and a private ferry, but it was afternoon when we crossed. Reaching the Mississippi, we found a number of the men waiting to get over, but Colonel Boggess had crossed and gone on. The crossing was tedious in the extreme, as the only means of doing so was to swim the horses by the side of a skiff, and this had to be done in the daytime, when you had to look out for gunboats. When over, it was very uncertain with whom you were going to travel, as every fellow, when he got his horse up the bank and over the levee on the west side, at once struck out for Texas. I lost Williams and never saw him afterwards.

The country between the Mississippi and Red River was practically afloat. We crossed a great many streams, how many I do not remember, and we found but one stream, Little River, where the bridge was not washed away. We travelled along near the Arkansas and Louisiana line, sometimes in one State and sometimes in the other. The first stream encountered after crossing the Mississippi was a large bayou in the bottom, which we crossed on a raft constructed of logs tied together. We ferried Ouachita River, two miles, crossed Little River on a bridge, and had to swim every other stream, averaging something like three a day. We struck Red River at Carolina Bluff, some twenty miles above Shreveport, and had to swim the overflow in several places to get down to Shreveport, where we found dry ground. We came through it all with but one serious accident, and that was the drowning of a negro boy. I travelled mostly with Dr. Blocker, of Harrison County, and three or four of the Third Texas from Smith County.

One morning I found my horse badly foundered, so that I could not keep up with my crowd. Coming to Magnolia, Ark., about noon, I had to sell one of my pistols in order to trade for a horse that was able to bring me on.

Upon reaching Henderson, about eleven o'clock one day, the first man I recognised on the street was Lieutenant-Colonel Jiles S. Boggess, of the Third Texas Cavalry. He abused me roundly for being behind, and threatened that I should never leave the town with whole bones unless I went down to his house and took a rest and dinner with him, and I yielded. Here I learned that the "owl train" gang had not yet reached Texas, that they crossed the river, had been arrested at Alexandria, perhaps, and were detained under guard at Shreveport. Through the influence of Colonel Boggess, however, they were soon afterwards released by General Smith and allowed to come home.

I reached Rusk a little before noon the next day.

The following is a true copy of the paper on which I came to Texas:

Hd. Qts. Ross Brig. Cav.,
Deasonville, Miss., Feb. 20, 1865.

Special orders
No. 2. Ext.

By authority from Lieutenant-General Taylor Leaves of absence are granted to the following named officers for Sixty (60) days. XXVII Lieutenant S. B. Barron, Company "C "Third Texas.

L. S. Ross,
Brig. Gen'l.

At the proper time I presented myself to Colonel Boggess at Henderson, and reported to him that I was ready to start back. He told me he had no idea that we could cross the river, as it was reported to be from five to twenty-five miles wide; that he had sent a man to ascertain whether it was possible for us to cross it, and if so he would let me know, and directed me to return to Rusk and remain until I heard from him. Thus matters stood until the startling news reached us that General R. E. Lee had surrendered his army in Virginia. This was followed in quick succession by the surrender of General Joseph E. Johnston in North Carolina, the other commanding officer, and finally by General E. Kirby Smith's surrender of the trans-Mississippi department.

And then—then the four years' war, with all its fun and frolic, all its hardships and privations, its advances and retreats, its victories and defeats, its killing and maiming, was at an end.

I am unable to give the losses of Ross' brigade sustained in the Atlanta campaign. If it was ever given out officially I never saw it. But our ranks were very much depleted as the result of this long campaign. Some went to the hospitals badly wounded, some were furloughed with wounds not considered dangerous, some were rolled in their blankets and buried where they fell, and others were carried to Northern prisons, there to die or remain until the close of the war.

Nor can I now give the loss we sustained in the Nashville campaign. It was carefully made up in detail, but I do not remember it. I remember that John B. Long, of Company C, was shot through both thighs, and I remember two gallant members of Company B, Bud McClure and Joe Robinson, were killed near Pulaski on the retreat.

The regulation that our horses should be listed and valued now and then, to show the estimation placed upon horseflesh in the currency of our Government, I give the following valuations made in the early part of the year 1864, of the officers and men then present for duty, *viz.*:

Captain John Germany, one bay horse, $2000; Lieutenant W. H. Carr, one sorrel horse, $1200; Lieutenant R. L. Hood, one sorrel horse, $1600: Lieutenant S. B. Barron, one black horse, $1400; one bay mule, $1000; First Sergeant John B. Long, one bay horse, $900; Second Sergeant R. L. Barnett, one sorrel mare, $1500: First Corporal D. H. Allen, one sorrel horse, $1600; S. D. Box, one bay horse, $1500; Stock Ewin, one sorrel horse, $2500; J. J. Felps, one brown mule, $900; Luther Grimes, one sorrel horse, $1400; J. B. Hardgraves, one sorrel horse, $1500; J. R. Halbert, one sorrel mare, $1200; J. T. Halbert, one grey horse, $1500; W. H. Higginbotham, one grey horse, $1200; J. H. Jones, one bay mare, $1000; W. H. Kellum, one brown mule, $900; S. N. Keahey, one grey horse, $1100; G. A. McKee, one sorrel mule, $1400; Jno. Meyers, one dark roan horse, $800; Tom Petree, one sorrel horse, $1100; J. B. Reagan, one black mule, $900; C. M. Roark, one sorrel horse, $1200; A. B. Summers, one black horse, $1500; J. W. Smith, one brown horse, $1600; E. S. Wallace, one bay horse, $1600; J. R. Watkins, one sorrel horse, $2000; C. Watkins, one cream horse, $1200; T. F. Woodall, one sorrel horse, $1000; R. F. Woodall, one sorrel horse, $1600; J. W. Wade, one grey horse, $1800; T. H. Willson, one grey mule, $1000; E. W. Williams, one sorrel horse, $1400; N. J. Yates, one black mule, $1000.

Ingram Content Group UK Ltd.
Milton Keynes UK
UKHW042112280423
420980UK00013B/189/J